— FIVE VIEWS —
ON
LAW
AND
GOSPEL

Books in the Counterpoints Series

►COUNTERPOINTS◄

— FIVE VIEWS —
ON
LAW
AND
GOSPEL

Greg L. Bahnsen

Walter C. Kaiser, Jr.

Douglas J. Moo

Wayne G. Strickland

Willem A. VanGemeren

Previously titled *The Law, the Gospel, and the Modern Christian*

ZondervanPublishingHouse
Grand Rapids, Michigan

A Division of HarperCollinsPublishers

Five Views on Law and Gospel
Copyright © 1993, 1996 by Wayne G. Strickland

Previously titled *The Law, the Gospel, and the Modern Christian*

Requests for information should be addressed to:

📖 ZondervanPublishingHouse
Grand Rapids, Michigan 49530

Library of Congress Cataloging-in-Publication Data

Law, the gospel, and the modern Christian.
    Five views on law and Gospel / Greg L. Bahnsen ... [et al.].
        p.   cm. — (Counterpoints)
      Originally published under title: The law, the gospel, and the modern
Christian, 1993.
      Includes bibliographical references and index.
      ISBN: 0-310-21271-5
      1. Law and Gospel.   2. Evangelicalism.   I. Bahnsen, Greg L.   II. Title.
III. Series: Counterpoints (Grand Rapids, Mich.)
    [BT79.L38   1996]
    241'.2—dc 20   96–21888
                                                    CIP

Printed in the United States of America

---

98 99 00 01 02 /❖ DH/ 10 9 8 7 6 5 4 3

CONTENTS

ABBREVIATIONS

BA	*Biblical Archaeologist*
BAGD	**Bauer, Arndt, Gingrich, and Danker,** *Greek-English Lexicon of the New Testament*
Bib	*Biblica*
BJRL	*Bulletin of the John Rylands Library*
BR	*Biblical Research*
BSac	*Bibliotheca Sacra*
CSR	*Christian Scholar's Review*
CT	*Christianity Today*
CTJ	*Calvin Theological Journal*
EJ	*Evangelical Journal*
GTJ	*Grace Theological Journal*
Inst	*Institutes of the Christian Religion*
Int	*Interpretation*
ISBE	*International Standard Bible Encyclopedia, Revised Edition*
JBL	*Journal of Biblical Literature*
JCR	*Journal of Christian Reconstruction*
JETS	*Journal of the Evangelical Society*
JSNT	*Journal for the Study of the New Testament*
JSNTSup	*Supplements* to *Journal for the Study of the New Testament*
NICNT	**New International Commentary of the New Testament**
NICOT	**New International Commentary of the Old Testament**

NIDNTT	*New International Dictionary of New Testament Theology*
NovT	*Novum Testamentum*
NTS	*New Testament Studies*
RevExp	*Review and Expositor*
RTR	*Reformed Theological Review*
SE	*Studia Evangelica*
SJT	*Scottish Journal of Theology*
ST	*Studia Theologica*
SupNovT	Supplements to *Novum Testamentum*
TDNT	*Theological Dictionary of the New Testament*
TJ	*Trinity Journal*
TNTC	Tyndale New Testament Commentary
TOTC	Tyndale Old Testament Commentary
Transf	*Transformation*
TynBul	*Tyndale Bulletin*
TZ	*Theologische Zeitschrift*
VT	*Vetus Testamentum*
VTSup	Supplements to *Vetus Testamentum*
WBC	Word Biblical Commentary
WCF	Westminster Confession of Faith
WEC	Wycliffe Exegetical Commentary
WTJ	*Westminster Theological Journal*
ZNW	*Zeitschrift für die neutestamentliche Wissenschaft*
ZTK	*Zeitschrift für die Theologie und Kirche*

PREFACE

The rise of the fortunes of biblical theology within evangelicalism has served to help preserve the dialogue concerning the proper relationship of Law and Gospel as well as the utility of the Mosaic law for the contemporary Christian. There are a multitude of key ancillary issues that are generated by the Law/Gospel question, such as the purpose of the Mosaic law in the Old Testament and Paul's treatment of the law. Indeed, this important complex of concerns has been the subject of numerous books in recent years. This fact serves to confirm the importance of the issue for the Christian church and underscores the fact that there is no consensus of understanding of the relationship between Law and Gospel. Differing systems of theology often have radically different conceptions of the proper relationship between Law and Gospel. Since one's understanding of these issues has a direct impact on the application to the life of the believer in Christ, I believe it is imperative and helpful to decide the proper relationship of Mosaic law to the saint.

With that in mind, it is the purpose of this volume to facilitate an objective and, I hope, a well-argued presentation of major alternatives regarding the Mosaic Law, its relationship to the Gospel, and the role it plays in personal sanctification as well as in ethical systems. Unlike other treatments of the Law and Gospel issue, this approach features differing views presented in one volume, together with responses designed to highlight and bring into sharper focus the differences, some of which are systemic. This format also gives the reader the opportunity to evaluate the relative strengths and weaknesses of the views presented. The reader may then decide which view best harmonizes with the biblical and theological evidence. At the same time, it may perhaps also serve to foster a greater degree of rapprochement between the advocates of the various systems which, despite their differences, share an evangelical heritage.

This dialogue is not intended as an exhaustive treatment or analysis, but rather is designed to introduce the very complex issues and provide a framework for the resolution of the issue by the reader. Ample documentation is provided in the essays for more in-depth reflection on the issues by the reader.

All of the contributors to this volume represent careful and articulate evangelical scholarship in biblical studies. Each contributor is committed to the primacy and authority of the Scriptures in framing the understanding of the Law/Gospel issue. Each advocate of a view has devoted extensive study to the issue and has written with great conviction. Yet each author has also written with an irenic spirit as befits Christ and Christian charity.

I would like to acknowledge those who have helped in this project. My deep thanks to the other participants who have helped to make this treatise a reality. Each contributor has appreciated the benefit of such an enterprise. They have engaged in this project enthusiastically and have made the task of editing a joy. I also wish to thank Leonard G. Goss and Stanley N. Gundry for their invaluable assistance at several points in the process of composition. I have especially valued the enthusiastic support shown by Len Goss from the inception of the project.

May this dialogue of brothers in Christ glorify God and encourage a life of holiness for his saints. *Tu solus sanctus.*

Wayne G. Strickland
General editor

Chapter One

THE NON-THEONOMIC REFORMED VIEW

Willem A. VanGemeren

THE LAW IS THE PERFECTION OF RIGHTEOUSNESS IN JESUS CHRIST: A REFORMED PERSPECTIVE

Willem A. VanGemeren

INTRODUCTION

In 1955 two outstanding Christians addressed the topic of the law of God. E. F. Kevan (1903–65), late principal of London Bible College, challenged the members of the Tyndale Fellowship for Biblical Research (Cambridge, England) with a lecture published as *The Evangelical Doctrine of Law*. Beginning his discussion with the place of God's law in the created order before the Fall, he affirmed that the law is "the *rule of life* of the redeemed."[1]

John Murray (1898–1975), the late professor of Systematic Theology at Westminster Theological Seminary, addressed the topic of ethics and the law in the Payton Lectures at Fuller Theological Seminary. These lectures were expanded and published in 1957 under the title *Principles of Conduct*.[2] In his characteristic manner, Murray set Christian ethics in the dual context of Scripture and the Westminster standards. Beginning

---

[1]E. F. Kevan, *The Evangelical Doctrine of Law* (London: Tyndale Press, 1956), 13 (emphasis mine). The same year he lectured at the Keswick Convention, resulting in the publication of *The Law of God in Christian Experience: A Study in the Epistle to the Galatians* (London: Pickering & Inglis, 1955).

[2]John Murray, *Principles of Conduct* (Grand Rapids: Eerdmans, 1957).

with the early chapters of Genesis, Murray argued for continuity in God's ordinances, also called creation ordinances.

Not all students of the Bible were then or are now in agreement with Kevan and Murray. Differences in theological perspectives on the law have existed for many centuries, as the Reformed theologian Jonathan Edwards (1703–58) observed, "There is perhaps no part of divinity attended with so much intricacy, and wherein orthodox divines do so much differ as stating the precise agreement and difference between the two dispensations of Moses and Christ."[3]

The issue of the observance and interpretation of the law has become more acute since 1955. Regrettably, while the academic discussion of the law has significantly advanced, the observance of the law has eroded. Growing individualism and narcissism, the closing of the American mind, and ignorance of the Bible have resulted in an ethical crisis, affecting even evangelical Christianity.

Indeed, there are many factors that have led to the modern crisis, and the issues are complex. Yet I believe that submission to God's law in the spirit of John Calvin and the Westminster standards may well create a deeper longing for God, develop a greater zeal for the interpretation of God's Word, kindle the flame of a renewed commitment to personal and societal ethics, rebuild relationships, and reconstitute vibrant Christian communities.

Special Approach to the Subject

I approach the subject on the Reformed view of the law as a pastor, a Reformed theologian, and a professor of Old Testament. As a pastor, I am concerned that God's children learn to discipline themselves after the teaching and model of the obedient Son of God, grow in righteousness by keeping the law in the power of the Spirit, and present themselves as an acceptable offering to the glory of the Father.

As a Reformed theologian, I affirm enthusiastically that the system of doctrine as set forth in the Westminster Confession and Catechisms is taught in the Scriptures. The Westminster Confession, with its clear and consistent formulation of covenant

---

[3]Jonathan Edwards, "Inquiry Concerning Qualifications for Communion," in *The Works of President Edwards*, 4 vols. 8th ed. (New York: Leavitt & Allen, 1858), 1:160. Cited by Daniel P. Fuller, *Gospel & Law: Contrast or Continuum? The Hermeneutics of Dispensationalism and Covenant Theology* (Grand Rapids: Eerdmans, 1980), 5–6.

theology, knows of only two basic covenantal structures: the covenant of works and the covenant of grace. The *covenant of works*, made with Adam, contained the promise of life "upon condition of perfect and personal obedience."[4] The *covenant of grace* extends from the Fall of humankind to the new creation and appears in two administrations: Law and Gospel. The administration (epoch) of *Law* was characterized by "promises, prophecies, sacrifices, circumcision, the paschal lamb, and other types and ordinances . . . all foresignifying Christ to come."[5] Israel's experience of salvation and the revelation of God was for them "sufficient and efficacious, through the operation of the Spirit, to instruct and build up the elect in faith in the promised Messiah, by whom they had full remission of sins, and eternal salvation." The administration of the *Gospel* is the era inaugurated by the incarnation of Jesus Christ. He is the reality and the substance of the covenant of grace. Yet Law and Gospel are not in opposition to each other because Law contains Gospel and the Gospel contains Law. Both Law and Gospel affirm the place of the moral law as a "perfect rule of righteousness."[6]

As a professor of Old Testament, I approach the law in the larger context of the covenants of God, the divine self-disclosure, and the progression of God's revelation and redemptive history.[7] Redemptive history is the unfolding of God's plan of salvation from Creation to the new creation; in the words of Murray, "progressive revelation, progressive realization of redemption, and progressive disclosure of the grace of the Spirit have been the method by which God's redemptive purpose in the world has been fulfilled."[8]

The Bible speaks of a beginning and an end. God's involvement with human beings is set within the two horizons of Creation *and* the new creation. Looking back to the one horizon, we reflect on God's involvement with and care for Adam and Eve. He gave them his law and one test. This test led to human transgression, expulsion from the Garden, and our present state of alienation from God.

Looking toward the other horizon, we see a new creation

---

[4]WCF, 7.2.
[5]WCF, 7.5.
[6]WCF, 19.2.
[7]W. A. VanGemeren, *The Progress of Redemption* (Grand Rapids: Zondervan, 1988).
[8]Murray, *Principles*, 18–19.

where God is present with the redeemed of all ages. They were defiled and guilty in Adam, but in Jesus Christ they are holy and pure. They belonged to the fallen creation, but are a new creation in Jesus Christ (Gal. 6:15). They were lawbreakers in Adam, but are now lawkeepers in Jesus Christ.

Jesus is the focus of both creation (John 1:3) and the new creation (Rev. 21:22). He is also the center of redemptive history. Jesus came, withstood the test, obeyed the law of God perfectly, bore the curse of the law upon himself in his death, and prevailed over Satan. He alone has made an acceptable atonement for sin, redeemed sinners, consecrated them, and shared his inheritance with the saints—an eternity of glory.

God's children prepare themselves for that inheritance by living to the glory of God; in the words of the Larger Catechism, "Man's chief and highest end is to glorify God, and fully to enjoy him for ever."[9] The total witness of the Old and the New Testament has a "basic unity and continuity of the biblical ethic."[10] Both Testaments contain the revelation of one God, given to people who live by faith, are sustained by his grace, enjoy communion with him as his covenant people, and persevere in faith.[11] Over the millennia, God has spoken through many servants and climactically through his Son, and he has repeatedly stated that there is one condition for entering into his eternal presence: "without holiness no one will see the Lord" (Heb. 12:14b).

Clearly, God expects his children in every epoch of redemptive history to love him, to obey from the heart, and to do his will gladly. Reformed theologians have rightly insisted that God is holy, that the moral law is holy, and that Jesus is the focus of the law. The history of redemption gives a perspective on the continuity and the discontinuity of this triad (God, law, Jesus Christ). Theological reflection on the law of God adds new dimensions by the issues raised in the history of the church. I plan to treat these two approaches separately with the hope that the reader may appreciate how the Reformed view of the law of God is the result of integration of exegesis and theology and is applicable to any age and to any culture.

---

[9] Larger Catechism, Answer to Question 1.
[10] Murray, *Principles*, 7.
[11] Ibid., 199–201.

THE LAW OF GOD IN THE HISTORY OF REDEMPTION

This section will focus on the place of the law of God in six major stages in redemptive history (Creation, Fall, Abraham, Moses, Jesus Christ, Paul). There is an underlying unity in biblical ethics. In every epoch of redemptive history, the Lord has loved people, and they have responded to his love by the triad of *love* for God (submission), *law* (obedience), and *life* (blessing). This linkage brings together the three ingredients of biblical ethics according to which the godly love the Lord: by *submitting* themselves to him, by *obeying* his law, and by depending on him alone for *life's blessings* (provision, guidance, protection). Any change in the order of the triad of love, law, and life leads away from theocentric ethics. Obedience separated from submission (i.e., obeying the law apart from a love for God) opens the door to mere legalism. Love of one's life apart from a prior love for God opens the door to subjectivism, antinomianism, or narcissism.

Creation[12]

A World of Order

This world has been created by one God, by whose wisdom creation is an orderly cosmos. He rules his creation, sustains it with his grace, and extends his grace to animals and to humans.[13] The Garden of Eden with its order ordained by the Lord is a reflection of the God who loves order. It remains a metaphor for harmony—a harmony between God and humans, between humans and nature, and between the various elements of nature.

The human being reflects God's image in a desire for balance, harmony, and order. God not only blessed Adam and Eve, but he also endowed them with his image, that is, all the qualities needed to maintain order and to live in harmony with God and with other people: love, commitment, compassion, forbearance, righteousness, justice, and goodness.

---

[12]VanGemeren, *Progress*, 40–66.

[13]The Lord made a covenant with creation, and the particular beneficiaries of this covenant were Adam and Eve. This covenant may be defined *as a sovereign administration of grace.* See W. J. Dumbrell, *Covenant and Creation: An Old Testament Covenantal Theology* (Exeter: Paternoster, 1984), 20–43.

Law and Order

The creation of humans in the divine image entails their being responsible. Adam and Eve were responsible for staying within the moral order. God gave them ordinances (creation ordinances) that are perpetually binding on all human beings.[14] The creation ordinances regulate rest, patterned after God's rest, establish responsible involvement (rule) over God's creation, and develop harmonious relationships with God, family members, and other human beings (Gen. 1:28; 2:2–3, 24; cf. Eph. 4:24). Because God endowed humans with his image and with his grace, they were capable of keeping and enhancing the spiritual, moral, and social order.

Order can only be maintained when humans acknowledge the triad love for God (submission), law (obedience), and life (blessing). The particular test of the first man's loyalty to the Lord was the prohibition not to eat from the tree in the midst of the Garden. It was a test of Adam's love for God: Would he be obedient to God's will and trust him for his life?

The Fall, Human Kingdoms, and the Law of God[15]

Rebellion in God's World

Order did not last. Sin shattered tranquility of the Garden. Sin is disobedience to God's law (Gen. 3). Adam and Eve deceived themselves into thinking that they could be more than they were. Instead of realizing some kind of higher potential and greater wisdom and happiness, Adam and Eve stood condemned before God. They were forced to leave the harmony of the Garden for a world filled with anxiety, alienation, and anguish.

The relationship between God and humankind is often an adversarial one, an ongoing contest between two wills. People repeatedly challenge God's legitimate sovereignty. Instead of building the kingdom of God, humans endeavor to construct their own kingdoms.

How do they do this? They live as if God has no relevance in their affairs and as if they are absolutely free to go their own way. Vestiges of the image of God remain, though shattered by the Fall. People still love order and seek to maintain it at any cost. Yet they also destroy order by advancing their own interests. Individuals

---

[14]For a fuller treatment of the creation ordinances, see Murray, *Principles*.
[15]VanGemeren, *Progress*, 68–97.

and nations have unjustly oppressed others in the pursuit of individual justice, happiness, and freedom.

The severity of the human condition evoked God's judgment on the generation of the Flood. Humankind had become corrupt. The Lord pronounced a terrible judgment on the human race because sin affected everyone. Humans had become so depraved that God observed "how great man's wickedness on the earth had become, and that every inclination of the thoughts of his heart was only evil all the time" (Gen. 6:5). Nevertheless, after the Flood, God permitted culture to continue in spite of human depravity: "every inclination of his heart is evil from childhood" (8:21).

The Bible portrays humans as unreliable and bent on independence. Another word for this human tendency toward self-rule is autonomy. *Autonomy* comes from two Greek words: *autos* ("self") and *nomos* ("law"). In other words, people love to develop their own laws by which to live and judge other humans. The spirit of autonomy came to expression at the Tower of Babel and revealed two aspects of the revolutionary nature of humanity, namely, that humans resist submitting themselves to God and exert themselves in self-development. The human race continues to be ambitious, to develop structures and institutions, to provide for itself, to protect itself, and to enrich itself.

Godliness before the Mosaic Law

Before the law of Moses was given, the godly walked with the Lord, loved him, and maintained order in his world. Enoch, Noah, and Abraham are representatives of the heroes of faith who observed the moral law by practicing a righteousness and blamelessness apart from the Mosaic law. Unlike their contemporaries, these heroes of faith were committed to God, sought his kingdom, and obeyed him (Heb. 11:5–19).

Enoch, the father of Methuselah, was a man of God. The phrase "walked with God" is found twice in the description of Enoch (Gen. 5:22, 24) and signifies his subordination of and commitment to the Lord.[16] Noah, too, "walked with God" (6:9) and found favor with the Lord (v. 8). He was a man of faith and of

---

[16]Victor P. Hamilton, *Genesis 1–17*, NICOT (Grand Rapids: Eerdmans, 1990), 258. G. J. Wenham suggests that "the double repetition of the phrase 'walked with God' indicates Enoch was outstanding in this pious family" (*Genesis 1–15*, WBC [Waco: Word, 1987], 127).

integrity, "a righteous man [ṣaddîq], blameless [tāmîm] among the people of his time" (v. 9). These two descriptive phrases—ṣaddîq and tāmîm—set Noah apart from the corruption and violence of his generation (v. 11). The word "righteous" denotes a commitment to God and an ethical integrity by which order is restored in this world. Those who are righteous separate themselves from the order of this world and advance God's "order" (cf. Ps. 1). Those who are "blameless" set before themselves the goal of "wholeness" of life; they live in harmony with God and with other human beings.

Abraham[17]

Faith and Law

Abraham, the father of faith, also walked with the Lord (Gen. 15:6; 17:1). Even though he did not receive the Decalogue, he kept the law of God. He was "blameless" (tāmîm) in that he adhered to God's unwritten law (17:1; 18:19). God himself comments to Isaac about Abraham's fidelity, when he confirmed the promises to him: "Abraham obeyed [šmʻ] me and kept [šmr] my requirements [mišmeret], my commands [miṣwâ], my decrees [ḥuqqâ] and my laws [tôrâ]" (26:5). The choice of nouns (miṣwâ, ḥuqqâ, tôrâ) and verbs (šmʻ, šmr) is significant in that they anticipate the revelation at Mount Sinai.

It is important to note that the "father of faith" was a lawkeeper. Abraham came to God in faith (15:6), walked with God in faith (17:1), had faith in God's word (cf. Heb 11:17–19), had faith in God as the Creator (v. 3; cf. Gen 14:22), and had faith in God's plan for a new creation (Heb. 11:13–16). As he walked with God, he demonstrated a living faith (cf. v. 17) by ordering his life in accordance with God's order. Abraham's interaction with relatives, kings, and people reveals that he had internalized the unwritten law. The "father of faith" demonstrated a righteousness apart from the written law of Moses. What then was the nature of the unwritten law Abraham kept?

The Unwritten Law of God

Philosophers and theologians have posited the existence of a moral order—or natural law—that reasonable human beings may discover. Some have explained this order as deriving from the will

---

[17]VanGemeren, *Progress*, 100–130.

of God (e.g., Scotus and Ockham) and others as deriving from the essence of things (e.g., Aquinas).[18]

John Calvin accepted the medieval concept of natural law, but redefined its meaning in two ways. First, natural law refers to the *order in nature* by virtue of God's creation. Calvin taught that natural law is "constant" in spite of human sin and rebellion, because it is God who graciously upholds creation.[19] Second, natural law is that *moral order* that God has enabled human beings to deduce from creation. It is "constant" insofar as it is rooted in the will of God, but "variable" in that the human conscience is an imperfect guide.[20] "Calvin did not mean that we could dispense with God's law and substitute a natural law," writes Cochrane. "His point is that God's law is in harmony with the true order of man's creatureliness *which is itself known from God's law.*"[21]

The Westminster Divines agreed with Calvin that God had endowed Adam and Eve with the ability to develop a moral order and, thus, to live in harmony with God's will. This law was "a perfect rule of righteousness."[22] If our first parents had obeyed it, they would have demonstrated a righteousness apart from the written law. The written law became necessary because of human sin and hardness of heart.

The moral law in its written form does not contradict or change the will of God. Rather, it makes explicit and amplifies that will as originally expressed in natural law. Since the will of God does not change, the law remains virtually the same throughout redemptive history.

---

[18]J. Van Engen, "Natural Law," *Evangelical Dictionary of Theology*, ed. W. Elwell (Grand Rapids: Baker, 1984), 751–52. Some have argued for a limited use of natural law (e.g., Karl Barth, T. F. Torrance); in the words of Wilhelm Niesel: "The law of nature has only one purpose: namely, to make man inexcusable before God" (*The Theology of Calvin*, trans. Harold Knight [Philadelphia: Westminster, 1956], 102). Others have argued for a more extensive place of natural law (e.g., Emil Brunner in his *Nature and Grace*); he holds that nature still contains the revelation of God and his will. See Arthur C. Cochrane, "Natural Law in Calvin," *Church-State Relations in Ecumenical Perspective*, ed. E. A. Smith (Louvain: Duquesne University Press, 1966), 176–80.

[19]Cochrane, "Natural Law," 204.

[20]Ibid., 197.

[21]Ibid., 206–7. For Calvin's view on the law apart from the written law, see I. John Hesselink, "Calvin's Concept and Use of the Law" (Ph.D. diss.; Basel, 1961), ch. V, 1–23.

[22]WCF, 19.2.

The moral law doth for ever bind all, as well justified persons as others, to the obedience thereof; and that, not only in regard of the matter contained in it, but also in respect of the authority of God the Creator, who gave it. Neither doth Christ, in the gospel, any way dissolve, but much strengthen this obligation.[23]

Natural law is not only the revelation of God's will, but it is also a revelation of his perfections—the divine qualities or attributes by which we may speak of the knowledge of God. He is good, loving, compassionate, faithful, merciful, patient, gentle, forbearing, just, and righteous. As the order of creation reveals the perfections of God, so does the moral order. Because God is good, loving, compassionate, faithful, and merciful, he expects his people to live out these same qualities in their relationship with him and with one another. The creation ordinances (worship, family, work, social relations) presuppose these qualities. Understandably, the entrance of sin has seriously affected the cultivation of the perfections and, hence, impeded the harmonious development of true religion, the family, society, and political and economic life in any culture.

Yet the concept of natural law explains the universal pursuit and appreciation of what is good, loving, compassionate, faithful, merciful, patient, gentle, forbearing, just, and righteous. Since the entrance of sin, man's knowledge of God and the discernment of his will are fallible, but God has extended his grace to humans. This grace, also known as common grace, explains God's restraint of evil and his supplying of human needs (food, drink), abilities, and a moral sense, including a sense of love and justice.

The concept of natural law also explains how Enoch, Noah, and Abraham responded to God's grace by keeping his law. Paul's distinction between the unwritten law and the written law is applicable to these men of faith: "Indeed, when Gentiles, who do not have the law, do by nature things required by the law, they are a law for themselves, even though they do not have the law, since they show that the requirements of the law are written on their hearts" (Rom. 2:14–15a).

The Father of Israel

Israel's roots and inheritance lie in their relation to Abraham. On the one hand, through Abraham Israel could have traced her roots back to the nations. The early chapters of Genesis show six

---

[23]WCF, 19.5.

universals of human existence: (1) *nature* is a part of an orderly universe created and sustained by one God; (2) humans are created in the *image of God* and with a sense of the moral law; (3) humans are affected by *sin* with its resultant corruption and rebelliousness; (4) God is the *sovereign and forbearing ruler*, who controls the nations, restrains sin, and upholds them by his grace; (5) humans are *responsible* for living in harmony with God's law in order to promote his order; and (6) humans are *accountable* to God and will have to submit to his judgment. Israel shared in these universals.

On the other hand, Israel shared in Abraham's inheritance. The Lord had called Abraham to leave the nations and to become the father of another people. His election was by grace, as was Israel's (Ex. 19:4; Deut. 7:6–8; 14:2). God intended to raise up a community of godly people who would follow Abraham's example of *love* for him, adherence to his *law*, and trust in his provisions for *life* (promises). He said, "For I have chosen him, so that he will direct his children and his household after him to keep the way of the LORD by doing what is right and just, so that the LORD will bring about for Abraham what he has promised him" (Gen. 18:19).

The Lord gave Abraham four promises: a large nation, a land, God's presence in blessing and protection, and the extension of blessing to the nations. The Lord covenanted to bring them to fulfillment (Gen. 12:2–3; 15:18–21; 17:1–8) and confirmed the promises to Isaac and to Jacob (26:3–4; 28:13–15; 35:11–12). This covenant, known as the Abrahamic covenant, is a sovereign administration of grace and promise. It is an administration of grace because the Lord promised that he would be present with his people (17:7; cf. Ex. 6:7; Deut. 29:13; Ezek. 11:20).[24]

The apostle Paul confirms the special benefits that had come to Israel as heirs of the promise: "Theirs is the adoption as sons; theirs the divine glory, the covenants, the receiving of the law, the temple worship and the promises. Theirs are the patriarchs, and from them is traced the human ancestry of Christ, who is God over all, forever praised! Amen" (Rom. 9:4–5).

---

[24]VanGemeren, *Progress*, 169–77.

The Mosaic Covenant[25]

Creation-order and law-order are correlative.[26] Law cannot be separated from the Lawgiver or from God's plan to bring order in creation. At Creation, God sent forth his word to create order. At Sinai, God sent forth his word to renew humans and prepare them for a new order. Psalm 147 reflects this holistic approach by relating God's word both to the natural order and to the moral life of God's people:

> He sends his command ['imrâ] to the earth;
> his word [dābār] runs swiftly. . . .
> He sends his word [dābār] and melts them;
> he stirs up his breezes, and the waters flow.
> He has revealed his word [dābār] to Jacob,
> his laws [ḥuqqîm] and decrees [mišpāṭîm] to Israel.
> (Ps. 147:15, 18–19; cf. Ps 19).

Far from looking at the law as a negative experience, saints in the Old Testament rejoiced in this revelation because obedience to the law was framed within the triad of love, law (obedience), and life.

In this section, I will develop a framework for looking at and interpreting the law of God. This framework includes five points of reference: (1) the fear of the Lord; (2) the God of the covenant; (3) the mediator of the covenant; (4) the covenant; and (5) the law of God.

The Fear of the Lord

Without the fear of God, obedience to the law reverts to legalism or to rebelliousness. Such was the case with Israel at the end of the forty years of wandering. The people needed a change of heart, "Oh, that their hearts would be inclined to fear [yr'] me and keep all my commands always, so that it might go well with them and their children forever!" (Deut. 5:29).

The fear of the Lord is not a phobia. Rather, it is that holy response to God by which the godly are inclined more and more to submit to and to imitate God (Deut. 6:2, 13, 24; 10:12; 31:12–13). The *fear* of the Lord comes to expression in four ways: (1) *faith*

---

[25]Ibid., 132–79.

[26]Oliver Barclay argues for a creation ethics ("The Nature of Christian Morality," in *Law, Morality and the Bible: A Symposium*, ed. Bruce Kaye and Gordon Wenham [Downers Grove: InterVarsity, 1978], 125–50).

and trust, (2) ethical integrity, (3) awe for God, and (4) reverence for God.

First, *faith and trust* in the Lord is the requisite for obedience to the law. Israel's rebellion in the wilderness showed that they did not trust him. Moses said, "But you rebelled against the command of the LORD your God. You did not trust him or obey him. You have been rebellious against the LORD ever since I have known you" (Deut. 9:23b-24). Trust is that childlike acceptance of the Father's will, depending solely on his ability to provide for one's needs.

Second, the fear of the Lord comes to expression in *ethical integrity*, which is the progress in sanctification whereby the individual aligns himself more and more with God's will. One's acts, speech, and thoughts externalize the internal work of the Holy Spirit. Living in ethical integrity involves being *tamîm* ("blameless") and *ṣaddîq* ("righteous"), like Noah and Abraham (Gen 6:8; 17:1). The word "blameless" denotes a wholeness of heart and an integration of one's self with God and other humans (cf. Ps. 18:24; 101:2, 6; 119:1; Matt. 5:48; Eph. 1:4; Phil. 2:15; Col. 1:22). The words "righteous" (*ṣaddîq*) and "righteousness" (*ṣedeq, ṣedāqâ*) relate to one's active obedience to the will of God.

Third, *awe for God* is a major motivating factor. Awe is that sense of respect, honor, and greatness that we cultivate toward a superior or a person in power. It is the emotional reaction to God's presence, miracles, and revelation. The revelation at Mount Sinai created this sense of awe for the condescension of the holy God (Ex. 19), and it was always to be in Israel's memory (Deut. 10:17, 20). The book of Hebrews calls attention to the difference between the revelation at Mount Sinai and the greater revelation of grace and glory in Jesus Christ (Heb. 12:18–27). The new covenant relationship in no way detracts from the holiness of God and of our response of awe and reverence (12:28–29). John Murray describes it this way: "The controlling sense of the majesty and holiness of God and the profound reverence which this apprehension elicits constitute the essence of the fear of God."[27]

Finally, the response to God's holiness comes to expression in *reverence for God*. This is entailed in the call: "Be holy because I, the LORD your God, am holy" (Lev. 19:2; cf. 11:44). Reverence involves consecrating oneself to the Lord for the purpose of living in harmony with God and with other people. The best expression of reverence is the imitation of God. His law teaches us in detail how

---

[27]Murray, *Principles*, 237.

to imitate God in being compassionate, gracious, forbearing, loving, faithful, forgiving, and just.

The God of the Covenant

Yahweh, the Creator of the cosmos and the God of the patriarchs, bound himself to the descendants of Abraham! He graciously committed himself to a relationship with them and assured them by the name *Yahweh* and by the revelation of his perfections.

The covenant name "Yahweh" ("the LORD") signifies that he is the God of the past, present, and future. The somewhat enigmatic phraseology *'ehyeh 'ᵃšer 'ehyeh* (lit. "I shall be who I shall be," Ex. 3:14) expresses God's sovereign freedom in his relationship with his people. It may best be rendered as "I will be whoever I will be," on the basis of the syntactically similar construction in Exodus 33:19: "I will have mercy on whom I will have mercy, and I will have compassion on whom I will have compassion." This doctrine of God's freedom has two implications. First, he is sovereign and unconstrained by creaturely limitations, acts of resistance, frustration, or expectation. Second, he is faithful in fulfilling his promise whenever and however he wills it.[28]

The perfections of God also assure his people of the constancy of his love. By nature Israel was stubborn and rebellious. Having been caught in the idolatrous worship of the golden calf (Ex. 32), Israel's future was in question. Though the people were subject to the sanctions of the law (22:20), the Lord dealt graciously with them by not destroying them. Israel's frailty threatened the continuity of the covenant relationship, but the revelation of the Lord's "goodness" (33:19) was and is the only reason for hope. His "goodness" is another expression for his "glory" (v. 18), that is, the wholeness of his perfections. Yahweh is "the compassionate and gracious God, slow to anger, abounding in love and faithfulness, maintaining love to thousands, and forgiving wickedness, rebellion and sin. Yet he does not leave the guilty unpunished" (34:6–7a; cf. Ps. 103). The divine perfections not only guarantee his commitment to creation, but also to redemption! God not only revealed his glory in creation (Ps. 57:11; Isa. 6:3), but also in his grace and forbearance with his people in the history of redemption (Isa. 44:23; 60:1–2).

---

[28]VanGemeren, *Progress*, 148–50.

Moses

Moses' position and revelation foreshadow the unique position and revelation of the Lord Jesus. Moses was God's servant (Ex. 14:31; Deut. 34:5; Josh. 1:1,2) and intimate friend (Ex. 33:11; Num. 12:6–8). He also served as the mediator of the covenant (Ex. 19:3–8; 20:18–19)[29] by whom the Lord administered his grace, confirmed the promises, consecrated Israel as his holy people, and gave the law with its sanctions.[30] Calvin rightly holds up the importance of Moses: "And Moses was not made a lawgiver to wipe out the blessing promised to the race of Abraham. Rather, we see him repeatedly reminding the Jews of that freely given covenant made with their fathers of which they were the heirs. It was as if he were sent to renew it."[31]

Moses' ministry prepared the people for the coming of Christ. Hebrews portrays him as a witness to the coming of Jesus Christ: "Moses was faithful . . . testifying to what would be said in the future" (Heb. 3:5). That future was nothing less than the coming rest in Jesus Christ (4:1–13), for whose sake Moses also suffered (11:26). Moses witnessed through his Torah to the spirituality of the covenant and to the need of a redeemer whose atonement would remove the burden of the law. He pointed to a transformation of God's people who would have the heart to fear the Lord (Deut. 5:29), having been transformed by the Holy Spirit (Num. 11:29; Deut. 30:5–10).

Moses painfully realized that his generation could not enter into the rest because of disobedience and rebelliousness (Deut. 4:21–25). He spoke of a new era opened up by God's grace (4:29–31; 30:5–10), an era of peace, tranquility, and full enjoyment of God's presence, blessing, and protection (12:9–10; 25:19; Ex. 33:14; cf. Heb. 4:1–11).

The Mosaic administration, therefore, was never intended to be an end in itself. It prepared people for the coming of Jesus Christ: "If you believed Moses, you would believe me, for he wrote about me" (John 5:46).

---

[29]Ibid., 158–60.

[30]For a treatment on the dynamics of law and grace, see Thomas E. McComiskey, *The Covenants of Promise: A Theology of the Old Testament Covenants* (Grand Rapids: Baker, 1985), 94–137.

[31]John Calvin, *Inst.*, 2.7.1.

The Mosaic Covenant

The Mosaic covenant is a development of God's covenant with creation (i.e., a sovereign administration of grace) and with Abraham (i.e., a sovereign administration of grace and promise). In other words, the Mosaic covenant is a sovereign administration of grace and promise by which the Lord consecrated a people to himself under the sanctions of his royal law. It is an administration of grace and promise, but also of law and sanctions.

The Mosaic covenant is an *administration of grace* in that the Lord dealt graciously with his people.[32] God forgave their sins, extended the benefits of the atonement for sin, consecrated the people to himself, gave them the joy of salvation, and renewed their spirits within them. During periods of their rebelliousness, he showed forbearance, love, and compassion. This administration was a means of grace for the godly in Israel, as it helped them to focus on the Lord and to await his salvation. The law was never intended to be the focus or the end in itself.

The Mosaic covenant is an administration of promise in that the Lord confirmed the promises, fulfilled them, and gave Israel a foretaste of the reality in Jesus Christ. The Mosaic covenant is not antithetical to the promises made to Abraham, nor is the Mosaic covenant a substitute for the Abrahamic covenant. Rather, the Mosaic covenant is a confirmation of the promises made to the patriarchs: "The LORD, the God of your fathers—the God of Abraham, Isaac and Jacob—appeared to me and said: I have watched over you and have seen what has been done to you in Egypt" (Ex. 3:16).

The Mosaic covenant is an *administration of law* in that the Lord bound individuals and tribes together into one nation by detailed regulations.[33] The law was God's means of shaping Israel into a "counter-community." Yahweh had consecrated Israel as a witness to the nations by showing them in the law how to mirror his perfections. The legal system of any other people reflects the culture of that people. Through God's law, however, the godly came to know how to reflect God's love, compassion, fidelity, and other perfections.

---

[32]See Francis I. Andersen, "Yahweh, the Kind and Sensitive God," in *God Who Is Rich in Mercy*, ed. P. T. O'Brien and D. G. Peterson (Homebush West, Australia: Lancer, 1986), 41–88; Gordon Wenham, "Grace and Law in the Old Testament," in *Law, Morality and the Bible*, 3–23.

[33]See Gordon Wenham, "Law and the Legal System in the Old Testament," in *Law, Morality and the Bible*, 24–52.

The Mosaic administration as a legal administration related to Israel as little children who did not quite understand the greatness and goodness of God's grace (Deut. 8:5; 32:7–15; Hos. 11:1; cf. Gal. 4:1–7, 21–31). Yet it is important to stress again that the Law of the Old Testament is not against the Gospel. It is an expression of God's care. In the interest of teaching his children how they should relate to him and how they should develop wholesome relations with one another, he detailed for them his expectations in laws, statutes, and ordinances.

God also threatened them with the sanctions (curses) in case of disobedience. The legal aspect of the Mosaic administration led people to look for the coming of Christ. The law was God's instrument to bring the godly closer to himself. They saw their need of the Savior because the Holy Spirit showed them their sins (Ps. 32:3–5), the awesome guilt that their knowledge of the law brought (51:3–5), and the imperfection of their offerings and sacrifices (vv. 16–17). They hoped for the righteous Redeemer, who is perfect in his obedience and able to bring redemption (cf. Isa. 11:1–9; 52:13–53:12). Indeed, he took upon himself the curse of the law by his death (Gal. 3:13–14). But for the unbelieving Israelites, the law was a burden that condemned them.

The Law of God

The Decalogue ("Ten Commandments") is found in Exodus 20:1–17 and Deuteronomy 5:6–21. These commandments, also called the "Ten Words" (4:13; cf. 5:22),[34] are the summary of the moral law and form the basic constitution of Israel in three ways. First, the opening provides a constant reminder that the context of law is God's work of redemption: "I am the LORD your God, who brought you out of Egypt, out of the land of slavery" (Ex. 20:2). Obedience to the commandments is in response to God's grace in being Israel's deliverer. Second, the Decalogue details how humans must express their love for the Lord and for their neighbor. Third, the Decalogue forms the basis of the other codes, of Moses' instructions, and of future judicial decisions. The laws

---

[34]Calvin divided the commandments into the two tablets of the law. The four commandments pertaining to our duty toward God were on the first, and the six commandments regarding our duties to humans were on the other (*Inst.*, 2.8.11). Meredith G. Kline has argued that the two tablets were identical copies of the covenant between Yahweh and Israel, on the pattern of the suzerainty treaty (*Treaty of the Great King: The Covenant Structure of Deuteronomy—Studies and Commentary* [Grand Rapids: Eerdmans, 1963], 13–26).

are in the form of imperatives ("you shall" or "you shall not") and are apodictic in form. Apodictic laws are permanent injunctions, prohibitions, or commandments. In contrast, casuistic laws (or case laws) give specific applications of the law under restricted circumstances. The laws of the Old Testament have also been commonly categorized as moral, ceremonial, and civil. Each one of the Ten Commandments expresses the moral law of God, whereas most laws in the Pentateuch regulate the rituals and ceremonies (ceremonial laws) and the civil life of Israel as a nation (civil laws).

The Book of the Covenant (Ex. 20:22–23:33)—with its regulations for worship (20:22–26; 23:14–19) and its civil laws (21:1–23:13)—extends the Decalogue in three directions. First, there is the complex development of *case law*. These laws begin with "if" or "when," and briefly describe a situation that may present itself in real life. For example, when the sixth commandment is applied to real life, the case laws differentiate between intentional and accidental homicide: "Anyone who strikes a man and kills him shall surely be put to death. However, if he does not do it intentionally, but God lets it happen, he is to flee to a place I will designate. But if a man schemes and kills another man deliberately, take him away from my altar and put him to death" (21:12–14).

Second, the *criminal laws* specify the penalty for breaking the commandments. In the example below, the laws reflect back on the Decalogue, render a judgment on a case by case basis, and specify a penalty:[35]

"Anyone who attacks his father or his mother must be put to death." [Fifth commandment]

"Anyone who kidnaps another and either sells him or still has him when he is caught must be put to death." [Eighth commandment]

---

[35]See T. Longman III, "God's Law and Mosaic Punishments Today," in *Theonomy, A Reformed Critique*, eds. W. S. Barker and W. R. Godfrey (Grand Rapids: Zondervan, 1990), 41–54. Longman rightly observes, "It is not a simple thing to apply the Old Testament law and its penalties to the New Testament period. We must take into account not only cultural differences, but also redemptive-historical differences. The latter will have a definite impact on how Old Testament civil laws, which have to do with the relationship between God and Israel, will be brought over into modern society. Each law and each penalty needs to be studied in the light of the changes between Israel and America, the old covenant and the new covenant. Theonomy tends to grossly overemphasize continuity to the point of being virtually blind to discontinuity" (48–49).

"Anyone who curses his father or mother must be put to death." [Fifth commandment] (Ex. 21:15–17).

Third, the Book of the Covenant reveals the *complexity of Israelite law*.[36] The moral laws (i.e., those reflected in the Decalogue) are intertwined with the civil laws, penal code, and ceremonial laws. For example:

[*moral*] Anyone who has sexual relations with an animal must be put to death.

Whoever sacrifices to any god other than the LORD must be destroyed.

Do not mistreat an alien or oppress him, for you were aliens in Egypt.

Do not take advantage of a widow or an orphan. If you do and they cry out to me, I will certainly hear their cry. [*penal*] My anger will be aroused, and I will kill you with the sword; your wives will become widows and your children fatherless.

[*casuistic/civil*] If you lend money to one of my people among you who is needy, do not be like a moneylender; charge him no interest. If you take your neighbor's cloak as a pledge, return it to him by sunset, because his cloak is the only covering he has for his body. What else will he sleep in? When he cries out to me, I will hear, for I am compassionate.

[*moral*] Do not blaspheme God or curse the ruler of your people.

Do not hold back offerings from your granaries or your vats.

[*ceremonial*] You must give me the firstborn of your sons. (Ex. 22:19–29)

The book of Leviticus further develops the law in three ways. First, the priests taught and applied the ceremonial laws: offerings and sacrifices (Lev. 1–7; 22); ritual purity (chaps. 11–15); feasts and festivals (including the Day of Atonement, chaps. 16; 23; 25), and laws of holiness (chaps. 17–27).

Second, the priests in particular modeled the high standard of ritual holiness and purity. They came into the very presence of God to represent the people. Whenever they served, they had to remember that God is holy and that he demands that all who approach him be whole and complete in observing his law: "You must distinguish between the holy and the common, between the unclean and the clean" (Lev. 10:10). Wholeness or completion is that state of consecration to the Lord in which the individual

---

[36]For the problems with a form-critical approach, see J. I. Durham, *Exodus*, WBC (Waco: Word, 1987) 315–18.

applies the law of God to every aspect of life.[37] Only when so prepared were the priests permitted to enter into God's presence: "'Among those who approach me I will show myself holy; in the sight of all the people I will be honored'" (10:3).

Such men of integrity were also set apart to be the teachers of God's people: "You must teach the Israelites all the decrees the LORD has given them through Moses" (Lev. 10:11). The power of their teaching was located in a lifestyle of "wholeness" as they were consecrated to the Lord. The purpose of their separation unto wholeness and of their role as teachers of God's holy law was to lead God's people into a wholeness of life, "to teach my people the difference between the holy and the common and show them how to distinguish between the unclean and the clean" (Ezek. 44:23; cf. Heb. 12:14–15).

For example, the commandment "love your neighbor as yourself" (Lev. 19:18) is defined in the context as an imitation of God: "Be holy because I, the LORD your God, am holy" (v. 2). Humans must be "holy" in their love for fellow humans. How can they avoid interpreting the commandment in such a way as to make it powerless? Apart from looking at God's repeated evidences of his love, the context of the commandment defines a wholeness of life. The godly act, speak, and think in submission to God's laws. Everything in their lives is integrated! The laws in Leviticus 19 specify that true love shows concern for the poor and the handicapped (vv. 9–10, 14), keeps the Decalogue (vv. 11–13), and upholds the sanctity of justice (v. 15), human dignity (v. 16), life (v. 17), and interpersonal relations (vv. 17–18a).

Third, the Lord taught his people through the law that they were guilty and under condemnation. This perfect instrument was designed to lead Israel to ethical perfection. However, no one could observe the law perfectly. Hence, the law itself pointed to the need of a more perfect high priest, better sacrifices, and a better atonement. The Lord taught them to look at the sacrifices and rituals as symbols of his grace in Jesus Christ.

Conclusion: Love, Law, and Life

Was the law the means of salvation? Was it the means of inheritance? Was the law an instrument of sanctification? I would

---

[37]M. Douglas has argued persuasively that holiness means ordering one's life in accordance with God's revealed order. Every regulation was a step toward the development of "the idea of holiness as order" (cited by Wenham, *Leviticus*, NICOT [Grand Rapids: Eerdmans, 1979] 24).

answer the first two questions in the negative, and the third in the positive. The law was never intended to be the means of salvation or of gaining the inheritance. God used the law to instruct his people to have a living faith in him, the source of the promise. He further taught them to express this faith in concrete acts of love by which they promoted a harmonious lifestyle of concern for God's honor and for the dignity of their fellow humans.

On the surface, it may appear that Leviticus 18:5 teaches that the inheritance is obtained by keeping the law: "Keep my decrees and laws, for the man who obeys them will live by them. I am the LORD" (cf. Ezek. 18:9). However, when we compare this text with the sermonic expansion in Deuteronomy 30:15–20, we find that the Lord himself is the source of life and that anyone who loved the Lord would gladly submit to his law in faith of the living God. Moses said:

> See, I set before you today life and prosperity, death and destruction. For I command you today to love the LORD your God, to walk in his ways, and to keep his commands, decrees and laws; then you will live and increase, and the LORD your God will bless you in the land you are entering to possess. . . .
>
> This day I call heaven and earth as witnesses against you that I have set before you life and death, blessings and curses. Now choose life, so that you and your children may live and that you may love the LORD your God, listen to his voice, and hold fast to him. For the LORD is your life, and he will give you many years in the land he swore to give to your fathers, Abraham, Isaac and Jacob. (Deut. 30:15–16, 19–20)

Moses defined the two ways of life in antithetical language. On the one hand, he associated love for God with life and inheritance of the promise. On the other hand, he showed that disregard for God is associated with death and destruction (vv. 17–18). Jesus Christ likewise used the same twofold way to proclaim of the gospel: "Enter through the narrow gate. For wide is the gate and broad is the road that leads to *destruction*, and many enter through it. But small is the gate and narrow the road that leads to *life*, and only a few find it" (Matt. 7:13–14, emphases mine).

In the Old Testament "law and love are not opposed but complementary."[38] The Lord is concerned with the heart attitude of his servants and expects them to readily practice whatever he requires. The internalization of the law is both a motivation by the Spirit of God and a wholehearted expression of love for God. Peter

---

[38]B. de Pinto, "The Torah and the Psalms," *JBL* 86 (1967), 173.

C. Craigie sees rightly law and covenant in the context of love: "The Decalog was representative of God's love in that its injunctions, both negative and positive, led not to a restriction of life, but to fullness of life."[39]

In addition to the Torah of Moses, the sages and prophets of Israel confirm the importance of the triad of love, law, life. They exhort, teach, and encourage people to love (seek) the Lord. Obedience to the law always begins with a heart that fears the Lord: "Trust in the LORD with all your heart and lean not on your own understanding; in all your ways acknowledge him, and he will make your paths straight. Do not be wise in your own eyes; fear the LORD and shun evil" (Prov. 3:5–7). The fear of the Lord comes to expression in acts of obedience: commitment (ʾemet), love for others (ḥesed), fairness to others (mišpāṭ), and righteousness (ṣedeq, ṣᵉdāqâ). Obedience to the moral law brings peace (Prov. 3:17; 12:20) and order with God and man: "You will win favor and a good name in the sight of God and man" (3:4; cf. Luke 2:52).

The Psalms view true spirituality in a holistic manner and adumbrate the godly who live in the shadow of the Almighty (Ps. 91:1). Psalm 15 asks, "LORD, who may dwell in your sanctuary? Who may live on your holy hill?" (v. 1). Similarly, Psalm 24 inquires, "Who may ascend the hill of the LORD? Who may stand in his holy place?" (24:3). In response, each psalm encourages the godly to develop a "wholeness" of life in which holiness is more than a personal separation from the world unto God and in which integration of one's whole being with the divine qualities (righteousness, justice, love, and fidelity) is the chief desire.

Isaiah also raises the question as to what the Lord expects from his saints: "Who of us can dwell with the consuming fire? Who of us can dwell with everlasting burning?" (Isa. 33:14b). By means of these questions, he encourages the godly to love the Lord and to obey his law by practicing wholeness of life: walking "righteously" (ṣᵉdāqôt) and speaking what is "right" (mêšārîm, v. 15). Such persons receive the promise of God's care for their lives: "This is the man who will dwell on the heights, whose refuge will be the mountain fortress. His bread will be supplied, and water will not fail him" (v. 16).

---

[39]P. C. Craigie, *The Book of Deuteronomy*, NICOT (Grand Rapids: Eerdmans, 1976). I agree with Craigie that "the commandments continue to be valid in the NT . . . and are still considered to be of vital importance to the contemporary Christian," 150.

According to Isaiah 57:15, the person who seeks the new order belongs to God's kingdom and has the assurance of God's presence: "I live in a high and holy place, but also with him who is contrite and lowly in spirit, to revive the spirit of the lowly and to revive the heart of the contrite." Truly, Isaiah proclaims the good news to anyone who lives in the spirit of the Beatitudes:

> This is what the LORD says:
> "Heaven is my throne,
>   and the earth is my footstool.
> Where is the house you will build for me?
>   Where will my resting place be?
> Has not my hand made all these things,
>   and so they came into being?"
>
> declares the LORD.
>
> "This is the one I esteem:
>   he who is humble and contrite in spirit,
>   and trembles at my word."
>
> (Isa. 66:1–2)

Micah, a contemporary of Isaiah, tersely sets forth an Old Testament ethic. He defines living faith as a walk of humble reliance on the Lord, expressed in acts of love (ḥesed) and justice (mišpāṭ). He rebukes the people for knowing but not responding to the Mosaic law: "He has showed you, O man, what is good." Then he asks rhetorically, "What does the LORD require of you?" (Mic. 6:8a), and in a climactic manner he summarizes the law of Moses: "To act justly (mišpāṭ) and to love mercy (ḥesed) and to walk humbly with your God" (v. 8b; cf. Hos. 6:6).

Finally, Zechariah, a post-exilic prophet, encourages the godly to be faithful to God's law in preparation for the age of restoration. He, too, calls on the people of his generation to submit themselves to the Lord and to demonstrate their love for God by loving their neighbor. The evidence of love is after all obedience to the law of love: "These are the things you are to do: Speak the truth to each other, and render true and sound judgment in your courts; do not plot evil against your neighbor, and do not love to swear falsely. I hate all this" (Zech. 8:16–17).

THE NEW COVENANT

So far we have seen that the law of God reflects the divine perfections and that anyone who wants to be like God must reflect the nature of God by practicing righteousness, love, compassion, justice, and patience (cf. Ps. 111; 112).[40] The laws provide details and make more explicit what these qualities mean. How is God's requirement for holiness through the law changed in the new covenant?

The new covenant is the sovereign administration of grace and promise by which the Father consecrates his people to himself by the blood of the Lord Jesus and by the presence of the Holy Spirit for the glory that he has prepared for the elect. This administration is the same in substance as the old covenant (the Mosaic administration), but different in form. The formal difference lies in the coming of Jesus Christ: his atonement, his present ministry, and the work of the Holy Spirit. While the saints before Christ enjoyed many benefits under the Law, the era of the Gospel presents even greater benefits. While the old covenant was an administration of grace, it was also rich in symbols (circumcision, temple, priestly service, the sacrificial system) pointing to the grace-to-come in Jesus Christ. While the new covenant has fewer symbols (baptism, Lord's Supper), it is an administration rich in grace.

Under both covenants, the Lord has one standard for ethics, namely holiness or wholeness of life. Wholeness of life is that integration of love for God and for human beings in which the blameless person grows in reflecting the perfections of God (e.g., love, fidelity, righteousness, justice, forgiveness, forbearance). Under both administrations God wants his people to *love* him, keep his *law*, and to depend on him wholly for *life*. The Ten Commandments, as a summary of the moral law, are a guide in the imitation of God. By the Spirit the letter becomes alive and powerful within the hearts of the godly.

Nevertheless there are formal differences in the triad love, law, and life. First, in the new covenant, the Father has demonstrated the *supreme act of love* in giving his Son. Jesus, too, so loved the Father that he was fully obedient, even unto death, and gave himself as a ransom for the church. In turn, love for God is an imitation of the love of Jesus Christ; it means a submission in which the individual Christian and the Christian community show

---

[40]W. A. VanGemeren, "Psalms," *Expositor's Bible Commentary* (Grand Rapids: Zondervan, 1991), 5:700–712.

the life of Christ in them by self-sacrifice, self-denial, and a readiness to serve (Eph. 5:1–2; Phil. 2:1–18).[41]

Second, Jesus Christ is the *perfection of the law* (Rom 10:4). Under the old covenant, the moral law was revealed at Mount Sinai in a composite and complex form. The Ten Commandments were supplemented by the ceremonial laws, civil laws, and a penal code. This complex form, together with the sanctions, often made the law a burden. Jesus carried that burden and is the perfection of righteousness. Under the new covenant, the law can never again be read, interpreted, or applied apart from Jesus Christ. He modeled the perfection of the law and simplified it. The ceremonial laws, civil laws, and the penal code have been abrogated, and the moral law has received further clarification in the person and teaching of Jesus Christ.

Third, *life in Christ* is richer because of his sufficiency, grace, and ministry, and because of the benefits that come to us on account of his death, resurrection, and glorification. We are new creatures in him, and the Christian life is richer in benefits and more spiritual than that offered to the saints before Christ.

Let us briefly look at the perspective on the law of God in the teachings of Jesus and Paul.

Jesus: The Cost of Discipleship

The apostle John seems to place Moses and Jesus in sharp contrast: "For the law was given through Moses; grace and truth came through Jesus Christ" (John 1:17). John was surely well aware that grace and truth were found in Moses, but in making the comparison he brings out the greatness of God's grace through Jesus Christ. When compared with Jesus, the era of Moses is law. As John Murray writes, "Grace and truth in complete manifestation and embodiment came by Jesus Christ."[42]

Jesus' teaching on the law has clear lines of continuity with

---

[41]Oliver Barclay develops a continuity of the creation ethics and Christ. He speaks of these as the "two poles of biblical ethics" ("The Nature of Christian Morality," 145).

[42]Murray (*Principles*, 150) devotes a whole chapter to law and grace (181–201), and this citation is representative of the spirit of Murray's argument: "The purity and integrity of the gospel stand or fall with the absoluteness of the antithesis between the function and potency of law, on the one hand, and the function and potency of grace, on the other" (186); see K. Chamblin, "The Law of Moses and The Law of Christ," in *Continuity and Discontinuity*, ed. J. S. Feinberg, (Westchester: Crossway, 1988), 194–95.

the law of Moses.[43] It is faithful to the law (Matt. 5:17; 17:27; 23:23), and Jesus challenges people to listen more carefully to Moses and the Prophets (Luke 24:27, 44; John 5:39–40, 46).[44]

Jesus gave a stricter interpretation of Moses than the rabbis. He rejected the mere observance of external concerns and complacency with tradition. The antithesis is, as Murray observes, "between his own interpretation and application of the law of the Old Testament and the externalistic interpretation of the rabbinic tradition."[45] In his application of the various laws, Jesus held people more accountable to the sanctity of the law. He upheld the spiritual intent of the Lawgiver; see his comments on the honor of God (Matt. 22:18–22), the Sabbath (Matt. 12:1–14; Mark 2:23–28; 3:1–6; Luke 13:10–21; 14:1–24), honor of parents (Mark 7:1–13), murder (Matt. 5:21–24, 43–48), divorce and adultery (Matt. 5:27–32; 19:3–12), fasting (Mark 2:18–22), and ceremonial rituals (Matt. 15:1–30; Mark 7:1–23; Luke 11:37–54). Clearly, Jesus did not abrogate the law! Indeed, he called for a more radical observance: "Anyone who breaks one of the least of these commandments and teaches others to do the same will be called least in the kingdom of heaven, but whoever practices and teaches these commands will be called great in the kingdom of heaven" (Matt. 5:19; cf. 7:17; Mark 10:17–22; Luke 6:45; 12:36).[46] As Ladd writes, "Jesus taught the pure, unconditioned will of God without compromise of any sort, which God lays upon men at all times and for all time."[47] John Gerstner similarly observes, "Christ's affirmation of the moral law was complete. Rather than setting His disciples free from the law, He tied them more tightly to it. He abrogated not one commandment but instead intensified all."[48]

Jesus linked together the law and the kingdom of God. His coming marked a new stage in the kingdom. With the death of John the Baptist one era in redemption history drew to a close (Matt. 11:11–13 = Luke 16:16–17), and the era of the greater

---

[43]See Murray, *Principles*, 149–80; Chamblin, "The Law of Moses," 187–92.

[44]See T. M. McComiskey, "The Law in the Teaching of Jesus," in *The Covenants of Promise*, 94–105.

[45]Murray, *Principles*, 158; see G. E. Ladd, *A Theology of the New Testament* (Grand Rapids: Eerdmans, 1974), 129–30.

[46]Murray writes that Jesus came "to realize the full measure of the intent and purpose of the law and the prophets . . . to bring to full fruition and perfect fulfillment the law and the prophets" (*Principles*, 150).

[47]Ladd, *Theology*, 128; see also 130–33.

[48]John H. Gerstner, "Law in the NT," *ISBE*, rev. ed., 3:88.

actualization of the kingdom was present in Jesus Christ (Luke 10:9). He described his ministry, "The good news of the kingdom of God is being preached. . . . It is easier for heaven and earth to disappear than for the least stroke of a pen to drop out of the Law" (Luke 16:16–17).

This explains why he urgently called on people to repent, to exercise faith in him, to keep the law, and to prepare themselves for the coming of the kingdom. Nothing on earth is so important that it can stand in the way of following Jesus (Matt. 6:33; 10:32–39; 16:24; Luke 9:58–61; 14:26, 33). The cost of discipleship is great, but the rewards of following Jesus are greater: "But love your enemies, do good to them, and lend to them without expecting to get anything back. Then your reward will be great, and you will be sons of the Most High, because he is kind to the ungrateful and wicked" (Luke 6:35; cf. v. 23; Matt. 5:19).

At the same time, Jesus simplified the complexity of the Mosaic law by focusing on one word ("love"). He had come to fulfill the law and the prophets (Matt. 5:18; Luke 24:44). Because he is greater than Moses (John 5:36–47), he authoritatively interprets Moses. As the Son of God, he authoritatively summarized the moral law of God in two commandments: to love God and to love one's neighbor (Matt. 22:37–40; cf. Lev. 19:18; Deut. 6:5).

Jesus further simplified the law by calling on his followers to follow him (Mark 10:21).[49] He has fulfilled the law and embodied the spirit of the law of God in his person. He said: "Come to me, all you who are weary and burdened, and I will give you rest. Take my yoke upon you and learn from me, for I am gentle and humble in heart, and you will find rest for your souls" (Matt. 11:28–29). The yoke of Christ is nothing other than the law of love (John 15:17). The Christian, having been incorporated in a relationship of love, embodies the love of God in his life:

> As the Father has loved me, so have I loved you. Now remain in my love. If you obey my commands, you will remain in my love, just as I have obeyed my Father's commands and remain in his love. . . . My command is this: Love each other as I have loved you. (vv. 9–10, 12)

Living from the strength of this relationship with God and keeping his focus on Jesus Christ, the disciple of Christ is in a better position to interpret and to apply the law of God.

---

[49]See Chamblin, "The Law of Moses," 191.

Paul: The Liberty of Law

I wholeheartedly agree with Ladd's frustration with Paul's view of the law: "Paul's thought about the Law is difficult to understand because he seems to make numerous contradictory statements."[50] The interpreters of Paul are many, and so are the positions on the Christian and the law. Having read several of Paul's interpreters and coming to the field of Pauline studies as an Old Testament scholar, I was glad to find a guide in Stephen Westerholm's recent work, *Israel's Law and the Church's Faith*.

Westerholm is helpful in defining essential terms that have confused the students of the apostle Paul: law, works of the law, faith, legalism, and Torah. He holds that Paul's usual meaning of law (*nomos*; Torah) is the Sinaitic legislation, though it may occasionally denote the Old Testament, the Pentateuch, or even "principle."[51] According to Westerholm, Paul openly deals with the deficiencies of the Mosaic administration.[52] Since this law cannot justify, works of the law—i.e., "deeds demanded by the Sinaitic code"—are opposed to faith in Jesus Christ.[53] He sees Christ's coming as the "end" of the Mosaic administration.[54] Westerholm concludes that the old covenant and the new are in contrast with each other and that consequently, the Mosaic law does not apply to the Christian.[55]

Westerholm's analysis aims at understanding what Paul himself says about the law rather than interpret Paul by his interpreters. Unfortunately, however, Westerholm is shackled by his reading of Paul from a Lutheran perspective, resulting in what Silva calls "a sharp and uncompromising discontinuity between 'Israel's law and the church's faith.' "[56] Even worse, Westerholm falls into the trap of making his Paul disagree with the Paul who said, "Keeping God's commands is what counts" (1 Cor. 7:19).

The contemporary scene gives little hope for achieving any unanimity on Paul's view of the law. Compare the contradictory

---

[50]Ladd, *Theology*, 495.

[51]S. Westerholm, *Israel's Law and the Church's Faith* (Grand Rapids: Eerdmans, 1988), 107–9.

[52]Ibid., 130–35.

[53]Ibid., 109–30.

[54]Ibid., 175–97.

[55]Ibid., 198–218.

[56]See Moisés Silva's review of Westerholm's work in *WTJ* 51 (1989), 177. See also the review by Andrew J. Bandstra, "Paul and the Law: Some Recent Developments and an Extraordinary Book," *CTJ* 25 (1990), 249–61.

conclusions of Westerholm and Thielman. Westerholm defines Paul's Christian understanding of the law as a total rejection of the Mosaic law, including the moral law: "Paul could not conceive of Torah as a mere guide for moral behavior. Once he had rejected the law as a means of salvation, then ethical conduct required different norms."[57] Over against this, Thielman connects Paul with the prophetic eschatology according to which the place of the law is heightened. He says that Paul's view of the law is not a novelty, but was rather "based on familiar ideas and echoed a familiar theme: the period of disobedience would end with the arrival of the eschatological age."[58]

Despite contradictory views, all interpreters will agree that Paul looks at the law in the light of Christ's coming[59] and that Paul is the apostle of liberty.[60] Let us now consider two aspects that have a bearing on Paul's view of the law of God: (1) the Spirit of Christ and (2) eschatology.

Law and the Spirit of Christ

Christ, the law, the Spirit, and love are integrated in Paul's theology.[61] Union with Christ makes a radical difference in lawkeeping. The Christian life is a life of dying to the old man and a growth in the new life: "Continue to live in him, rooted and built up in him, strengthened in the faith as you were taught, and overflowing with thankfulness" (Col. 2:6b–7). Ridderbos calls this lifestyle a "training oneself in the *militia Christi*."[62] The moral law is still relevant as a mirror condemning our negative passions characteristic of the old man and as a mirror of God's perfections (cf. Gal. 5:17–18). A Christian wars against and puts to death the old passions that are prohibited by the moral law: "sexual immorality, impurity, lust, evil desires and greed, which is idolatry. . . . anger, rage, malice, slander, and filthy language" (Col. 3:5, 8, 9; cf. Gal. 5:19–20). He also develops new passions:

---

[57]Westerholm, *Israel's Law*, 218.

[58]Frank Thielman, *From Plight to Solution: A Jewish Framework for Understanding Paul's View of the Law in Galatians and Romans*, SupNovT 61 (Leiden: Brill, 1989), 122.

[59]Ladd, *Theology*, 495–96.

[60]See Herman Ridderbos on Paul's view of liberty and conscience in his *Paul: An Outline of His Theology*, trans. John Richard de Witt (Grand Rapids: Eerdmans, 1975), 288–93.

[61]Ibid., 286–88.

[62]Ibid., 252; see his discussion on the new life (205–52).

"compassion, kindness, humility, gentleness and patience" (Col. 3:12).

The Spirit of Christ guides the Christian in all truth and godliness. However, the Spirit does not operate in a vacuum. He applies the word of God to the heart of the Christian who is in union with Christ. In this way, Christians grow in a new lifestyle that shows a concern for being in harmony with the will of God[63] by living in obedience to the law of God (Gal. 5:18; cf. vv. 22–23). Here I agree with Ladd when he says, "more than once he [Paul] asserts that it is the new life of the Spirit that enables the Christian truly to fulfill the Law (Rom. 8:3–4; 13:10; Gal. 5:14)."[64]

Elsewhere, the apostle explains that the Spirit illumines and applies the word, "in order that the righteous requirements of the law might be fully met in us, who do not live according to the sinful nature but according to the Spirit" (Rom. 8:4).[65] Guidance by the Spirit without the appropriate use of the law of God is dangerous to Christian growth, as E. F. Kevan observed, "It must never be forgotten that Law and obedience are merely the form of the moral life. . . . To ignore the form is to lapse into a mystical type of piety which may soon become a cloak for impiety."[66]

The purpose of the law is Christian growth in grace, not justification or merit. In Galatians 3:21, Paul draws a contrast between the law and the promise: "Is the law, therefore, opposed to the promises of God? Absolutely not! For if a law had been given that could impart life, then righteousness would certainly have come by the law." Silva determines that this text is the crux of Paul's interpretation of the law. Paul does not oppose promise and law, but rather he sees promise and obedience to the law as a way of receiving the promise. Hence, the law leads those who are already alive to life and righteousness, but it does not have the power to give life when unaccompanied by the work of grace.[67] Grace is necessary for obedience to the law, but sole dependence on grace without the responsible use of the law leads to antinomianism, as John Murray cautioned:

---

[63]Ladd, *Theology*, 518.

[64]Ibid., 517.

[65]See John Murray's fine treatment in the chapter entitled "The Dynamic of the Biblical Ethic" (*Principles*, 202–28); Chamblin, "Law of Moses," 192–94.

[66]Kevan, *The Evangelical Doctrine of the Law*, 28.

[67]M. Silva, "Is the Law Against the Promises? The Significance of Galatians 3:21 for Covenant Continuity," in *Theonomy: A Reformed Critique*, 165.

It is not only the doctrine of grace that must be jealously guarded against distortion by the works of law, but it is also the doctrine of law that must be preserved against the distortions of a spurious concept of grace. This is just saying that we are but echoing the total witness of the apostle of the Gentiles as the champion of the gospel of grace when we say that we must guard grace from the adulteration of legalism and we must guard law from the depredations of antinomianism.[68]

The Christian advances in wisdom as he or she crucifies the old nature by the Spirit and conforms to the new nature of Jesus Christ. The apostle Paul instructed Timothy to live by the Scriptures, including the Old Testament law, as God's prescription for growth in grace: "All Scripture is God-breathed and is useful for teaching, rebuking, correcting and training in righteousness, so that the man of God may be thoroughly equipped for every good work" (2 Tim. 3:16–17).

Love is obedience to God.[69] The apostle of liberty summed up his perspective on the law as a debt of love:

> Let no debt remain outstanding, except the continuing debt to love one another, for he who loves his fellowman has fulfilled the law. The commandments, "Do not commit adultery," "Do not murder," "Do not steal," "Do not covet," and whatever other commandment there may be, are summed up in this one rule: "Love your neighbor as yourself." Love does no harm to its neighbor. Therefore love is the fulfillment of the law. (Rom. 13:8–10; cf. Gal. 5:14; see Ex. 20:13–15, 17; Lev. 19:18; Deut. 5:17–19, 21)[70]

Love motivates one to keep the law (Phil. 2:12). As Christ obeyed unto death (Phil. 2:5–11; 2 Cor. 8:9), so Christians should develop a new lifestyle of obedience (Phil. 2:12) and a commitment to please the Father (v. 13). They are empowered by God's work in them (v. 13) and are transformed by the Spirit to a lifestyle of humility (v. 14). They become "blameless and pure" (v. 15), like Christ.

---

[68]Murray, *Principles*, 182.

[69]See Ridderbos on Paul's view of the new obedience (*Paul*, 253–326).

[70]See McComiskey, "The Law in the Teaching of Paul," in *The Covenants of Promise*, 106–37.

Law and Eschatology

Paul holds that the new age has begun with Jesus' resurrection (1 Cor. 15). *Union with Christ* explains the change from the old man to the new man (Eph. 2:1–22; 3:1–4) and from the old era to the new. Christ has abrogated the ceremonial laws in his death (Col. 2:11–15) and has liberated us from the "shadow of the things that were to come" (v. 17). In Christ the follower of Christ already shares in the new age (2 Cor. 5:17), the eschatological gift of the Spirit, and in the communion of the saints ("God's chosen people, holy and dearly loved"; Col. 3:12). The new nature by the Spirit actively pursues righteousness (Rom. 8:10) without being seduced by the things of the present age, which is "passing away" (1 Cor. 7:31). Having been a *doulos* ("slave") to sin (Rom 6:16), the Christian has been transformed to be a *doulos* to righteousness (v. 18). The Christian will experience in the members of his body the tension of being in the kingdom (new creation) and yet awaiting the kingdom (the age to come), as Paul expressed in Romans 7:6: "But now, by dying to what once bound us, we have been released from the law so that we serve in the new way of the Spirit, and not in the old way of the written code."

Frank Thielman develops the place of the law in Pauline eschatology, unlike some of Paul's interpreters who disregard the eschatological perspective of law.[71] He concludes, I believe rightly, that Paul's doctrine of the two ages may explain some of Paul's contradictory statements on the law. Since the Christian already belongs to the new creation, the law of God, when internalized by the Spirit of God, is an effective instrument of righteousness and a means of shaping the new community. Thielman observes, "Paul . . . reserves a place for the law among the eschatological community of believers and claims that the eschatological Spirit enables believers to fulfill the law of love."[72]

This fits well with the Old Testament prophets. They had spoken of the correlation of the messianic age and the law.[73] For example, Isaiah said, "Many peoples will come and say, 'Come, let us go up to the mountain of the LORD, to the house of the God of Jacob. He will teach us his ways, so that we may walk in his paths.' The law will go out from Zion, the word of the LORD from

---

[71]Thielman, *From Plight to Solution* (see footnote 58).

[72]Ibid., 118.

[73]Willem A. VanGemeren, *Interpreting the Prophetic Word* (Grand Rapids: Zondervan, 1990), 354–89.

Jerusalem" (Isa. 2:3). Jeremiah also pointed to a new age when the law would be internalized: "I will put my law in their minds and write it on their hearts. I will be their God, and they will be my people" (Jer. 31:33b).

The law is not replaced by the Spirit in the eschatological age. The Spirit opens people up to the law and transforms them to live by a higher ethics. We may even speak of eschatological ethics as an application of the moral law, by which the believers live in the present age with their eyes focused on the coming of the kingdom. While all people belong to the present age and are made responsible for keeping its mores, Christians live by the higher ethics of the kingdom. Paul speaks of this tension in his ministry: "To those not having the law I became like one not having the law (though I am not free from God's law but am under Christ's law [*ennomos Christou*]), so as to win those not having the law" (1 Cor. 9:21).[74] The law is God's instrument in transforming the Christian into a servant of the kingdom of God, as E. F. Kevan wrote, "Any change in relation to Law that occurs in Christianity is not in the Law but in the believer. . . . To say that Christian conduct is now governed by holy principles is . . . incorrect . . . if it meant any withdrawal or modification of the Law."[75]

THEOLOGICAL REFLECTIONS ON THE LAW OF GOD

Of what relevance is the law of God from a Reformed perspective? This biblical-theological survey of the major moments in the history of redemption has presented several overarching and connecting themes. (1) At Creation God revealed the natural law in the order of creation and in the moral law. Both the order in creation and the moral law reveal God's will and nature (his perfections). (2) Humans were especially endowed to respond to God's will, to reflect his perfections, and to live morally, in harmony with God, other humans, and creation. (3) Sin and rebelliousness keep humans from reflecting the divine perfections and from understanding the moral law as revealed in creation. (4) God sustains creation, including humans, with his grace. (5) Before the law at Mount Sinai, the Lord gave special grace and raised up people who walked with him and kept his command-

---

[74]See Herman Ridderbos on Paul's view of the third use of the law (*Paul*, 278–88, especially 284–85).

[75]Kevan, *The Evangelical Doctrine of the Law*, 25.

ments. (6) The law at Mount Sinai made much more explicit the moral law and supplemented the moral law with ceremonial and judicial regulations. (7) The old covenant was an administration of grace and promise, as well as of law. (8) The new covenant in Jesus Christ is an administration of grace and promise, but also contains law. (9) The laws point to Jesus Christ as the complement of the law. (10) The law may never be separated from covenant, grace, Jesus Christ, or the Spirit of God.

In this section I shall develop the concept of God's law in Reformed theology.[76] In the discussion of the law of God, Reformed theologians discuss it in the context of (1) the covenant, (2) grace and gospel, and (3) redemption.

The Law and Covenant[77]

The Reformed view of the law is integrated with an understanding of covenant.[78] *Covenant* denotes a relationship that the Lord sovereignly and graciously establishes and maintains, whereas *law* denotes the order that is required for that relationship to be meaningful. For example, the Lord sovereignly established a relationship with creation, holding everything together by his grace (Col.1:15–20). His maintaining orderly coherence in nature permits the meaningful existence of all life.

Likewise, in God's relationship with humans, the moral law reveals his will and character, the observance of which enhances order. Adam and Eve were expected to submit themselves to the Lord and obey this law in anticipation of God's reward. In the words of the Westminster Confession, "God gave to Adam a law, as a covenant of works, by which He bound him and all his posterity, to personal, entire, exact, and perpetual obedience, promised life upon the fulfilling, and threatened death upon the breach of it, and endued him with power and ability to keep it."[79]

God maintains covenant and order. After the Fall of our first parents, he continued to be gracious to creation. He confirmed his covenant with creation (Gen.6:18; 8:15–17), even though humans had occasioned the Flood by their corruption. Though they

---

[76]For a review of the place of the law in the Reformation period, see Geoffrey H. Greenhough, "The Reformers' Attitude to the Law of God," *WTJ* 39 (1976–77), 81–99.

[77]See B. K. Waltke, "Theonomy in Relation to Dispensational and Covenant Theologies," in *Theonomy: A Reformed Critique*, 59–86.

[78]Hesselink, "Calvin's Concept," ch. VI, 1–69.

[79]WCF, 19.1.

continue to wreak havoc by destroying the moral and social order, the Lord maintains the cosmos by his grace, upholding all creatures and blessing humanity with health, offspring, and prosperity (Acts 17:26–28). Nevertheless, he still holds all humans responsible for keeping the moral law: "This law, after his fall, continued to be a perfect rule of righteousness."[80]

God's special grace extends to the beneficiaries of the covenant of grace of which Christ is the Mediator. The Father extends the benefits of Christ's atonement to all the saints, both those before and those after Jesus' first coming. All recipients of God's grace are obedient to his will and willingly keep the moral law. Even saints such as Enoch, Noah, and Abraham, who lived before the revelation of the law at Mount Sinai, observed the moral law blamelessly and walked with God.

The moral law was written down in the Ten Commandments and incorporated in the Mosaic covenant. The Decalogue summarizes the moral law and is clearer, more fixed, and more effective than the natural law.[81] Since the Decalogue is incorporated into the covenantal structure, it is an instrument of grace. As Berkouwer observes, "Law and grace—a perfect harmony; but law without gospel, or thora without the covenant, must always clash with grace."[82] But if grace is contained in the law, why does Paul identify the promise with the Abrahamic covenant and law as something added to the Mosaic covenant? Let us consider how law and grace and Law and Gospel relate within the covenantal structure.

Law, Grace, Gospel

Law and Grace

The relationship between law and grace is crucial in Reformed theology because both are operative in the covenants. The seeming paradoxical approach to law comes to a particular focus in reading Reformed theologians on the relation of the Abrahamic to the Mosaic covenant.

Calvin keeps law and grace in balance. The covenant, even the Mosaic covenant, is an administration of grace: "God made a gratuitous covenant which flows from the fountain of his pity . . .

---

[80]WCF, 19.2.

[81]Hesselink, "Calvin's Concept," ch. III, 11–13.

[82]G. C. Berkouwer, *Faith and Sanctification* (Grand Rapids: Eerdmans, 1952), 191.

from God's mercy. . . . It has its cause, stability, execution and completion solely in the grace of God. . . . Whenever God's covenant is mentioned, his clemency, goodness or inclination to love is also added."[83] Even the law has a gracious dimension because it is incorporated in a gracious covenant; "in the promulgation of the law, he also established his grace."[84]

The ambivalent relation between law and grace has come to the fore during the latter half of this century in the writings of John Murray and Meredith G. Kline. In defining the relationship between the Abrahamic covenant and the Mosaic covenant, Murray is more sympathetic to continuity, whereas Kline favors discontinuity.

Murray defines covenant as a "sovereign administration of grace and promise"[85] and focuses on the sovereignty of God in extending his grace and realizing his promise to Abraham and his heirs. He carefully argues for continuity between the Abrahamic and the Mosaic covenant because under both covenants obedience is an overt evidence of love for God and a condition for blessing.[86]

On the other hand, Meredith G. Kline holds that the Abrahamic and Mosaic covenants differ from each other in form. The Abrahamic covenant is a "promise-covenant" in that God made the promise and swore to fulfill it (Gen. 22:16–17). The Mosaic covenant (e.g., Ex. 24) is a "law-covenant" in that God made the promise and Israel made an oath to keep God's law.[87] The law-covenant is "an administration of God's lordship, consecrating a people to himself under the sanctions of divine law."[88] In Kline's definition, grace or promise is subject to law.[89] In comparison with the Abrahamic promise-covenant, the Mosaic law-covenant is inferior; it is an "administration of law, bondage,

---

[83]Calvin's comment on Daniel 9:4 (cited by Hesselink, "Calvin's Concept," ch. VI, p. 3).

[84]Calvin's comment on Psalm 111:9.

[85]John Murray, *The Covenant of Grace* (London: Tyndale, 1954), 31.

[86]Murray writes, "Not only is holiness, as expressed concretely and practically in obedience, demanded by the covenant fellowship; we must also bear in mind that holiness was itself an integral element of the covenant blessing" (*Principles*, 198).

[87]Meredith Kline, *By Oath Consigned: A Reinterpretation of the Covenant Signs of Circumcision and Baptism* (Grand Rapids: Eerdmans, 1968), 16–17.

[88]Ibid., 36.

[89]Kline writes, "Coherence can be achieved in Covenant Theology only by the subordination of grace to law" (ibid., 35).

condemnation, and death."[90] Consequently, the Mosaic era as a law-covenant is a parenthesis, being wedged in between two promise-covenants: the Abrahamic and the new covenant.

These positions have not been without criticism. Mark Karlberg censures Murray for subordinating law to grace in the Mosaic covenant and for not relating the curse sanctions of the Mosaic administration to the covenant of works.[91] Karlberg concludes correctly that the law is an administration of death and that the sacrifices, feasts and festivals, ceremonial and civil laws, ordinances, and promises point to the need for Christ's atonement. The Mosaic administration by itself is incomplete but has an eschatological and Christological focus.[92] O. Palmer Robertson, while expressing agreement at some basic points with Murray and Kline,[93] disagrees particularly with Kline's distinction between promise- and law-covenants.[94]

This brief treatment on the relation between law and grace in Reformed theology confirms the importance of maintaining the tension, as Robertson states, "Always grace and promise operate in the framework of God's law."[95] How then does the Mosaic covenant differ from the gospel?

Law and Gospel[96]

The Mosaic covenant as an administration of Law is the same in substance as the Abrahamic covenant and as the new covenant—namely the same God, Christ, Spirit, inheritance, salvation, rule of faith and life, hope of immortality, church, doctrine, and adoption.[97] It contains grace and promise. As Calvin explains, "the promise stands first because God chooses rather to invite his people by kindness than to compel them to obedience from

---

[90]Ibid., 25.

[91]Mark W. Karlberg, "Reformed Interpretation of the Mosaic Covenant," *WTJ* 43 (1980–81), 53.

[92]Ibid., 51–53.

[93]O. Palmer Robertson, "Current Reformed Thinking on the Nature of the Divine Covenants," *WTJ* 40 (1977–78), 63–76.

[94]Ibid., 70–74.

[95]Ibid., 74.

[96]See Andrew J. Bandstra, "Law and Gospel in Calvin and in Paul," in *Exploring the Heritage of John Calvin*, ed. D. E. Holwerda (Grand Rapids: Baker, 1976), 11–39.

[97]Hesselink, "Calvin's Concept," ch. VII, 10–42.

terror."[98] How then does it differ from the Gospel? How is the gospel of Jesus Christ superior to the gospel of Moses?

In the Mosaic administration both promises and threats were attached to obedience to the law. Positively, the threats themselves were intended to stimulate sinners to repent and to seek his grace.[99] The threats, nevertheless, open up a function of the Law that is antithetical to the Gospel. The Law renders us without excuse, excludes us from the promises of life,[100] condemns us (cf. Rom. 5:20; Gal. 3:19), "holds us far away from the blessedness that it promises its keepers,"[101] and cannot be fulfilled in the flesh on account of the weakness of our own nature (Rom. 8:3).[102]

Hope only lies in the Gospel, because Moses' law demands perfect obedience and righteousness (cf. Rom. 10:5).[103] The Law is not defective, but people are. They cannot be justified by the works of the law because they fail to keep the law: "The law and the promise do not contradict each other except in the matter of justification, for the law justifies a man by the merit of works whereas the promise bestows righteousness freely."[104] By this Calvin meant that if one kept the law perfectly, one could be justified by law. However, no one could, except for the Lord Jesus. Every child of God under the old covenant was justified by the promise in Christ. The Law without Christ and the Spirit is dead and brings condemnation.[105]

The balance between Law and Gospel is found in Jesus Christ. He gives a true perspective on the Law by the good news that sin is atoned for and that guilt is removed. He holds the administrations of Law and Gospel together, "for both attest that God's fatherly kindness and the graces of the Holy Spirit are offered us in Christ."[106] The crux is in the words "in Christ."

---

[98]Cited by Hesselink, ibid., ch. VI, 38.

[99]Ibid., ch. VI, p. 38. Calvin commented on Jeremiah 11:3: "A curse is added. . . . In the law God followed another order; for he first embraced them with a rule of living well and even added promises. . . . Finally he appended curses."

[100]*Inst.*, 2.7.3.

[101]*Inst.*, 2.7.4.

[102]*Inst.*, 2.7.5.

[103]I disagree with Daniel P. Fuller, according to whom the inheritance of the promise depends on the *obedience* of faith (*Gospel & Law*), 103–5.

[104]Calvin's comment on Gal. 3:17, cited by Hesselink, "Calvin's Concept," ch. VI, 5.

[105]*Inst.*, 2.7.7.

[106]*Inst.*, 4.14.26.

Calvin understood any act of divine grace as contingent on Christ's obedience and death. The benefits under the old covenant came on account of the work of Christ, the mediator of the covenant of grace.[107] The coming of Christ is like a bright light in comparison to the lamp of the Mosaic era.[108]

The Law in The Context Of Redemption

The law is God's instrument of conforming us to the image of Jesus Christ. It is the school of faith by which the Holy Spirit leads us into conformity to God's will.[109]

The Law and Jesus Christ

The law is "the heart and core of Scripture."[110] It used to be a pedagogue (Gal. 4:1–3),[111] but now that Christ has come, he is the focus, the perfection, the complement, the fulfillment of the law (cf. Rom.10:4).[112] Using "the law and the prophets as our foundation we live in Christ, for Christ, and by his Spirit."[113] Thus we may learn to develop what John Hesselink calls the "well-ordered life."[114]

Christ, the focus of the law, is the Lawgiver. He is the true mediator of the covenant of grace, of which Moses was the custodian.[115] Whatever perfections the law has, they reveal Christ. As Hesselink states, "Calvin is saying that what is said of God in the Old Testament can without any twisting, manipulating or

---

[107]Hesselink, "Calvin's Concept," ch. VII, 36–38.

[108]Calvin's comment on Daniel 9:25.

[109] Significantly, Calvin discussed the law in the second book of the *Institutes*, entitled "The Knowledge of God the Redeemer in Christ" (see Hesselink, "Calvin's Concept," ch. IV, pp. 8–9, 18–21; WCF, 7–8.

[110]Hesselink, "Calvin's Concept," ch. VII, p. 13. He further adds that "the prophets and psalmists, *apostles and Christ himself* are all nothing but expounders and interpreters of the law." See also *Inst.*, 4.8.6–8.

[111]See Ridderbos on the law as disciplinarian (*Paul*, 149–53).

[112]Hesselink, "Calvin's Concept," ch. VI, p. 17. He writes, "The whole of the law then—not only the covenant but also its promises and threats, rules and regulations, sacrifices and ceremonies—finds its meaning in Christ who is its life, soul, spirit, substance, fulfillment and goal" (p. 19).

[113]I. John Hesselink, "Calvin, the Law, and the Christian: An Unexplored Aspect of the Third Use of the Law in Calvin's Theology," in *Reformation Perennis: Essays on Calvin in Honor of Ford Lewis Battles*, ed. B. A. Gerrish (Pittsburgh: Pickwick, 1981), 20.

[114]Ibid., 19.

[115]Hesselink, "Calvin's Concept," ch. VI, 14–15.

allegorizing be applied to Christ in the New Testament because when God is referred to in the Bible, Christ is presupposed!"[116]

The Law Is Spiritual

God is Spirit, and his law is by definition spiritual. His purpose was to lift the minds of the saints before Christ from the ceremonies and institutions to himself, because only "spiritual worship delights him."[117] Moreover, the Spirit of God is the "inner light," who works in the believers to make the law a joy. The demands of the law are such that they require a love for God and the power of the Holy Spirit: "The love of the Law thus created in our hearts by the Holy Spirit is a sure sign of our regeneration and adoption."[118] Otherwise the law becomes a burden and unprofitable.[119]

What then is the power of the moral law since the outpouring of the Holy Spirit? Negatively, it no longer has the power to bind (Rom. 7:6; Matt. 5:17–18)[120] or condemn us, because Christ has released us from "the bonds of harsh and dangerous requirements, which remit nothing of the extreme penalty of the law, and suffer no transgression to go unpunished."[121] Positively, the law has the power to exhort believers "to shake off their sluggishness, by repeatedly urging them, and to pinch them awake to their imperfection."[122] As such the law remains inviolable. By its teachings, admonishments, reproofs, and corrections, the law is the instrument of growth in faith and in sanctification (2 Tim. 3:16–17).[123] Berkouwer correlates these three aspects in the "golden triad of faith, sanctification, and law."[124]

The Moral Law Is an Instrument of Perfect Righteousness

In this section, I shall discuss the limits of the moral law, its use, and its function in sanctification.

---

[116]Ibid., ch. VI, 14.

[117]Inst., 2.7.1.

[118]Wallace, Calvin's Doctrine of the Christian Life (Edinburgh: Oliver & Boyd, 1959), 121.

[119]For the correlation of law and Spirit in Calvin, see Hesselink, "Calvin's Concept," ch. VI, 11–12; ch. VII, 42–59.

[120]Inst., 2.7.14. See Ridderbos on Paul's view of the bondage of the law (Paul, 143–49).

[121]Inst., 2.7.15.

[122]Inst., 2.7.14.

[123]Ibid.

[124]Berkouwer, Faith and Sanctification, 184.

The Limits of the Moral Law. The moral law is summarized in the Ten Commandments and was supplemented by the ceremonial and judicial laws. The ceremonial laws applied the first four commandments to the context of Israel's existence as a nation. Regulations of sacrifices, laws of holiness and purity, and the priestly system protected the worship of God. With the coming of Jesus Christ, the ceremonial laws have been abrogated,[125] having been nailed to the cross (Col. 2:14). The judicial laws applied the last six commandments to the context of Israel's existence as a nation. The regulations pertained to the judicial and political life of Israel as a nation. They have also been abrogated.[126]

The Three Uses of the Moral Law. The law as an instrument of righteousness warns, convicts, and condemns us of our unrighteousness.[127] As a pedagogue it instructs sinners concerning the will of God. This is the *usus elenchticus*.[128] The law has also the power to restrain us by reminding us of the consequences of our disobedience (cf. 1 Tim. 1:9–10).[129] This is the *usus politicus*.[130] Thirdly, the law is an instrument of the Holy Spirit by which he teaches believers to understand and to do God's will. Sometimes he may use it as a "rigorous enforcement officer"[131] to bring us into conformity with the will of God.[132] This use, the *usus in renatis* or the *usus normativus*, is the most important use of the law.[133]

The Moral Law in Sanctification. The moral law is "the rule of perfect righteousness."[134] The Decalogue reveals God's will and tells us how we must grow in our love for him and for our neighbor: "There are these two chief things in our life—to serve God purely, and then to deal with our fellow men with all

---

[125]*Inst.*, 2.7.16–17.

[126]WCF, 19.4. The confession permits the use of the "equity" of the law, but for the definition of equity as a technical term, see S. B. Ferguson, "An Assembly of Theonomists? The Teaching of the Westminster Divines on the Law of God," in *Theonomy: A Reformed Critique*, 315–49. See this book for a fair discussion of all the issues raised by theonomy.

[127]*Inst.*, 2.7.6.

[128]Hesselink, "Calvin's Concept," ch. VIII, 3–33.

[129]*Inst.*, 2.7.7–11.

[130]Hesselink, "Calvin's Concept," ch. VIII, 33–49.

[131]*Inst.*, 2.7.13.

[132]*Inst.*, 2.7.12.

[133]Hesselink, "Calvin's Concept," ch. VIII, 49–84. See especially Ralph Roger Sundquist, Jr., "The Third Use of the Law in the Thought of John Calvin: An Interpretation and Evaluation" (Ph.D. diss.; Columbia University, 1970).

[134]*Inst.*, 2.8.5.

integrity, and uprightness, rendering to each what is his due."[135] The first four commandments are "the beginning and foundation of righteousness,"[136] while the other six give a framework for demonstrating love toward our fellow humans.[137] These commandments put our love for God to the test, because it is all too easy to assume that one's relationship with God is good. The second table is especially the test by which we must check our love for God. Love for our fellow human beings is the only real evidence, the "infallible proof that the heart is right with God."[138]

Christ appointed the law as "a godly and righteous rule of living,"[139] as the appointed instrument of sanctification[140] that instructs us in righteousness. Because God is holy, righteous, perfect, good, and gracious, his will is holy, righteous, perfect, good, and gracious. God is not pleased with any other righteousness than that which conforms to the requirements of his will. Through the law we may learn obedience, freedom, perfect righteousness, and order.

(1) The law forms the basis for obedience. Calvin agrees with Augustine that obedience is "the mother and guardian of all virtues, sometimes their source."[141] The law instructs us to have reverence for God's righteousness, and, as Murray puts it, "Obedience is the principle and secret of integrity."[142]

(2) Obedience to the law brings real freedom. Freedom is not license, nor is it the liberty to interpret and apply the law as one pleases. Rather, freedom is the exercise of that spontaneous love for God by a sinner, who has been a *doulos* to sin and has become a *doulos* to righteousness (Rom. 5:21; 6:12).[143] The Christian is absolutely free in the Augustinian sense, "Love God and do as you like." Love for neighbor may not be restricted because one's neighbor is the whole human race.[144] Berkouwer expresses it

---

[135]Calvin's sermon on Deuteronomy 5:16, cited by Wallace, *Calvin's Doctrine*, 114.

[136]*Inst.*, 2.8.11.

[137]Ibid.

[138]Wallace, *Calvin's Doctrine of the Christian Life*, 116.

[139]*Inst.*, 2.7.1.

[140]See Hesselink, "Calvin's Concept," ch. IV, 1–25.

[141]*Inst.*, 2.7.5.

[142]Murray, *Principles*, 239.

[143]Berkouwer, *Faith and Sanctification*, 180–81.

[144]*Inst.*, 2.8.55.

pointedly, "There is no difference between Christian liberty and being 'under the law of Christ.'"[145]

(3) Perfect righteousness is not sinlessness, but "blamelessness" in the Hebraic sense. Perfection is a commitment to God and other people by which an individual serves God with "wholeheartedness, integrity, and sincerity" and seeks to understand, apply, and keep the whole law, while living by the grace of God (cf. Eph. 2:10).[146]

(4) Perfect fulfillment of the law brings true order; that is, "a true harmony between the outward life and the feelings of the heart, and a true relationship between the fulfillment of our duty towards God and our duty towards man."[147] Unlike the refined qualities that some people have because of their upbringing or social standing, the Holy Spirit perfects the saints by "the bond of perfection," that is, a restoration of wholeness (James 3:17–18).[148]

Principles of Interpretation and Application

Rather than giving a rigid system of ethics, Reformed theology offers a method of interpreting and applying the law of God. When the moral law is applied in the light of God's perfections, Jesus' teaching and life, and the whole Bible, the commandments of the Decalogue become relevant in any time or in any situation. The genius lies in Calvin's two principles of interpretation:[149] (1) The commandment addresses "inward and spiritual righteousness";[150] (2) the "commandments and prohibitions always contain more than is expressed in words."[151]

Let us apply these principles to God's prohibition of murder in the sixth commandment, "You shall not murder" (lōʾ tirṣaḥ; Ex. 20:13). What is "murder"? According to the first rule, God is addressing the matter of "inward and spiritual righteousness." Because the law is spiritual (Rom. 7:14) and reveals the character of the Lawgiver, the commandment must first be applied to the heart. Through the law, God calls on his children to discipline themselves in "obedience of soul, mind, and will" and not to be

---

[145]Berkouwer, *Faith and Sanctification*, 183.

[146]Wallace, *Calvin's Doctrine of the Christian Life*, 122.

[147]Ibid.

[148]Ibid.

[149]For Calvin's exposition of the Decalogue, see *Inst.*, 2.8.13–50. See also Hesselink, "Calvin's Concept," ch. VI, 42–43.

[150]*Inst.*, 2.8.6.

[151]*Inst.*, 2.8.8.

satisfied until they meet the law's demand for "an angelic purity, which, cleansed of every pollution of the flesh, savors of nothing but the spirit."[152] This interpretation is in the light of Christ's high view of the law of God. Over against the Pharisaic view, Jesus applies the prohibition against murder to the attitude of the heart (Matt. 15:19), to anger (5:22), and to malicious speech (5:22). John applies it to hatred (1 John 3:15). James argues that anyone who shows favoritism may be guilty of associating with a murderer (James 2:5–8; 5:1–6) and consequently be a lawbreaker (2:11). Other texts in Scripture apply the sixth commandment to the oppression of the poor (Ps. 94:6) and to the comfort and defense of the poor (Isa. 1:16–17).

Murder forcibly removes, reduces, or restricts the vitality of one's self or another. This commandment prohibits suicide as well as homicide, the neglect of life, sinful expressions of the emotions (anger, envy, revenge, excessive passions), distracting cares, improper care of the body (food, drink, work, recreation), hurtful words or abusive language, and behavior that brings discord or hurt.[153]

According to the second principle, the negative commandment also entails positive duties. In other words, if something displeases God, then the opposite pleases him, and vice versa.[154] The sixth commandment promotes the physical, psychological, mental, and spiritual vitality of human beings. This is consonant with the biblical teaching of a person being in the image of God. Because humans are in God's image, we have the duty to protect everything that is associated with the divine image. Hence, obedience to the law requires the preservation of physical life; the defence of the innocent or powerless; the comfort of the distressed; the proper care of one's body (food, drink, sleep, work, recreation); and the cultivation of the fruits of the Spirit in one's being (love, compassion, meekness, gentleness, kindness), in one's speech and behavior (peaceable, mild, courteous), and in one's attitude to one's neighbor (forbearance, readiness to forgive, doing good for evil).

---

[152]*Inst.*, 2.8.6.

[153]The Westminster Larger Catechism is a helpful guide to the interpretation and application of all the commandments. In dealing with the sixth commandment, it begins on a positive note by asking, "What are the duties required in the sixth commandment?" and thereafter it deals with "the sins forbidden in the sixth commandment" (Questions 135–136).

[154]*Inst.*, 2.8.8.

The application of these two principles to the sixth commandment opens up a discussion on the sins and the duties. The examples above reflect issues relevant in the sixteenth and seventeenth century as well as the twentieth. While there are certain common problems that people have in any age, we may further apply the commandment to unique problems in the twentieth century. The sins prohibited include negative competition in sports and business; oppressive relations between employer and employee, husband and wife, parents and children; parental abuse of children; neglect of the disabled and elderly; discrimination based on anyone's race, religion, social status, or sex; abortion; addictive behavior (alcohol, smoking, drugs); and a cover-up of one's bearing an infectious disease such as AIDS.

The duties include the development of positive business and professional relations; the cultivation of harmonious relations between employer and employee, husband and wife, parents and children; protection of the dignity of children, the handicapped, and the elderly; care for mothers-to-be and unborn babies; the encouragement of positive behavioral patterns; and the responsible handling of issues that involve AIDS, such as testing and communication between the medical profession and the patients.

In accordance with the above-mentioned three uses of the law (conviction, restraint, guidance), the commandment convicts us of sins of omission and commission. The Spirit convicts us so that we may learn to discipline our sinful thoughts, speech, and behavior. Resistance to conviction may lead to hardening, which ultimately stifles our progress in sanctification. When we are filled with the Spirit, the law will not only convict us, but will also lead us to look at Jesus Christ. He is the perfection of righteousness who guides us by his Spirit into the proper behavior, including one's response to others. Guidance is that work of the Holy Spirit whereby he illumines the law to our hearts, helps us see our need of Christ, and makes us responsible and accountable followers of Jesus.

CONCLUSION

This short study on the law of God in Scripture and in Reformed theology leads me to a deep sense of gratitude to God. Because he is so gracious in relating to fallible and rebellious human beings, he can involve us in fellowship with himself and extends his kingdom through weak vessels. The greatness of God's love arouses in me a consciousness of a need for more grace (Rom. 8:31–39). In response to his great love, we must fear him by growing in (1) faith, trusting him for all our needs and submitting wholly to him, (2) ethical integrity, (3) awe for God, and (4) reverence.

Ethical integrity is a wholeness of life. As we keep the moral law, pursue the perfection of righteousness in union with Jesus Christ, and walk by the power of the Spirit, we develop wholeness, a wholeness that involves the integration of our heart, speech, acts, and manners with the mind of Christ. Our vision, too, becomes holistic as we look back at the order of the original creation, at the glory of the new creation, and at Jesus, who holds creation and the new creation together. In our longing to give glory to the Father, to have communion with the Son, and to receive the power from the Holy Spirit, we must readily sacrifice self. Moreover, knowing the deceptions of our hearts, we must constantly check ourselves by the moral law to see whether we truly love our neighbor as ourselves. Love for neighbor is the thermometer by which we check the extent of our *love* for God, obedience to his *law*, and our dependence on the Lord for *life*.

Let me end on a personal note. I cannot keep God's law unless I live by the grace of God, in the light of the gospel of Jesus Christ, and by the power of his Spirit. I need his grace every day to help me in the discipline of my heart and in imaging the perfections of the Lord Jesus. It is my prayer that by God's grace I may enhance order where there is harmony and promote order where there is discord. Come, Lord Jesus, come!

Response to Willem A. VanGemeren

Greg L. Bahnsen

Our hearts surely beat in tune with the recurring and tender note throughout Dr. VanGemeren's essay that Spirit-given understanding of the Law of God serves to magnify our need and love for the Gospel of God's grace in Christ. Certainly we should all stand together here. Although the Law has its appropriate glory, it pales in comparison for those upon whom has dawned the light of the Gospel of the glory of Christ (2 Cor. 3:7–11, 18; 4:4, 6). The Gospel unmistakably exceeds in glory (3:9)! And for me personally, VanGemeren's ending note expresses my own heart: "I cannot keep God's law unless I live by the grace of God, in the light of the gospel of Jesus Christ, and by the power of his Spirit. I need his grace every day to help me in the discipline of my heart and in imaging the perfections of the Lord Jesus." These themes in VanGemeren's essay, echoing our shared Reformed heritage in theology, are sweet music indeed.

The task the editor expects me to perform in this response, however, is to identify and analyze any possible sour notes in VanGemeren's symphonic sweep of biblical and theological matters pertaining to the law of God. There are a few, regrettably, but in general terms the basic assumptions and positive approach to the law which he rehearses are in harmony with my own. Let me draw together out of different places in his essay a number of particular comments or insights where we agree.

VanGemeren speaks of an "underlying unity" or "basic unity and continuity" in biblical ethics between Old and New Testaments. For him the moral ordinances of God were known from the

59

time of creation and "are perpetually binding on all human beings." From the outset "sin is disobedience to God's law." The moral law of God was known and obeyed by godly people even before the revelation of the Mosaic law. Human sinfulness made it necessary for God's will to be communicated in written form. However, "since the will of God does not change, the law remains virtually the same throughout redemptive history." Receiving this law in written form at Sinai was not "a negative experience," but rather the Old Testament saints "rejoiced in this revelation"— even though "for the unbelieving Israelites, the law was a burden that condemned them." The law "teaches us in detail how to imitate God"; "the Law of God reflects the divine perfections." Furthermore, God even intended to show the nations "in the law how to mirror his perfections." For VanGemeren, the Mosaic covenant was "not antithetical to" nor a "substitute" for the Abrahamic promise, but it looked ahead to the unique Redeemer and Mediator of the covenant, Jesus Christ. Even "the Mosaic covenant is a sovereign administration of grace." He insists that "the law was never intended to be the means of salvation" (even at Lev. 18:5). To all of this we reply with a hearty "amen." And there is more.

What about after Christ came and established the new covenant? VanGemeren maintains rightly that it is "in substance" the same as the Abrahamic and Mosaic covenants, although differing "in form." In particular, "under both covenants, the Lord has one standard for ethics," and "Jesus' teaching on the law has clear lines of continuity with the law of Moses" (giving a "stricter interpretation" of the law than the rabbis). However, where the old covenant was "rich in symbols," the new covenant is "rich in grace," bringing with it "greater benefits." Christ has accomplished promised redemption and given us his Holy Spirit. Yet the moral law continues to have a place. Today "Christ, the focus of the law, is the Lawgiver," and "Christ appointed the law as 'a godly and righteous rule of living.'" "The law is not replaced by the Spirit in the eschatological age." "The purpose of the law is Christian growth in grace, not justification or merit." Moreover, he agrees with Ladd in the statement, "it is the new life of the Spirit that enables the Christian truly to fulfill the Law." The Holy Spirit "works in the believers to make the law a joy." According to VanGemeren, neither grace nor guidance by the Spirit should be separated from the law, lest we end up with antinomianism and a cloak for impiety. "Love motivates one to keep the law." "The law of God, when internalized by the Spirit of God, is an effective instrument of righteousness." He thus quotes E. F. Kevan who argued against any modification of the law in the governing of Christian conduct: "Any change in relation to Law that occurs in Christianity is not in the Law but in the believer." These kinds of remarks in VanGemeren's essay provide a broad foundation for agreement.

At this juncture, though, we need to turn to points of disagreement that call for further reflection and dialog. The task of critically analyzing VanGemeren's entire essay (as opposed to scattered comments), however, is made almost impossible by his manner of presentation. To go right to the point: there is simply nothing like an argument here—no discursive and systematic unfolding of a particular and clearly defined conclusion (or interrelated set of conclusions). VanGemeren does not develop and defend a distinctive thesis about the law of God and the modern Christian. His essay is more a cursory (although organized) survey of bits and pieces of information related in a variety of different ways to a broad topic or subject of discussion (namely, the law of God, although even here he tends to roam more widely). The specific focus of the debate in this book is not fixed in VanGemeren's discussion, thus leaving the respondent somewhat unsatisfied. It is sometimes not easy to find natural transitions, logical connections or subordination between points, interfacing of interpretations of texts, conceptual synthesis, or precision.

Some statements are elusively vague or mere truisms: for example, "Creation-order and law-order are correlative," or the sixth commandment requires from us "positive" behavioral patterns. Some outlining divisions confuse the reader, not being clearly distinct: for example, the Reformed view of law is discussed under the heading of "grace" *as well as* the [coordinate?] heading of "redemption." Many of the comments made in the text (even if true) just seem to sit next to each other without obvious relevance to each other, nor do they seem to serve a specific conclusion. Why some subjects are taken up within subsections but others are not is not evident to the reader. Nor is the rationale or meaning for certain concepts (e.g., "the triad" of love, law, and life that does not tolerate "any change in the[ir] order"), organizing devices (e.g., "order," "wholeness," and "integration," used throughout the essay in ways that are extremely vague and/or equivocal, in addition to lacking exegetical backing), or proposed frameworks (e.g. the framework "for looking at" the law of God within the Mosaic covenant includes five subjects [why these?], the last of which is "the law of God" *itself*!). Finally, if there is any theological synthesis given to the many brief and undeveloped comments or insights throughout the essay, providing a distinctive position, it is very faint.

Under these circumstances about all we can do is to examine a disjointed number of points about which there would be some criticism.

In the title of his essay VanGemeren says he is offering "a" Reformed perspective on the law of God, but within a few paragraphs he claims more for himself, saying that he here approaches the subject of "the" Reformed view of the law. A little later he announces that his "plan" is to utilize two kinds of treatment so that the reader may appreciate how "the Reformed view of the law of God" integrates exegesis and theology. Such overstatement should not go unchallenged. His is not the only Reformed understanding of God's law available (and neither is mine). VanGemeren's views are indisputably within the conventional orbit of generic Reformed theology, but so are those of a number of Reformed thinkers (past and present) who would dissent from certain of his distinctive or debatable claims; and in some areas of conceptualization and application regarding the Old Testament law there is no consensus anyway. Indeed, at certain points VanGemeren omits or departs from the views of traditional Reformed stalwarts like John Calvin or the Westminster divines, even clashing with a few conclusions that many leading Puritans found compelling.[1] Given his own particular slant, VanGemeren could claim to be presenting "the" Reformed view of the law only by gerrymandering the historical evidence. But let's move on.

VanGemeren's discussion of "natural law" needs clarification

---

[1]For instance, in VanGemeren's essay there is no acknowledgment, much less development, of a "political" use of God's law in civil society, despite this being a renowned element of the understanding of law in the Reformed tradition. One suspects this is because the author is uncomfortable with that aspect of historic Reformed thinking and practice. To take a different kind of example, even though VanGemeren gives consideration to Calvin's guides for interpreting the law, he reduces Calvin's explanation of the second guide (*Institutes* 2.8.8) to the principle of opposites (e.g., a negative prohibition entails a corresponding positive duty)— overlooking the Reformer's discussion of the need to seek the "reason or purpose" of each commandment in order to ascertain its "substance." One would not expect this oversight in a presentation of "the" Reformed view of the law, as this insight becomes a key to the Puritan and Westminster handling of the Old Testament judicial laws (holding onto their "equity"). But then VanGemeren's essay shortchanges the whole subject of judicial law, saying (quite mistakenly) that Reformed theology sees it as "abrogated."

and correction, I believe. The diligent reader realizes that some confusion is present when the author, having just referred to the medieval debate between voluntarist and essentialist schools of thought, writes "John Calvin accepted the medieval concept of natural law, but redefined its meaning. . . ." First, given the disputes over the subject, there was no such thing as "the" medieval concept of natural law. And second, it makes no sense to say Calvin accepted some concept "but redefined its meaning"; to say that one redefined the meaning of some fundamental concept (like "natural law") is just to say that he was engaged in a theoretical reconstruction or shift, *not* accepting previous theory.

But there is a more important confusion in VanGemeren's discussion. It does not seem that the author is himself very clear on what he means by "natural law." Sometimes he simply means "the unwritten law of God"—in which case he should have more accurately spoken of "natural revelation" (rather than "natural law"). Sometimes it is the expression of the will of God, but elsewhere it is "rooted in" the will of God. Sometimes it is the objective divine will that God communicates (being universal and perfect), but at other points it is something humans "discover" or "deduce from creation," given their "ability to develop a moral order"—thus amounting to a human being's subjective perception of God's will (being "variable" and "imperfect"). It is just not clear what kind of thing VanGemeren thinks natural law is. He treats it like a kind of metaphysical structure (created order), but by contrast as "the order *in* nature" (yet at another place he speaks oddly of "nature" being "part of" an orderly universe). He treats natural law as an epistemological instrument, but then on the other hand as a "moral order" in itself (whatever that could be), yet also as a psychological impulse that "explains the universal pursuit and appreciation of what is good" (which VanGemeren goes on to confuse theologically with "common grace"). The author needs to stop, analyze, and make clear just what he wishes to mean by speaking of "natural law." Until he does, the reader cannot tell whether the claims and inferences made about natural law by VanGemeren are theologically trustworthy, exegetically justified, or even cogent.

There are problems in the essay with the treatment given to other "kinds" (or categories) of law as well. VanGemeren sometimes calls the Decalogue "the summary" of God's "moral law," but at other places he says the moral law was "written down in the Ten Commandments," treating them as though they were the whole of the moral law by themselves. Of course logically you cannot have it both ways. In line with the "summary" conception of the Decalogue, VanGemeren holds that it was "the basis of the other codes" and "judicial decisions"; with this I concur, for the judicial code is simply the application of the Decalogue (and thus an unpacking of its meaning). But later VanGemeren claims the judicial laws are abrogated, while the Ten Commandments which they apply are not. Logically, again, you cannot have it both ways. At one point the author conceives of the judicial laws as something categorically different from the moral law: "Each one of the Ten Commandments expresses the moral law of God, *whereas* [other] laws in the Pentateuch regulate . . . the civil life of Israel as a nation" (emphasis added). But at another point he claims instead that "the judicial laws applied the last six command-ments" of the Decalogue. Once again: logically, you cannot have it both ways.

So VanGemeren needs to regiment his thinking and draw more careful distinctions regarding the relationship of the moral to the judicial law to preserve his position from internal contradic-tions (and thus self-refutation). Let me add that it seems to me his distinction is artificial when he says the first four commandments of the Decalogue are applied by the ceremonial law, while the judicial law applies the last six. The civil penalty for blasphemy given in Leviticus 24:16 surely seems "judicial," even though it is an application of the third commandment; and the ritual for averting the defilement of the land with innocent blood, where a murderer cannot be identified (Deut. 21:1–9), is "ceremonial" in character and purpose, and yet obviously applies the sixth commandment. The author is again somewhat artificial, or his point is overly and misleadingly general, when he contrasts the "specific" details and "restricted circumstances" of the case laws to the apodictic generality of the Decalogue. The Ten Command-ments themselves mention specific cultural circumstances: "idol," "animals," "alien within your gates," "the land the LORD your God gives you," and the neighbor's "ox or donkey."

Another criticism related to VanGemeren's discussion of the corpus of Old Testament laws can be mentioned. The author draws particular attention to the way in which the Mosaic literature extends beyond the Decalogue to other codes, instruc-tions, decisions, and penalties, all of which are "intertwined" with each other. He speaks of the "complex development" of the case laws, says the old covenant law from Sinai was "in a composite and complex form," and states that "the Book of the Covenant reveals the *complexity of Israelite law*" (his emphases). Now then, according to VanGemeren this detailed revelation of God's will was not a blessing or advantage to God's people—contrary to the testimony of David who found his "delight" in meditating upon God's law and had high regard for "all your commands" (Ps. 1:2; 119:6). The increase in moral revelation was an increase in light by which to live for the psalmist (119:105, 130); it was liberating (119:45), not a shackle. The greatness of Israel's wisdom in the sight of the nations was found precisely in "all this law"—the whole package of "statutes and ordinances"—that Moses taught the people (Deut. 4:5–8). Even today, when God's people get embroiled in moral dilemmas, they desire more inspired law (guidance), not less. It is surely no blessing to be left only with broad generalities: e.g., see how many people are blessed and happy by trying to play a basketball game under the single rule of "Play fair"!

Yet consider the quite different evaluation and attitude of VanGemeren toward the detailed and complex character of the law: "This complex form, together with the sanctions, often made the law a burden"—a burden. This sentiment is diametrically opposed to the teaching of God's own Word about the law. Moses wrote: "What I am commanding you today is *not too difficult for you*," nor is understanding it so far off that Israel could not do it (Deut. 30:11–14). John agreed when he wrote: "His commands are not burdensome" (1 John 5:3). VanGemeren makes his error even worse by claiming, based on Romans 10:4, that Jesus carried away this "burden" of complexity in the law by "simplifying" it. Later he says "Jesus simplified the complexity of the Mosaic law by focusing on one word ('love')." I am dubious that he can make anything like a credible exegetical case for taking Romans 10:4 in this manner. It is difficult to believe that Jesus intended to end the complexity of the Old Testament law when He declared that every "smallest letter" and "least stroke of a pen" of it should be obeyed and taught (Matt. 5:18–19). In the teaching of Jesus (as well as of Paul), love does not replace the law (or its complexity then), but provides a summary statement. A summary does not abrogate that which it summarizes. Jesus requires that even the minor points ought not to be left undone (Matt. 23:23).

Reference to Jesus' endorsement of every minute detail of the law—indeed of "the least of these commands"—in Matthew 5:17–19 leads me to broach what I think is the most glaring and significant error in VanGemeren's essay. He categorically states that the civil (judicial) laws and penal code of Moses have been "abrogated." I cannot find anywhere in his essay where he offers qualification or further refinement. Plain and simply, the judicial is deemed abrogated, without anything further needing to be said about it. Deep into his essay, following a similar claim about the ceremonial laws, VanGemeren points to the judicial laws and tersely, simply states: "They have also been abrogated." That would appear to fly directly in the face of the authoritative teaching of Christ, who said he did not come to abrogate the law, that not the slightest stroke of the commandments has passed away, and that anybody who dared to teach the loosening of the least of the commandments would be demoted to least within the kingdom. Those are strong and inspired words, and VanGemeren's statements seem to contradict them. I can understand someone holding that these words require us to presume the continuing validity of the Old Testament commandments, *but then also* finding qualifications or alterations in the further teaching of Christ and the New Testament (I myself appeal to such). But here is what the diligent reader must note. VanGemeren categorically sweeps away the judicial law without the slightest bit of biblical warrant even attempted. He sets forth no evidence for the reader at all. If he did, we would certainly need to take it into account and assess its strengths or weaknesses. But he gives no exegetical and theological proof. To this we can only reply that Dr. VanGemeren does not have the authority to dismiss a portion of God's law on his own. That really is the end of the story for those who believe they need biblical backing for their theological conclusions.

But there is more. Not only does VanGemeren's unsupported judgment that the judicial laws of the Old Testament are "abrogated" seem, on the face of it, to contradict the teaching of Jesus in Matthew 5, it also seems to negate what VanGemeren himself teaches in his essay—amounting to self-contradiction. VanGemeren writes: "Clearly, Jesus did not abrogate the law!" (note "clearly" and the exclamation). He endorses John Gerstner's statement that Christ did not set his disciples free from the law: "He abrogated *not one commandment*" (emphasis added). And he quotes Ladd: This is laid by God "upon men at all times and for all time." When therefore VanGemeren goes on to say that not just one, but many, of the Old Testament commandments (the whole judicial law) have been abrogated, there is a lethal and unresolved incoherence in his own theological outlook.

He also reduces his own position to ethical absurdity. In discussing the Mosaic covenant, VanGemeren offers as an example of a civil case law the distinction drawn in Exodus 21:12–14 between intentional and accidental homicide. Then later in his essay VanGemeren declares that the civil or judicial laws of Moses have been abrogated. If we were to be consistent with this reasoning, it would be necessary to conclude that it is no longer morally obligatory to distinguish between deliberate and accidental homicide. Common sense tells us that VanGemeren cannot really mean what he has written in his essay. He has not thought through his theological position carefully enough.

Not only does VanGemeren's "abrogation" of the judicial laws contradict the teaching of Jesus, as well as VanGemeren's own teaching elsewhere, but it contradicts the teaching of the Westminster Confession of Faith as well. The authors of that stupendous theological achievement carefully distinguished between the ceremonial law, which they said was "abrogated," and the judicial law which, by contrast, they said had "expired" (compare 19.3 with 19.4). The former was conceived of as abolished in its authority by the work of Christ, whereas the latter still had moral authority but its specific cultural form was disengaged by the passing away of the "state" or "body politick" for which it was worded. "Expired" cannot mean freedom from moral obligation to what those commandments taught. In the first place, the Westminster writers went on to cite the judicial laws at points in their exposition of God's law found in the Larger Catechism (e.g., #135, including duties of civil magistrates, as at the end of #108) because they saw them as "moral" in character (with specific applicatory form). Moreover, at the very place in the Confession where they spoke explicitly and directly to the question of in what way "the liberty of Christians is further enlarged" over Old Testament Jews, they list "freedom from the yoke of the ceremonial law, to which the Jewish Church was subjected"—but self-consciously do *not* include "the judicial law" (which, as noted, they treated as binding when expounding the Ten Commandments). The judicial law was not, then, "abrogated." Nevertheless, what was binding in the judicial laws was not their specific cultural form, but their underlying principle or purpose: "not obliging any other now further than the general equity thereof may require" (19.4). Note that, when applicable, this general equity of the judicial law is "required"—something that cannot be said of an "abrogated" law.

The most significant evidence for how the Puritans understood this comes from the pen of George Gillespie, the Scottish delegate to the Westminster Assembly itself and universally regarded as the most influential and authoritative theologian there. Addressing the question "whether the Christian Magistrate is bound to observe the judicial laws of Moses," Gillespie wrote that "he is obliged to those things in the judicial law which are unchangeable and common to all nations." In particular, "the Christian magistrate is bound to observe these judicial laws of Moses which appoint the punishments of sins against the moral law." It was Gillespie's weighty opinion that "the will of God concerning civil justice and punishments is nowhere so fully and clearly revealed as in the judicial law of Moses. This therefore must be the surest prop and stay to the conscience of the Christian Magistrate." Does he not treat them the same way as the ceremonial law, as VanGemeren does? "Though we have clear and full Scriptures in the New Testament for abolishing the ceremonial law, yet we nowhere read in all the New Testament of the abolishing of the judicial law, so far as it did concern the punishing of sins against the moral law." For Gillespie, then, "he who was punishable by death under the judicial law is punishable by death still."[2] VanGemeren's blunt dismissal of the Mosaic judicial law as "abrogated" does not find support in the Westminster Standards, and it departs from leading Puritan theologians.

Finally, a comment is appropriate and needed in reply to a point in the essay where the author directly addresses theonomic ethics (specifically as it touches on the judicial and penal laws). VanGemeren quotes with approval a generalization by T. Longman III, who charges that theonomy so "grossly" overemphasizes continuity between the old and new covenants that it is "virtually blind to discontinuity." But this is an exaggeration, as anybody who looks at my books,[3] or even the essay in this book, can readily see. Longman made this extreme statement in an essay for a book with other authors—a volume that I answered in a book of my own. My book included a direct response to the very statement in question here:

> "Virtually blind" to discontinuity? Longman does not tell us [neither does VanGemeren] just exactly what he sees that is relevant to refuting the theonomic approach, but which theo-

---

[2]"Wholesome Severity Reconciled with Christian Liberty" (London, 1645), reprinted in *Anthology of Presbyterian and Reformed Literature*, vol. 4, ed. Christopher Coldwell (Dallas, Tex.: Napthali Press, 1991), 182–83.

[3]*Theonomy in Christian Ethics* (Nutley, N.J.: The Craig Press, 1977, 1984); also *By This Standard: The Authority of God's Law Today* (Tyler, Tex.: Institute for Christian Economics, 1985), in which chapter 16 is actually entitled "Discontinuity Between the Covenants on the Law."

nomists blindly overlook. Longman's co-author, Dennis Johnson, readily enough corrects this accusation of gross blindness: "Both theonomists and their critics acknowledge continuity and discontinuity between the old covenant and the new. . . . No theonomist of whom I am aware actually contends that the law's applicability remained utterly unchanged by the coming of Christ. . . . So the difference between theonomists and non-theonomists is not that one group sees nothing but continuity between the Mosaic order and the new covenant, while the other sees nothing but discontinuity." . . . Johnson easily offers a number of such important discontinuities spoken of in my writings.[4]

I believe VanGemeren should not echo such a false argument.[5] Resorting to knocking down a straw man is a futile and inadequate defense against the serious exegetical and theological critique that theonomic ethics makes of the defects in VanGemeren's view of the Old Testament civil and penal law.

---

[4]*No Other Standard: Theonomy and Its Critics* (Tyler, Tex.: Institute for Christian Economics, 1991), 48.

[5]Elsewhere, VanGemeren again mentions the book that he has cited (*Theonomy: A Reformed Critique*, ed. W. S. Barker & W. R. Godfrey [Grand Rapids: Zondervan, 1990]), commending it "for a fair discussion of the issues raised by theonomy." For a much different evaluation of that volume—a technical evaluation much more detailed and more objectively based on extensive analysis and consideration of sources—compare *Theonomy: An Informed Response*, ed. Gary North (Tyler, Tex.: Institute for Christian Economics, 1991), to which a number of authors contributed.

Response to Willem A. VanGemeren

Walter C. Kaiser, Jr.

VanGemeren's essay is marked with a lot of good exegetical sense and theological savvy on how Law and Gospel are related to each other. With typical Reformed logic, VanGemeren distinguishes the covenant of works made with Adam from the covenant of grace that covers everything from the fall of Adam to the new creation.

The covenant of grace is divided into two "administrations": Law and Gospel, even though neither administration is devoid of either Law or Gospel, since Law contains the Gospel and Gospel contains the Law. Therein lies the uniqueness and the attractiveness of the Reformed position on Law and Gospel.

One might wish to quibble that the Bible itself does not actually talk about these two different "covenants," as posed here, but there is nothing in that manner of formulating the issues of Law and Gospel that would detract from the central concerns that need to be addressed. The problem of imposed versus inductively derived theological grids needs to be handled in another context.

The focus of biblical ethics remains very much the same for both the Old and New Testaments in VanGemeren's representation of the matter. It is the call for holiness of life. Since God is holy, his moral law is holy. In fact, "without holiness no one will see the Lord" (Heb. 12:14b). Again, we are in wholehearted agreement with this assessment of the biblical witness.

There are four rather minor issues that I would like to comment on. One is only touched on briefly, for the topic is brought up almost as an aside, but since I object to it strenuously in the other essays, it is only fair to note its presence here. The other issues will be raised by way of making a small contribution to the on-going conversation on the topic of Law/Gospel. The four issues are: (1) the history of redemption and the law; (2) the Abrahamic and Mosaic covenants in covenant theology; (3) the hypothetical offer of salvation for keeping the law perfectly; and (4) the principles of interpretation and application of the law. Each of these will be taken up in turn.

The History of Redemption and the Law

VanGemeren arranges his discussion of Law and Gospel within the grid of the history of redemption. There are six major stages in redemptive history: Creation, Fall, Abraham, Moses, Jesus Christ, and Paul. In each of these six stages of redemption, VanGemeren finds the triad of love, law, and life operating and forming the essential ingredients of biblical ethics in each.

Following the lead of Calvin, VanGemeren argues for the existence of a moral order in creation prior to the publication of the will of God in the Mosaic covenant. This natural law does not replace or make the written law of God unnecessary, but is in harmony with that same order that is now made known in God's law. Thus, since the will of God is as unchanging as his nature, that will remains constant throughout all of redemptive history.

This natural law reveals both the will of God and his attributes. It is for this reason that the human race was accountable to the same standard of righteousness even prior to the publication of the law of God under Moses.

I find this to be an especially strong argument. It is well to be reminded of the fine heritage that evangelical theology has in this contribution from Reformation theology. Sadly, however, few are being exposed to this type of thinking, even, at times, within the ranks of Reformed theology. Surely, natural law was the basis for Paul's indictment of all persons, even those who have never seen the law of God, in Romans 2:14–15a. This too will explain why Scripture notes that Enoch, Noah, and Abraham kept God's requirements, laws, commands, and statutes (e.g., Gen. 26:5), even when the law of Moses had not yet been published. This type of argumentation goes a long way towards softening the criticism that the law of Moses was (in all aspects, including its moral law) added *after* the promise had been given to Abraham. The Pauline reference (Gal. 3:17) to the law being introduced 430 years later than the promise to Abraham of the birth of the seed clearly refers to those aspects of the law that supplemented the moral law of God. To argue otherwise is to deny natural revelation as defined here and to leave the enigma of explaining just what kind of law it was that Abraham and those who came before the patriarchs observed. VanGemeren has reminded us of a most important component in the Law/Gospel debate.

The discussion of the importance of the role that the "fear of God" plays in any proper observance of the Mosaic law in order to prevent law-keeping from reverting to sheer legalism was another major coup for VanGemeren. This will tie in wisdom literature all the more with the history of redemption and provide a major link in the long sought center of biblical theology.

VanGemeren treated the Mosaic covenant as an administration of promise, even if it was a legal administration that came with sanctions for disobedience, with casuistic (i.e., case) laws, with specific applications for very special circumstances, and with ceremonial and ritual observances. But the Mosaic law, VanGemeren correctly assures us, was not intended as a means of salvation. It was, instead, intended as an instrument of salvation. We could not be in more hearty agreement.

Rather than treating the new covenant as being different in substance from the old covenant of the Mosaic era, VanGemeren set forth a strong case for its being the same in substance. It is true that he slipped at this point and does mention that it was the same in substance with the Mosaic *administration*, but it is clear that he meant the Mosaic covenant itself. He does not specifically treat the issue of whether it is the same *tôrâ* that Moses gave that will be placed on the heart of the New Covenant believer. But from what he says, it is clear that it is the same moral law that will be written on the heart of the believers during the days of the new covenant.

While VanGemeren, like most of us, is frustrated with the apostle Paul on his discussion of the law, he finds the central teaching of Paul on this issue in Galatians 3:21—"Is the law, therefore, opposed to the promises of God? Absolutely not!" He also cites Paul's advice in 1 Corinthians 7:19—"Keeping God's commands is what counts."

The best way to explain Paul's apparent contradictory statements on the law is to note Paul's doctrine of the two ages. As such, the Christian belongs to the new creation of God and therefore may use the law of God only as it is internalized by the Holy Spirit in producing righteousness and in creating a new community that fulfills the law of love. This is not to argue for some new replacement theology wherein the Spirit now replaces the law, but it is to recognize the key role that the Holy Spirit plays in transforming us to apply the moral law of God. The change, then, explains VanGemeren, quoting E. F. Kevan, "is not in the Law but in the believer."

This section on the history of redemption is extremely well written and should provide the basis for a very healthy discussion of the key issues for many years to come.

The Abrahamic and Mosaic Covenants in Reformed Theology

The least satisfying discussion in VanGemeren's otherwise helpful essay is his treatment of the relationship between the Abrahamic and Mosaic covenants. He describes the ambivalent attitude that has been expressed within the Reformed community on this matter, as represented by Meredith Kline, by John Murray, and now more recently by Mark Karlberg. Kline treats the period of Mosaic Law as a parenthesis, marked by aspects of strong discontinuity, while Murray favors more continuity. However, Karlberg criticizes Murray for putting grace under law in the Mosaic era and for not relating the curses found in the Mosaic Law to the covenant of works. Palmer Robertson expresses partial agreement with Murray and partial agreement with Kline.

Disappointingly, VanGemeren decided to conclude this discussion by calling for the maintenance of a tension between law and grace. But what does that signify in this context? Does he mean both Kline and Murray are correct? Is the Mosaic covenant a parenthesis, marked by discontinuity in some, all, or none of its substance? If it is totally parenthetical, will not Reformed theology now differ very little, if at all, with the dispensational option? If it is partial, then what will the criteria be for distinguishing between the different aspects? It is unfair for Old Testament scholars to imply that there are some distinctions here without putting their hand to the task to give us some guidance on just how the laity may discern these differences.

Interestingly enough, just at the point where Reformed theology exhibits its greatest strength (in maintaining the unity of the plan of salvation through the history of redemption), there arises a reluctance to forge ahead on the manner in which the Abrahamic promise relates to the law of Moses. Is this reluctance in any way related to a prior theological move that has replaced Israel with the church? In retrospect, would that pose some problems and confusions of identity, mission, and purpose of the Mosaic materials? Here is a problem worth exploring. The point, however, remains that the fine discussion of the way Law and Gospel were related in the history of redemption is not followed up with a theological discussion that can tell us just how the Abrahamic covenant relates to the Mosaic covenant—except to conclude that a tension must be maintained. That sounds like saying everybody on this issue must be right. But how can that be, given such contradictory conclusions?

The Hypothetical Offer of Salvation for Perfect Law-keeping

VanGemeren appears to quote Calvin with approval when the latter opined, "The law and the promise do not contradict each other except in the matter of justification, for the law justifies a man by the merit of works whereas the promise bestows righteousness freely." VanGemeren explains this amazing quote from Calvin by claiming that Calvin meant that if one kept the law perfectly, one could be justified by the law. However, since no one has, or ever, will keep the law perfectly, justifying faith will never come by keeping the law.

But my response to Calvin, as well as VanGemeren, is the same as it is to dispensational forms of theology that I will evaluate elsewhere in this volume: Paul flatly denied that there ever was any such offer, hypothetically or really, of the gospel in Galatians 3:21b. Did he not affirm, "For if a law had been given that could impart life, then righteousness would certainly have come by the law"? Does that not slam the door shut on any and all proposals about a theoretical offer of salvation made available to all who would properly take up the task of observing and obeying the law to its perfection? We are just amazed to see such an argument raising its head in Reformed thinking. It is for this reason that some, like Daniel Fuller, have rightly charged that when push comes to shove, there is not all that much difference in many of the solutions given to the Law/Gospel problem between dispensational and covenant theologies.

Of course, balance can be found between Law and Gospel in Jesus Christ, as VanGemeren points out. But the presence of Christ in both Testaments has been assumed in all of Reformed thinking. That must mean that something else is out of place or missing, if we are to account for the fact that at the end of the day there is little difference on some of the solutions between covenant and dispensational theologies on the relationship of law and grace in Moses, Jesus, and Paul.

Principles of Interpretation and Application of the Law

The distinction of the three uses of the law has long been a stable facet of Reformed theology. In particular, the third use of the law, known in the Latin phrases as the *usus in renatis* or the *usus normativus*, remains the most useful for the believer's growth in sanctification. This third use of the law guides believers in righteousness, provides the basis for obedience, yet does so without enslaving any who are so bound to this, which may now also be called the "law of Christ." On these matters, we are in full agreement, for this is precisely what we think the biblical text teaches.

But how shall we interpret and apply the law of God? Here VanGemeren appropriately resorts to Calvin's two principles of interpretation: "(1) The commandment addresses 'inward and spiritual righteousness'; and (2) "the 'commandments and prohibitions always contain more than is expressed in words.'" Both of these principles get at the heart of the matter with unusual insight. Evangelicalism would have been saved from a lot of its fears about the contemporary use of the law had the generation that grew up in the middle and the end of this century been taught such principles and appreciation for the law of God. We applaud VanGemeren's inclusion of them in this collection of essays.

Conclusion

God's law can only be kept by his grace. Moreover, as VanGemeren concludes, it may only be appreciated in the light of the gospel of Jesus Christ and kept by the power of the Holy Spirit—all this is true for either Testament!

The current evangelical generation has been raised almost devoid of any teaching on the place and use of the law in the life of the believer. This has resulted in a full (or perhaps semi-) antinomian approach to life. Is it any wonder that the unbelieving society around us is so lawless, if those who should have been light and salt to that same society were themselves not always sure what it was that they should be doing?

The time for a powerful proclamation of the proper uses of the law is now long overdue. Meanwhile, the moral character of the living God continues to be what it has ever been, even before it was codified and given to Moses by revelation. It is time for the dispute to come to an end; instead, let a good share of the energies be focused on discerning, by the work of the Holy Spirit, how that law of God can be further interpreted and applied to the whole of life in a way that is both honoring to Scripture and to the grace of God that brought us so great a salvation!

Response to Willem A. VanGemeren

Wayne G. Strickland

In the Reformed tradition, VanGemeren has articulated a model that preserves the continuity between Law and Gospel by suggesting they are two administrations of the one covenant of grace. He has approached the issue of the role of the Mosaic law in the church age from the perspective of covenant theology and has argued for the abiding enforcement of at least a portion of the Mosaic law. He has purposed to demonstrate that the responsibility to keep the moral aspect of the Mosaic law is biblical and faithful to the tradition of both Calvin and the Westminster Divines. His approach has been to give a fairly comprehensive survey, and he has contributed many helpful insights into the issue.

VanGemeren has properly recognized the principle of natural law as the standard of behavior for saints prior to the Mosaic economy (though he makes no serious attempt to validate the concept from the biblical testimony, appealing instead to John Calvin and the later Westminster theologians). As early as the creation of the human race, there were standards to be followed that he labels creation ordinances.[1] Thus, God's moral demands

---

[1]Some of these ordinances are not explicitly presented in Scripture, but must be drawn from implications and assumed. VanGemeren has accepted the concept as drawn from John Murray, *Principles of Conduct* (Grand Rapids: Eerdmans, 1957), 27–44. For example, the Sabbath ordinance is drawn from Genesis 2:2–3, but it only states that God himself rested on the seventh day and does not prescribe this

were known to people prior to the giving of the Mosaic law; later, that ethic was codified in various ways in the different dispensations.

VanGemeren has also provided insight into the nature of the Mosaic covenant from a biblical theological perspective. He accurately paints a picture of the Mosaic covenant as an administration of grace. Certainly the Mosaic compact is not to be understood as antithetical to or a substitute for the promises made to Abraham. He has rightly presented the two covenants as complementary. This discussion serves as warning not to arrive at simplistic summaries that suggest either wholesale continuity or discontinuity. The elements of grace and promise underscore that there is a certain level of continuity between Law and Gospel, since the Gospel, like Law, is clearly characterized by grace and promise. In response to VanGemeren, the emphasis in Scripture is on discontinuity, but there are several aspects of continuity.

VanGemeren has given a helpful survey of the purposes of the Mosaic law. In harmony with the Reformed tradition, he has made it clear that the law was not a means of salvation in the Old Testament. However, he claims that the Mosaic law was the instrument of *sanctification* for the Old Testament believer. Concerning the present day uses of the Mosaic law, VanGemeren appreciates its applicability in the pedagogical sense. It serves to indict the sinner and inform regarding the need for the righteousness of God; it also serves to bring about civil restraint. It is these revelational purposes that continue into the present.

Although accepting the threefold division of moral, civil, and ceremonial aspects of the Mosaic law, VanGemeren does acknowledge the complexity of Israelite law and the special difficulty of dividing it into distinct sections based on this principle of separation.

A major difference that continues to distinguish most covenantal and dispensational approaches to the Mosaic law surfaces in VanGemeren's discussion of the treatment of the law by Jesus Christ. To VanGemeren, Jesus Christ did not bring an end to the Mosaic law. Rather, the moral law "received further clarification in the person and teaching of Jesus Christ." Further, he disagrees with Westerholm's treatment of law, who presents a case for a strong discontinuity between Israel's law and the church's faith.

---

behavior for others (see the discussion of this issue later in my response). The idea of a *Sabbath* creation ordinance cannot be sustained.

At this point he believes that Westerholm has been unduly influenced by Lutheran theology, and VanGemeren expectedly opts for the Reformed paradigm. He charges Westerholm with "making his Paul disagree with the Paul who said, 'Keeping God's commands is what counts' (1 Cor. 7:19)." However, in agreement with Westerholm, we must emphasize that Paul clearly develops the discontinuity theme in several passages (e.g., Rom. 6:14–15; 9:31–10:8, esp. 10:4; 1 Cor. 9:19–23; 2 Cor. 3:3, 6–18; Gal. 2:19; 3:1–5, 10–29; Phil. 3:7–9).

In response to Westerholm's presentation of Paul's sharp contrast between law and faith, VanGemeren raises 1 Corinthians 7:19 as proof that Paul adhered to the abiding validity of the Mosaic moral law.[2] The question that must be raised is whether the phrase "God's commands" (*entolōn theou*) actually refers to the Mosaic commandments. If so, then Westerholm is guilty as charged, making Paul disagree with himself. Yet, Paul does not always use the term *entolos* ("commandment") to refer to the Mosaic law (e.g., Col. 4:10; 1 Thess. 4:2; Tit. 1:14).

For several reasons, it seems unlikely in 1 Corinthians 7:19 that Paul is referring to the Mosaic law; rather, he seems to be referring to his own instructions. In 6:1–11, Paul has been dealing with the issue of Christians taking other Christians to court. It is significant to note that not once does he appeal to Mosaic legislation to handle this problem, but rather appeals to an argument based on the principle of believers judging unbelievers in the eschaton. Likewise in the following section, when Paul treats the effect of immorality on the body, he does not appeal to Mosaic decrees that prohibit such behavior, but instead appeals both to the unique relationship whereby the believer is a member of Christ (6:15) and to the relationship that has been established with the Holy Spirit (6:19). Paul himself gives a commandment that he considers binding on the church: "Flee immorality" (6:18). In chapter 7 Paul continues giving instructions, this time dealing with marriage. Again he repeatedly refrains from appealing to the appropriate Mosaic codes and instead appeals to the Lord Jesus Christ (7:10–11) and his own authority (7:12). Paul himself commands the believer to remain with the unbeliever in a marriage unless the unbelieving spouse deserts, in which case separation is permitted (7:12–15). No Mosaic legislation was

---

[2]See also E. B. Allo (*Première Epître aux Corinthiens* [Paris: J. Gabalda, 1956], 172) for a defense of "commandments" in 1 Cor 7:19 as a reference to the Decalogue.

applicable to this situation since marriage with non-Jews was prohibited by the law (Ex. 34:15–16; Deut. 7:3; Ezra 10:2; Neh. 13:23–27). Following general instructions to remain in the state that God has assigned, Paul states that the important thing is to follow the commandments of God (1 Cor. 7:19). As can be seen, the context demands that the commandments of the Lord and Paul are in view rather than the Mosaic law. Certainly if Paul were referring to the Mosaic law when he uses the term "God's commands," then there is an internal contradiction in the verse, since the requirement to be circumcised, which Paul suspends, was a commandment of God. Perhaps, of course, VanGemeren wants to delimit the term "command" in 7:19 to mean the moral part of the Mosaic law. If so, the problem is minimized, although there is no evidence to support understanding *entolos* as restricted to the moral aspect of the Mosaic law.

An additional problem for the continuity view is the insufficient attention given to the nature of the Mosaic law itself. It was given in the form of a covenant, directed to a particular people, and intended as prescription for the Israelites, with whom God entered into a contractual agreement. VanGemeren's view of law does not totally satisfy the epochal shift that has transpired. He suggests that the new covenant administration "is the same in substance as the old covenant (Mosaic administration), but different in form." The similarity in substance extends also to the Abrahamic covenant. All three share "the same God, Christ, Spirit, inheritance, salvation, rule of faith and life, hope of immortality, church, doctrine, and adoption. It contains grace and promise."[3] Yet, VanGemeren goes on to admit that the covenants have different purposes. The new covenant is primarily a soteriological covenant, whereas the old covenant purposed to regulate life in the theocracy. This alone should demonstrate that they differ in substance. The Abrahamic covenant is patterned after the royal grant that is unconditional in nature, whereas the Sinaitic covenant is patterned after the sovereign-vassal treaty form that is conditional in nature.[4] Again this fundamental difference in

---

[3]See Knox Chamblin, "The Law of Moses and The Law of Christ" in *Continuity and Discontinuity: Perspectives on the Relationship between the Old and New Testaments*, ed. John S. Feinberg (Westchester, Ill.: Crossway, 1988), 181-202, for a similar assertion that the covenants are the same in substance and different in form.

[4]Moshe Weinfield, "The Covenant of Grant in the Old Testament and in the Ancient Near East," *Journal of the American Oriental Society* 90 (1970), 184–203; and George E. Mendenhall, "Covenant Forms in Israelite Tradition," *BA* 17 (1954), 50–

substance argues for some measure of discontinuity. Further, the author of Hebrews presents substantive differences between the two covenants related to promises—the new covenant is based on better promises (Heb. 8:6).

Since there has been an abrogation of the entire Mosaic law with the coming of Christ, it follows that the Mosaic law is not the required code for growth in grace among church-age believers. The so-called third use of the law does not withstand the scrutiny of Paul's testimony. VanGemeren appeals to Galatians 3:21 to make the point that the law was not designed to procure salvation but to lead "those who are already alive to life and righteousness." Yet, an examination of this passage demonstrates that Paul does not encourage the church-age believer to obey the Mosaic law. To be sure, he argues that the law was added after the Abrahamic covenant because of sin and that the law was not designed or able to save. Rather, the law was designed to be a custodian or *paidagōgos* until faith came, until Christ came (3:23–24). This purpose of the law has ended, however, with the arrival of Christ. Paul concludes, "Now that faith has come, we are no longer under the supervision of the law" (3:25). Thus, VanGemeren is partially correct in that Paul denies the saving ability of the law, but neither does the apostle give the law sanctifying ability.

VanGemeren raises a crucial point regarding the relationship of the Holy Spirit and the law. A significant area of discontinuity between the Mosaic economy and the church age is the promise to the believer of a permanently indwelling Holy Spirit. This Spirit uses the internal law to convict the modern believer of sin and to encourage godly behavior. Yet it is not the moral law of the Mosaic code that the Holy Spirit employs to supervise the believer; rather, it is the law of Christ that is made imperative by the Spirit. Perhaps greater attention could have been paid to the passages treating the law of Christ. Why is it labeled "the law of Christ?" How does it relate to the Mosaic law? VanGemeren merely alludes to it once in reference to 1 Corinthians 9:21, where the phrase *ennomos Christou* ("in-lawed to Christ") is used.[5] The contribution of Galatians 6:2 also needs to be weighed.

---

76. See D. Patrick, *Old Testament Law* (Atlanta: John Knox, 1985), 224, for one who rejects the idea of the biblical material being patterned after Hittite suzereignty treaties.

[5] See C. H. Dodd, "ENNOMOS CHRISTOY," in *Studia Paulina*, eds. J. N. Sevenster and W. C. Van Unnik (Haarlem: De Erven F. Bohn, 1953), 96–110, for a discussion of the law of Christ as Jesus' instruction.

Finally, a problem for the Reformed position is the proper understanding and contribution of the Sabbath to the applicability of the Mosaic law. The issue provides a mechanism for testing the accuracy and coherency of the Reformed paradigm with regard to the applicability of the law in ethics.

VanGemeren and other covenant theologians argue that the moral aspect of the Mosaic law is expressed in the Decalogue. Thus the Sabbath commandment is a binding ethic. Yet this commandment is dissimilar to the other nine commandments, thus creating special problems. It is the only Decalogue imperative that is not reissued in the New Testament. Also, Paul discusses the controversy in the church surrounding Sabbath observance several times and never prescribes obedience to the Sabbath command or even to Sunday as the recipient of the Sabbath shift (Rom. 14:5; Gal. 4:10–11; Col. 2:16–17). Not only is it not repeated, but the church does not observe the seventh day of the week. Very early in its history the church worshiped on the first day of the week (Acts 20:7; 1 Cor. 16:2).

It is argued that the permanent obligation of Sabbath observance stems from the fact that conformance was prescribed at the creation. Specifically, the Sabbath was instituted by the example of God himself and is one of the creation ordinances prescribed for people. Appeal as an "ordinance" is based on Genesis 2:2–3. Yet these verses do not prescribe or command adherence to the Sabbath for rest. Thus the principle of weekly Sabbath rest cannot be based on the so-called creation ordinance. Further the institution of the Sabbath rest comes with the travel to the promised land (Ex. 16:23) and the Sinai legislation (Ex. 20:11).

Likewise, there is no biblical evidence for Sabbatarianism that argues that the Sabbath rest has been transferred from the seventh day to Sunday. In the New Testament era, worship on Sunday was never described or understood as a Christian Sabbath. Additional complications are caused by Sabbatarians who argue that Christ brought an end to the "existing Sabbath ceremonial" in Matthew 12:8.[6] Thus the Sabbath principle should be enforced by moving it to Sunday or without prescribing a particular day. There is in fact no Sabbath transfer or shift taught in Scripture. This constitutes a hermeneutical shift inasmuch as the meaning of the other nine commandments are not modified or qualified in this way in the New Testament. If the Decalogue is perpetually

---

[6]Chamblin, "The Law of Moses," 196.

binding, including in the church age, how is it that this commandment can be eradicated or altered?

A preferable solution is to understand that no command to
observe the Sabbath day of rest is given until Israel is in the
wilderness on the way to the promised land, where they will be
governed as a theocracy. God established the principle of rest, and
such weekly rest is patterned after God's original creative rest. The
worship of God on Sunday is not in any way fulfillment of the
Sabbath command. That command is not repeated, and thus there
is no obligation to include such a rest period. However, the
principle of Sabbath rest is established as a wise course of action,
and the Sabbath rest of the Mosaic law serves to remind us of the
rest into which the believer has already entered (Heb. 4:1–11).

In conclusion, VanGemeren has presented an eloquent case
for the continuing binding nature of the moral aspect of the
Mosaic law. He rightly has stated the requirement of the proper
heart and motivation in the keeping of the law. There must be
submission and obedience. Yet the submission and obedience
must be to the law of Christ rather than to the law of Moses.

Response to Willem A. VanGemeren

Douglas Moo

My colleague Willem VanGemeren has provided us with a clear and comprehensive sketch of the traditional Reformed perspective on the law in its relationship to the various stages of salvation history. This perspective is deeply embedded in our common Protestant heritage; most of us, perhaps without even knowing it, have absorbed into our theology many of the elements of the Reformed perspective on the law. It is a perspective with many clear strengths, and these strengths are evident in VanGemeren's essay. Before I indicate some points at which I would disagree with VanGemeren, then, I want to acknowledge the very many points at which I agree.

First, I commend VanGemeren for insisting on the clear and unchanging standards of God's moral law. In an era of "alternative lifestyles" it is more important than ever that Christians cling tenaciously to the moral law of God as our absolute and unquestioned standard. Second, I commend VanGemeren for maintaining the traditional Reformed separation between faith and the promise on the one hand and works and the law on the other. As I indicate in my essay, some Protestant scholars are now combining "faith" and "law" in such a way that endangers what I think is central to New Testament teaching: that salvation is "by faith alone" and "by grace alone."

VanGemeren's balance between discontinuity and continuity in salvation history is a third point that I endorse and, indeed, applaud. His comprehensive and helpful survey of biblical history stresses, in typical Reformed fashion, the continuity of God's plan and the oneness of God's people. At the same time, he acknowledges discontinuities in salvation history as God's plan unfolds. Preparatory and propaedeutic elements such as the ceremonies of the Mosaic law and the unique national status of Israel fall away while God's people come to better understand his purposes and to experience a fuller measure of blessing and liberty. Fourth, I appreciate VanGemeren's attention to the unwritten, or natural, law. Some Protestants, following Barth, have downplayed the role of natural law, while others have given it too much credit, according to it virtually salvific functions. VanGemeren, representing again here a traditional Reformed perspective, strikes a good balance on this debated point.

I could extend this list of agreements beyond these four to many other more detailed points in the essay. Suffice to say that I endorse its general theological approach and even most of its specific points about the law. But there is one point with which I disagree: I do not think that the Christian is directly responsible to obey any part of the Mosaic law. Or, to put the matter differently, I think the Mosaic law as a whole was given to Israel for a limited time and purpose and is no longer immediately authoritative for the Christian. VanGemeren, reflecting again at this point a typical Reformed perspective, disagrees, maintaining that within the Mosaic law the Ten Commandments function as eternal moral law, authoritative for believers in every age. I will concentrate on this difference of opinion in the rest of my response.

First, I want to make clear that I am not denying that the Mosaic law, especially the Ten Commandments, contains principles and requirements that reflect God's eternal moral will. My point, rather, is that the Mosaic law is not identical with this eternal moral law. It is part of a covenant document entered into with the nation Israel and is therefore specifically addressed to Israel—and not to the new covenant community. Reformed theologians such as VanGemeren admit that the greater part of the Mosaic law was given to Israel and is no longer directly authoritative for the Christian—the "casuistic" laws, or the "civil" and "ceremonial" law. But they insist that part of the law is directed to the community of believers in every age—the "apodictic" laws or the "moral" law, which is found especially (or only) in the Ten Commandments. VanGemeren therefore insists on a continuity of the "moral law" within the larger discontinuity of the Mosaic covenant and its law. It is just this treatment of one part of the Mosaic law in a way different from the rest of it that I question.

What is the evidence for treating the Ten Commandments as eternal moral law in distinction from the rest of the Mosaic law? VanGemeren provides little. He notes that these "ten words" are apodictic in form, expressing therefore principles upon which the rest of the law is built. But this in itself does not require that they be eternal moral law. VanGemeren appears to assume the traditional Reformed triadic division of the law into "moral," "civil," and "ceremonial" without arguing the case. Yet this distinction, vital to his whole argument, is nowhere clearly stated in the Bible. In fact, as we have argued elsewhere, there is good reason to think that Jesus and the New Testament authors treated the Mosaic law as a whole. Jewish theology refused to allow a "picking and choosing" among the commandments of the law, and passages such as Galatians 5:3 and James 2:8–13 suggest that the New Testament adopted the same perspective. This is not to deny that Jews sometimes discussed the relative importance of the Mosaic commandments. But these discussions never assumed that the more important commandments were in a separate category from the others such that, at some future date, they would continue in force while the others would drop away. Jesus followed this Jewish tradition closely when he claimed that some commandments were more "weighty" than others and yet that even the "lighter" commandments still must be done (Matt. 23:23).

Nevertheless, without demonstrating from Scripture the existence of the distinction between such elements as the "ceremonial" and the "moral" law, VanGemeren employs it in exegeting key passages. He argues, for instance, that it is only the ceremonial law that Paul is speaking of when he claims that Christ [or God] "canceled the written code, with its regulations, that was against us and that stood opposed to us; he took it away, nailing it to the cross" (Col. 2:14). That Paul here refers to the Mosaic law is probable (cf. the word *dogmata*, used also in Eph. 2:14). But that we can confine his reference to the "ceremonial law" is unlikely, for Paul's point here is to show that Christ's cross cancels the debt we owe to God for the sins we have committed (*cheirographon* is a "certificate of indebtedness," an "IOU"). It is the law that defines these sins and is, because of that, "against us." Clearly, then, Paul would not be thinking only of sins committed against the ceremonial law; he must be thinking of the Mosaic law as a whole.

VanGemeren again speaks of the "moral law" in connection with Galatians 5:17–18, citing this text as evidence that the "moral law is still relevant as a mirror condemning our negative passions characteristic of the old man. . . ." These verses read:

> For the sinful nature desires what is contrary to the Spirit, and the Spirit what is contrary to the sinful nature. They are in conflict with each other, so that you do not do what you want. But if you are led by the Spirit, you are not under law.

Now we can see that this passage itself says nothing positive about the law in any sense. VanGemeren apparently refers to the moral law here because it is what defines the desires of the sinful nature (see vv. 19–20). But the text certainly does not justify the conclusion that the moral law remains in force as a condemning power. In fact, Paul suggests in this text that it is what "the Spirit [desires]" that reveals the desires of the sinful nature. Furthermore, even if we allow that what "the Spirit [desires]" may be equivalent to the moral law, there is no reason to think that Paul would consider the Mosaic law to be the source of this moral law. Now VanGemeren does not make clear in this paragraph that he thinks of the Mosaic law as the source for this moral law. If he does not intend this connection, then these texts give no basis at all for thinking that the Mosaic law has any continuing function in the life of the believer. Such a conclusion would be unwarranted unless one were to argue that the Mosaic law is the only possible source for moral law—a conclusion that VanGemeren would not allow, since he rightly argues for the existence of an "unwritten law."

On the other hand, if VanGemeren is suggesting that the moral law he speaks of here has its source in the Mosaic law, formidable objections loom. Rather than affirming the role of the Mosaic law in the life of the Christian (as VanGemeren seems to imply), Galatians 5:17–24 rather clearly denies it. Paul claims explicitly that Christians, led by the Spirit and subject to the "law of Christ" (see 5:18 and 6:2), are not "under law" (almost certainly, in light of the Galatians' situation, the Mosaic law). At the least, however, Galatians 5:17–18 provides no basis for the concept of a Mosaic "moral law," and certainly not, then, for its continued relevance to the Christian.

VanGemeren himself appears to agree elsewhere with the holistic approach to the Mosaic law that we are advocating. He claims that Jesus taught "a stricter interpretation of Moses than the rabbis," "simplified the complexity of the Mosaic law," and "upheld the spiritual intent of the Lawgiver." As illustrations of the last point, VanGemeren mentions Jesus' teaching on the

Sabbath, murder, and ceremonial rituals. Jesus speaks to each of these issues; and none of them is left unchanged, for even the Decalogue's prohibition of murder is extended by Jesus to include anger. In other words, as VanGemeren's approach suggests, Jesus does not ignore any part of the Mosaic law in his sovereign reinterpretation. He treats it as a whole, selecting illustrations from all parts of it to use as a means of affirming his own kingdom ethics. There is no evidence that Jesus isolated the Ten Command-ments from the rest of the Mosaic law and put them in a separate category. He came to "fulfill" the law as a whole, in all its parts.

In this regard, VanGemeren's claim that "Jesus did not abrogate the law!" must be carefully nuanced. For among the instances VanGemeren has just cited to illustrate Jesus' upholding of the spiritual intent of the Lawgiver is Jesus' debate with the Jews about ceremonial rituals in Mark 7:1–23. Yet it is this very text that the evangelist himself notes, "In saying this, Jesus declared all foods clean" (v. 19b). In other words, Mark is telling us that Jesus teaches that his followers need no longer obey large sections of the Mosaic law. I am not necessarily claiming that this is "abrogating" the law. But I am insisting that it means that we, as new covenant believers, no longer obey the law in the form it was originally given; we are not directly under its authority. When we say then (as VanGemeren does) that Jesus "called for a more radical observance" (citing Matt. 5:19), we must interpret this carefully. It certainly cannot mean observance of the Mosaic law as such, for we no longer are subject to, for example, the food laws. Perhaps VanGemeren would argue that it means more radical obedience to the "moral law" (this seems to be a fair deduction from the Gerstner quotation that follows). But one must then again ask: Where has this category come from? What clues are we given that we can put a prohibition against murder into the category of a "moral" issue while putting fasting or the Sabbath into a different category? VanGemeren's own approach here suggests, rather, that Jesus treated them all together as part of the single entity—the Mosaic law.

Perhaps VanGemeren would reply at this point that Jesus' own treatment of the different commandments reveals just such a distinction. He absolves his followers from obeying the ceremonial law, while he reiterates and sharpens the moral laws. But this is just my point. It is only as we look at the way that Jesus and the writers of the New Testament treat the commandments of the Mosaic law that we can know which ones continue to apply directly to us and which ones no longer do. The Mosaic commandments, then, are not *directly* applicable to us, but only as they are passed on to us by Christ. He is the "filter" through which the whole law must go, and it is he who determines which of those laws must still be followed and which ones need not be.

The Sabbath commandment affords an excellent illustration of the point I am trying to make.[1] VanGemeren asserts that "each one of the Ten Commandments expresses the moral law of God." I am not sure that VanGemeren ever deals with the matter directly, but I would suspect that he holds to a traditional Reformed interpretation of the Sabbath: that it is no longer to be observed on "the seventh day" but on the first day, to commemorate the resurrection. Furthermore, he may, as many Reformed authors do, argue for an easing or reinterpretation of the prohibition of work. Yet worshiping on the first day of the week is not what the fourth commandment requires: It explicitly requires cessation of work on the *seventh* day. Here, then, VanGemeren would apparently argue that we need no longer obey an eternal moral law of God in the way that it was first given to us. Furthermore, he would presumably claim that we can do so because it is sanctioned in the New Testament. But this leads to one of two conclusions: either (1) the Ten Commandments are not the "eternal moral law of God," or (2) the "eternal moral law of God" is subject to revision. Since VanGemeren explicitly affirms the former, I would assume that he adopts the latter. Perhaps he would argue that the Ten Commandments "express" the eternal moral law of God but do so in the form of general principles that can be applied in different ways. Thus, the Sabbath commandment expresses the need to dedicate part of every week to the worship and recognition of God. This is the principle, and the day on which it is done is incidental.

Now this may be a fair interpretation of the matter. But I would submit that our only basis for knowing it to be the case is the New Testament interpretation of the commandment. In other words, on this view, the "eternal moral law of God" is not *directly* applicable to us. May we not, then, make a similar claim for the other Ten Commandments? I am arguing, then, that the Sabbath commandment is a crucial "test case," suggesting that the Ten Commandments, in their Mosaic form, were not intended by God to be eternally binding on all people everywhere. All ten were

---

[1]This is made clear in great detail in the volume edited by D.A. Carson, *From Sabbath to Lord's Day* (Grand Rapids: Zondervan, 1982).

expressions of God's will for his people Israel; and we know, from the New Testament, that nine of them state commands that continue to be binding on New Testament believers. They are binding on us not because they are in the Ten Commandments but because the New Testament makes clear that they are expressions of God's eternal moral law. Following the pattern Paul suggests in 1 Corinthians 9:20–22, I would advocate the following scheme for relating the eternal moral law of God to the Mosaic law and to New Testament "law":

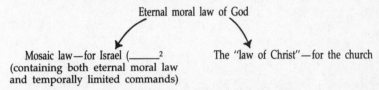

Eternal moral law of God

Mosaic law—for Israel (_____²   The "law of Christ"—for the church
(containing both eternal moral law
and temporally limited commands)

The "law" under which Christians live is continuous with the Mosaic law in that God's eternal moral norms, which never change, are clearly expressed in both. But there is discontinuity in the fact that Christians live under the "law of Christ" and *not* under the Mosaic law. Our source for determining God's eternal moral law is Christ and the apostles, not the Mosaic law or even the Ten Commandments. It is, then, the commandments of Christ and the apostles to which Paul is referring in 1 Corinthians 7:19 when he claims that "keeping God's commands is what counts." Contrary to VanGemeren, then, this text is thoroughly consistent with the opinion that the Mosaic law does not apply directly to the Christian.³

Speaking of continuity and discontinuity, however, let me conclude with a final note of continuity between VanGemeren and myself. Our perspectives on the matter of the Christian's relationship to the Mosaic law differ, and this difference affects matters such as theological synthesis and the interpretation of several key texts. Nevertheless, our "bottom lines" are very similar. With him, I call on Christians to a deeper and more radical obedience of the eternal moral law of God, an obedience that our increasingly anti-Christian culture makes at the same time both more difficult

---

²As I argue elsewhere, some continuity between the Mosaic law and the law of Christ is necessary to maintain. This is what this line represents.

³VanGemeren is here citing the view of Stephen Westerholm, *Israel's Law and the Church's Faith* (Grand Rapids: Eerdmans, 1988). My own view is similar to Westerholm's, and I consider this volume one of the best surveys of the issue.

and more important. And even our differences about whether we discover that eternal moral law of God directly in the Ten Commandments or not have very little, if any, effect on the "bottom line": what Christians are actually to do to reverence God in this life.

Chapter Two

THE THEONOMIC
REFORMED VIEW

Greg L. Bahnsen

THE THEONOMIC REFORMED APPROACH TO LAW AND GOSPEL

Greg L. Bahnsen

LAWFUL AND UNLAWFUL APPROACHES TO THE LAW

According to Scripture, what role does the Mosaic law have in the life of the modern believer? We cannot arrive at a God-glorifying and theologically faithful answer to that question if we do not take into account the fullness and complexity of the New Testament witness and the diversity in its usage of the word "law." The New Testament does not yield an answer to our question easily and without problems. Nevertheless, we can discover the answer clearly and confidently with cautious study.

Some passages in the New Testament seem to advocate a positive attitude toward the Old Testament law. Paul affirms that "the law is holy, and the commandment holy, righteous and good" (Rom. 7:12); he cites the Old Testament law as authoritative warrant for his ethical judgments (e.g., 1 Cor. 9:9; Eph. 6:1–2). Paul candidly wrote, "In my inner being I delight in God's law" (Rom. 7:22). James teaches that his readers do well to fulfill "the royal law," and warns them against breaking any one point of it (James 2:8–10); according to him our place is to be doers, not judges, of the law (4:11–12). Peter calls believers to sanctified living based upon the demand of the law (1:15–16), and John identifies keeping the law with both knowing and loving God (1 John 2:3–4; 5:3; 2 John 6). In some important sense for Christian living, the Old Testament law is indisputably upheld by the writers of the New Testament.

Notwithstanding such endorsements of the law, the New

Testament equally speaks of the law in a negative fashion and appears to dismiss it. Paul declares, "I died to the law so that I might live for God" (Gal. 2:19). He describes himself as not being "under the law" (1 Cor. 9:20). His readers "are not under law, but under grace"—indeed, "we have been released from the law" (Rom. 6:14; 7:6). Elsewhere Paul says that Christ abolished "the law with its commandments and regulations" (Eph. 2:15). In some way that is vital to the gospel message, therefore, the Old Testament law is indisputably opposed by the writers of the New Testament.

This ambivalence and apparent conflict in the New Testament attitude toward the Old Testament law begins to find its clarification and resolution when Paul declares in 1 Timothy 1:8, "But we know that the Law is good, if one uses it lawfully" (NASB). It is Paul's infallible testimony that there should be no doubt about the inherent goodness of the moral instruction contained in the commandments of the Old Testament law. The ethical demands of the law reflect nothing less than the very holiness, righteousness, and goodness *of God himself* (1 Pet. 1:15–16; cf. Rom. 6:18, 22 with 7:12–14). Paul affirmed "that the law is spiritual" (Rom. 7:14), so that those who "live . . . according to the Spirit" will indeed fulfill the ordinance of the law, whereas the mind of the sinful nature "is hostile to God. It does not submit to God's law" (Rom. 8:4, 7). Since the law is a transcript of God's character, one's response to the law is one's response to God himself. So of course the law's moral prescriptions must be seen as good.

However, the goodness of the law is sullied if it is used in a way that God never intended. Paul qualifies his categorical assertion of the law's goodness by adding: "if one uses it *lawfully*" (NASB). The law must be used according to its own character, direction, and intention. This obviously implies that people can misuse the law—can interpret it and put it to a use that is contrary to God's purpose. In that case the law would be perverted into something against its nature and intent, making it ungodly and evil. This kind of abuse of God's good law is openly and repeatedly condemned in the pages of the New Testament. What is this unlawful approach to the law? We find it in the attitude of the Pharisees and Judaizers who promoted self-merit before God through performing works of the law.

It was incredible pride and self-deception that caused the Jews to "rely on the law" and to be confident that they possessed "in the law the embodiment of knowledge" that made them self-righteous teachers of others (Rom. 2:17–21), when in fact these who "brag about the law" were notoriously guilty of transgressing the law and dishonoring God (vv. 23–24). The Pharisees were infatuated with justifying themselves before men (Luke 16:15), trusting in themselves that they were indeed righteous (Luke 18:9); they felt they no more needed a Savior than a healthy person needs a physician (Matt. 9:12–13). Nevertheless, God thoroughly knew their hearts; regardless of outward appearances of righteousness, they were inwardly polluted, full of iniquity, and spiritually dead (Matt. 23:27–28). Seeking to establish their own righteousness, such Jews could not submit to the genuine righteousness of God (Rom. 10:3).

In the earliest days of the Christian church, a party arose from among the Pharisees who refused to abandon this perverse and unlawful use of the law of God and to recognize the way in which the redemptive accomplishment of Christ had put out of gear those portions of the law that foreshadowed his person and work. As a result, the people of this persuasion wanted to compel the Gentiles to live "like the Jews" (Gal. 2:14 NASB; lit., "to Judaize"). The Judaizers insisted that the Gentiles could not be saved without becoming circumcised and keeping the covenantal distinctiveness of the Mosaic law (Acts 15:1, 5). Grace needed to be supplemented by works of the law, that is, by self-righteous submission to Jewish ceremonies.

Paul was no stranger to the attitude of the Pharisees and Judaizers toward the law of Moses. It had been his own mind-set prior to conversion. He was brought up as a Pharisee concerning the law (Phil. 3:5), and at the feet of Gamaliel he was "thoroughly trained in the law of our fathers" (Acts 22:3). His testimony was: "I was advancing in Judaism beyond many Jews of my own age and was extremely zealous for the traditions of my fathers" (Gal. 1:14). He knew what it was to make his boast in the law (cf. Rom. 2:17–20, 23). From the perspective of a man who is spiritually dead, Paul once claimed that as far as "legalistic righteousness" was concerned, he was "faultless" (Phil. 3:6). That is, he was once, apart from a true perception of the law, so self-deceived as to think that he was spiritually alive and righteous. Only under the influence of God's convicting Holy Spirit did the commandment finally come home to his consciousness and kill his self-righteous complacency. "Once I was alive apart from the law; but when the commandment came, sin sprang to life and I died" (Rom. 7:9).

WHAT DOES THE LAW ITSELF SAY?

Here is something remarkable, something that theologians must not miss if they want to understand correctly the divine intention regarding the Old Testament law. Paul knew from his personal experience that he needed to die to legalism, to the use of the law as a means of self-merit or justification before God. And just how *and where* did Paul learn that crucial lesson? Listen to Galatians 2:19: *"Through the law* I died to the law so that I might live unto God."* It was *the law itself* that taught Paul not to seek righteousness and God's acceptance through law-works! The Old Testament law was never legalistic in character or intention, though the Jews perverted it to that self-serving end. They simply did not see that "Christ is the end of the law so that there may be righteousness for everyone who believes" (Rom. 10:4). Paul lamented that "to this day . . . when the old covenant is read . . . when Moses is read, a veil covers their heart" (2 Cor. 3:14–15).

Paul clearly categorized and included the Mosaic covenant— the *law* covenant, which had erected a wall between Jews and Gentiles and alienated the uncircumcised from "citizenship in Israel"—as part and parcel of what he called "the covenants of the *promise*" (Eph. 2:12). There were many Old Testament covenants (plural), but they were all administrations of the one underlying promise (singular) of God. Theologians may properly speak of "law" and "grace" as convenient tags for the two different covenantal administrations (namely, old and new covenants), but the Bible asserts emphatically that *both* are administrations of God's *grace* (or promise) as the only way of acceptance before him. The law-covenant was a manifestation of God's promise, not of legalism.

The old covenant administration of law (or the Mosaic administration itself) did not offer a way of salvation or teach a message of justification that differs from the one found in the gospel of the new covenant. Recognizing that in God's sight no one could be justified (Ps. 143:2), the old covenant promised justification grounded in "the LORD Our Righteousness" (Jer. 23:6). The old covenant witness was that righteousness had to be *imputed*, even to the great father of the Jews, Abraham (Gen. 15:6; cf. Rom. 4:3; Gal. 3:6). Accordingly, the literature of the Old Testament provides abundant evidence that God's saints were people *of faith* (cf. Heb. 11). Paul came to understand very clearly that the old covenant itself taught that the just shall live by faith (Hab. 2:4; cf. Rom. 1:17; Gal. 3:11). Isaiah the prophet proclaimed:

"In the LORD all the descendants of Israel will be found righteous" (Isa. 45:25); and later, "This is the heritage of the servants of the LORD, and this is their vindication from me, declares the LORD" (54:17).

If we allow the Bible to interpret itself and not infuse it with a preconceived theological antithesis between old and new covenant (Law[1] and Gospel), we are compelled to conclude that the old covenant—indeed, the Mosaic law—was a covenant of *grace* that offered salvation on the basis of grace through faith, just as does the Good News found in the New Testament. The difference was that the Mosaic or law-covenant looked ahead to the coming of the Savior, thus administering God's covenants by means of promises, prophesies, ritual ordinances, types, and foreshadowings that anticipated the Savior and his redeeming work. The Gospel or the new covenant proclaims the accomplishment of that which the law anticipated, administering God's covenant through preaching and the sacraments. The substance of God's saving relationship and covenant is the same under the Law and the Gospel.[2]

Scripture does not present the Mosaic or law-covenant as fundamentally opposed to the grace of the new covenant—an erroneous view (essentially dispensational in orientation) that is at the heart of so much misguided thinking about the law today. For example, consider Hebrews 3–4. According to the New Testament, why was God displeased with the Israelites so that they could not enter the promised land? The answer is that they were disobedient (Heb. 3:18), but this is the same as to answer that they were lacking faith (3:19)! They had the gospel preached to them, even as we do (4:2), but they failed to enter into God's promised provision because they failed to have faith (4:2)—that is, they were guilty of disobedience (4:6)! You cannot pit faith and obedience against each other in the old covenant; they are

---

[1]It is important for the reader to notice here that the expression "the Law," when set over against "the Gospel," is being used to denote an administration of God's covenant with humankind: particularly, the Mosaic covenant, or more broadly the entire old covenant. "The Law" does not in this context mean the moral demands or ethical instructions of God as such (e.g., "You shall not steal").

[2]The substance of God's grace is the same in both Old and New Testaments, even as the substance of God's moral will is the same in both (cf. Westminster Confession of Faith 7.5–6; 19.1–2, 5–6). These theological truths do not, however, minimize the clear differences between the testaments in terms of their outward character or order. "The law was given through Moses; grace and truth came through Jesus Christ" (John 1:17).

different sides of the same coin, just as in the new covenant (James 2:14–26).

Therefore Paul could ask quite incredulously, "Is the law, therefore, opposed to the promises of God?" Should the grace of the Abrahamic covenant be seen as contradicted by the law revealed by Moses? The apostle's answer was an emphatic "Absolutely not!" (Gal. 3:21). The law was never intended to be a way of works-righteousness, as Paul goes on to say. By their self-righteous effort to gain merit and favor before God through obedience to the law, the Israelites did not attain the law at all! (Rom. 9:31) And why not? "Because they pursued it [righteousness] not by faith but as if it were by works" (v. 32).

If we listen to the law itself, we would be warned away from any idea that God's law was intended to be a way of self-merit or self-justification before God. The gracious salvation of the new covenant is the flowering, unfolding, or realization of the promises and grace anticipated and foretold in the old. "For no matter how many promises God has made, they are 'Yes' in Christ. And so through him the 'Amen' is spoken by us to the glory of God" (2 Cor. 1:20). In the greatest Bible lesson of all time, Christ expounded, "beginning with Moses and all the Prophets . . . what was said in all the Scriptures concerning himself" (Luke 24:27). Indeed, "Moses was faithful as a servant in all God's house, testifying to what would be said in the future" (Heb. 3:5). The Mosaic law does not stand in antithesis to the Gospel of Christ that was afterward proclaimed—any more than it contradicts the Abrahamic promise that was given 430 years previously (Gal. 3:15–17). Christ was the focus and aim of the Mosaic law or old covenant (Rom. 10:4), just as he was of the Abrahamic covenant and promises of old.

Paul insists that the Mosaic administration, the law, did not disannul the Abrahamic promise, but was rather added "until the Seed to whom the promise referred had come" (Gal. 3:17, 19)—that is, it was added until the coming of Christ (v. 16). Before the arrival of Christ, the object of our faith, God's people "were held prisoners by the law" (v. 23). That is to say, the law became a "tutor . . . to Christ, that we may be justified by faith" (v. 24 NASB). Again we see that Pauline theology sees the Mosaic covenant—the law—as pointing to Christ and itself teaching the same message of justification as does the Gospel or new covenant.

The aspect of the law that most distinguished the Mosaic administration and performed this function of pointing ahead to Christ and the doctrine of justification by faith was what is often called today the "ceremonial" law, the redemptive rituals and ordinances of the old covenant (e.g., circumcision, priesthood, temple, sacrifices: cf. Col. 2:11–13; Heb. 7–10). The tutor or schoolmaster to which Paul alludes in Galatians 3:24–25 was the Mosaic administration, "the law," particularly in its ceremonial foreshadowing of Christ. The following is clear from Paul's letters: Paul was engaged in theological controversy with the Judaizers, who insisted on circumcision (Gal. 2:3–4; 5:2–4); he chose as his particular example the ceremonial calendar of the Jewish law (Gal. 4:10); he also spoke of those "basic principles" (Gal. 4:3, 9), which Colossians 2:16–17 further describe as "a shadow of the things that were to come," the reality or substance of which is Christ; finally, he described the law as governing and teaching the Jews that justification comes through faith in Christ (Gal. 3:24)— something not accomplished by moral stipulations like "you shall not steal" but by sacrificial ordinances that vividly illustrated the way of salvation. Paul insisted that now that Christ has come as the object of our faith, we are no longer under [this] tutorship of the Mosaic law (Gal. 3:25). The Mosaic administration, appropriate to God's people in the early stage of their education and containing only beggarly foreshadowings of redemption, has now given way to the mature liberty of God's sons who place their faith in his Son (Gal. 3:26; 4:1–7, 9).

In recapitulation, we have found that the old covenant law *itself* teaches us to die to legalism or self-merit, since the law, consistent with the Abrahamic promise, looked ahead to Christ and taught justification by faith. The Gospel may not be pitted against the Law with respect to the doctrine of salvation. Nevertheless the Gospel is a glorious superseding of and an advancement over the Mosaic administration with its ceremonial ordinances. While in the establishment of the new covenant there is no change from the gracious character of the salvation promised and foreshadowed in the days of Abraham or Moses, there is still a vanishing away of the obsolete administration and order of the old covenant (Heb. 8:13). It remains for us to see, now, that the *moral* instructions found in the law—God's commandments revealed in the old covenant—have not been laid aside along with the redemptive instructions for circumcision, priesthood, sacrifice, and temple.

DISCONTINUITIES WITH THE OLD TESTAMENT LAW

Is it theologically legitimate to make contemporary use of the Old Testament law in its moral instruction? This is not an easy question. On the one hand, to deny that the divinely revealed dictates of the Mosaic law are unchanging moral absolutes is implicitly to endorse the position of cultural relativism in ethics— "they were morally valid for that time and place, but invalid for other people and other times"; this position is diametrically contrary to the united testimony of Scripture (Ps. 89:34; 111:7; 119:160; Eccl. 12:13; Mal. 3:6; Rom. 2:11). On the other hand, to affirm that the laws of the Old Testament are binding in our day and age might suggest to some people that one should recognize no differences between the old and new covenant, or between an ancient agrarian society and the modern computer age. After all, in the Old Testament we read instructions for holy war, for kosher diet, for temple and priesthood, for cities of refuge at particular places in Palestine, for goring oxen, and for burning grain fields.

Obviously, there are some kinds of discontinuity between these provisions and our own day. However, the evangelical literature that touches on this subject often teems with hasty generalizations, exegetically unwarranted premises, and fallacious conclusions. We need to draw a distinction from the very outset if we want to avoid confusing ourselves about the contemporary use of the Old Testament law.

Some discontinuities with the Mosaic law (or laws) are *redemptive-historical* in character and pertain to the coming of the new covenant and the finished work of Christ, while others are *cultural* in character and pertain to simple changes of time, place, or lifestyle. The latter are conceptually unrelated to the former. There are cultural differences not only between our society and the Old Testament, but also between modern America and the New Testament (e.g., its mention of whitewashed tombs, social kisses, and meats offered to idols); indeed, there are cultural differences even *within* the Old Testament (e.g., life in the wilderness, in the land, and in captivity) and *within* the New Testament (e.g., Jewish culture and Gentile culture). Such cultural differences pose important hermeneutical questions—sometimes vexing, since the "culture gap" between biblical times and our own is so wide.[3]

---

[3]Is that gap as wide as the Grand Canyon or merely a crack in the sidewalk? (alternatives suggested by Rodney Clapp, "Democracy as Heresy," *CT* 31 [Feb. 20,

However, these differences are not particularly relevant to the question of ethical validity. That is, it is one thing to realize that we must translate biblical commands about a lost ox (Ex. 23:4) or withholding pay from someone who mows fields (James 5:4) into terms relevant to our present culture (e.g., about misplaced credit cards or remuneration of factory workers). It is quite another thing to say that such commands carry no ethical authority today! God obviously communicated to his people in terms of their own day and cultural setting, but what he said to them he fully expects us to obey in our own cultural setting, lest the complete authority of his word be shortchanged in our lives.

Moreover, it should be obvious that in teaching us our moral duties, God as a masterful Teacher often instructs us not only in general precepts (e.g., "You shall not murder," Ex. 20:13; "love one another," 1 John 3:11), but also in terms of specific illustrations (e.g., rooftop railings, Deut. 22:8; sharing worldly goods with a needy brother, 1 John 3:17), expecting us to learn broader, underlying principles from them. Again, those biblical illustrations are taken from the culture of that day. After the New Testament story of the good Samaritan, Jesus said, "Go and do likewise" (Luke 10:37). It does not take a lot of hermeneutical common sense to know that our concrete duty is not thereby to go travel the literal Jericho road (rather than an American interstate highway) on a literal donkey (rather than in a Ford) with literal denarii in our pockets (rather than dollars), pouring wine and oil (rather than modern antiseptic salves) on the wounds of those who have been mugged. Indeed, one can be a modern "good Samaritan" in a circumstance that has nothing to do with travel and muggers. Unfortunately, however, this same hermeneutical common sense is sometimes not applied to the cultural illustrations communicated in Old Testament moral instruction.[4] For

---

1987]: 22.) It would be misleading to answer either way. First, the "gap" obviously varies from precept to precept in the Bible; some are more distant to our lifestyle than others. Clapp's question calls for dangerous oversimplification. Second, the metaphors suggested are obviously extreme; between those extremes there surely exist other, more reasonable answers, pointing to mediating degrees of difference. Finally, one would be seriously misled to think that this question of culture gap is any more uncomfortable for, or critical of, theonomists than it is for any other school of thought committed to using the ancient literature of the Bible in modern society. The alternative—which any believer should find repugnant—is simply to dismiss the Bible as anachronistic.

[4]Just here Christopher J. H. Wright has misconceived and thus badly misrepresented the "theonomic" approach as calling for a "literal imitation of

instance, the requirement of a rooftop railing (Deut. 22:8), relevant to entertaining on flat roofs in Palestine, teaches the underlying principle of safety precautions (e.g., fences around modern backyard swimming pools), not the obligation of placing a literal battlement on today's sloped roofs.

There are, then, *cultural* discontinuities between biblical moral instruction and our modern society. This fact does not imply that the ethical teaching of Scripture has been invalidated for us; it simply calls for hermeneutical sensitivity. In asking whether it is theologically legitimate to make contemporary use of biblical (especially Old Testament) precepts pertaining to civil law, then, our concern is more properly with *redemptive-historical* discontinuities, notably between the old and new covenants. Clearly, the Scriptures teach us that a new day arrived with the establishment of Christ's kingdom (Jer. 31:31–34; Luke 22:20; Heb. 8:7–13; 10:14–18) and the age of the Spirit (Luke 3:16–17; Acts 2:16–36), a day anticipated by all the old covenant Scriptures (Luke 24:26–27; Acts 3:24; 1 Pet. 1:10–11).

What differences with the old covenant era have been introduced? Only the King, the Lord of the covenant, who speaks by means of the Holy Spirit, is in a position to answer that question with authority, and thus we look, not to sinful speculation or cultural tradition, but to the inspired Word of Christ to guide our thoughts regarding it. There we are taught that the new covenant surpasses the old covenant in (1) power, (2) glory, (3) finality, and (4) realization. Such discontinuities must not be overlooked, and yet, in the nature of the case, they presuppose an underlying unity in God's covenantal dealings. The historical changes in outward administration and circumstance grow out of a common and unchanging divine intention.

(1) The old covenant law as written on external tablets of stone accused humankind of sin, but it could not grant the internal ability to comply with those demands. By contrast, the new covenant written by the Holy Spirit on the internal tables of the human heart communicates life and righteousness, giving the *power* to obey God's commandments (Jer. 31:33; Ezek. 11:19–20; Rom. 7:12–16; 8:4; 2 Cor. 3:3, 6–9; Heb. 10:14–18; 13:20–21).

That the new covenant surpasses the old covenant in power

Israel," one that simply lifts its ancient laws and transplants them into the vastly changed modern world ("The Use of the Bible in Social Ethics: Paradigms, Types and Eschatology," *Transf* 1 [January/March 1984]: 17).

we see in the Pentecostal outpouring and the dynamic ministry of the Holy Spirit (also active in the old covenant, to be sure). The new covenant promised by Jeremiah will write the law upon the very tables of the human heart (Jer. 31:33), or, as Ezekiel puts it, God will "put a new spirit in them. . . . Then they will follow my decrees and be careful to keep my laws" (Ezek. 11:19–20). Paul sees the difference between the old order and that which has been instituted by Christ in the same way. "For what the law was powerless to do, in that it was weakened by the sinful nature, God did by sending his own Son in the likeness of sinful man to be an offering for sin. And so he condemned sin in the sinful man, in order that the righteous requirements of the law might be fully met in us, who do not live according to the sinful nature, but according to the Spirit" (Rom. 8:3–4).

(2) The surpassing power of the new covenant is not unconnected with the surpassing *glory* of redemption. Although the old covenant had its glory, the sin-laden Jews requested Moses to veil his face when revealing its stipulations, for it was fundamentally a ministration of condemnation. But the new covenant redemptively brings life and confidence before God (Rom. 8:3; 2 Cor. 3:7–4:6; Heb. 4:15–16; 6:18–20; 7:19; 9:8; 10:19–20), thus exceeding in unfading glory (2 Cor. 3:9, 18; 4:4–6; Heb. 3:3).

(3) Furthermore, unlike God's word to old covenant believers, special revelation will not be augmented further for new covenant Christians; it has reached its *finalized* form until the return of Christ. This New Testament word brings greater moral clarity (removing Pharisaical distortions of the law, Matt. 5:21–48; 23:3–28, and demonstrating unmistakably the meaning of love, John 13:34–35; 15:12–13) and greater personal responsibility for obedience (Luke 12:48; Heb. 2:1–4; 12:25).

(4) Finally, the new covenant surpasses the old in the *realization* of redemption. To understand this, we must take account of the fact that the laws of the old covenant served two different purposes. Some laws defined the righteousness of God to be emulated by humans (thus being moral in function), while other laws defined the way of salvation for the unrighteous (thus being redemptive in function). For example, the law forbidding us to steal shows what righteousness demands, whereas the law stipulating animal sacrifice shows what must be done by a thief to gain redemption. This distinction between laws that define justice and expound redemption was proverbially expressed by the Jews: "To do what is right and just is more acceptable to the LORD than

sacrifice" (Prov. 21:3). It was evident in the prophetic declaration from God: "I desire mercy, not sacrifice, and acknowledgment of God rather than burnt offerings" (Hos. 6:6; cf. Matt. 9:13; 12:7). These biblical statements would make no sense whatsoever if the Israelites could not tell the difference between (what we call today) moral and ceremonial laws. Surely the ancient Israelites had the mental acumen to understand a difference between laws that bound Jews and Gentiles *alike* (e.g., the death penalty for murder, Lev. 24:21–22) and laws that bound Jews *but not* Gentiles (e.g., the prohibition of eating animals that died of themselves, Deut. 14:21). Whether the Jews used the labels of "moral" and "ceremonial" is quite beside the point.

As we have already observed, the New Testament teaches that some portions of the Old Testament law were "shadows" of the coming Messiah and his redemptive work (Heb. 9:9; 10:1; Col. 2:17). They were considered weak and miserable principles that served as a tutor to Christ and taught justification by faith (Gal. 3:23–4:10). Paul called them "the law with its commandments and regulations" that imposed a separation of Jews from the Gentile world (Eph. 2:14–15). These descriptions, however, do not accurately apply to moral laws of the Old Testament, such as those that forbid adultery or oppressing the poor. Such laws do not foreshadow the redemptive work of Christ, show us justification by faith, or symbolically set apart the Jews from the Gentiles. That laws pertaining to the priesthood, temple, and sacrificial system do accomplish those ends, however, and are to be considered "put out of gear" by the coming of Christ is demonstrated by the author of Hebrews (esp. chaps. 7–10). For instance, the coming of Christ has brought a change of law regarding the priesthood (Heb. 7:12), and the administrative order of the old covenant is vanishing away (8:13). By bringing to realization the salvation foreshadowed in the old covenant, the new covenant supersedes the details of the old covenant redemptive dispensation. We no longer come to God through animal sacrifices, but now through the shed blood of the Savior; both dispensations do acknowledge, however, that "without the shedding of blood there is no forgiveness" from the guilt of sin (Heb. 9:22).

In connection with the superseding of the old covenant shadows, the redemption secured by the new covenant also redefines the people of God. The kingdom that was once focused on the nation of Israel has been taken away from the Jews (Matt. 8:11–12; 21:41–43; 23:37–38) and given to an international body, the church of Jesus Christ. The New Testament describes the church as the rebuilding of Israel (Acts 15:15–20), "the commonwealth of Israel" (Eph. 2:12 NASB), "Abraham's seed" (Gal. 3:7, 29), and "the Israel of God" (6:16). What God was doing with the nation of Israel was but a type looking ahead to the international church of Christ. The details of the old order have passed away, giving place to the true kingdom of God established by the Messiah, in which both Jew and Gentile have become "fellow citizens" on an equal footing (Eph. 2:11–20; 3:3–6).

It is important for biblical interpretation to bear the above analysis in mind because certain stipulations of the old covenant were enacted for the purpose of distinguishing Israel as the people of God from the pagan Gentile world. Such stipulations were not essentially moral in function (forbidding what was intrinsically contrary to the righteousness of God), but rather symbolic. This accounts for the fact that Gentiles were allowed to do the very things forbidden to the Jews (e.g., Deut. 14:21). Accordingly, given the redefinition of the people of God in the new covenant, certain aspects of the old covenant order have been altered. (1) The new covenant does not require political loyalty to Israel (Phil. 3:20) or defending God's kingdom by the sword (John 18:36; 2 Cor. 10:4). (2) The land of Canaan foreshadowed the kingdom of God (Heb. 11:8–10; Eph. 1:14; 1 Pet. 1:4), which is fulfilled in Christ (Gal. 3:16; cf. Gen. 13:15); this fulfillment rendered inapplicable old covenant provisions tied to the land (such as family divisions, location of cities of refuge, and the levirate).[5] (3) The laws that symbolically taught Israel to be separate from the Gentile world, such as the dietary provisions (Lev. 20:22–26), need no longer be observed in their pedagogical form (Acts 10, esp. v. 15; see also Mark 7:19; Rom. 14:17), even though the Christian does honor their symbolized principle of separation from ungodliness (2 Cor. 6:14–18; Jude 23).

It is from the perspective of our preceding discussion of biblically-defined differences with the old covenant that we ought

---

[5]Ronald J. Sider is thus mistaken in imagining that the validity of the Old Testament law entails the necessity of a Jubilee restoration of land to original owners today; he forgets the special place and treatment given to the Palestinian promised land and the (objective) New Testament rationale for alteration regarding it ("Christian Love and Public Policy: A Response to Herbert Titus," *Transf* 2 [July/September 1985]: 13). He goes on, without exegetical justification, to treat the sabbatical and Jubilee provisions as though they were matters for civil coercion, in addition to being enforced by direct imposition of supernatural judgment (p. 14).

to understand the words of Paul in two passages popularly used by dispensational writers to prove that "the law of Moses has been set aside" in the present dispensation[6]—Romans 6:14 and 1 Corinthians 9:19–23. (1) Paul says in Romans 6:14, "For sin shall not be your master, because you are not under law, but under grace." House and Ice confuse matters by alluding to Galatians 3:23, thus interpreting Paul's words in Romans 6:14 to mean that "Christians are not 'under *the* law' as a rule of life."[7] This is a serious misreading. Unlike Galatians 3, Romans 6:14 does not refer to "the law" of Moses (cf. Gal. 3:19) or to the Mosaic law as a particular administration of God's covenant (cf. Gal. 3:17, 24). There is nothing like this in the immediate textual context of Romans 6:14 to supply a specifying sense to Paul's words; to be technically precise, one should observe that Paul there does not speak of being under "*the* law," but rather to being "under law" (generically, without any definite article). He teaches that those whose personal resources are merely those of law, without the provisions of divine grace, are for that reason under the inescapable dominion of sin; "there is an absolute antithesis between the potency and provisions of law and the potency and provisions of grace."[8] The "dominion of law" from which believers have been "released" is forthrightly explained by Paul to be the condition of being "in the sinful nature," being "controlled" by "sinful passions . . . so that we bore fruit for death" (7:1–6). From this spiritual bondage and impotence, the marvelous grace of God, through the death and resurrection of Jesus Christ, has set believers free; but it has not set them free to sin against God's moral principles.

When Paul speaks of not being "under law," even House and Ice cannot consistently interpret him to mean "law" in the sense of a "rule of life" (moral demands) since they themselves insist that believers *are* under a law in that sense, "the law of Christ."[9]

---

[6]For example, see H. Wayne House and Thomas Ice, *Dominion Theology: Blessing or Curse?* (Portland, Ore.: Multnomah, 1988), 113–15.

[7]Ibid., 118. Their discussion also suffers from self-contradiction. They claim that to be biblically precise, Old Testament Israel was *not* "under grace," but later they turn around and say that "the stipulations of Sinai were . . . to a people under grace" (p. 128).

[8]John Murray, *The Epistle to the Romans* (Grand Rapids: Eerdmans, 1959), 1:229. The reader is also recommended to study Murray's discussion of "Death to the Law (7:1–6)" as an excellent exegetical treatment of this issue (pp. 239–47).

[9]House and Ice, *Dominion Theology*, 85, 179.

Their interpretation would have Paul denying that the believer has any such "law" (in the sense of a rule of life), thus contradicting themselves. Moreover, "law" in Romans 6:14 *cannot* refer to the Mosaic administration or dispensation in particular, for, as we have seen, "under law" is equivalent to being under the dominion of sin. House and Ice would have to say then that all those saints who lived under the law of Moses were under sin's dominion—an idea that is absurd and unbiblical. One last point: It is clear to all schools of interpretation that Paul in Romans 6:14 teaches that believers should not be controlled by sin (cf. vv. 1–2, 6, 11–13, 15–18). How, then, did Paul himself understand what sin was? "I would not have known what sin was except through the law" (7:7). Consequently, far from dismissing the authority of the law, Romans 6:14 teaches that believers should not transgress the law and thereby sin. It is precisely the mind of the sinful flesh that "does not submit to God's law" (8:7). But Christians have the mind of the Spirit, who leads and enables them to meet fully "the requirements of the law" (8:4).

(2) Dispensationalists also turn at times to 1 Corinthians 9:19–23 to support the claim that believers are released from the moral authority of the Mosaic law, but there is really nothing like that claim found in this passage. When Paul spoke of himself as being "myself . . . not under the law," yet being willing to act "like one under the law" for the sake of those who are under the law, he is clearly referring to his relations with the Jews. "To the Jews I became like a Jew to win the Jews" (v. 20). But he was just as willing to act "like one not having the law" in dealing with "those not having the law" (v. 21), a reference to the Gentiles. "I have become all things to all men so that by all means I might save some" (v. 22). Clearly then, the law that Paul could adopt or ignore, depending upon whether he was among Jews or Gentiles, could not at all have been "the whole Mosaic law" as alleged by House and Ice. Even they recognize that much of the Mosaic law enshrined moral principles (learned through general revelation) that bind the Gentiles as much as the Jews.

Nor can we imagine that Paul is confessing to acting with duplicity, according to a double standard of morality ("law as a rule of life," say House and Ice). Notice, for instance, how "becoming like a Jew" is placed in parallel to "becoming like one under the law" in verse 20. Paul states this even though only *some* of the regulations of "the law" imposed a difference between Jewish and Gentile lifestyles (e.g., Deut. 14:21); in most cases the law's stipulations bound Jew and Gentile alike (cf. Rom. 1:32;

2:14–15; 3:19). Alteration in Paul's conduct was permissible because he was not morally bound by the ceremonial code in the first place, thus leaving him free to follow or ignore its provisions for symbolizing Jewish separation according to the governing principle that he should become all things to all people in order to gain some for Christ. It would be absurd to think that Paul intended to teach that he was allowed to break God's moral law (by stealing, raping, blaspheming, etc.) among the Gentiles, but was obligated to refrain from doing so among the Jews, in order that both groups might be drawn to Christianity! The only "law" that distinguished Jews from Gentiles, yet without involving inherent moral principle, was what we call today the ceremonial law. Only in this light can the passage make sense. When ministering among the Jews, Paul would conform to certain ceremonial provisions that had been set aside (e.g., purification rites and vows, cf. Acts 18:18; 21:20–26), even though it was not antecedently obligatory for him to follow those regulations; but while ministering among the Gentiles there was no need for him to do so.

Although the two passages we have just discussed do not support the notion that New Testament believers are released from moral obligation to the Old Testament law, we do not want to minimize or forget that the redemptive dispensation and form of the kingdom that was present in the old covenant has dramatically changed in the age of the new covenant. The new covenant surpasses the old in power, glory, finality, and realization. In short, the new covenant is a better covenant "founded on better promises" (Heb. 8:6). Even those aspects of the old covenant law that typified the kingdom of God and the way of redemption (e.g., priesthood, sacrifice, temple, promised land, symbols of separation, and purity) were speaking to the promises of God, preparing for and foreshadowing the salvation and kingdom to be brought by the Messiah.

Regarding the promises pertaining to redemption, then, we may rightly speak of the "better promises" of the new covenant. They differed from the old covenant provision by being the fulfillment of that to which it looked ahead, giving both covenants the same intention and objective. The differing covenantal administrations of God's promise are due precisely to the historical character of his redemptive plan.

THE CONTINUING VALIDITY
OF GOD'S MORAL DEMANDS

Unlike what we have just seen regarding God's promises, one nowhere reads in Scripture about God's law that his moral stipulations share the same kind of historical variation. For example, the Bible never speaks of the new covenant instituting "better commandments" than those of the old covenant. Far from it. Instead, Paul declared that "the [Old Testament] law is holy, and the commandment is holy, righteous and good" (Rom. 7:12). He took the validity of the law's moral demands as a theological truth that should be obvious and presupposed by all, stating unequivocally: "We know that the law is good" (1 Tim. 1:8).

Contrary to those today who are prone to criticize the Old Testament moral precepts, there must be no question whatsoever about the moral propriety and validity of what they revealed. The starting point for Christian ethics, the standard by which we judge all other opinions, should be that the law's moral provisions are correct. "I consider all your precepts right" (Ps. 119:128). Accordingly, James reminds us that we have no prerogative to become "judges of the law," but are rather called to be doers of the law (James 4:11). And when Paul posed the hypothetical question of whether the law is sin, his immediate outburst was, "Certainly not!" (Rom. 7:7).

God's holy and good law is never wrong in what it demands. It is "perfect" (Deut. 32:4; Ps. 19:7; James 1:25), just like the Lawgiver himself (Matt. 5:48). It is a transcript of his moral character. Thus the suggestion that theonomists concentrate on abstract impersonal laws instead of on knowing the Lawgiver is not only a serious misunderstanding of our position, but it also rests upon a devastating theological error. God's law is not abstract (if it were, fewer people would be offended by it), nor is it impersonal. It so perfectly reflects God's own holiness (Rom. 7:12; 1 Pet. 1:14–16) that the apostle John categorically dismissed anyone as a "liar" who claimed to know God and yet did not keep his commandments (1 John 2:3–4). God's law is a highly personal matter—so much so that Jesus said, "If you love me, you will obey what I command" (John 14:15; cf. vv. 21, 23; 15:10, 14). True believers have the law written upon their heart and delight inwardly in it (Ps. 1:1–2; Jer. 31:33; Rom. 7:22), just because they so intimately love God, their Redeemer.

Paul teaches elsewhere that all human beings—even pagans who do not love God and do not have the advantage of the written oracles of God (cf. Rom. 3:1–2)—know the just requirements of God's law. They know what the Creator requires of them. They know it from the created order (1:18–21) and from inward conscience, the "requirements of the law" being written upon their hearts (2:14–15). Paul characterizes them as knowing "God's righteous decree" (1:32) and therefore being "without excuse" for refusing to live in a God-glorifying fashion (1:20–23).

This discussion indicates that the stipulations of God's moral law, whether known through Mosaic (written) ordinances or by general (unwritten) revelation, carry a universal and "natural" obligation that is appropriate to the Creator-creature relationship, apart from any question of redemption. Their validity is by no means restricted to the Jews in a particular time period. What the law speaks, it speaks in order that "the whole world [may be] held accountable to God" (3:19). God is no respecter of persons here. "*All* have sinned" (3:23), which means they have violated the law of God, that common standard of moral integrity for everyone (3:20).

A good student of the Old Testament would have known as much. The moral laws of God were never restricted in their validity to the Jewish nation. At the beginning of the book of Deuteronomy, when Moses exhorted the Israelites to observe God's commandments, he clearly taught that the laws divinely revealed to Israel were meant by the Lawgiver as a model to be emulated by all the surrounding Gentile nations:

> See, I have taught you decrees and laws as the LORD my God commanded me, so that you may follow them in the land you are entering to take possession of it. Observe them carefully, for this will show your wisdom and understanding to the nations, who will hear about all these decrees and say, "Surely this great nation is a wise and understanding people." . . . what other nation is so great as to have such righteous decrees and laws as this body of laws I am setting before you today? (Deut. 4:5–8)

"All the nations," not just the Israelites, should follow the manifestly righteous requirements of God's law. In this respect, the justice of God's law made Israel to be "a light to the nations" (Isa. 51:4).

Unlike many modern Christian writers on ethics, God did not have a double standard of morality, one for Israel and one for the Gentiles (cf. Lev. 24:22). Accordingly, God made it clear that the reason why the heathen tribes were ejected from the promised land was precisely because they had violated the provisions of his holy law (Lev. 18:24–27). This fact presupposes that the Gentiles were antecedently obligated to obey those provisions. Accordingly, the psalmist condemned "all the wicked of the earth" for departing from God's statutes (Ps. 119:118–19). Similarly, the book of Proverbs, intended as international wisdom literature, directs all nations to obey the laws of God: "Righteousness exalts a nation, but sin is a disgrace to any people" (Prov. 14:34). Isaiah also looked forward to the day when the Gentile nations would stream into Zion, precisely in order that God's law would go forth from Jerusalem into all the world (Isa. 2:2–3).

Clearly the Gentiles were obligated to the same moral requirements as the Jews, even though the Jews alone enjoyed the privileges of a special covenantal relationship with the Lord. On the one side, the Old Testament indicated that Israel had a special, redemptive relationship with God, for he himself said, "You only have I chosen of all the families of the earth" (Amos 3:2). On the other side, the nations of the world were morally bound to God's commandments, just as were the Jews. Thus Isaiah 24:5 reads, "The earth is defiled by its people; they have disobeyed the laws, violated the statutes, and broken the everlasting covenant." E. J. Young comments on this verse:

> Just as Palestine itself, the Holy Land, had become profane through the sin of its inhabitants (Num. 35:33; Deut. 21:19; Jer. 3:9; and Ps. 106:38), so also the entire earth became profane when the ordinances given to it were violated. . . . Transgression is against the law of God, and this is expressed by the terms *law, statute, everlasting covenant.* The laws which God has revealed to His people bind all mankind; and hence, the work of the Law of God written on the human heart, for example, may be described under such terms.

> The Law was not specifically revealed to the Gentiles as it was to the Jews at Sinai. Nevertheless, according to Paul, the Gentiles do by natural instinct those things which are prescribed by the Law. . . . and this fact shows that the work of the Law is written on their own hearts. In transgressing those things prescribed in the Law, however, it may be said that the Gentiles were actually transgressing the Law itself. Here, the plural is used to show that the Gentiles had transgressed divine commands and ordinances, and also that their sins were many and varied. We may say that the Gentiles transgressed specific items of the Law, a thought which the plural form of the noun would also support. It is a transgression of the divine will generally, or as Calvin puts it, "all the instruction contained in the Law."

The mention of "statute" is perhaps intended for the sake of specificity, for inasmuch as both commandment and promise are included in the Law, this word stresses the commandment. . . .

Lastly, we are told that men frustrated or made void the everlasting covenant. . . . It must be noticed, however, that those who have frustrated the eternal covenant are not merely the Jews but the world generally. The frustrating of the covenant is something universal. For this reason we may adopt the position that the eternal covenant here spoken of designates the fact that God has given His Law and ordinances to Adam, and in Adam to all mankind. . . . Isaiah uses the language which is characteristic of the Mosaic legislation, and thus describes the universal transgressions of mankind.[10]

The Bible repeatedly illustrates that the pagan nations were judged by the same moral standard as the Mosaic law. Amos, Nahum, and Habakkuk all declared the Lord's judgment on Gentile nations for violating moral standards found in the law of Moses—for example, such mundane and specific matters as slave trafficking (Amos 1:6; cf. Ex. 21:16; Deut. 24:7), witchcraft (Nah. 3:4; cf. Ex. 22:18; Lev. 19:21), and loan pledges (Hab. 2:6; cf. Ex. 22:25–27; Deut. 24:6, 10–13). John the Baptist declared the moral standard of the Mosaic law to Herod with these words: "It is not lawful for you to have your brother's wife" (Mark 6:18). The moral standards of the Mosaic law were not unique to Israel, even though the Mosaic covenantal administration was.

Two premises about the law of God are thus abundantly clear if we want to be faithful to the infallible testimony of Scripture: (1) The law of God is *good* in what it demands, being what is natural to the Creator-creature relationship. (2) The demands of God's law are *universal* in their character and application, not confined in validity to Old Testament Israel.

Consequently, it is unreasonable to expect that the coming of the Messiah and the institution of the new covenant would alter the moral demands of God as revealed in his law. Why, we must ask, would God feel the need to change his perfect, holy requirements for our conduct and attitudes? Christ came, rather, to atone for our transgressions against those moral requirements (Rom. 4:25; 5:8–9; 8:1–3). And the new covenant was established precisely to confirm our redeemed hearts in obedience to God's

---

[10]E. J. Young, *The Book of Isaiah* , NICOT (Grand Rapids: Eerdmans, 1969), 2:156–58.

law (Rom. 8:4–10; 2 Cor. 3:6–11). May we sin because we are under the grace of God? Paul declared unequivocally, "By no means!" Being made free from sin we must rather now become the "slaves of righteousness" (Rom. 6:15–18). The grace of God has appeared, and Jesus Christ has given himself to "redeem us from all lawlessness and to purify for himself a people . . . eager to do what is good" (Tit. 2:14; cf. Eph. 2:8–10).

While the New Testament condemns any legalistic (i.e., Judaizing) use of God's law to establish one's personal justification or sanctification before him, and while the New Testament rejoices in the fact that the work of Christ has surpassed the legal foreshadowings and rituals of the old covenant, we never find the New Testament rejecting or criticizing the *moral demands* of the Old Testament law. They are at every point upheld and commended.[11] Thus Paul firmly taught that "all Scripture" (i.e., the inspired Old Testament) was "useful for . . . training in righteousness," in order that we might be equipped perfectly for every good work (2 Tim. 3:16–17). James is equally clear that if someone is guilty of breaking even one commandment of the law, that person has broken all of them (2:10); by this he indicates our obligation to every one of them. Jesus rebuked Satan (and many modern ethicists) by declaring that all people should live "on every word that comes from the mouth of God" (Matt. 4:4). This is the uniform New Testament perspective and presumption regarding the laws of the Old Testament. God certainly has the prerogative to alter his commandments. His word teaches, however, that we should countenance such change in particular cases *only when* God himself teaches such. We may not arbitrarily assume that his commandments have been repealed, but only where, when, and how he says so.

The decisive word on this point is that of our Lord himself as found in Matthew 5:17–19. Since the moral demands of God's law continue to be deemed good and holy and right in the New Testament, and since those demands were from the beginning obligatory upon Jews and Gentiles alike, it would be senseless to think that Christ came in order to cancel humankind's responsibil-

---

[11]The antitheses of Matthew 5:21–48 are not an unfair *ex post facto* condemnation of the Pharisees by a higher standard than that which they already knew. They prove to be a series of contrasts between Jesus' interpretation of the law's full demand and the restrictive, external, distorted interpretations of the law by the Jewish elders (cf. 5:20; 7:28–29; e.g., 5:43, a verse that does not even appear in the Old Testament).

ity to keep them. It is theologically incredible that the mission of Christ was to make it morally acceptable now for humans to blaspheme, murder, rape, steal, gossip, or envy! Christ did not come to change our evaluation of God's laws from that of holy to unholy, obligatory to optional, or perfect to flawed. Listen to his own testimony:

> Do not think that I have come to abolish the Law or the Prophets; I have not come to abolish them but to fulfill them. I tell you the truth, until heaven and earth disappear, not the smallest letter, not the least stroke of a pen, will by any means disappear from the Law until everything is accomplished. Anyone who breaks one of the least of these commandments and teaches others to do the same will be called least in the kingdom of heaven. (Matt. 5:17–19)

Several points about the interpretation of this passage are clear. (1) Christ twice denied that his advent had the purpose of abrogating the Old Testament commandments. (2) Until the expiration of the physical universe, not even a letter or stroke of the law will pass away. (3) Therefore, God's disapprobation rests on anyone who teaches that even the least of the Old Testament laws may be broken.[12] In all of its minute detail ("the smallest letter" and "the least stroke of a pen"), the law of God should be reckoned to have an abiding validity, unless the Lawgiver reveals otherwise.

There is no exegetical stalemate or standoff here, as though non-theonomists can adduce equally strong, universal, and pointed statements from Jesus or the apostles that every single jot and tittle, indeed even the greatest commandment, have been revoked by the advent of the Messiah and the establishment of the new covenant. Whatever statements we find about the setting aside of the law or any particular commandments will have to be integrated into the broader and absolute dictum of the Messiah himself. Christ speaking in the Scriptures does not permit silence to revoke the law.

Moreover, we should not be misled into thinking that

---

[12]Attempts are sometimes made to evade the thrust of this text by editing out its reference to the moral demands of the Old Testament—contrary to what is obvious from its context (5:16, 20, 21–48; 6:1, 10, 33; 7:12, 20–21, 26) and to the references to "the Law" (v. 18) and "the commandments" (v. 19). Other attempts are made to extract an abolishing of the law's moral demands from the word "fulfill" (v. 17) or the phrase "until all things have happened" (v. 18). These, however, render the verses self-contradictory in what they assert.

Scripture pits the summary or comprehensive commandments of God's law—i.e., to love God and one's neighbor (Lev. 19:19; Deut. 6:5; cf. Matt. 22:36–40)—against the law's specific details. The whole law in its various stipulations hangs on the two summary commands, but the summary does not abrogate or discount that which it summarizes. It would make no sense to say that we must follow the summary command to love our neighbor as ourselves (Lev. 19:19), but that it is unimportant whether I refrain from violating the detailed stipulation not to place a stumbling block before a blind man (see v. 14)! To trip the blind is precisely to show a lack of love. Jesus bids us to live "on every word that comes from the mouth of God" (Matt. 4:4), even "the least of these commandments" (5:19). And when our Lord called upon us to recognize "the more important matters of the law" (Matt. 23:23), he immediately added that the lesser matters should not be neglected. Breaking even one point of the law makes us guilty of breaking the whole law (James 2:10). In fact, the minor specifics of the law help to define and clarify the more important or summary commandments of love and justice. To use Jesus' words again, "If you love me, you will obey what I command" (John 14:15).

A NECESSARY WORD OF CAUTION

Nothing that has been said above means that the work of Christian ethics is a pat and easy job. Even though the details of God's law are available to us as moral absolutes, they still need to be properly interpreted and applied to the modern world. It should constantly be borne in mind that no school of thought, least of all the theonomist outlook, has all the answers. Nobody should get the impression that clear, simple, or incontestable "solutions" to the moral problems of our day can be just lifted from the face of Scripture's laws. A tremendous amount of homework remains to be done, whether in textual exegesis, cultural analysis, or moral reasoning—with plenty of room for error and correction. The work of Christian ethics must not be carried on thoughtlessly or without sanctified mental effort. Moreover, in all of it we need each other's best efforts and charitable corrections. Only after our ethical senses have been corporately exercised to discern good and evil by the constant study and use of God's law, only after we have gained considerably more experience in "the teaching about righteousness" (Heb. 5:13–14), will we achieve greater clarity, confidence, and a common mind in applying God's law to the ethical difficulties that beset us today. Nevertheless, even with the mistakes that we may make in using God's law today, I prefer it as the basis for ethics to the sinful and foolish speculations of human beings. It would be absurd for anyone to resign himself or herself to poison just because medical doctors occasionally make mistakes with prescription drugs!

THE TRANSFORMATIONAL NATURE
OF CHRIST'S KINGDOM

We must now face the question how the continuing validity of the Old Testament law should be applied to the controversial area of politics today. Is some modification of the conclusions that we have reached required when the Christian faces the questions of contemporary socio-political ethics? Although the rather automatic and unthinking response of many Christians would be to say yes (indeed, to insist upon it with vehemence), I believe that sober theological reflection leads toward another conclusion, especially if we are concerned to eschew arbitrariness and inconsistency.

Any conception of the role of civil government that claims to be distinctively "Christian" must be explicitly justified by the teaching of God's revealed Word.[13] Anything else reflects what the unbelieving world in rebellion against God may imagine on its own. If we are to be Christ's disciples, even in the political realm, it is essential that we abide in his liberating word (John 8:31). In every walk of life a criterion of our love for Christ or lack thereof is whether we keep his words (John 14:23–24), instead of founding our beliefs upon the ruinous sands of other opinions (Matt. 7:24–27). And as those especially in the Reformed heritage confess, to the extent that our view of civil government (or any matter) does adhere faithfully to Scripture, that view stands above any and all

---

[13]God's Word is, of course, found not only in special revelation (Ps. 19: 7–14), but also in natural revelation (vv. 1–6). And to whatever degree unbelievers do civic good, and whenever a reasonably just government exists in non-Christian lands, it is to be credited to common grace and natural revelation. Scripture is nonetheless our final authority. In a fallen world where natural revelation is suppressed in unrighteousness (Rom. 1:18, 21), special revelation is needed to check, confirm, and correct whatever is claimed for the content of natural revelation. Moreover, there are no moral norms given in natural revelation that are missing from special revelation (2 Tim. 3:16–17); indeed, the content and benefit of special revelation exceeds that of natural revelation (cf. Rom. 3:1–2).

challenges that stem from human wisdom and tradition (Rom. 3:4; 9:20; Col. 2:8).

Thus Christians who advocate what has come to be called the "theonomic" (or "reconstructionist") viewpoint[14] reject the social forces of secularism that too often shape our culture's conception of a good society. The Christian's political standards and agenda must not be set by unregenerate pundits who wish to quarantine religious values (and thus the influence of Jesus Christ as recorded in the Scripture) from the decision-making process of those who set public policy. Theonomists equally repudiate the sacred/secular dichotomy of life that is the effect of certain extra-scriptural, systematic conceptions of biblical authority that have recently infected the Reformed community[15]—conceptions implying that present-day moral standards for our political order may not be taken from what the written word of God says directly about society and civil government. Those stances involve a theologically unwarranted and dangerous curtailing of the scope of the Bible's truth and authority (Deut. 4:2; Ps. 119:160; Isa. 40:8; 45:19; Matt. 5:18–19; John 17:17). We theonomists exhort people not to be conformed to this world, but to be transformed by the renewing and reconciling work of Jesus Christ so as to prove the good, acceptable, and perfect will of God in their lives (Rom. 12:1–2; 2 Cor. 5:20–21). We call on them to be delivered out of

---

[14]From the theonomist's standpoint there really is no need for a new or distinctive label, since the position is deemed essentially that of Calvin (cf. his sermons on Deuteronomy), the Reformed confessions (e.g., the Westminster Confession, chaps. 19; 20; 23, and the Larger Catechism's exposition of the Ten Commandments), and the New England Puritans (cf. *JCR* 5 [Winter 1978–79]). Even as hostile an opponent as Meredith Kline concedes that the theonomic view was that of the Westminster Confession of Faith (see his review-article in the *WTJ* 41 [Fall 1978]: 173–74).

[15]Two pertinent illustrations are found in (1) the Dooyeweerdian scheme of dichotomizing reality into modal spheres, each one having its own peculiar laws, and (2) Meredith Kline's idea of dichotomizing the canonical authority of various elements of Scripture, both between and within the two Testaments. In the former case, explicit biblical texts pertaining to civil government may not provide a Christian view of the state, for Scripture is said to apply directly only to the modal sphere of "faith" (cf. Bob Goudzwaard, *A Christian Political Option* [Toronto: Wedge, 1972], 27). In the latter case, the moral authority of certain elements of Scripture is arbitrarily dismissed on the basis of the author separating, without conceptual cogency or exegetical justification, faith-norms from life-norms, individual-norms from communal-norms, and "common-grace" principles from "eschato-logical-intrusion" principles—implying that the most explicit biblical directions about political ethics may not be utilized today (*The Structure of Biblical Authority* [Grand Rapids: Eerdmans, 1972]).

darkness into the kingdom of God's Son, who was raised from the dead in order to have preeminence in *all* things (Col. 1:13–18). We must "demolish arguments and every pretension that sets itself up against the knowledge of God, and we must take captive every thought to make it obedient to Christ" (2 Cor. 10:5), in whom "are hidden all the treasures of wisdom and knowledge" (Col. 2:3). Thus we exhort believers to be holy in all manner of living (1 Pet. 1:15) and to do whatever they do for the glory of God (1 Cor. 10:31). Doing so requires adherence to the written word of God since our faith does not stand in human wisdom but rather in the work and teaching of God's Holy Spirit (1 Cor. 2:5, 13; cf. Num. 15:39; Jer. 23:16; 1 Thess. 2:13). That teaching, infallibly recorded in *every* Scripture of the Old and New Testaments, is able to equip us for *every* good work (2 Tim. 3:16–17), including work in public, community life.

For these reasons theonomists are committed to the transformation or reconstruction of every area of life, including the institutions and affairs of the socio-political realm, in accordance with the holy principles of God's revealed Word (theonomy). It is toward this end that the human community must strive if it hopes to enjoy true justice and peace.

The apostle John opens the book of Revelation by introducing the resurrected Savior, Jesus Christ, not only as the head of the church with whom he is sovereignly present (Rev. 1:12–20), but also as "the ruler of the kings of the earth" (v. 5). One is reminded of the closing of Matthew's gospel, where, once again, not only does Christ promise to be with the church "to the very end of the age," but also claims for himself "all authority . . . on earth" (Matt. 28:18–20). These are bold claims. They forcefully counteract the popular tendency to restrict the exalted reign of our Lord to some transcendent spiritual domain or to the confines of the institutional church. Christ is entitled to, and settles for, nothing less than immanent authority over all things, including the political potentates of this earth, "because he is Lord of lords and King of kings" (Rev. 17:14).

Not only are the above claims bold, but they are also somewhat bewildering. At the very time that Christ claimed all authority upon earth, he simultaneously indicated that the nations still needed to be made his disciples. At the very time when John wrote of Christ as the ruler of earthly kings, he was about to launch into a lengthy portrayal of the brutal hostility of those political leaders in his own day to the Savior and his people. How can this paradox be resolved? Is Christ actually the King over present earthly rulers, or do they reign in unbelief and defiance of him? That both things are true can be readily understood in terms of (1) the broader teaching of Scripture about God's kingdom and (2) the specific teaching of Psalm 2.

The Kingdom of God in Scripture

(1) To avoid befuddling ourselves over the biblical teaching regarding God's "kingdom," we need to recognize some conceptual distinctions regarding it, which many writers today fail to do. First, Scripture leads us to differentiate the *providential* kingdom of God (his sovereign dominion over every historical event, whether good or evil, as in Dan. 4:17) from the *Messianic* kingdom of God (the divine rule that secures redemption and breaks the power of evil, as in Dan. 7:13–14). Second, the Bible distinguishes three historical phases of the Messianic kingdom: the past phase of its Old Testament *anticipation* or foreshadowing (cf. Matt. 21:43), the present phase of its *establishment* at Christ's first coming (e.g., 12:28), and the future phase of its *consummation* at Christ's Second Advent (e.g., 7:21–23). Finally, as closely allied as the church is with God's kingdom (e.g., it holds the keys of entrance to its blessing, 16:18–19), the presently established Messianic kingdom is still not equated with the church (see Acts 28:23); the scope of that kingdom, unlike that of the church, is the entire world, including the doers of iniquity (13:38, 41).

But how can this last point be the case? How can unbelievers who reject the Savior and live wickedly on the earth nevertheless be under the dominion of the Messiah? We can relieve the perplexity of that question by remembering a few relevant points. First, we may distinguish between an objective state of affairs and the subjective recognition of it (e.g., between having tuberculosis and admitting it to yourself). Secondly, there is a difference between reigning *by right* and reigning in *actual fact*, as is evident in any nation at a time of revolution against constituted authority. Accordingly, unbelievers often resist subjectively acknowledging the reign of Jesus Christ over them, but objectively and by right that rule belongs to him nevertheless; to that end he was appointed by the Father (Luke 22:29; 1 Cor. 15:27–28), and his resurrection and ascension certified it (Matt. 28:7, 18; Acts 17:30–31; Rom. 1:4; Phil. 2:9–11; Heb. 1:3, 8–9; 2:7–9). Furthermore, like the gospel, which is a savor unto both life and death (2 Cor. 2:14–16), the reign of the Messiah presently breaks the power of sin and rebellion in two different ways: one in *redemptive blessing* (John

3:3, 5; Rom. 14:17; Col. 1:13), but the other in *judgmental curse*, experienced both now (Mark 9:1; cf. 13:1–30; Ps. 72:4, 12–14; Acts 12:21–23; Rev. 18; 19:15–16) and later in its full fury (Matt. 13:41–42, 49–50; 25:31–34, 41, 46; 2 Thess. 1:4–9). As a result, unbelievers who repudiate the Messiah's dominion are nevertheless under his reign in the form of wrath and curse.

Finally, we should not forget the growth dimension of the present, unconsummated Messianic kingdom. It will gradually become large and transform all things (Matt. 13:31–33). That is, the objective reign of the Messiah by right, involving judgment upon rebels, will more and more become a recognized reign in actual fact as it spreads redemptive blessing. Though in this age the wheat will always live in the presence of weeds (Matt. 13:36–43),[16] it will become increasingly evident that this world is Christ's wheat field (kingdom), not a weed field. Christ is presently reigning, and he must continue to do so until every enemy has been subdued under his feet (1 Cor. 15:25; Heb. 10:12–13), progressively spoiling Satan's house and rescuing the nations from deception (Matt. 12:29; cf. Rev. 20:1–3). In the power of the gospel and the Holy Spirit, "the gates of Hades will not overcome" the onward march of the church of Christ (Matt. 16:18). Many sinners will be saved (Rom. 11:12–15, 25–26), nurtured in the commandments of Jesus (Matt. 28:20), and they will give Christ preeminence in all things (Col. 1:13–20), including

---

[16]The pluralist attempt to find biblical support, however meager, for its unique political tenets looks desperate when it reaches for the parable of the wheat and weeds. Surveying the text of this eschatological lesson turns up not the slightest intimation that it pertains to the nature or function of civil government, nor does it bear upon such issues by logical implication. The type of punishment dealt with in the parable is not temporal, but rather the judgment of eternal damnation (the weeds are collected in "bundles to be burned," Matt. 13:30). Moreover, the temporal judgments of the civil magistrate have nothing to do with the discerning of human hearts so as to divide the unregenerate ("the sons of the evil one," v. 38) from the regenerate ("the sons of the kingdom"), but rather with punishing lawbreakers while protecting lawkeepers. In restraining premature separation of wheat and weeds, Jesus was not condemning the moral judgments and divine vengeance expressed through the civil magistrate, or else Paul is actually pitted against him (cf. Rom. 12:19; 13:4). Surely even pluralists would not protect any and all criminal behavior (e.g., molesting children in professed subservience to the evil one) for the sake of safeguarding the freedom of religion for all citizens! Accordingly, it is ridiculous for them to suggest that they alone conform to the teaching of this parable, while those who advocate civil enforcement of God's law regarding crime somehow do not.

the things pertaining to this present world (cf. 1 Tim. 4:8).[17] The nations will be discipled and will obey the Lord's word (Matt. 28:18–20). The kingdom of Christ will come to dominate the kingdoms of this world (Rev. 11:15). And as God's kingdom comes, his will shall be more and more done on earth (Matt. 6:10), both in the church (Mal. 1:11) and in the political realm (Ps. 72). "The government will be on his shoulder. And he will be called . . . Prince of Peace. Of the increase of his government and peace there will be no end. He will reign on David's throne and over his kingdom, establishing and upholding it with justice and right-eousness from that time on and forever. The zeal of the LORD Almighty will accomplish this" (Isa. 9:6–7). The knowledge of the Lord is destined to cover the earth as the waters cover the sea (Isa. 11:9). Concomitantly, the people of God will with Christ exercise the authority of persuasion and of right, rather than military might, over the nations (Luke 22:29–30; Eph. 2:5–6; Rev. 2:26–27; 3:21; 5:10; 20:4–6).

These biblical convictions about the kingdom of Christ will help us understand how it can be that, though many kings of this earth rebel against the Savior, he is nevertheless their higher authority and ruler (as Matt. 28:18 and Rev. 1:5 teach). Christ is indeed the "King of kings" in a sense that is both *ethical* (all rulers ought to obey him, and they stand under historical and eternal judgment if they refuse to do so; see 2 Thess. 2:8) and *eschatologi-cal* (throughout history Christ's reign, proclaimed in principle, will see more and more kings submit to it; e.g., Rev. 21:24).[18]

---

[17]The much-abused statement of Jesus in John 18:36, "My kingdom is not of [*ek*: out from] this world," is a statement about the *source*, not the nature, of his reign, as the epexegetical ending of the verse makes obvious: "but now is my kingdom not from hence [*enteuthen*]" (KJV). The teaching is not that Christ's kingdom is wholly other-worldly, but rather that it originates with God himself, not with any power or authority found in creation.

[18]My own eschatological view of Christ's kingdom (notably its growth dimension) is historic postmillennial. Premillennial and amillennial fellow believers apply many of the victorious elements of the kingdom mentioned in my discussion to a time *after* Christ returns. This is not the place to debate such questions. It is crucial to note, though, that one's eschatological (especially millennial) interpreta-tion of the kingdom has no logical bearing upon the ethical aspect of the present, unconsummated kingdom. We should all agree that human beings, including their political leaders, *ought* to submit obediently to the will of Jesus Christ, regardless of our differing views about whether or when many will do so. There are premillennialists and amillennialists who are just as theonomic as some postmillen-nialists; likewise, there are postmillennialists who are not theonomic.

The Teaching of Psalm 2

(2) These general truths about Christ's kingdom receive specific expression in the majestic words of the second psalm. David opens with a scene showing the tumultuous nations united in their agitation against God (Ps. 2:1; cf. 74:22–23). This political opposition, stemming from "the kings of the earth . . . and the rulers" (v. 2), is directed against the Lord. These rulers in particular set themselves contrary to the Most High, devising evil schemes against him—specifically "against his Anointed One," his Christ (cf. the conceiving of a wicked plot against the everlasting King in 21:11). Loving to exercise authority over others themselves (cf. Matt. 20:25), the rulers of this world are hostile to any claim that God has chosen Someone to exercise authority over them. This antipathy, characteristic of all unbelieving kings, was clearly and definitively expressed during the earthly ministry of Jesus Christ and the founding of his church (see Acts 4:23–31). The rebellion against God's Christ that David spoke of in Psalm 2 is applied there to (1) the crucifixion of the Savior (Acts 2:27–28) and (2) the persecution of those who proclaim his sovereignty (vv. 29–30). The civil judges who condemned Christ to die were united with the covenant people of God, who in apostasy called for the crucifixion of God's Son by their statement: "We have no king but Caesar" (John 19:12, 15). Likewise, when the church of Christ preached that he is Savior and Lord, the response of the world was (and continues to be) that this is "defying Caesar's decrees, saying that there is another king, one called Jesus" (Acts 17:7).

That against which the rulers of this world rebel is the claim that Christ, God's Anointed, is the supreme King to whom all earthly magistrates must obediently submit. David indicated this in Psalm 2:3, saying that the specific political counsel taken "against the LORD and against his Anointed One" had as its purpose to "break their chains . . . and throw off their fetters." Unbelieving rulers despise being ruled by a higher, divine authority; they want to rule according to their own dictates and autonomous desires. They choose to "break their chains" with God, thus disregarding and transgressing the law of God (cf. Jer. 5:5). God responds to this political impudence with laughing derision (Ps. 2:4; cf. 37:13; 59:8) and wrathful displeasure (2:5). The Creator laughs at those rulers who vainly attempt to assert their independence of Christ and his rule, and he places them under his dreadful curse. No one can escape the objective fact that, by divine right, Jesus Christ is God's established King (2:6), figuratively described as enthroned upon the Lord's holy hill (the temple) in the "city of the Great King" (cf. Ps. 48:1–2). God has anointed him "with the oil of joy" above all his companions and placed him upon an everlasting throne, the scepter of whose kingdom is "a scepter of justice" (Ps. 45:6–7)—a clear reference to Christ's ascension (Heb. 1:8–9; cf. v. 3). Likewise, the divine affirmation "You are my Son, today I have become your Father" (Ps. 2:7)—a truth made manifest at Christ's baptism, transfiguration, and resurrection (Mark 1:11; Luke 9:35; Acts 13:32–33)—reaches its culmination at Christ's ascension (Heb. 1:5; 5:5–6).

Consequently, the second psalm portrays God honoring his Son, the Christ, by enthroning him as the supreme King, which took place especially at the ascension, in spite of the autonomous rebellion against Him by the kings and rulers of the earth. The divine response to this political opposition is to assert the eschatological (Ps. 2:8–9) and ethical (vv. 10–12) character of Christ's reign, the same two aspects of his kingdom that we have seen above. Eschatologically, the Lord promises his Anointed One that all the nations will become his ultimate inheritance and possession. Jesus Christ will, as exalted King, come to have victory over the nations of this world, both by way of crushing historical judgment against disobedience (v. 9) and by way of giving blessed refuge to the humble (v. 12). Elsewhere in the psalms David spoke of "the LORD" sitting David's Lord at his right hand until all his enemies are subdued (110:1), again in the twofold fashion of either turning them to himself in repentance (v. 3; cf. Ps. 22:27; 65:2; 67:7) or crushing them "on the day of his wrath" (vv. 5–7).

Ethically speaking, the second psalm portrays God responding to political opposition against Christ by calling upon "the kings . . . [and] rulers of the earth" to become wise and to be warned (v. 10). It is utter moral folly to disobey the King whom the Lord has enthroned. It is noteworthy that this verse is addressed, not simply to the magistrates of theocratic Israel, but to all of the kings and judges "of the earth," especially to those who dare to exercise civil rule in defiance of Jesus Christ. We cannot escape the clear biblical truth that each and every earthly ruler stands under the divinely established moral obligation declared in this psalm: "Serve the LORD with fear and . . . kiss the Son" (vv. 11–12). Serving the Lord with fear without question means obeying his commandments (cf. Deut. 10:12–13; Josh. 22:5; Ps.

119:124–126). Doing homage to "the Son"[19] in the form of a kiss was an ancient ritual by which the authority of a leader was acknowledged (e.g., 1 Sam. 10:1).

We cannot help but see, then, how far the infallible moral instruction of this psalm is removed from the "pluralist" political theories of our day. By contending that civil policy should not be based on or favor any one distinctive religion or philosophy of life but rather balance the alleged rights of all conflicting viewpoints, pluralism ultimately takes its political stand with secularism in refusing to "kiss the Son" and to "serve the LORD with fear." The pluralist approach transgresses the first commandment by countenancing and deferring to different ultimate authorities (gods) in the area of public policy. Instead of exclusively submitting to the Lord's law with fear and openly following God's enthroned Son, the pluralist attempts the impossible task of honoring more than one Master in civil legislation (Matt. 6:24)—a kind of "political polytheism." The Bible warns us how our ascended and supreme King, Jesus Christ, will react to political refusal to do homage to him and obey his law: he will become "angry [with a wrath readily kindled] and you [will] be destroyed in your way" (Ps. 2:12). The only safe and obedient political option for the kings of the earth is to "take refuge in him." Our own rulers should no more take refuge in themselves instead of the Lord than we should (Ps. 118:9; 146:3).

THE CIVIL GOVERNMENT IS TO ENFORCE GOD'S CRIMINAL LAW

If, as we have seen, all present-day civil magistrates are obligated to obey the will of the Lord and serve his Son, they need to know the standard by which their duty before God is determined. Where do civil magistrates find the political dictates of God? Surely not in varying subjective opinions, personal urges, the human wisdom of some elite group, the majority vote, or even a natural revelation that is suppressed and distorted in unrighteousness. It stands to reason that God's objective and unchanging standards for civil government are found in the infallible, inscrip-

---

[19]The traditional interpretation of the Hebrew is defended in standard commentaries by Hengstenberg, Delitzsch, and Leupold; Kidner prefers to read it "do homage purely (sincerely)"—which will, in light of vv. 6–9, imply submitting to the Son anyway.

turated Word of God, in those passages where it speaks about political ethics. And only someone ignorant of the literary content of the Scriptures could fail to recognize that the Bible says a great deal about public policy, especially in the law of Moses—much of it direct and detailed, which is precisely why it offends many people today. If the moral stipulations of the Mosaic revelation are axiomatically good and universal in character and are upheld by Christ in their moral validity even in the least commandment, unless God reveals otherwise, then all civil magistrates today must be guided and regulated by those laws. To be properly understood, this conclusion calls for drawing a distinction between "social ethics" (in general) and "political ethics" (in particular). The failure to observe such a distinction is perhaps the most damaging oversight in contemporary evangelical thinking about the ethics of life in community.

A distinction between social and political ethics helps us mark off, within the context of public moral duties and responsibilities, a delimited realm where the state has authority to enforce civil sanctions against misbehavior. Not all sins against the law of God should be treated as crimes, and therefore we must (in an objective fashion) circumscribe the authority of the state to inflict punishment upon its citizens. This viewpoint stands diametrically opposed to the axiom of Lenin, who said, "We have no more private law, for with us all has become public law." Were the sphere of sin (even public or interpersonal sin) to be equated with the sphere of the state's legal prerogative to impose punitive sanctions, the state would be placed in the position of God himself. But the state does not have the right to scrutinize and judge every social misdeed, nor does it have the responsibility to produce every social virtue. The state is neither competent nor empowered to judge the private lusts of an individual's heart or even one's selfish use of money in light of a neighbor's need.

The special characteristic that marks off the state from other institutions within society is its *moral* authority to inflict public penalties for disobeying civil statutes. It is an institution distinguished by coercive authority. Paul accordingly symbolized the distinctive function of the state as that of bearing "the sword" as a "terror" and "agent of wrath" to evildoers (Rom. 13:3–4), a prerogative denied to both the family (Deut. 21:18–21) and the church (2 Cor. 10:3–4). Because the state possesses this awesome prerogative to use compulsion in enforcing its dictates (whether by threat of death, monetary fine, or imprisonment), it must be carefully and ethically limited in its proper jurisdiction. If the state lacks moral warrant for imposing a civil penalty on someone for violating a public statute, whatever punitive action it takes reduces to the situation where the will of the stronger overwhelms the desires of the weaker. "Without justice, what are states but great bands of robbers?" asked Augustine. Without a moral warrant for its use of force in particular cases, the state's use of capital punishment is indistinguishable from murder, imprisonment is no different from kidnaping, and extracting a monetary fine is equivalent to theft. Therefore, lest our states become lawless beasts (cf. 2 Thess. 2:3; Rev. 13:16–17), there must be objective limits to legal coercion, a law above the civil law to which appeal can be made against injustice and oppression. This objective criterion is the revealed law of God in its prescriptions of civil penalties for misdeeds. God's law enables us to distinguish consistently and on principle sin from crime, personal morality from civil legality, social from political ethics, and areas where the state may properly legislate from areas where it must not interfere.[20]

Evangelical ethicists of both politically conservative and liberal varieties have transgressed the principle offered above.

---

[20]David Basinger faults this criterion on the ground that sincere Christians disagree in interpreting the Bible as to what are punishable crimes ("Voting One's Christian Conscience," CSR 15 [1986]: 143–144). But given that reasoning, the Bible should equally be precluded from being the basis for theology, doctrinal truth, or church polity—again, because sincere believers have unresolved disagreements in these areas. Moreover, even Basinger's own suggestion of a political standard (namely, those values that all people, believers and unbelievers, propound in common) would fall under his own censure; it is surely not a "common value" among all that political power should be restrained by values that are agreed upon by everyone! Besides, the only truly "common" values that are explicitly endorsed by every single individual are unhelpful verbal abstractions (e.g., "fairplay," "justice"); these lack particular applications.

Ronald Sider suggests that the guiding principle for distinguishing between social sins (that the church alone must deal with) and crimes (that the state must also punish) is the libertarian ideal: "Persons should be free to harm themselves and consenting associates . . . as long as they do not harm others or infringe on their rights" ("An Evangelical Vision for Public Policy," Transf 2 [July/September 1985]: 6). Such a principle is not only ambiguous, arbitrary, and inconsistently applied (see Greg Bahnsen, Homosexuality: A Biblical View [Grand Rapids: Baker, 1978], chap. 6), it is simply not derived from the Bible. This is a fatal defect for a Christian. Not surprisingly, it leads Sider to a complete reversal of the explicit teaching of God's law: applying to the state what is appropriate only to the church (e.g., penal redress of racial discrimination in a matter of private property), and restricting to the church what God's law actually requires of the state (e.g., redress of adultery and homosexuality)!

Those with conservative leanings have tended to promote ethically commendable goals (sobriety regarding alcoholic beverages, restriction of smoking, intervention to curtail the geopolitical spread of Communism) by less than ethical means, calling upon the state to exercise its power of compulsion where no biblical warrant for it can be cogently adduced. Likewise, those with liberal political leanings have tended to promote ethically commendable goals (racial integration, food or medical care for the poor, public education) by less than ethical means, calling upon the state to exercise its power of compulsion where no biblical warrant for it can be cogently adduced. No matter how ethically good these various projects may be, attempting to get the civil authorities to enforce them without warrant from God's Word is to capitulate to the unprincipled position of Thrasymachus, who taught that what counts as "justice" is simply whatever happens to be in the interest of the stronger faction in society. Ironically, when the strong arm of the state is courted in the name of "public justice," as defined by some evangelical's personal opinion (whether conservative or liberal), it is usually at the cost of depriving others of their genuine rights (e.g., to choose for what causes to contribute their lives or earnings), as revealed by the just Judge of all the earth (cf. Gen. 18:25; Deut. 2:4).

The state that overextends its authority by promoting or enforcing whatever aims it wishes, however otherwise commendable (e.g., sexual harmony between husbands and wives, prudent financial savings plans, regular brushing of one's teeth), is a state that has abused the power delegated to it from God (Rom. 13:1; John 19:11). God explicitly forbids kings to swerve to the right or to the left from the well-defined path of his law (Deut. 17:18–20). Indeed, the memorable words of our Lord in Matthew 22:21 inescapably teach that there must be a defining limit on "what is Caesar's." When Caesar demands of his subjects more than is owed to him (Rom. 13:7), Caesar's government inevitably acts as a "corrupt throne . . . that brings on misery by its decrees" (Ps. 94:20).

The state's "sword," therefore, which should not be used "in vain" (Rom. 13:4 RSV), is not under the capricious or autonomous direction of the civil magistrates. They will eventually give an account of their judicial actions to the "King of kings" (1 Tim. 6:15), the "ruler of the kings of the earth" (Rev. 1:5). The fact that the civil magistrate makes a law does mean it receives God's sanction. When civil magistrates (God's servants, cf. Rom. 13:4) exceed the limits of delegated power, enforcing laws not authorized by God, they come under his wrath and curse: "Woe to those who make unjust laws" (Isa. 10:1). The proper domain and divine calling of the state is that of civil justice, protecting its citizens against violence (whether in the form of foreign aggression, criminal assault, or economic fraud). In order that people may live together in tranquility and peace (1 Tim. 2:2), the state has been empowered with "the sword" for the specific purpose of avenging wrath against those who do evil (Rom. 13:4). This is why taxes may be legitimately collected (v. 6). Beyond this a magistrate may not go. He or she must establish the land by justice that is steadfastly followed in the courts (Prov. 29:4; Amos 5:15). God's Word does not, however, authorize civil rulers to be agents of charitable benevolence, financial welfare, education, and mercy. Nor does it grant the state the prerogative of promoting or enforcing the Gospel, much less to be a "policeman of the world." States that assume such functions take on a Messianic complex, attempting to save humans or the world in ways that God never intended for them.

When our Christian reflections on political theory are guided by all of Scripture and only Scripture, we must conclude that, in submission to the presently established Messianic kingdom, all political leaders are ethically obligated to enforce those civil provisions in the moral law of God, and only those provisions, where he has delegated coercive power of enforcement to rulers. In short, it is the civil magistrate's proper function and duty to obey the Scripture's dictates regarding crime and its punishment. The law of God is not a "textbook" of statecraft, as though all the statutes any culture would ever need (e.g., traffic laws), precisely in the wording a complex technological society might require (e.g., computerized theft, copyright infringement) can be read verbatim right out of Deuteronomy and into every country's civil code. As noted previously, much homework remains to be done in interpreting and applying God's laws to our modern world. However, what modern legislators, magistrates, and judges should be concerned to apply and enforce in the state are the precepts of God's law.

Although this idea has long been a virtual staple of the Reformed social and political outlook, many respond to it today with intellectual shock and adamant personal rejection. A common reason for doing so is that people adhere to a particular interpretation of church/state separation that actually parallels the sacred/secular distinction we previously found biblically unacceptable. Some writers will concede that God's law is valid in personal, ecclesiastical, or social ethics, but they go on to deny its continuing validity in *political* ethics. Such a distinction hardly arises from the literature and teaching of the Bible, much less the ancient and medieval worlds. It is much more in tune with the mentality of modern, Enlightenment-sponsored rationalism that quarantines politics, along with other material concerns such as history and natural science, from religious revelation.

That mentality has been especially fostered by one misguided American conception: the "separation of church and state." Such a slogan is not biblical in wording, nor is it conceptually unambiguous.[21] We should think that the institutional separation of the state from the church (something both crucial and biblical) has any logical bearing on the transcendent moral authority of Jesus Christ over each and every sphere of life, whatever their institutional forms. The doctrine of church-state separation does not entail the separation of the state from ethics, and it is precisely to such ethical concerns that God's law speaks. Ironically, it is precisely those who do *not* acknowledge God's law as their political norm who readily disregard and overturn the proper separation of church and state. They do so by taking ethical norms addressed to, and intended appropriately for, the church (a redemptive institution characterized by mercy and persuasion) and applying them instead to the state (a natural institution characterized by justice and coercion). Thus the moral obligations addressed to the church (e.g., to care for the poor and practice racial non-discrimination) are transferred to the civil state in general.[22]

The relevant moral question is whether the infallible Word of God countenances an exemption from God's law for modern civil magistrates. Such an alleged exemption must be read into the text of Scripture rather than being taken from it. It thus reveals not the mind of God but the extraneous presuppositions of the inter-

---

[21]Cf. Greg L. Bahnsen's taped lecture "Separation of Church and State" (#346 from Covenant Tape Ministry: Auburn, Calif.) for an analysis of the different issues that are commonly grouped together under the rubric of "separation of church and state." This collection of multiple senses under one expression is easily conducive to logical equivocation.

[22]E.g., Richard J. Mouw, *Politics and the Biblical Drama* (Grand Rapids: Eerdmans, 1976), chap. 4, where God's will for the church is explicitly used as a model for civil political theory. This results in Mouw criticizing civil legislation, for instance, against sexual promiscuity (which God's law prescribes) and commending redistributive economic legislation (which God's law prohibits).

preter. The assumption that today's political leaders are exempt from obligation to the relevant dictates of God's revealed law falsely assumes that the political validity of God's law applied solely and uniquely to Israel as a nation. Of course, there were many unique aspects of Israel's national experience; important discontinuities existed between Israel and the pagan nations. Only Israel as a nation stood as such in an elect, redemptive, and covenantal relationship with God; only Israel was a type of the coming kingdom of God—having its kingly line specially chosen and revealed, being led by God in holy war, and so on. But the relevant question before us is whether Israel's standards of political ethics were *also* unique. Did they embody a culturally relative kind of justice, valid only for this ethnic group? Happily, not all Christians take that assumption for granted,[23] though many thoughtlessly do.

The error of that assumption is evident from what the Bible teaches about the civil magistrates in the Gentile nations surrounding Israel. If God expected them to uphold and enforce the civil provisions of his law, the natural inference would be that magistrates outside of Old Testament Israel in the modern world are likewise charged with obedience to the same provisions. From our previous discussion of Psalm 2, we have already made it clear that Gentile and pagan magistrates were morally obligated to submit to the rule of God, even though they were, in the nature of the case, operating outside of Old Testament Israel. Similarly, referring to the kings outside of Israel, the psalmist of Psalm 119 declared that he would "speak of [God's] statues before kings and . . . not be put to shame" (v. 46). This statement clearly assumes the validity of that law for such kings. We know too from David's last words that he was convinced that God endorses "one who rules over men in righteousness . . . in the fear of God" (2 Sam. 23:3, where the categorical thrust of the words "over men" is especially to be noted).

The wisdom literature of the Old Testament, intended for practical guidance on an international scale, reinforced this

---

[23]"Though we cannot address secular society in the terms God addressed Israel, nor presuppose a covenant relationship, it is nevertheless valid to argue that what God required Israel as a fully human society, is consistent with what he requires of all men. It is therefore possible to use Israel as a paradigm for social ethical objectives in our own society" (Christopher J. H. Wright, "The Use of the Bible in Social Ethics III: The Ethical Relevance of Israel as a Society," *Transf* 1 [October/December 1984]: 19).

perspective of David: "Kings detest wrongdoing, for a throne is established through righteousness" (Prov. 16:12). Israel's own throne was to be established on righteousness (Ps. 72:1–2), because that quality is the foundation of God's throne (Ps. 97:2). Thus all rulers were seen as belonging to God (Ps. 47:7–9). Indeed, in "all the nations" God himself stands in the assembly of "gods" (judges, rulers) and "gives judgment among" them (Ps. 82:1, 6–8). They are expected to "defend the cause" of the afflicted and needy (vv. 3–4). "Justice" here does not mean welfare payments and redistribution of wealth; it rather means refusing to show "partiality to the wicked" and thereby "deliver [the weak and needy] from the hand of the wicked" (vv. 2, 4). This can only be accomplished by the "gods" handing down judgments based on God's law, the law of the Most High and final Judge of all humankind.

In that light, the personified Wisdom of God declared: "By me kings reign and rulers make laws that are just; by me princes govern, and all nobles who rule on the earth" (Prov. 8:15–16). Consequently, God's Word teaches that every political ruler of the earth is subordinate to the moral authority of God and the holiness of his throne. They have been established to deal with the transgressions of a country (Prov. 28:2) and are morally required in their sphere of authority to condemn the wicked (Prov. 17:15). To this end they must rule according to the just dictates of God's law.

The law revealed by Moses to Israel was intended as a model for surrounding cultures. As we saw earlier, Moses declared in Deuteronomy 4:5–8 that "this [entire] law body of laws I am setting before you today" (v. 8)—not simply the personal, familial, redemptive, or ecclesiastical aspects of it—was meant to be imitated by the Gentiles. Accordingly, the Old Testament prophets applied the very same standards of political ethics to pagan nations (Hab. 2:12) as they did to Israel (Mic. 3:10), and their prophetic condemnations for disobedience to God were applied to pagan cultures as a whole, including the sins of Gentile kings and princes (e.g., Isa. 14:4–20; 19:1, 13–14, 22; 30:33). By contrast, Ezra the post-exilic scribe praised God for inspiring the pagan emperor to establish magistrates beyond Israel who would punish criminals according to the law of God (Ezra 7:27–28; cf. vv. 25–26).

In light of this cantata of evidence, it is futile to think that Gentile rulers in the Old Testament were exempt from the politically relevant stipulations of God's law. And if so, what biblical rationale might be advanced for exempting rulers today who operate outside of the theocratic land of Old Testament Israel? The only conceivable one is the argument that the New Testament introduces a completely new regime of deontological ethics from that of the Old Testament, a hypothesis that we have already refuted. In fact, the New Testament itself teaches that civil magistrates, even those outside of the Jewish nation, are morally bound to obey the political requirements of God's law. Note that the most evil political ruler imaginable, "the beast" of Revelation 13, is negatively described as substituting his own law, figuratively written on the forehead and hand, for God's law (Rev. 13:16–17, in contrast to Deut. 6:8). Those who oppose this wicked ruler are, in contrast, twice described as believers who "obey God's commandments" (12:17; 14:12). Paul condemns this wicked ruler precisely as "the man of lawlessness" (2 Thess. 2:3), indicating his guilt for repudiating the law of God in his rule.

THE PENAL SANCTIONS OF THE LAW

The way that Paul regarded civil magistrates, even the emperor in Rome, was that they should behave as "God's servant[s]" (Rom. 13:4) who "bring punishment on the wrongdoers." In this passage the punishment is clearly intended to be God's (cf. 12:19; 1 Pet. 2:14), and wrongdoing is defined by God's law (cf. 13:8–10). Unless civil rulers serve God by enforcing his just laws against criminal behavior, they will indeed "bear the sword for nothing" (v. 4). This political use of God's law to punish and restrain crime is precisely how Paul illustrates a proper use of the law in 1 Timothy 1:8–10 and cannot, therefore, be deemed out of place in New Testament ethics. Since civil magistrates have been commissioned to bear a sword for the punishment of wrongdoers according to the avenging wrath of God, they will need God's law to inform them how and where God's wrath is to be worked out in the state. Magistrates who repudiate the penal directives of that law are therefore rebelling against being God's servants. They retain the form of the civil office without its substance and thereby deify their own political wisdom or desires.

Some just take it for granted, as a starting point in their political theorizing, that the penal sanctions of God's law must not be enforced by modern magistrates, recoiling from the very idea of it. Ronald Sider, for example, without presenting any argument or evidence, treats this assumption as an adequate benchmark for testing and rejecting the theonomic view,[24] as though it is somehow a priori obvious that the civil penalties prescribed by God's law are morally horrid. Such an approach implicitly ridicules the political wisdom of God himself. That attitude is sometimes fueled by our own misinterpretation of what God's civil law actually does and does not require. To use Sider again, he continues the common error of thinking that the Old Testament prescribed civil punishment for failing to worship God, which would in turn imply the positive enforcement of religious belief today. But the only warrant for this preconceived negativity toward God's law is cultural tradition or personal disdain; for that reason it comes under Christ's censure in Matthew 5:19. Moreover, there is no better political standard to offer than God's law. Without it we are left with either unredressed criminal anarchy or arbitrary and manipulative penalties determined by sinful overlords.

The attitude we are considering stands squarely against that of the apostle Paul, who insisted, "If . . . I am guilty of doing anything deserving death, I do not refuse to die" (Acts 25:11). In fact, Christ himself excoriated those who laid aside the provisions of the law in order to honor their own human traditions (Matt. 15:3–5). The Bible stands squarely against the personally chosen starting point of those who recoil from the penal sanctions of God's law. The Word of God insists that "the law is good" (1 Tim. 1:8–10). According to its infallible teaching, it is necessary to execute civil penalties against criminal behavior (Prov. 20:2, 8; 1 Pet. 2:14), and to do so without exception or mercy (Deut. 19:13, 21; 25:12). Moreover, God requires that those civil penalties be equitable, neither more nor less than civil justice dictates (cf. according as "his crime deserves" in Deut. 25:2; "guilty of a capital offense" in 21:22; and "eye for eye," etc., in Ex. 21:23–25). On this issue the teaching of Hebrews 2:2 is especially pertinent. There we find explicit New Testament endorsement of the "binding" justice of the penal sanctions prescribed in the law of Moses. According to God's evaluation, "every violation and disobedience received its just punishment" in the law delivered from Sinai.

The very justice of God is at stake in the appeal to the Old Testament civil sanctions by the author of Hebrews 2:2. If in any of the punishments God prescribes for transgression he is arbitrary, harsh, lenient, or changeable, then one could indeed entertain the possibility that he or she can "escape" the threat of eternal

---

[24]Ronald Sider, "Christian Love and Public Policy," 13.

condemnation for spurning so great a salvation offered in the Gospel (Heb. 2:3). If universally valid and unchanging justice does *not* characterize even the capital crimes of the old covenant order, then the new covenant, especially with its greater power or emphasis upon grace, could indeed enunciate threats that do not apply to everyone or apply for all time. Hell may be threatened, but God could change his mind again about the absolute justice of his sanctions, just as he has supposedly done with the civil code. After all, if God has not insisted upon the universal, unchanging justice of the lesser (civil penalties), how much more could we expect that he would relent on the justice of the greater (eternal penalties)! This interpretation would be a perverse reversal of the very point made by the author of Hebrews. The divine justice of all the penalties of the Mosaic order—civil, ecclesiastical, eschatological, etc.—is precisely the premise on which the author founds his argument.

Therefore, to repudiate the penal sanctions of the Mosaic law is to be impaled upon the horns of a painful ethical dilemma: one either gives up all civil sanctions against crime, or one settles for civil sanctions that are not just. Both options are clearly unbiblical and produce abusive political effects in practice.

According to another popular line of thinking today, the Old Testament penal sanctions served the purpose of drawing a line between God's covenanted people and the unholy world, purging the covenant community of God-insulting and unholy sinners; for this reason those penal sanctions are applicable today solely to the church, only in the form of excommunication.[25] Such reasoning leaves us wondering several things right from the outset: (1) Were Gentile crimes not also in some way insulting to the holiness of God? (2) Why were only selected forms of sin in Israel insulting to the holiness of God so as to require cutting off? (3) Why is the holiness of God less protected on earth after the Incarnation rather than more strictly or universally protected? (4) Why does one form of Old Testament "cutting off" (religious ostracizing) come over into the church today, whereas another form of "cutting off" (execution) is abrogated? (5) How can anyone holding this view logically avoid cultural relativism in the matter of civil penology?

---

[25]Cf. Greg L. Bahnsen, "M. G. Kline on Theonomic Politics: An Evaluation of His Reply," *JCR* 6 (Winter 1979–80), 195–221, as well as appendix 4 in my book, *Theonomy in Christian Ethics* (Phillipsburg, N.J.: Presbyterian and Reformed, 1984).

This line of reasoning is popular today, but it looks arbitrary on further analysis.

On the major theological issues pertaining to the Old Testament law and the modern Christian, Dr. Walter Kaiser has expressed a position that is much like that of theonomic ethics.[26] The one area where there seems to be a genuine disagreement has to do with the penal sanctions prescribed for civil magistrates in the Old Testament. Kaiser writes: "While it is true that the law is given for all nations, times and peoples, I cannot agree that each of the capital punishments is still in vogue." The one exception he would make is that capital punishment for murder is still obligatory, since it "has as its reason a moral principle: People are made in the image of God."[27] This reasoning is faulty, however. All of the capital crimes of the Old Testament have similar "moral principles" invoked as the reason for the severity of their penalty: for example, "you must purge the evil from among you" (Deut. 22:21); "you will not be guilty of bloodshed" (19:10); "I am the LORD" (Lev. 19:37). If this were the extent of Kaiser's argument, it would readily be overturned by further study of the penology of the Old Testament. None of God's penalties are arbitrary (Heb. 2:2). They require only what justice demands for each crime (Ex. 21:23–25). Those who are punished with death in God's holy law are executed only because they are "guilty of a capital offense" (e.g., Deut. 21:22). It is moral principle that requires the penalties to be what our holy God has prescribed them to be—not just in the case of murder, but in all the cases.

Elsewhere Dr. Kaiser offers further reasoning for opposing the theonomic view of the Old Testament penal sanctions. He maintains that the penalties of the law do not continue to be an integral part of the law today. However, Kaiser makes it clear that he does not take this position for anything like the reasons offered by Meredith Kline:

> Kline's intrusionism does not appear to differ much from distinctive dispensationalist approaches to the law. . . . We are

---

[26]Walter C. Kaiser, Jr., "God's Promise Plan and His Gracious Law," *JETS* 33 (September 1990): 289–302.

[27]Ibid., 297. The difficulties of trying to retain only the penal sanction for murder have been explored in *Theonomy in Christian Ethics*. Kaiser does not answer these problems. Nor does he respond to the point offered in *Theonomy* that reference to the image of God in Genesis 9:5–6 does not explain why murder is punished in this fashion, but rather why any person has the prerogative to inflict such a punishment (given the fact that all life belongs to God).

still left without an explanation as to how these legal texts function for the contemporary Christian. . . . Furthermore the details of the text usually are swallowed up in a wide-sweeping generalization about the history of salvation being fulfilled in Christ.[28]

Why, then, does Kaiser himself not affirm the continuing validity of the Old Testament penal sanctions? To his theological credit, Kaiser's argument attempts to be exegetically based, appealing specifically to Numbers 35:31 rather than to emotion or popular sentiment.[29] Theonomic ethics teaches that we cannot dismiss the Old Testament civil code as somehow horrible in its severity; Kaiser goes on to indicate his full agreement: "This is not to argue that we believe that the OT penal sanctions were too severe, barbaric or crude, as if they failed to match a much more urbane and cultured day such as ours is. Bahnsen appropriately notes that in Heb. 2:2 'every violation and disobedience received its just [or appropriate] punishment.'" Theonomy teaches that only the Lawgiver has the prerogative to modify or revoke his laws; Kaiser again says the same thing: "only God could say which crimes might have their sanctions ransomed."[30]

Furthermore, what Kaiser is arguing is not that there has been a change in the penal sanctions from the Old to the New Testament, but rather that *even within the Old Testament itself* the law of God did not necessarily or absolutely require the death penalty for all the crimes where that penalty is mentioned. Accordingly, Kaiser claims to be championing the same thing that he believes the Old Testament law taught for the Old Testament. This is significant, for if the law taught what Kaiser claims, then a theonomist is committed to advocating his interpretation as the moral standard for civil governments in our day.[31]

This leaves us with the question of whether Dr. Kaiser is correct in his interpretation of the Old Testament law. He may be, though I am not yet convinced. According to him,

---

[28]Ibid., 292–93. Of course, I applaud Kaiser for these important observations against Kline's treatment of the Old Testament.

[29]Ibid., 293.

[30]Ibid.

[31]The reader should also not overlook the fact that Kaiser's interpretation does not demonstrate that the death penalty is impermissible today in connection with the crimes specified in the Mosaic law, but only that such a penalty in those cases is not necessary. They might still be utilized under appropriate circumstances.

the key verse in this discussion is Num. 35:31. . . . Only in the case of premeditated murder did the text say that the officials in Israel were forbidden to take a "ransom" or a "substitute." This has been widely interpreted to imply that in all the other fifteen cases the judges could commute the crimes deserving of capital punishment by designating a "ransom" or "substitute."[32]

This reasoning involves at least two errors that need correcting. (1) It involves a fallacious argument from silence: namely, since the law did not forbid commuting the capital penalty for crimes other than murder, the penalty for those crimes may be commuted. This argument is analogous to the following line of reasoning: Christ applies to certain specific sins the explicit censure of hellfire (e.g., Matt. 5:22, 29–30; 23:15, 33; 25:41), but does not explicitly mention this in connection with every particular sin; therefore, the punishment of hell applies only to a few particular sins. We would surely reply to such logic that (a) the particular sins mentioned are but an example of how every sin will be treated by God, and (b) there are texts in Scripture that more generally teach that God's eternal wrath will be visited upon all sins in general. Likewise, Kaiser has not dealt with the real possibility that the prohibition of taking a substitute (and thus commuting the penalty) in the case of murder was intended to teach us how every capital crime should be treated—that is, it should be treated as illustrative for the rest of the class. Moreover, Kaiser has not made any response to the texts in Scripture that generally teach that the penalties of the law were all just, precisely what the crime deserved and apparently not to be commuted. Thus judges were ordered by God: "Show no pity: life for life, eye for eye, tooth for tooth, hand for hand, foot for foot" (Deut. 19:21; cf. 25:12). Hebrews tells us that those who broke the relevant portions of the Mosaic law "died without mercy on the testimony of two or three witnesses" (Heb. 10:28).

(2) Furthermore, his argument rests upon an incorrect prem-

---

[32]Ibid., 293. The only confirmatory evidence offered by Kaiser for this interpretation is the fact that Paul did not prescribe capital punishment in the case of the incestuous fornicator in 1 Corinthians 5. This kind of argument from silence has been refuted in my books, *Theonomy in Christian Ethics* and *By This Standard* (Tyler, Tex.: Institute for Christian Economics, 1985). Are we to believe that Paul was "commuting" the sentence of the person guilty of incest, or rather that he was not attempting to pass civil sentence at all? The answer should be obvious. Excommunication is not a civil penalty, but on Kaiser's view it would prove to be the commuted sentence.

ise, one that needs to be at least modified, if not negated. His premise, inferred from Num. 35:31, is that "only in the case of premeditated murder" was the death penalty absolutely required. However, we know from the teaching of the Old Testament elsewhere that this is simply not accurate. Consider two examples. Exodus 22:18 says, "Do not allow a sorceress to live." This says much more than simply that a convicted, practicing witch should be assigned some civil penalty; it specifically forbids allowing such a criminal to continue living (which she would do if any other penalty than capital punishment were inflicted). The next verse, Exodus 22:19, teaches, "Anyone who has sexual relations with an animal must die." This too cannot be interpreted as simply calling for some kind of civil penalty for bestiality. The original text uses an idiomatic Hebrew expression that communicates the certainty of that which is being required: "dying he shall die," an expression that is commonly and properly translated, "he shall *surely* die." God's explicit command is that the crime of bestiality shall without question be punished with death. Variation is not allowed in cases like witchcraft and sexual perversion.[33] We need not pursue our study of Old Testament penology any further in detail here.

The argument offered by Dr. Kaiser on the narrow point of the penal sanctions, therefore, is doubly unsound. It rests on a false premise, and it requires a fallacious argument from silence. There may, nevertheless, be flexibility *within* the penal code of the Old Testament that biblical scholars need to take account of. But the fact that there was some flexibility or judicial discretion built into the penal provisions of the law of God as revealed by Moses does nothing whatever to suggest that those provisions have therefore been abrogated today.

_____

[33]Given the apparent transition in Exodus 21:29–30 to penal instructions where the death penalty could be used but ransom was permitted, some commentators have suggested that the death penalties in verses 12–25 (e.g., for kidnaping, violent attacks upon one's parents) are mandatory ones. This would not mean that all cases that prescribe the death penalty make it the mandatory punishment; there may be cases where the law should be read (in context, local or wider) as making the death penalty the maximum allowable sentence a judge may impose, allowing a lesser sentence where circumstances warranted it. However, we can only determine this on a case by case basis, requiring sound biblical reasoning in each instance before determining that the prescription of execution is not absolutely required. (For example, Matthew 1:19 could be used to show that justice did not demand the death penalty in every case of sexual relations with a betrothed woman.)

We are driven to conclude that the Bible offers no justification for teaching that, as a category, the "political" provisions of God's Old Testament law have been abrogated. All the relevant biblical evidence, whether about Old Testament Gentile rulers, New Testament magistrates, or necessary and equitable penal sanctions, moves entirely in the opposite direction. God is never pictured as having a double standard of political ethics, as though it was any less necessary to punish rapists, kidnapers, and murderers with a "just punishment" (cf. Heb. 2:2) in Old Testament Israel than across the geopolitical line into Gentile territory or across the time line into the New Testament era. The justice of God's law, even as it touches political matters like crime and punishment, is not culturally relative. It is not surprising that our most pressing criminal problems today (e.g., disdain for the integrity of life, for proper sexual relations, and for property) are precisely those matters that are addressed with firmness and clarity in God's law. Its divine direction has been set aside, however, in favor of the "enlightened" speculation and self-destructive fashion of this world.

LAWFUL MANNER OF POLITICAL REFORM

Biblical Christians are not "legal positivists" who deny any conceptual connection between civil law and morality. We realize that all civil law arises from, and gives expression to, a particular moral point of view (or more widely, a world-and-life view). The question is not, therefore, *whether* the state should enforce some definable and coherent conception of ethics, but rather *which* ethical system it should enforce. It is impossible for the state to avoid constraining the behavior of its subjects according to statutes that reflect some moral philosophy. We have argued above that for the Christian, this moral philosophy should be taken from the infallible Word of God as recorded in the Old and New Testaments. It must not be based upon the autonomous philosophical speculation or human social traditions, both of which are afflicted by our fallen condition and can therefore offer no reliable ethical guidance.

The fact remains, however, that within society there are plenty of unbelieving people who would readily challenge the veracity and authority of God's Word. The Christian lives in the midst of a world in rebellion against the Lord and his Christ, a world where non-Christians often outnumber or carry more influence than believers within a particular society. A plurality of perspectives compete with each other for a following. If the law of God is the moral ideal that ought to be followed politically, and if the practice of one's political order is contrary to it, what measures should believers take if they hope to correct the situation? This question, as every other ethical question, must be addressed by the law of God itself. That moral code not only sets forth standards to be followed by those in political power, but it also lays down principles of conduct to be followed by those who wish to bring about a more just political order.

Accordingly, let me end this essay by observing that a commitment to the law of God does not encourage, but rather forbids, the use of violence (Matt. 26:52; 2 Cor. 10:4) and revolution (Rom. 13:1–2; Tit. 3:1) to institute closer conformity to the will of God. Simply put, the law of God must not be "imposed" by force upon an unwilling society. Of course, there will always be individuals upon whom the laws of society need to be imposed, whether these are precisely the laws of God or not. That is, there will always be a criminal element who will not regulate their actions by the restraints of civil law. Imposing society's civil (not ecclesiastical or personal) standards upon these individuals through the application or threat of penal sanction is both right and inevitable (Prov. 20:8, 26; Rom. 13:3). The kind of imposition that we disapprove of, however, is the use of coercion or violence to compel a corporate society to submit to the dictates of God's law. That very law directs God's people to rely upon and utilize, instead, the means of regeneration, reeducation, and gradual legal reform to bring about a reformation of their outward political order.

Christian political concern will advance very little indeed if it ignores the fundamental spiritual human need to have hearts changed from above. Hence we would make evangelism, prayer, and education critical planks in the Christian's strategy for eventual political change. At the same time as we are offering Christian nurture and reeducation to converts (including education in socio-political morality), we must likewise engage in intellectual persuasion and apologetic appeals to the unconverted, aiming to change and correct their value systems and to promote the advantages of the Christian view on political issues.

Beyond this, Christians should use the lawful means that are available in any particular society to work toward reconstruction of the legal, judicial, and political framework of that society. Christian legislators, judges, magistrates, and aides ought to work for progressive amendment of the statutes and legal proceedings of the state, bringing them more and more into harmony with the principles of God's law for political authorities. Complementary and necessary to such reform is every believer's moral obligation to make use of his political voice and vote to support those candidates and measures that best conform to the rule of God's law. In all of this, it should be manifest that peaceful means[34] for political change should be utilized by those committed to the law of God and its modern application—not anything like "holy war," revolutionary violence, or "the abolition of democracy."[35]

SUMMARY OF THE THEONOMIC APPROACH TO GOD'S LAW

1. The Scriptures of the Old and New Testaments are, in part and in whole, a verbal revelation from God through human words, being infallibly true regarding all that they teach on any subject.

2. Since the Fall it has always been unlawful to use the law of God in hopes of establishing one's own personal merit and justification. Salvation comes by way of promise and faith; commitment to obedience is the lifestyle of faith, a token of gratitude for God's redeeming grace.

3. The Word of the Lord is the sole, supreme, and unchallengeable standard for the actions and attitudes of everyone in all areas of life; this Word naturally includes God's moral directives (law).

4. Our obligation to keep the law of God cannot be judged by any extrascriptural standard, such as whether its specific require-

---

[34]This restriction to peaceful means of (positive) political transformation or reform does not, as such, address the issue of (negative) self-defense against the illegal assaults of state officials (for example, in a Christian school) or against a murderous political regime which is beyond judicial correction (for example, in Hitler's Germany or Idi Amin's Uganda).

[35]Rodney Clapp misleadingly says this about theonomists ("Democracy as Heresy," 17). Surely Mr. Clapp is aware that the word "democracy" is susceptible to a wide range of definitions and connotations (e.g., from an institution of direct rule by every citizen without mediating representatives, to a governmental procedure where representatives are voted in and out of office by the people, to the simple concepts of majority vote or social equality). The definitions of democracy are so varied that J. L. Austin once dismissed the word as "notoriously useless." While there are some senses of "democracy" that theonomists (and all Christians, even Mr. Clapp) would want to shun, we are certainly not opposed to "democratic procedures" as commonly understood.

ments are congenial to past traditions or modern feelings and practices.

5. We should presume that Old Testament standing laws[36] continue to be morally binding in the New Testament, unless they are rescinded or modified by further revelation.[37]

6. In regard to the Old Testament law, the new covenant surpasses the old covenant in glory, power, and finality, thus reinforcing former duties. The new covenant also supersedes the old covenant shadows, thereby changing the application of sacrificial, purity, and "separation" principles, redefining the people of God, and altering the significance of the promised land.

7. God's revealed standing laws are a reflection of his immutable moral character and are absolute in the sense of being non-arbitrary, objective, universal, and established in advance of particular circumstances; thus they are applicable to general types of moral situations.

8. Christian involvement in politics calls for recognition of God's transcendent, absolute, revealed law as a standard by which to judge all social codes.

9. Civil magistrates in all ages and places are obligated to conduct their offices as servants of God, as agents of divine wrath against criminals, and as those who must give an account on the Final Day of their service before the King of kings, their Creator and Judge.

10. The general continuity that we presume with respect to the moral standards of the Old Testament applies equally to matters of socio-political ethics as it does to personal, family, or ecclesiastical ethics.

11. The civil precepts of the Old Testament (standing "judicial" laws) are a model of perfect social justice for all cultures, even in the punishment of criminals. Outside of those areas where God's law prescribes their intervention and application of penal

---

[36]"Standing law" is used here for policy directives applicable over time to classes of individuals (e.g., do not kill; children, obey your parents; merchants, have equal measures; magistrates, execute rapists), in contrast to particular directives for an individual (e.g., the order for Samuel to anoint David at a particular time and place) or positive commands for distinct incidents (e.g., God's order for Israel to exterminate certain Canaanite tribes at a certain point in history).

[37]By contrast, it is characteristic of dispensational theology to hold that old covenant commandments should be a priori deemed as abrogated, unless they are repeated in the New Testament (e.g., Charles Ryrie, "The End of the Law," *BSac* 124 [1967]: 239–42).

redress, civil rulers are not authorized to legislate or use coercion (e.g., in the economic marketplace).

12. The morally proper way for Christians to correct social evils that are not under the lawful jurisdiction of the state is by means of voluntary and charitable enterprises or the censures of the home, church, and marketplace, even as the appropriate method for changing the political order of civil law is not through violent revolution, but through dependence on regeneration, reeducation, and gradual legal reform.

Response to Greg L. Bahnsen

Willem A. VanGemeren

I commend Bahnsen for the reasonable treatment of theonomy. Theonomists have many points in common with the classic Reformed view of the law of God. They are committed to: (1) the authority of the whole Bible (*tota Scriptura*) as the sole basis (*sola Scriptura*) for the development of faith (i.e., doctrine) and life (i.e., ethics); (2) the excellence of the new covenant and the relevance of the law as the revelation of God's perfections; (3) the necessity of regeneration as a prerequisite of transformation and the need for a transformation based on the law of God; and (4) the correlation of faith and obedience (*sola fide*).

It was not a surprise to me that in reading the first part of the chapter—the correlation of Law and Gospel—I noted my agreement with Bahnsen in the margins. Indeed, the New Testament substantiates the positive and the negative approaches to the law of God. This ambivalence does not arise from inconsistencies in the teachings of the apostles, but from the rhetorical contexts. When the Lord and the apostles eyed the practitioners of the law, who held that their righteousness would justify them with God, they spoke harshly against the (traditions of the) law and the Mosaic administration. Other times, they spoke of the excellence of the new era of grace and of the blessings inherent in Christ's coming and in the outpouring of the Holy Spirit. The new era is superior and much more glorious in comparison with the Mosaic era. The negative portrayal and the comparison of the old with the new do not have a bearing on the essence of the Mosaic covenant as an administration of grace. At this point, I agree with Bahnsen:

"Scripture does not present the Mosaic or law-covenant as fundamentally opposed to the grace of the new covenant."

I take issue with Bahnsen at three points. First, he does not give sufficient attention to the guilt of the law. The law was a ministry of condemnation and death (2 Cor. 3:9), from which Christ has delivered us. He came not only to forgive sins, but also to empower spiritually all who believe on his name. The Mosaic administration did not have the power to give or sustain life. It is true that God promised life to all who loved him and submitted themselves to doing his will. But the fulfillment of the promise was contingent on the coming of his Son and his atonement on the cross. The administration of law was a continual reminder of the ugliness, of the power, and of the consequences of sin. Bahnsen could have helped us by looking more closely at the sufficiency of Christ's sacrifice, the new position of the believer in Christ, and the freedom of the Spirit. Calvary has a bearing on the place and the practice of the law.

Second, Bahnsen introduces the distinction between "standing laws" and "particular directives." This sounds so similar to what Old Testament scholars call apodictic and casuistic laws,[1] though that is not quite what he has in mind. The standing laws are "policy directives applicable over time to classes of individuals" and are morally binding, whereas particular directives are commands addressed to particular individuals or unique events. This classification is too broad and does not do justice to the complexity of the laws in the Old Testament. Instead, I would maintain that the category of "standing" laws be broken up into two classes: apodictic and casuistic laws. The former includes the Decalogue, laws with the "thou shalt" and the "thou shalt not" language, laws that have a generalized subject ("anyone who"), laws that begin with the formula ("cursed is he"), and laws that demand the penalty of death. The casuistic laws further delineate the circumstances under which the law must be applied. Apart from this distinction, the *application* of the law is at issue. I maintain that God is free in commuting the sentence, in changing his law, and in abrogating his law. The Old Testament itself shows flexibility in the application of the law.[2] Therefore, we cannot

---

[1]See my chapter in this book, "The Law Is the Perfection of Righteousness in Jesus Christ: A Reformed Perspective."

[2]See T. Longman III, "God's Law and Mosaic Punishments Today," in *Theonomy, A Reformed Critique*, ed. W. S. Barker and W. R. Godfrey (Grand Rapids: Zondervan, 1990), 41–54.

presume that the standing laws of the Old Testament continue to be morally binding.

The appeal to the continuity of the law (Matt. 5:17–18) hits a sensitive nerve with Reformed people. The confessional statements address the issues of continuity and of abrogation of the laws. For example, article 25 of the Belgic Confession reads:

> We believe that the ceremonies and figures of the law ceased at the coming of Christ, and that all the shadows are accomplished; so that the *use* [emphasis mine] of them must be abolished among Christians: yet the truth and substance of them remain with us in Jesus Christ, in whom they have their completion. In the meantime we still use the testimonies taken out of the law and the prophets, to confirm us in the doctrine of the gospel, and to regulate our life in all honesty to the glory of God, according to his will.

Similarly, the Westminster Confession of Faith allows for "the equity" of the law.

At issue is the extent of continuity between the two covenantal administrations. Bahnsen stands squarely within the Reformed camp by holding to the *continuity* of the moral law of the old covenant and to the *discontinuity* of the old covenant. From this perspective of continuity, he argues that we should *presume* that the law's moral stipulations are binding during the present era. What are the moral stipulations? They are the regulations revealed in the written and in the natural law. Does Bahnsen really mean that all the commandments of the law, including the ceremonial and civil laws, are still to be observed?

As the argument progresses, it appears that he broadens the confessional meaning of the moral law to include all laws "known through Mosaic (written) ordinances or by general (unwritten) revelation." These laws "carry a universal and 'natural' obligation." This definition excludes the ceremonial laws, but includes all the other regulations of the Mosaic law, as well as what may be properly deduced from the natural law. But how are we to interpret the laws properly and to apply them to a new cultural and political context? On the basis of Bahnsen's logic, Vern Poythress has asked whether Leviticus 19:19—"Do not mate different kinds of animals. Do not plant your field with two kinds of seed. Do not wear clothing woven of two kinds of material"—is still applicable.[3] These laws are in the form of apodictic laws ("thou shalt not") and should, on the basis of theonomic ethics, be morally binding. Bahnsen's answer is simple: Do your homework and allow for mistakes in judgment and in exegesis. After all, the issue is black and white: Live by God's law or by "the sinful and foolish speculations of human beings."

Bahnsen takes the confessional ambiguity as a warrant for holding that his position is Reformed and that the label "theonomic" is unnecessary. However, S. B. Ferguson has effectively demonstrated that the Westminster divines used the word "equity" in the technical sense of an application of the law to a new context.[4] Like Bahnsen, they saw a connection between the Mosaic law and the natural law, but unlike Bahnsen, who begins with the written law, they looked for the general equity in the natural law. In the practice of the principle of equity, they freely applied the natural law to a new situation by developing laws and by making the offenses punishable, without tying their hands to the Mosaic laws. The punishments for the crime likewise were subject to cultural changes. Ferguson writes, "Mosaic punishments may be altered not only in mode of administration but in severity of action."[5]

Third, the issue before us is further complicated by the historic connection of the law to Israel, to the land, and to the cult. The relation between God and Israel was primarily a covenant relationship, but it was regulated by the sanctions of law.[6] The Mosaic law bound the people by regulating in detail all aspects of their existence in the land and of their relationship to the cult. What Thomas F. Torrance wrote concerning the correlation of people, land, and law—"There is an intrinsic connection between the People and the Land and also between the People and the Book"[7]—equally applies to the cult. The purpose of the law was to teach Israel something of obedience, respect, and love for God and

---

[3]V. S. Poythress, "Effects of Interpretive Frameworks on the Application of Old Testament Law," in *Theonomy, A Reformed Critique*, 104–10.

[4]S. B. Ferguson, "An Assembly of Theonomists? The Teaching of the Westminster Divines on the Law of God," in *Theonomy, A Reformed Critique*, 315–52.

[5]Ibid., 333.

[6]W. A. VanGemeren, *The Progress of Redemption* (Grand Rapids: Zondervan, 1988), 146–77.

[7]Thomas F. Torrance, "Vocation and Destiny of Israel," in *The Witness of the Jews to God*, ed. David W. Torrance (Edinburgh: Handsel Press, 1982), 103.

for their fellow human beings "in the land that you are crossing the Jordan to possess" (Deut. 6:1). Within this land there was a center of worship, the temple. The law regulated all aspects of society, including civil life and the ceremonial aspects of the cult. The teaching of the law was a pedagogical tool by which the Lord instructed his people to begin to relate every aspect of their lives to him in a particular time and place.

The law was not primarily intended as a document for the nations or for civil governments. It was intended to bring the kingdom of God—that is, the will of God—closer to earth *in the theocracy of Israel*. That kingdom was not, however, actualized in Israel. Jesus Christ alone fully executed the will of God and was obedient in all aspects of the law (moral, civil, ceremonial). He loosened believers from the guilt of the law and brought them into the freedom of the mature experience of sonship. As the church extended into the Gentile world, the ancient connections apparent in the Old Testament were broken up. That is, the Gentile mission loosened the connection between the Book and the Land and, hence, between Christians and the Land. The apostolic teaching prepared the early church to anticipate these dissolutions. Peter spoke of the exile existence of the church (1 Pet. 1:1). The author of the letter to the Hebrews explained most clearly the abrogation of the ceremonial laws. The apostle Paul addressed the matter of the new creation, the new birth, and the life of the Spirit. The civil law was *disconnected* from its links with the old people of God, Jerusalem, and the land. Hence, as referred to above, the Belgic Confession speaks of the abrogation of the ceremonial and civil laws. In the apostolic teaching, however, the book (moral law) was *reconnected* with the teachings of Jesus Christ, his suffering and present glory, the work of the Holy Spirit, and the new people of God.

The crisis of the fall of Jerusalem in A.D. 70 had a different impact on the history of Christianity and Judaism. Rabbinic Judaism reconnected with the *tôrâ* in their diaspora existence, having experienced two forms of dissolution: the bond of people and the cult in the destruction of the temple in A.D. 70, and of people and land in the exile of the Jews from Judea in A.D. 135. By this latter date, Christianity had already established new points of connection through the teaching and ministry of Jesus Christ, as transmitted in the apostolic teaching. He had taught that his kingdom is being established when people come to him in *living faith* and do the Father's will, as summarized in the command-ments to love God radically and to love people sacrificially.[8]

In conclusion, both non-Reformed[9] and Reformed critics of theonomy have observed that the theonomic approach diverges from the Reformed view of the law. I agree with the authors of *Theonomy: A Reformed Critique,* as well as other critics of theonomy, that the Reformed answer to Bahnsen's question "What role does the Mosaic law have in the life of the modern believer?" is different from his.

---

[8]See D. G. McCartney, "The New Testament Use of the Pentateuch: Implications for the Theonomic Movement," in *Theonomy, A Reformed Critique,* 129–52.

[9]See Christopher J. H. Wright, "The Ethical Authority of the Old Testament: A Survey of Approaches (Part 1)," *TynBul* 43 (1992), 110.

Response to Greg L. Bahnsen

Walter C. Kaiser, Jr.

The theonomic approach to the Law/Gospel debate urges believers to begin with the truth of 1 Timothy 1:8—"We know that the law is good if one uses it properly." The fact that there is a certain ambivalence and apparent conflict in the New Testament towards the law is the reason why Paul cautions that believers must use it in a manner that accords with "its own character, direction, and intention."

With this beginning we are in solid agreement. However, we could have wished that Dr. Bahnsen would have gone on to describe how the context of 1 Timothy 1:8–11 supported his contentions. It is not uncommon to hear, even as one or more of the chapters in this book testify, that the 1 Timothy 1:8 reference to the law could hardly be aimed at believers and their use of the law in sanctification, since verses 9–11 of this context *seem* to clearly rule this option out:

> We also know that law is made not for the righteous but for lawbreakers and rebels, the ungodly and sinful, the unholy and irreligious; for those who kill their fathers or mothers, for murderers, for adulterers and perverts, for slave traders and liars and perjurers—and for whatever else is contrary to sound doctrine that conforms to the glorious gospel of the blessed God, which he entrusted to me.

It would have been helpful if Bahnsen had treated the full context, thereby avoiding what seems like a proof-texting or lifting out of the context a readily available sentence to act as a slogan for a particular campaign.

But setting this criticism aside for the moment, an especially fine part of Bahnsen's argument is the section where he sets forth those ways in which the new covenant surpasses the old covenant in (1) power, (2) glory, (3) finality, and (4) realization. Here are some of the finest sentences contributed to the Law/Gospel discussion in the recent past.

However, in spite of our appreciation for the major case set forth by Bahnsen on many points, we must nevertheless object to three issues that are so serious that they will affect his overall system and all the good he has done in rightly evaluating the place of law for the New Testament believer. These issues are: (1) the new covenant redefines and replaces Israel as the people of God with the new people of God—the church; (2) the political ethics and agenda of God can and will be realized more and more by the kings of the earth even prior to the eschaton; and (3) the penal sanctions of the law are still in force today. Each of these affirmations is of enormous significance and consequence both for Christian theology and exegesis, and for the question of the place of the law in the life of the believer.

The Church Replaces Israel as the New People of God

Dr. Bahnsen takes a critical step in the wrong direction when he assures us that

> the redemption secured by the new covenant also redefines the people of God. The kingdom that was once focused on the nation of Israel has been taken away from the Jews (Matt. 8:11–12; 21:41–43; 23:37–38) and given to an international body, the church of Jesus Christ. [In its place, Bahnsen argues that] the New Testament describes the church as the rebuilding of Israel (Acts 15:15–20), "the commonwealth of Israel" (Eph. 2:12 NASB), "Abraham's seed" (Gal. 3:7, 29), and "the Israel of God" (6:16).

Bahnsen's alleged continuity has exceeded the bounds of Scripture. If the promise made to Abraham, Isaac, and Jacob about the seed and the gospel (e.g., Gen. 12:2–3, 7; 15:4) was "eternal," by what rule of hermeneutics and logic is it possible to extract or to somehow factor out the significant part that the people to whom the promise was made would play, while maintaining the rest of the features, included in the same covenant, remained unchanged? In Genesis 15:9–21, God, as a "smoking fire pot with a blazing torch," passed between the pieces of the animals that had been split into two to form an aisle. By this process, the divine promisor obligated himself, and himself alone, to bring about all that he had promised in the covenant, since Abraham was not also obligated to pass between the pieces (and in effect pledge that if he failed to keep his part of the bargain, both his life and the promises of the covenant would be forfeited). Clearly, the pledge to Abraham was a unilateral, unconditional covenant and not a bilateral, conditional one!

Even after Israel returned from the Babylonian exile, God was still promising that he would not replace, redefine, or remove them from being his people or having the land he promised to give to them, for in 518 B.C. (eighteen years after their return from Babylon), the word is still in effect in Zechariah 10:6–12. Nor has it changed in New Testament times, for Paul makes it abundantly clear that "God's gifts and his call [to Israel] are irrevocable" (Rom. 9–11, esp. 11:29).

To teach that the church will replace national Israel will lead to exegetical difficulties, not only in understanding God's program of future events (e.g., the regrafting of Israel into the olive tree in Rom. 9–11), but it will also lead to a confusion of the political agenda marked out for the nation with those personal and social responsibilities given to the individual and the church.

There is, however, a side to the argument that Bahnsen makes that must not be missed. The titles he cites for the church do demonstrate that the believing community is made up of only *one* "people of God." All who believe, be they Jew or Gentile, are part of "Abraham's seed." That had been God's intention from the beginning, as Genesis 12:3 bears eloquent testimony. Nevertheless, granting the biblical fact that there is only *one* people of God in both Testaments is not equivalent to replacing Israel with the Church or to denying that it is impossible to still observe that that one people of God may be made up of several *aspects*, with the Jewish contingent of believers being one of the more noticeable ones, since God is not finished with them as yet.

The Transformational Nature of Christ's Kingdom and Nations

This section is obviously one of the distinguishing features of this approach to law. It is also a difficult area in that it has not been as well charted in biblical studies of recent days, and there is the possible damage that might result from the replacement theology of applying to the church what had previously been directed to the nation Israel. Theonomists are committed to the transformation or reconstruction of all areas of life, but especially the institutions and affairs of the political and educational arena.

Let it be said in defense of the type of theonomy that Bahnsen projects, that he has been exceedingly clear (and in our estimation, correct) in the distinctions he has made between the *providential* kingdom of God and the *Messianic* kingdom of God. As for the providential kingdom, God is sovereign over all historical events in all times. And the Messianic Kingdom of God must be divided, as he noted, into three phases: the past with its foreshadowing of the kingdom, the present with its establishment of that kingdom, and the future with its consummation at Christ's second advent. Bahnsen is still more precise when he notes that the Messianic kingdom is not biblically related to the church, for the scope of the Messianic kingdom is the whole world and includes judgment of the workers of iniquity.

Nevertheless, it is precisely at this point where the slippery aspects of Bahnsen's thought develop. He claims that the Bible teaches that "political leaders are ethically obligated to enforce those civil provisions in the moral law of God . . . where he has delegated coercive power of enforcement to rulers. . . . it is the civil magistrate's proper function and duty to obey the Scripture's dictates regarding crime and its punishment."

Our only objection at this point is the very specific reference to the "civil provisions" of the law. Let it be abundantly clear that we have no argument with the sovereign rule of God over the nations (as described by Bahnsen in his exegesis on Ps 2). Scripture does teach that there are moral responsibilities and duties for government. But to take all the civil duties of the theocracy and to urge the church to hold present day (non-theocratic) forms of government responsible for carrying all of these charges is to slip categories and to confuse Israel with the church and a theocracy with every form of government.

There is no debate over all the other passages cited by Bahnsen to support God's demand of righteousness, justice, and equity from all earthly governments. The problem would seem to come with the "civil provisions," by which I believe Bahnsen would want to imply the "covenant code" of Exodus 21–23 as a chair or teaching passage. Interestingly enough, Bahnsen never directly cites this section, but that must be one of his key texts, for there Israel is instructed in the civil aspects and some of the penalties of God's law.

If the case that was being made here was simply that human governments had better conform to the standards of justice, righteousness, and equity that God has revealed, both in natural and special revelation, I would see no problem. But when the position held by Israel is entirely replaced with the church, and the theocratic provisions specifically delivered to Israel are now transferred directly to the church, there is every possibility for a major hermeneutical disaster waiting in the wings of history. Of course both Testaments teach that civil magistrates must obey the political requirements of God. But our only question is whether these may also be found in the covenant code and in the formulation of the theocracy as it was specifically delivered to that ancient nation. And to be perfectly clear, we do not even doubt that both the so-called civil law and the ceremonial law carry principles within them that are still normative for our day. But that is not where the debate centers; instead, it is a question about how *closely* we may follow these civil provisions. Are we bound to follow, for example, even the sanctions of the law that provided for some sixteen to twenty situations where the state is required to take a person's life (capital punishment)?

The prophets did apply moral standards when they urged pagan national leaders to measure up to God's norms for political ethics. But every one of those lists (e.g. Amos 1–2; Mic. 3:9–12; Hab. 2:6–19) have such distinctively moral rootage that it is impossible to see how they could have shared in any of the more unique features of the theocratic government God gave to Israel. That very difference within the Old Testament itself is another clue to the fact that the political ethics for the nations were not identical with the instructions given to Israel, even during the days of the Old Testament itself. The only possible way that a new confusion could be introduced in modern times is to equate ancient Israel with the modern church, thereby granting to the latter all the benefits and responsibilities of the former. And even though believing Israel and the believing church share much, that is in no way a cause for making them identical or for giving to one the previous political agenda of the other.

The Penal Sanctions of the Law Are Still in Force Today

We agree that civil magistrates are to "bring punishment on the wrongdoer," for they do not "bear the sword [read: 'guns'] for nothing" (Rom. 13:4). Nor do we argue, as some incorrectly do, that the punishments demanded by God at this time or another, were arbitrary, harsh, lenient, or changing.

But we do not agree, therefore, that one is caught on the horns of an awful dilemma that insists that either we adopt as valid for us today all the civil sanctions and penalties specified for crimes committed during the theocracy, or we claim that the case for the use of any part of the law for today's believers is destroyed! If the logic of that argument were true, then the dispensationalist's case for a monolithic law would also hold! I doubt if Bahnsen really wants to pursue such an all-or-nothing logic, for he himself has already acknowledged that there are certain legitimate kinds of discontinuity in our use of the provisions of the law. He allows *cultural* differences between our day and the New Testament as well as cultural differences even *within* the Old Testament itself. Of course, none of these impacts the question of the *ethical validity* of these laws, but that indeed is the point. It continues to be a *hermeneutical* question, and not a theological one, as to how we shall treat the question of the penalties or sanctions of the law.

In this connection, I offered a way out of the hermeneutical trap that I thought theonomy was building for itself when I called attention to a provision *within the law itself* for enforcing the sanction of capital punishment. Numbers 35:31 merely *insists* that no one accept any "ransom" (i.e., a "substitute") in lieu of the required capital punishment when the charge was first-degree murder, and it was proven beyond any reasonable doubt that the offender had committed it. What this text clearly *inferred*, however, was that in all of the other fifteen to nineteen cases (depending on how they were counted) where the penalty called for the judges to take someone's life, a "ransom" or "substitute" was possible.

Some do not like the idea that we are dependent on an inference, but we have argued elsewhere that if inference is not made a legitimate part of the theological endeavor, how are we to account for Nadab and Abihu's responsibility in Leviticus 10:1–3 when there had been no explicit prohibition in the Scripture for the act they had committed? And was it not by inference that our Lord expected that the message of the burning bush would extend beyond what appeared on the surface? Therefore, to resist the legitimate use of inference in theologizing is to take sides against an approach used by our Lord. And what is more, Numbers 35:31 pointedly makes an exception to a well-known set of dreaded sanctions. The point could hardly have been lost on that generation!

But examine Numbers 35:31 more closely. Is the inference fairly made in this case when it closes the door forever on any persons or cultures thinking that the penalty for first-degree murder may be anything other than capital punishment while leaving the door open, both in Old Testament times and in our own day, that in all other cases where capital punishment was required there could be a substitute at the discretion of the judges? Dr. Bahnsen seems to vacillate ever so slightly, but waver he does; he says: "I am not *yet* convinced" (emphasis ours). But suddenly, Bahnsen recovers and decides this is an argument from silence (rather than one from legitimate inference)! Moreover, the added evidence that Paul did not insist on capital punishment but church discipline in the case of an incestuous relationship in 1 Corinthians 5 is dismissed by deciding that Paul was not "commuting" the sentence against the man and his mother, since he was in no position to pass a civil sentence on either. Excommunication is an ecclesiastical penalty, not a civil penalty, Bahnsen concludes. But this is a most unusual conclusion, since, on Bahnsen's view, civil Israel has become the church.

Though I do not approve of Bahnsen's replacement theology, it was a delight to see him refuse to put into operation a hermeneutical decision that I have objected to already. What I would counsel Bahnsen to do here is to note that the issue of incest was no longer a civil issue, as it had been in the theocracy, but an ecclesiastical one. It was not a matter of "commuting the sentence of a crime" or of sensing that the interest of the state still had to be satisfied even after the interest of the church had been met. Nor was it a matter that the legal case against the woman had broken down when the witnesses disappeared, as for example in the case of the woman taken in adultery (John 7: 53–8:11). The case was fully substantiated: there were no questions about whether the charges were correct or whether the case could be substantiated. Therefore, we think Bahnsen has dismissed an important hermeneutical clue with the label "argument from silence" that could have opened the door to realizing that the morality of the law abides while the sanctions may change. Reluctantly, Bahnsen allows that "there may, nevertheless, be flexibility *within* the penal code of the Old Testament that biblical scholars need to take account of" (emphasis his). But this in no way suggests that this flexibility or judicial discretion exists today, he demands! What more can be done to help if this is the way the argument will go?

Surely, an argument for such flexibility does not mean that either the church of God now approves of a double standard for political ethics and that rapists, kidnapers, and abusers of all sorts are to be let go free. This is no more a setting aside of the law of

God now than it was in the days of the Old Testament. God's law is still relevant for all peoples and for all times.

Conclusion

Our reflections on Bahnsen's understanding of the law indicates that there are a lot more areas of agreement than disagreement. But when it came to the area of political ethics, the replacement of Israel with the church, and the sanctions of the law, we move into areas of major disagreement. However, even in these problem situations, it is still possible for a major break-through. Bahnsen's theory as to what constitutes the Messianic kingdom makes it possible for both of us to get our views together with each other; it will only take further dialogue on what is the relationship of Israel to the church and in what sense do we continue, or discontinue, what was given to Israel in the covenant code.

As for our debate over the penalties of the law, the issue of silence versus inference on Numbers 35:31 and the related texts that invoke a similar inference is going to take an extended period of time for reflection and further theological work. But let the reader observe closely that Bahnsen did not close the door altogether, for he said he was not convinced that Numbers 35:31 applied to this situation "yet," even though "there may . . . be [some] flexibility" in the application of the penalties of the Old Testament. Those are signs of a possible breakthrough, even though they may also be signs of scholarly reserve and academic humility.

Response to Greg L. Bahnsen

Wayne G. Strickland

As with most theological paradigms, theonomy presents considerable variation in the expressions of its models. Greg Bahnsen has presented a model that avoids some of the excesses and extremes of other presentations of the reconstructionist model.[1] This is manifest, for example, in his allowance for change of application based upon cultural discontinuities. Likewise, the ceremonial laws are not applicable to the Christian today for Bahnsen, whereas Rushdoony argues for its abiding validity. Bahnsen also allows for some changes in the application of penal sanctions found in the Mosaic law.[2]

I agree with the Bahnsen essay in substantial areas. He is correct in asserting that the Mosaic law reflects the character of God himself and in observing that Mosaic law is not the means of salvific justification. It is critical to observe with Bahnsen that the Mosaic law does "not offer a way of salvation or teach a message of justification that differs from the one found in the gospel of the new covenant." Likewise, there has been *no* change in the gracious character of salvation.[3] Further, the Mosaic law is not

---

[1]See R. J. Neuhaus, "Why Wait for the Kingdom? The Theonomist Temptation," *First Things* 3 (May 1990), 13–21, for a similar assessment.

[2]Greg Bahnsen, *By This Standard: The Authority of God's Law Today* (Tyler, Tex.: Institute for Christian Economics, 1985), 6–7, 345–47. Bahnsen's final summary of the theonomic approach in his essay is taken from pages 345–47 of this book.

[3]See the section in my essay on the dispensational approach entitled "Demonstration of God's Graciousness." I believe that Bahnsen has either

opposed to grace; God's grace was mediated through the Mosaic law. Finally, Bahnsen recognizes the importance of hamartiological defection and the importance of obedience to God.

Despite these areas of agreement, there are significant points of disagreement. While many of these disagreements focus on the exegesis of significant passages, we must first note a methodological flaw. His first major section is entitled, "What Does the Law Itself Say?" and he briefly focuses on Galatians 2:19 as his answer to this question. However, if the law is to speak for itself, then the support should be marshaled from the sections of the *Old Testament* dealing with the law. He focuses primarily on the New Testament passages and only briefly alludes to six Old Testament passages.

There is fundamental disagreement regarding the Pauline treatment of the Mosaic law. The solution to resolving the apparent contradiction or at least tension in Paul's theses on the Mosaic law, according to Bahnsen, is 1 Timothy 1:8. He claims that Paul's disparaging comments in this verse are directed toward unlawful approaches to the law, such as that of the Pharisees. Yet Bahnsen links 1 Timothy 1:8 with Romans 7:4 (and 8:4, 7), suggesting that the law provides guidance for sanctification.[4] First, this appears to be an example of illicit juxtaposing of Pauline passages, reading Romans 7:4 into 1 Timothy 1:8. Paul states that the law can be used unlawfully, but further gives explicit testimony *himself* regarding the true *purpose* of the law in 1 Timothy 1:9—to indict the unrighteous. This fits his treatment of the law in Galatians, which has to do with bringing about condemnation and exposing the need for salvation. In other words, the lawful use has to do with exposing the sinfulness of the unrighteous person. But Bahnsen has read Pharisaism into 1 Timothy 1:9 rather than letting the context inform the meaning. Pharisaism was a significant problem, although Paul is not focusing on that in this passage, but rather its purpose of exposing the sinfulness of a person.

---

misunderstood or misrepresented House and Ice at this point. In his essay he argues that House and Ice contradict themselves by arguing that Old Testament Israel was *not* "under grace" (ibid., 118) and later saying they were a people under grace (p. 128). Yet House and Ice do not say that Israel was not under grace on p. 118. Further, Bahnsen implies they actually use the phrase "under grace" on p. 118, but this is not the case at all.

[4]G. Bahnsen, *Theonomy in Christian Ethics*, rev. ed. (Phillipsburg, N.J.: Presbyterian and Reformed, 1984), xiii.

Moving to Galatians 3:23–24, Bahnsen argues that it is the law's utility as tutor to Christ that is temporary. He limits Paul's reference to the "ceremonial foreshadowing of Christ," rather than the entire Mosaic law. These ceremonial aspects are accordingly pictures and illustrations of Mosaic principles. Yet the argument and context demonstrate that Paul is speaking of the entire law in this passage, not merely the ceremonial aspects. In 3:17 Paul argues that *nomos* in its entirety came 430 years later, not merely the ceremonial portion. Second, the discussed inheritance is based on *nomos*, not merely ceremonial aspects or sacrifices (v. 18). In verse 21, Paul is thinking of the whole law in terms of an administration; this is confirmed by 4:4–5, where Paul states that Christ was born during the time of the Mosaic law. Likewise, 3:24 makes it apparent that Paul is not simply thinking of one aspect of law, but of the entire law in an epochal sense. Two epochs are being compared.

According to Galatians 3:22, the law epoch brought knowledge of sin ("the Scripture [i.e. the law] declares the whole world is a prisoner of sin"). And in verse 23, Paul employs the term *sugkleiō* ("to keep prisoner"), a word that stresses the idea of constraint. This harmonizes with the so-called "moral" and "civil" aspects of the law better than merely the ceremonial aspects. The sacrificial system provided *remedy* for violations of the custody of the law, but the Decalogue provided the actual constraints on the behavior of the Old Testament saint.

Another disagreement arises over whether the Mosaic law "defined the way of salvation for the unrighteous" person or not. The covenant was addressed to a graciously redeemed nation and presented principles of sanctification. It came in alongside the promises of the Abrahamic covenant that included spiritual deliverance (Gal. 3). Since its purpose was not salvific, it certainly would not have "defined" the way of salvation, but would have foreshadowed the concept of substitutionary atonement.

A persistent problem with theonomy in general and Bahnsen's presentation in particular is the internal contradiction within the system.[5] Based on passages such as Matthew 5:17–19; 23:23; and James 2:10, he argues that the *entire* law is binding (even to

---

[5]Others have noted this problem: John W. Robbins, "Theonomic Schizophrenia," *Trinity Review* 84 (February 1992), 1–4; Bruce Waltke, "Theonomy in Relation to Dispensational and Covenant Theologies" in *Theonomy: A Reformed Critique*, eds. W. S. Barker and W. R. Godfrey (Grand Rapids: Zondervan, 1990), 81.

the jot and tittle);[6] yet using the same model when treating other details of the law (e.g., the ceremonial aspects), he argues that the law is not applicable.[7] If the law is not applicable, then it is not binding. That is not to say that moral principles may not be extracted, but the law as it stands is not enforced. Bahnsen notes that "we no longer come to God through animal sacrifices," and argues that land provisions are "inapplicable," as are dietary provisions. If the law is binding to the jot and tittle, then the escape of the principle of inapplicability is not available.

Further tension in Bahnsen's model is evident in his treatment of Matthew 23:23. Christ's pronouncement (the definitive speaker on law, according to Bahnsen) is that lesser features of the law are to be neither neglected nor abrogated. Yet Bahnsen earlier implied that God *can* alter or repeal a commandment. Would laws concerning sacrifice fit under the category of lesser matters? If so, they should not be neglected.

James 2:10 is often marshaled by Bahnsen as support for the notion that the Christian is obligated to keep the law. At one point Bahnsen argues that James 2:10 obligates the Christian to keep every (moral) commandment of the Mosaic law. Yet this verse would seem to argue too much—James would seem to argue one must keep the *whole* law (*holon ton nomon*), which would include the ceremonial aspects.

At times, Bahnsen also *equates* the Mosaic law with the moral standards of God. He presents the idea that the Mosaic law was binding on Jew and Gentile alike and is universal in character and application. The coming of Christ furnishes no good reason for God "to change his perfect, holy requirements for our conduct and attitudes." To be sure, God's moral standards are expressed in the Mosaic law, but they should not be absolutely equated. To posit the cessation of the Mosaic law is not equivalent to abolishing God's moral standards. For example, one may obey God's moral standard of no sexual immorality without feeling the obligation to obey the Mosaic law per se. Certainly Bahnsen would allow for the idea that moral dictums and demands existed prior to the giving of the law to Moses. In like manner, God's moral standards and demands may continue to exist with the cessation of the Mosaic law. The standards do not change, but the codification and expressions may. This distinction would preserve

---

[6]See also Bahnsen, *Theonomy*, xiii, 314.
[7]See also ibid., 212.

Bahnsen from self-contradiction. The concrete expressions of the moral standards are often temporally and culturally bound. Bahnsen admits this difference himself when he states, "It is unreasonable to expect that the coming of the Messiah and the institution of the new covenant would alter the moral demands of God as revealed in his law." Yet later in the same discussion he admits, "God certainly has the prerogative to alter his commandments." Bahnsen should not shift from moral demands to altering commandments themselves.

A major concern is Bahnsen's emphasis on Matthew 5 as the definitive statement on the usefulness of the Mosaic law. Elsewhere he has argued this as the *crux interpretum* for theonomy, yet as demonstrated in my essay on the dispensational approach, this passage is misinterpreted by theonomists.[8] In addition, Bahnsen argues that the other statements on law are to be evaluated on the basis of Christ's statement. This seems to imply the illegitimate concept of a canon within a canon. Bahnsen seems to suggest that the testimony of Christ is more authoritative than Paul's. Why not rather present an argument based on the principle of progressive revelation—subsequent revelation is clearer and more complete revelation—so that for the church, we should be guided by Paul's assertions. In any event, the testimony of Paul should not be rendered less authoritative than Christ's statements. Keep in mind that Christ operated during the law epoch, not the church age, so that much of his teaching is addressed to people living during the law period.

Further, Bahnsen has given several misleading presentations of non-theonomist views. At one point he clearly implies that some interpreters pit "the summary or comprehensive commandments of God's law . . . against the law's specific details."[9] However, the New Testament commands to love God and to love one's neighbor are based on the same moral standards as the Mosaic law. They are different expressions of the same moral standard, not competing standards. Generally, those who emphasize the law of Christ do *not* suggest that it is pitted against the detailed Mosaic law.

Another "straw man" is the implication that those who argue

---

[8]See the section in my essay, "The Mosaic law and the Christian," which treats Matthew 5:17–19.

[9]A similar charge is levied against dispensationalism by B. Waltke, "Theonomy in Relation to Dispensational and Covenant Theologies," 69.

for cessation of the Mosaic law are somehow arguing for the cessation of God's moral demands: "it is theologically incredible that the mission of Christ was to make it morally acceptable now for humans to blaspheme, murder, rape, steal, gossip, or envy!" The question may be fairly asked, "Who argues this?!" The expression and codification of the moral standard of God has changed leading to the cession of the *Mosaic* law, but the standard itself has not changed. There is ample New Testament pronouncement of specific moral prescriptions explaining the law of Christ to prevent adoption of such antinomianism. No evangelical argues that it is morally acceptable to blaspheme, etc. No Christian argues they are without any law whatsoever.

Bahnsen's statement that Old Testament standing laws continue to be morally binding in the New Testament unless rescinded or modified by further revelation is one that may be harmonized with this dispensational view. Simply put, the New Testament explicitly presents the Old Testament Mosaic law in its entirety as abrogated and replaced by a similar law, the law of Christ, which places greater premium on dependence on the indwelling Holy Spirit.

My chapter in this book on the dispensational approach includes an extensive section dealing with passages arguing for cessation of the Mosaic law. Bahnsen's rejection of Romans 6:14 as presenting discontinuity with Mosaic law is based on the lack of article with *nomos*. To him, it does not discuss Mosaic law. Yet there are ample examples of *nomos* without the article that clearly represent the Mosaic law (e.g., Luke 2:23–24; Acts 13:39; Rom. 4:13). The identical expression *hupo nomon* (without the article) is found in 1 Corinthians 9:20, where it clearly refers to the Mosaic law that bound the Jews. The term *nomos* appears without the article in Romans 10:4, a passage Bahnsen admits refers to the Mosaic law.[10]

The church should be appreciative of the encouragement toward transformation given by theonomy. The church certainly cannot escape being involved in transformation as it fulfills the Great Commission. As individual citizens, Christians also often have a forum for influencing the ethic of society. Yet the focus on transformation must be balanced with the fact that the mission of the church centers on spiritual redemption (Matt. 28:19). It is encouraging that Bahnsen recognizes the crucial role of regeneration and suggests that the methodology of transformation is

---

[10]G. Bahnsen, *Theonomy*, 129.

educative rather than coercive. One is not required to become a theonomist to influence society and government toward a biblical ethic.

The model of perfect social justice should not be understood as that presented in the Mosaic law. Since the civil sanctions are part of the Mosaic law and the law has been abrogated, it stands that the civil sanctions included in the law are likewise not in force. Bahnsen suggests that "to repudiate the penal sanctions of the Mosaic law is to be impaled upon the horns of a painful ethical dilemma: one either gives up all civil sanctions against crime, or one settles for civil sanctions that are not just." Yet is there not another option? Is it not possible to repudiate the Mosaic law and give a new law based on the same ethical principles, yet updated to account for administrative and societal differences, such as the fact that God is no longer dealing exclusively with a theocracy (Israel), but with the church? In addition, the contribution of the Mosaic law to penology and government may be retained as presenting principles in a descriptive, not normative, sense.

That the Old Testament law of Israel was not intended to be the model of justice for all time is validated when we recognize the special nature of Israel. Although its uniqueness is minimized by theonomists, the testimony of Scripture is that Israel as a nation was special, chosen by God (Deut. 7:6). The law was designed for the *covenant* nation of Israel, given to Moses for a *holy* nation (Ex. 19:5–6). Any appeal to Deuteronomy 4:6–8 in support of the Mosaic law and administration being normative for all nations fails to recognize that the passage does not say, "Be like Israel," or "We (other nations) will be like Israel." It was given to Moses for a special nation that would be a kingdom of priests. It is likewise telling that the New Testament does not apply Old Testament law to civil discussions (Matt. 22:17; Rom. 13:1–10; 1 Pet. 2:13–17).

Rather than suggesting that Mosaic legislation is normative for all governments, natural law (as found in general revelation) provides the basis for ethics in government. There is a natural sense of rightness and wrongness that resides in the conscience (Rom. 2:14–15). Although this sense of right and wrong has been effaced by sin (1:32), it is nevertheless able to serve as the moral guide. It should be noted that Paul does not say that God embraces a particular form of government, but rather states, "The authorities that exist have been established by God" (13:1).

It is these and other concerns with theonomy as presented by Bahnsen that give cause for rejection of the paradigm of the Mosaic law as the rule of life for the Christian today.

Response to Greg L. Bahnsen

Douglas Moo

Defenders of the theonomic approach set forth the eternal authority of the Mosaic law as a barrier against the flood of ethical relativism that is threatening to drown our cultures and churches. Their concern is understandable: Christians too often make ethical judgments on the basis of expediency. We sidestep teachings in the Bible that challenge our worldview or desired course of action by subjectively applying various hermeneutical devices: "That requirement was limited to the first-century church"; "Jesus was obviously exaggerating"; "Jesus was speaking only of the apostles." It is not that such considerations are necessarily improper; it is that our basis for applying them seems too often the degree of difficulty that we would have in obeying the teaching under discussion. And thus Scripture is defanged, and our laudable insistence on the authority of Scripture becomes meaningless in practice.

Bahnsen and other theonomists want to replace this highly subjective picking and choosing of biblical teachings with a more objective procedure. Boiled down to its essentials, their position is that the Old Testament laws, reflecting as they do God's unchanging moral character, remain in force until further revelation modifies or cancels them. As Bahnsen sees it, such modification occurs only with respect to the laws having to do with sacrifices and purity. Therefore all other Old Testament laws remain in full force, spelling out the conduct expected of God's people and setting forth a blueprint for the nature and procedures of civil government.

As others have pointed out, the claim of theonomists to have found an assured alternative to the dangers of subjectivism in ethical interpretation is illusory. Bahnsen admits that many Old Testament laws, while still in force, cannot now be applied in the same way that they were in the Old Testament. The subjectivity that is ostentatiously ushered out the front door is therefore smuggled in through the side door again. The Christian must still decide just how a particular authoritative Old Testament law is to be put into practice in vastly changed cultural circumstances.

But this point is a minor one. The fact that a degree of subjectivism remains in the theonomic approach does not invalidate the viewpoint any more than the claim to objectivity proves it. As Bahnsen claims, the truth or falsehood of theonomy must be demonstrated on the pages of the New Testament. And it is just here that theonomy is weakest. As I argue in my own essay, the New Testament does not allow the conclusions reached by Bahnsen and other theonomists. In this response, I will reiterate and expand on some of the points in that essay that apply particularly to the theonomic position. I will also offer a critique of the best known and distinctive element in the theonomic approach: the application of Old Testament civil laws to contemporary government.

In his attempt to prove that the New Testament endorses a theonomic perspective, Bahnsen makes two main points, one "defensive" and the other "offensive." Defensively, he argues that statements appearing to deny the continuing applicability of the Mosaic law do not apply to the law as a whole. He then goes on the offensive to argue that the New Testament teaches the continuing applicability of the Mosaic law to believers. I will look at each point in turn.

If the theonomic position is to find acceptance, the many New Testament verses that appear to teach that believers are no longer subject to the direct authority of the Mosaic law must be interpreted otherwise. Bahnsen treats only a few of these texts, but his basic approach is clear enough: the word "law" (*nomos*) in these verses refers not to the Mosaic law as a whole, but to (1) the Jewish legalistic misuse of the law as a means of justification (e.g., Gal. 2:19); (2) the ceremonial requirements of the law (e.g., 1 Cor. 9:20–21; Gal. 3:23–25; Eph. 2:14–15); or (3) the spiritual bondage produced by reliance on law of any kind (e.g., Rom. 6:14). Bahnsen's method of handling such passages is a popular one; it is a staple of traditional Reformed exegesis. This hermeneutical move is attractive because it solves the tension between positive and negative evaluations of the law in the New Testament. The negative assessments apply only to a part of, to a function of, or to a misuse of the law, while the positive ones refer to the law as God gave it.

Now the interpreter must certainly be alive to possible nuances in the use of the word "law" (*nomos*) in the New Testament. But as I point out in my essay, these nuances will have to be demonstrated from context and not simply assumed. Because the point is so important and so easily obscured by the history of interpretation, we must insist again: First-century Jews viewed the law as a unity. It was the *tôrâ*, given by God through Moses to the people of Israel as their guide for the whole of life. Jews did not make any fundamental distinction between "moral" and "ceremonial" laws or "moral" and "redemptive" laws.[1] We must assume, unless there is clear evidence to the contrary, that Jesus and Paul maintained this same basic perspective: Not only were they themselves Jews, but they were speaking to or writing to Jews or people who were influenced by Jewish views. The burden of proof, then, rests on those who claim that "law" means anything less than the Old Testament law as a whole.

We must then ask if Bahnsen has made a convincing exegetical case for limiting the scope of the word "law" in those texts that speak of the believer's freedom from the law. Bahnsen actually deals exegetically with only a few of the key passages; and I do not have space to deal even with those. I will therefore look at several that I think are representative.

Regarding Galatians 2:19 Bahnsen gives essentially different meanings to the two occurrences of the word "law": "I through the *law* died to *legalism*." Yet the Greek word in both cases is *nomos*, and both are without the article. The other occurrences of the word in this context seem clearly to refer to the Mosaic law as a whole (three occurrences in v. 16; v. 21). What is the justification for giving this one occurrence of the word a nuanced meaning? Bahnsen gives none; and, to be fair, he does not make the verse an important one in his argument. But it illustrates the tendency evident in his essay: to give the word "law" a limited or nuanced meaning on the basis not of exegetical evidence but on the basis of the logic of his general position. Too many crucial texts lack any

---

[1] I deal with this point in more detail in my response to Walter Kaiser's paper.

exegetical discussion at all (e.g., Rom. 2:12–16; 7:4–6; Gal. 5:18; 6:2; Eph. 2:15).[2]

This criticism cannot, however, be leveled against his restriction of the word "law" in Galatians 3:24–25 to refer to the law "particularly in its ceremonial foreshadowing of Christ." Bahnsen gives several reasons for this restriction. Nevertheless, I find none of them convincing. That the focus of the controversy in Galatia is circumcision and that calendrical observances also were involved (Gal. 4:10) is clear. But it is equally clear that in Galatians 2:16–4:7 Paul treats these issues as part of the larger question of the place of the law, as a whole, in salvation history. (Bahnsen himself tacitly admits this elsewhere in his essay, recognizing that "the law" in Gal. 3:19 is the law of Moses.) Why, then, should the meaning of "law" be restricted in Galatians 3:23–24? Bahnsen's main argument is that Paul here is discussing the function of the law as "governing and teaching the Jews that justification comes through faith in Christ." But this function, Bahnsen claims, is accomplished only by the ceremonial law. It is only this part of the law, then, that believers are no longer "under" (see v. 23).

There are two problems with this view. First, it is not at all clear that it is only the ceremonial law that teaches about justification by faith. As Romans 4:15, Galatians 3:13, and other texts make clear, the law as a whole has functioned to show people their inability to please God by works and has thereby worked to teach us about our need for justification by faith. But, second, it is doubtful that Paul is even talking about this function of the law here. Bahnsen's interpretation appears to rest on a meaning of the word *paidagōgos* that is today generally dismissed ("tutor"; see my essay for elaboration and bibliography). We are left, then, with no reason to think that "law" in this text means anything different than what it plainly means throughout Galatians 2–4: the Mosaic law, the *tôrâ*, in its entirety.

Bahnsen can make a better case for a restriction of the meaning of "law" in Romans 6:14–15. For Paul here associates not being "under law" with being free from its confining and

---

[2]Bahnsen's understanding of "law" in some contexts to refer to "the attitude of the Pharisees and Judaizers who promoted self-merit before God through performing works of the law" assumes what many modern scholars would not assume: that the Pharisees, or Judaism generally, held such a view. Since I myself think that, properly nuanced, there was a strain of "legalism" in much first-century Judaism, I do not make this a point of direct critique. But Bahnsen's failure even to mention the problem is disturbing.

condemning power (see 7:1–6). Following a typical Reformed exegesis, then, Bahnsen claims that the text teaches only that believers are free from the spiritual condition of bondage and impotence. As I have indicated in my essay, I am sympathetic to, but finally unconvinced by this interpretation. In my view Paul is claiming here that believers are no longer subject to the binding authority of the law; a salvation historical shift has occurred and the Mosaic law is no longer central to God's administration of the promise. However this may be, Bahnsen is surely wrong in suggesting that Paul may not even here be speaking directly about the Mosaic law. As we have seen, "law" in the New Testament denotes the Mosaic law unless there are good reasons to the contrary; no "specifying" additions to the word are needed. Moreover, Paul's immediately preceding (5:13, 20) and following (7:1–25; see esp. v. 7) uses of "law" clearly refer to the Mosaic law.[3]

Another key text appearing to claim that Christians are no longer directly subject to the ruling authority of the Mosaic law is 1 Corinthians 9:19–23, in which Paul claims not to be "under the law."[4] Here again Bahnsen avoids this conclusion by arguing that he (Paul) is referring only to the ceremonial law. He bases this conclusion on the context: Paul is contrasting his behavior when evangelizing Gentiles from his behavior in working with Jews; and it is only the ceremonial law that distinguishes Jews and Gentiles. But Bahnsen's argument misses the first-century and Pauline context. Jews believed that only they had been given the Law of Moses; the Gentiles at best had been given some general moral requirements (often traced back to the time of Noah and hence called the "Noahic commandments"). The distinction between Jews, who had been given the law, and Gentiles, who had not, was fundamental at that time and one that Paul himself clearly assumes (see Rom. 2:12–16, where the focus, if anything, is on the "moral law"). Bahnsen fails to ground his interpretation in the first-century context and in Pauline usage.

---

[3] Nor is the lack of an article significant. As writer after writer has pointed out, no conclusions about the meaning of the word *nomos* in Paul can be based on the presence or absence of the article.

[4] Bahnsen may give the wrong impression by referring to "dispensationalists" in his discussion of Romans 6:14–15 and 1 Corinthians 9:19–23. In fact, scholars from a wide theological spectrum—including Roman Catholics, Anglicans, Lutherans, Baptists, and charismatics—hold views similar to those I argue in the text.

But there is another and more serious issue here. Bahnsen's main reason for confining the reference in this text to the ceremonial law is not exegetical but theological: Paul could not have claimed that he or other Gentiles were free from the Mosaic law as a whole because that law enshrined moral principles that reflect God's own character and that are therefore universally applicable. This virtual equation of the law of Moses with God's eternal moral law is very important for Bahnsen's whole argument, and it comes up repeatedly. For instance, Bahnsen claims that Paul could not in Romans 6:14–15 be asserting that believers are free from the law of Moses generally because Paul elsewhere claims to be subject to "the law of Christ."

Similar is the subtle but critical move Bahnsen makes in discussing the applicability of the law to Gentiles in the Old Testament. He begins by arguing, correctly, that the Bible holds Gentiles to the same basic moral standards as it does the Jews and that God's moral laws are, therefore, universal. But he then uses this argument to claim continuity for the law of Moses. Now it is plain that this argument works only if one assumes that the Mosaic law is equated with the moral law of God. Bahnsen's argument, in other words, seems to be:

God's moral law is found in the law of Moses;

God's moral law is universally applicable;

Therefore: the Mosaic law is universally applicable.

Now it is clear that this argument works only if an "only" is supplied in the first line. For if God's moral law is found in other than the Mosaic form, then the argument fails. Yet Bahnsen never tries to prove this "only." And, in fact, the presence of God's law in other than Mosaic forms seems clearly to be argued or assumed by Paul in texts such as Romans 2 and 1 Corinthians 9:21–22. The Mosaic law has been given only to the Jews; thus Gentiles are those who are "apart from the law" and those "not having the law" (Rom. 2:12; 1 Cor. 9:21). Nevertheless, the Gentiles are not without "law," for God has revealed in nature and in conscience his moral will for all people (Rom. 2:14–15). Similarly, Paul as a Christian, while no longer "under the law," is still subject to "God's law"—but now not in its Mosaic, but "Christian" form: he is subject to "Christ's law" (1 Cor. 9:20–21). This point is fundamental to my disagreement with Bahnsen. He assumes that "law of God" is equivalent to the Mosaic law; therefore, to be without the Mosaic law is to be without any divine imperative and to fall into subjective and humanistic autonomy. But I see God's moral imperatives for human beings coming in various forms:

through the law of Moses for the Jewish nation, through nature and the conscience for all human beings, and through "the law of Christ" for Christians. Theonomy is misnamed, for I, and I am sure all contributors to this volume, believe in "the law of God." A better name for Bahnsen's position would be "Mosonomy."

This same issue emerges in some of the texts that Bahnsen uses to show that the Mosaic law continues to be applicable to believers. Only if references to "the commandments" (e.g., John 14:15; 1 Cor. 7:19; 1 John 2:3–4) refer to the commandments of the Mosaic law do such texts support Bahnsen's position. In my view these are better taken to refer to the commandments issued by Christ: commandments that are by no means identical with those of the Mosaic law. Nor do the other texts Bahnsen cites to prove the continuing validity of the Mosaic law support his position. No one doubts that the Mosaic law is "holy, righteous and good" (Rom. 7:12); the question is what the function of that holy law is for the Christian. Even Bahnsen admits that the ceremonial parts of that law are no longer directly authoritative for us; yet presumably this does not remove their holiness or goodness.

The New Testament presumes that the law functions to reveal sin and to imprison people under it. But never is this function applied to Christians (note that Paul is speaking of his life under the law in Romans 7:7, while 1 Timothy 1:8 is speaking of unbelievers). Nor can Matthew 5:17–19 be used to demonstrate the eternal, direct applicability of the Mosaic law. As my exegesis of this text shows, Jesus is here endorsing the continuing validity of the Mosaic law (vv. 18–19) while at the same time claiming that his teaching is the true goal of that law (v. 17). As I point out in my essay, it is quite remarkable, if Bahnsen's position is right, that Paul does not fill his letters with references to the Old Testament law as a necessary foundation for teaching his new Gentile converts how they are to please God. The fact that the New Testament contains so few references brings into serious question the whole "Mosonomic" viewpoint.

"Theonomy" is a basic element in the movement known as "reconstructionism," whose advocates want to "reconstruct" society on the basis of God's (the Mosaic) law. In the Mosaic law, so Bahnsen and others claim, we have instructions about how to govern society—instructions that most Christians have wrongly ignored by artificially confining God's law to certain spheres of life. It is this insistence on the continuing applicability of the Mosaic laws about government that sets theonomy apart from more "mainstream" Reformed theology. It has, accordingly, sparked a lively debate. Among most Reformed theologians, the problem is how much of the Mosaic law continues to be authoritative for the new covenant community. Most Reformed scholars have answered: the "moral" law only. Bahnsen and other theonomists answer: the "moral" *and* the "civil" law. My position is, of course, different: I argue that Christians are no longer *directly* subject to any of the Mosaic law, with only those Mosaic commandments that are "reapplied" to Christians being authoritative for us. My response to the thenomists on this point, then, will also be different.

I can agree with the reconstructionists that God desires to remake all of society and not just the individual. (I do not share, however, their optimism about the likelihood of this happening before the return of Christ.) It is surely wrong for the Christian to think "Christianly" about sexual ethics and business morals and not to think "Christianly" about what political philosophy to endorse and what candidate to vote for. Where I disagree with the theonomists is on their insistence that our decisions on such matters ought to be made on the basis of the Mosaic law. Bahnsen and other reconstructionists argue, for instance, that Christians should not support government welfare programs because the Bible does not endorse such a coercive role for the government. Not only, then, are contemporary governments to enforce all the laws found in the Mosaic law; they are wrong to enforce any laws that are *not* found in the Mosaic law.

Of course, this logic is persuasive only if it can be shown that everything God wants government to be is revealed in the Mosaic law; it is the final word. As I have argued, I find this to be a most unlikely reading of the biblical teaching about the Mosaic law and its fulfillment in Christ. The theonomists would have us believe that the Christian who is also a leader in government is to be guided only by the Mosaic law; ethical and moral considerations revealed in the New Testament are to play no part. At this point, it seems to me, theonomists bring in by the back door the kind of Lutheran "two-kingdom" ethics that they seem to deplore. As a private person, I can fulfill Christ's law of love by giving financial assistance to a neighbor; but as a Christian leader, I could not vote to tax rich people so as to give money to poor people—even if my vote to do so would represent the will of my constituents.

My basic problem with theonomy at this point, then, is their assumption that the Mosaic law gives complete and final guidelines for the functioning of human government. Yet this is never taught in either Old or New Testament. Bahnsen and other theonomists again often argue quite generally at this point: Civil government must have clear divine guidance; that guidance can be found only in the Mosaic law; therefore, the Mosaic law must be intended to give such guidance. We may, however, have to live with a situation in which we are not given such clear guidance about the form and function of government. The alternative is not, as theonomists sometimes assert, an unquestioned adherence to secular political theory. The only alternative we have, and one that many thoughtful Christians follow, is to seek divine wisdom in translating the moral teaching of Scripture into the civil realm. That the process is subjective and that we will disagree on many points is clear. But we are not thereby absolved from the task nor should we cease seeking the unity of mind that the Spirit can bring.

Chapter Three

THE LAW AS GOD'S GRACIOUS GUIDANCE FOR THE PROMOTION OF HOLINESS

Walter C. Kaiser, Jr.

THE LAW AS GOD'S GRACIOUS GUIDANCE FOR THE PROMOTION OF HOLINESS

Walter C. Kaiser, Jr.

The classic theme of all truly evangelical theology is the relationship of Law and Gospel. In fact, so critical is a proper statement of this relationship that depicts both a believer's standing in Christ and his or her acting and living, that it can become one of the best ways to test both the greatness and the effectiveness of a truly biblical or evangelical theology.

Indeed, the contrasts between the Law (which many seem to attribute solely to Moses) and the Gospel or grace and truth (which also at times is unfairly limited to the New Testament) seem to be legion. Some describe the relationship between Law and Gospel as one in which the law is no longer obligatory (2 Cor. 3:11; Eph. 2:15; Col. 2:14 are cited as sample proofs). Accordingly, we are delivered both from the law's usefulness, now that the promise has come (cf. Rom. 7:6; Gal. 3:19–25; 4:1–5), and from its dominion (cf. Rom. 6:14; 7:4), because Christ has fulfilled the righteousness of the law in us (Rom. 8:3–4; 10:4). These statements appear to be so definitive for many that there is no need for any further investigation of the issue.

However, such a presentation of the Law's relationship to the Gospel of grace is too absolute, antithetical, and one-sided for a great number of other Pauline passages, let alone the rest of the Bible. Simply ask the apostle Paul the question: "Has grace 'annulled' the law?" He will answer without qualification: "Never!" On the contrary, through faith "we uphold the law" (Rom 3:31). In fact, "removed" was the very word Paul used in 2 Corinthians 3:11 and 14 to speak of the "fading away" of the glory of the "ministry" of Moses and the "removal" of the veil that still persists over the minds of Jews who read the old covenant, even up to the present day.[1] Thus, for Paul, the law (or to speak more accurately, the *tôrâ*) would not "fade away" or be "removed" (or "annulled") by the presence of grace, faith, or the promise. Paul asked the same question in the Galatian correspondence: "Is the law, therefore, opposed to the promises of God? Absolutely not!"(Gal. 3:21a). In other words, any solution that quickly runs the law out of town certainly cannot look to the Scriptures for any kind of comfort or support.

Neither can the law be made the scapegoat for our problem with sin, for the law itself is "holy," "righteous," "good," and "spiritual" (Rom. 7:7, 12–14). The law was never intended as an alternative method of obtaining salvation or righteousness—not even hypothetically.[2] "For if a law had been given that could impart life, then righteousness would certainly have come by the law" (Gal. 3:21). Clearly, then, the law never was intended to be a means by which people could earn eternal life; thus, it never was viewed as being in opposition to the promises and grace of God.

Typical of the muddled thinking that exists on this topic is the atomistic approach that tends to select an array of biblical phrases as a systemic statement on the relationship of Law and Gospel. Such phrases are: "a righteousness from God, apart from law, has been made known" (Rom. 3:21), "So, my brothers, you also died to the law" (7:4), "by dying to what once bound us, we have been released from the law so that we serve in the new way of the Spirit" (7:6a), "we serve . . . not in the old way of the written code" (7:6b), and "Once I was alive apart from law; but when the commandment came, sin sprang to life and I died" (7:9).

The full intent of the apostle's own explanation does not lie more than a few verses away in the very context from which the phrase has been lifted. Thus, Paul's use of "apart from law" in Romans 3:21 is amplified in 3:28 as "apart from the works of the

---

[1]For a more extensive argumentation of this point, see Walter C. Kaiser, Jr. "The Weightier and Lighter Matters of the Law: Moses, Jesus and Paul," in *Current Issues in Biblical Interpretation: Studies in Honor of Merrill C. Tenney Presented by His Former Students*, ed. Gerald F. Hawthorne (Grand Rapids: Eerdmans, 1975), 176–92.

[2]The text that usually is cited as being the basis for a hypothetical offer of salvation in the Old Testament is Leviticus 18:5. For a discussion of the impossibility of this argument, consider Walter C. Kaiser, Jr., "Leviticus 18:5 and Paul: 'Do This and You Shall Live' (Eternally?)," *JETS* 14 (1971), 19–28.

law" (NASB). In fact, even 3:21 itself had gone on to say that this very righteousness of God is witnessed to by the law and the prophets. Clearly, "apart from observing the law" had nothing to do with the Torah God had revealed to Moses.

Likewise, our death to the law and discharge from it in Romans 7:6a is to be linked with the death of Christ for all who believe. Accordingly, 8:1 announces that "there is now no condemnation [which was the curse of the law] for those who are in Christ Jesus." Christ has ended that forever. Furthermore, while redeemed persons no longer served "in the old way of the written code," (7:6b), yet "in [their] mind[s] [they were] slave[s] to God's law" (7:25).

Few things have changed since the day of John Wesley when he gave his series of three sermons on "The Original [sic], Nature, Property, and Use of the Law."[3] Wesley concluded, "Perhaps there are few subjects within the whole compass of religion so little understood as this."[4] More recently, C. E. B. Cranfield came to the same conclusion about the state of modern biblical scholarship and its teaching on the law:

> The need . . . exists today for a thorough re-examination of the place and significance of law in the Bible. . . . The possibility that . . . recent writings reflect a serious degree of muddled thinking and unexamined assumptions with regard to the attitudes of Jesus and St. Paul to the law ought to be reckoned with—and even the further possibility that, behind them, there may be some muddled thinking or, at the least, careless and imprecise statement in this connection in some of the works of serious New Testament scholarship [not to speak of OT scholarship also!] which have helped to mould the opinions of the present generation of ministers and teachers.[5]

THE CHAIR TEACHING PASSAGE[6] ON
A HOMEMADE LAW

One of the more helpful surveys on the various issues and positions held by recent interpreters on the question of Paul,

---

[3]John Wesley, *Sermons: On Several Occasions*, First Series (London: Epworth, 1964), 381–415.

[4]Ibid., 381.

[5]C. E. B. Cranfield, "St. Paul and the Law," *SJT* 17 (1964), 43–44.

[6]The importance of appealing to the *sedes doctrine*, or the so-called "chair passages," for the development of theology, this author argued for in his *Toward an*

Christ, and the law is Brice L. Martin's *Christ and the Law in Paul*.[7] Martin conveniently summarizes the following views on Paul's use of the law: those who saw contradictions in Paul's view on the law (E.P Sanders, Heikki Räisänen); those who saw development in his view (John W. Drane, Hans Hübner, Ulrich Wilchens, Heikki Räisänen, E. P. Sanders, W. D Davies); those who argued that the law was no longer valid for believers (Albert Schweitzer, H. J. Schoeps, Ernest Käsemann, F. F. Bruce, Walter Gutbrod); and those who argued that the law was valid for believers (C. E. B. Cranfield, George E. Howard, C. Thomas Rhyne, Robert Badenas, Ragnar Bring, Hans Conzelmann, George Eldon Ladd, Richard Longenecker, and Hans Hübner). There is such a veritable Babel of voices and positions that one wonders what the waiting and watching church must think and make out of all this confusion on the part of her scholars!

In Paul's thirteen books, he used *nomos* ("law") in only six of them. But in two of those books, it is clear that this concept forms a central theme, for *nomos* occurs 33 times in Galatians and 74 times in Romans.[8] It is fair, then, to concentrate on these two books for our primary understanding of what it is that Paul is trying to get at with this term.

At the heart of Romans, Paul's most systematic statement of soteriology (for who would doubt that the book of Romans is just that?), is his important exposition in 9:30–10:13. If times had been different, we would have preferred to have begun our argument on the law with the Pentateuch.[9] However, most contemporary Christians cannot overcome the impression that the apostle Paul

---

Exegetical Theology (Grand Rapids: Baker, 1981), 134–40, 161–62, and in his article, "Hermeneutics and the Theological Task," *TJ* 12 n.s. (1990), 3–14.

[7]Brice L. Martin, *Christ and the Law in Paul* (Leiden: Brill, 1989). Note particularly his second chapter, 21–68.

[8]Ibid., 3.

[9]See Walter C. Kaiser, Jr., "Images for Today: The Torah Speaks Today," in *The Old Testament and the World: Festschrift for David A. Hubbard*, eds. Robert L. Hubbard, Jr., Robert K. Johnston, and Robert P. Meye (Dallas: Word, forthcoming). Also see Walter C. Kaiser, Jr., "A Single Biblical Ethic in Business," in *Biblical Principles and Business: The Foundations*, ed. Richard C. Chewning (Colorado Springs, Co.: NavPress, 1989), 76–88. Two more essays I have written can be consulted to see how I would have preferred to have begun this article: "The Place of Law and Good Works in Evangelical Christianity," in *A Time to Speak: The Evangelical-Jewish Encounter*, eds. A James Rudin and Marvin R. Wilson (Grand Rapids: Eerdmans, 1987), 120–33; and "James' View of the Law," *Mishkan* 8/9 (1988), 9–12.

taught that we were finished with the law; therefore, it is necessary that we begin with Paul's argument.

In Romans 9:30–10:13 we have one of the clearest expositions of what Paul meant as he used *nomos*. Unfortunately, this text has also been a favorite battleground, for its pivotal text, "Christ is the *telos* of the law" (Rom. 10:4), has become a slogan for the two contrasting ways of regarding how the law is to be viewed. One side concludes that Christ's first coming marked the "termination" of the law, while the other side contends just as vigorously that his coming was the "goal" toward which the whole law was aimed. Only a careful exegesis of the passage can answer which position is correct.

Paul customarily signaled the next stage in his argument in the book of Romans with the repeated phrase, "What then shall we say?" (Rom. 9:30). And the problem he proposed to deal with in 9:30–10:13 was this: How did it happen that the Gentiles attained "righteousness . . . by faith" (*ek pisteōs*) while the Jewish people failed to attain the same righteousness even though they pursued it "by works" (*ek ergōn*)?

Surprisingly enough, the failure of Israel to attain the righteousness of God can be traced to five specific indictments that the apostle charges against his own fellow Jews. They are:

1. Instead of receiving this righteousness of God by faith, Israel "[made] a law [out] of righteousness" (*nomon dikaiosynēs*) (9:31).
2. They pursued righteousness not by faith, "but as if it were by works" (9:32).
3. In contrast to many of the Gentiles, they refused to believe in Christ, the "stone that causes men to stumble and a rock that makes them fall" (9:33; quoted from Isa. 8:14 and 28:16).
4. Even though Paul's fellow Jews were extremely zealous for God, "their zeal [was] not based on knowledge" (10:2).
5. Finally, in place of the righteousness that came from God, all too many Jews had decided "to establish their own" righteousness (10:3).

How could Paul have warned us any more clearly than he did here that not everyone who follows the law, no matter how zealously his or her efforts mount up, is talking about or obeying the same law that God had given to Moses?

One of the most critical decisions to make in this central passage is the meaning of *nomon dikaiosynēs*. Even though most exegetes understand *nomos* in this phrase to refer to the Old

Testament law,[10] neither the context nor the special word order of the Greek phrase will permit such a facile equation. This is only the beginning of troubles in this text—indeed, in the whole problem of relating Law and Gospel. Notice that Paul puts the word *nomon* first in the phrase and then the genitive *dikaiosynēs*. This cannot mean "a law that promises righteousness" or "a law that results [either truly or falsely] in righteousness."[11]

The most serious flaw with most exegetical discussions of this passage, however, is the false connection of *nomon dikaiosynēs* with "the righteousness that is by law" (*tēn dikaiosynēn tēn ek [tou] nomou*) in Rom. 10:5. Not only is the order of the two phrases reversed, but everything that is said about the one type of law (referred to in 9:30) stands over against what is said about the type of law that Moses is commending in two passages from the Pentateuch (Lev. 18:5 and Deut. 30:10–14, both quoted in Rom. 10:5–8).

The context of Romans 9:30–10:13 is clearly contrasting two ways of obtaining righteousness—one that the Gentiles adopted, the way of faith; the other, a works method, that many Israelites adopted—all to no avail! The problem with the righteousness that Israel was advocating was that it was attainable by works and not by faith, without Christ as its object, driven by a zeal that was not backed up by knowledge. It was homemade in every sense of the word and turned in on itself in such a way that righteousness was made into a law rather than the Israelites finding the righteousness that God had intended to come from the law of Moses.

God's righteousness could never have been attained by works. Paul concluded that in Galatians 3:21—"For if a law had been given that could impart life, then righteousness would certainly have come by the law." Therefore, whatever Israel thought they were doing by trying to attain righteousness by working for it, it certainly did not originate with God and his law as described by God's revelation to Moses. A further indication that Israel was off on the wrong footing could be seen in their refusal to believe in the Messiah. If they would only have trusted in the One promised to Eve, the patriarchs, and David, they would not have been put to shame, stumbled, or been made to fall—just as the prophet Isaiah had predicted in 8:14 and 28:16.

---

[10]Martin, *Christ and the Law*, 135.

[11]See the extensive bibliography on these and several other ways of interpreting this phrase in ibid., 135–38 (nn. 36–57).

It is alarming to witness how many contemporary evangelical believers have likewise misunderstood the fact that the *object* of faith in the Old Testament was basically the same as that of the New Testament! While it is generally agreed that the apostle Paul taught in Romans 4 that Abraham and David were justified by faith, there is little understanding about who or what, if anything, the Old Testament saints thought was the *object* of that saving faith. The only sign that something might be out of line has come as modern evangelicals answer the question as to whether the "hidden peoples" of the earth will be saved if they do not believe in Jesus as their personal Savior. All acknowledge that Acts 4:12 teaches that "there is no other name [than the name of the Jesus] under heaven given to men by which we must be saved." However, in spite of the general acquiescence that most will give to this principle, many will go on immediately to say that for those who have never heard of this name, they may cast themselves on the mercy of God and probably experience salvation just as the Old Testament saints did by merely believing in God, even though they did not call upon the name, person, and work of Jesus Christ. Such a conclusion is unwarranted from the text of Scripture.

Even the use of the most famous of all texts that is generally appealed to, Genesis 15:6 ("Abram believed the LORD, and he credited it to him as righteousness"), is appealed to incorrectly to sustain this particular argument since most forget to notice that God has just promised to give the Seed to Abram,[12] which Seed was the line of the Messiah. That was the object, substance, and focal point of Abram's faith; it was not a faith in faith nor the fact that Abram became a theist for the first time as he merely believed in God in general. Thus to argue that remote peoples today may be converted under a more minimalistic set of beliefs—and especially without having Jesus as the definite object of their salvation—is to compound the earlier error of a poor exegesis of Genesis and the Old Testament. No, the Jews must not stumble or trip over the divinely-placed "Stone" or "Rock" that was laid in Zion for them to believe in.

---

[12]For a detailed argument and exegesis of this point, see Walter C. Kaiser, Jr., *Toward Rediscovering the Old Testament* (Grand Rapids: Zondervan, 1987), 121–28. Also see his *The Communicator's Commentary: Micah to Malachi* (Dallas: Word, 1992), in the section on Habakkuk 2:4c; and "Salvation and Atonement: Forgiveness and Saving Faith in the Tenak," in *To the Jew First: The Place of Jewish Evangelism in the On-going Mission of the Church*, ed. James I. Packer (Grand Rapids: Baker, forthcoming).

Israel had another fault: they insisted on establishing their own righteousness rather than using the righteousness that had already been described by Moses under God in the Torah. If this contrast does not speak of two "laws" that are about as antithetical to each other as laws can be, then language has no more normative qualities to it, and we are left without any valid way of communicating with each other, much less having a way for God to address us.

It is serious enough to miss the point that a homemade law of righteousness is not equivalent to the righteousness that is from the law of God. But when a sharp antithesis is placed between Romans 10:5 and 10:6–8, it is clear that the exegete must either opt for the fact that Moses (and consequently God, the revealer of the word) contradicted himself, or that the Torah actually described the righteousness that comes from the law in two ways that stand at odds with each other. However, this sharp antithesis cannot be sustained either from the grammatical *gar . . . de* construction or from the Old Testament contexts from which both of these texts originate.

"Moses describes" (Rom. 10:5) does not introduce a contrasting set of citations (as if the translation should be: "for . . . but"), but a coordinating set of citations: "for . . . and." The fact is, as George E. Howard so clearly pointed out,[13] that *gar . . . de* does not mean "for . . . but," but as Romans 7:8–9; 10:10; 11:15–16, and Wisdom of Solomon 6:17ff show, it means "for . . . and." For example, "believing" in Romans 10:10 does not involve placing believing with the heart against believing with the mouth; instead, it is "*and* with the mouth." In the same way, verse 5 is connected with verses 6–8.

Associated with this error is a similar one that views Romans 10:5 and its citation of Leviticus 18:5 as urging perfection and the obtaining of eternal life by means of some type of deeds or works. But this view fails to consider the following:

1. The translation of Romans 10:5 that understands "the man who does these things will live *by them*" (italics ours) in an instrumental mode should be replaced by a locative

---

[13]George E. Howard, "Christ the End of the Law: The Meaning of Romans 10:4ff," *JBL* 88 (1969), 331–32.

concept that says, "the man who does these things shall
live *in the sphere of them*."[14]

2. The context from which this passage comes in Leviticus 18
   begins and ends (vv. 1, 30) with the theological
   affirmation, "I am the LORD your God." Thus, this citation
   in verse 5 does not address the matter of how one might
   earn his or her salvation; instead, it deals with Israel's
   sanctification—the grand evidence that the Lord they
   claimed as their Lord was indeed just that.

3. In the context of Leviticus 18, the customs of the pagans
   were contrasted with the happy privilege that Israel had of
   perpetuating a life already begun by their continuing to do
   the law. This is similar, then, to John 10:10—"I have come
   that they may have life, and have it to the full."[15]

In what sense, then, is Christ the *telos* of the law (Rom. 10:4)?
Paul uses *telos* thirteen times in his letters. In general, the
medieval and Reformation church understood Greek *telos* (and
Latin *finis*) either in a perfective/completive sense or a teleological
sense, but it did not choose to give the meaning of Romans 10:4 a
temporal/terminal sense. "Erasmus, Calvin, and Bucer took it in a
perfective sense, while Luther, Melanchthon, and Beza took it in a
teleological sense."[16] However, the Anabaptists (who tended to
see the New Testament as superseding the Old Testament), later
Lutherans (who applied some of Luther's negative views on the
law from other contexts than Rom. 10:4), eighteenth-century
interpreters (with their lower views on Scripture), and nineteenth-
century liberals all tended to view *telos* in Romans 10:4 as an
abrogation and termination of the law for the Christian.

The debate here cannot, and should not, be settled by an
appeal to a word study of the thirteen uses of *telos* in Paul. Much
greater significance should be placed on the context with its

---

[14]See J. Oliver Buswell, *A Theology of the Christian Religion* (Grand Rapids:
Zondervan, 1963), 1:313. Buswell summarized his study of this word by saying,
"The words, *en autē*, [Rom. 10:5] and the corresponding words in Galatians 3: 12,
en autois, where the same Old Testament passage [Lev. 18:5] is quoted, should not
be construed as instrumental, but locative, indicating the sphere or horizon of the
life of a godly man. . . . Moses is obviously describing not the means of attaining
eternal life, but the horizon within which an earthly godly life ought to be lived."

[15]For a more extensive set of arguments, see Kaiser's "Leviticus 18:5 and
Paul."

[16]Brice L. Martin, *Christ and the Law in Paul*, 129, citing Robert Badenas, "Christ
the End of the Law: Romans 10:4," in *Pauline Perspective*, JSNTSup (Sheffield: JSNT,
1985), 6–38.

affirmation that "Christ is the *telos* of the law for everyone who believes [*eis dikaiosynēn panti tō pisteuonti*]." That phrase is extremely close to the ones in Romans 10:6, *dikaiosynēn de tēn ek pisteōs* (lit. "and the righteousness that is by faith"), and Romans 10:10, *pisteuetai eis dikaiosynēn* ("you believe unto righteousness"). Clearly, the righteousness being talked about in these contexts is the one that comes by faith, by believing; it is the opposite of appealing to homemade righteousness and of using works to establish it!

That former type of righteousness is what the Jewish people have been missing all along: Christ was the single object of focus for those who were believing. The Gentiles seized on this method of obtaining righteousness even while Israel continued to miss the point. Meanwhile, Paul asserts explicitly, the identical point about this very same righteousness was made by Moses in the Torah: "Moses describes in this way the righteousness that is by the law" (Rom. 10:5). But Martin is most insistent that "it is fallacious to argue that since 'righteousness by faith' in 10:6–8 is actually taken from the law itself (Deut. [30:12–14]) then Christ must be the fulfillment of the Torah in 10:4. Räisänen points out that for the author of Hebrews the old covenant is superseded, yet he bases his argument on the OT."[17] But this type of argumentation allows us to see just what is being confused here. The writer to the Hebrews clearly shows that what he saw as being abrogated from the first covenant were the ceremonies and rituals—the very items that had a built-in warning from God to Moses from the first day they were revealed to him. Had not God warned Moses that what he gave him in Exodus 25–40 and Leviticus 1–27 was according to the "pattern" he had shown him on the mountain (e.g., Ex. 25:40)? This meant that the real remained somewhere else (presumably in heaven) while Moses instituted a "model," "shadow," or "imitation" of what is real until that reality came!

The net result cannot be that for the writer of the Hebrews, the whole old covenant or the whole Torah had been superseded. Thus, it is persuasive that the very righteousness being debated can be substantiated in the Torah of Moses—and it was this Moses and this law that described the righteousness that Paul was urging that his Jewish compatriots now adopt. It was the same righteousness that found its purposeful completion and perfection

---

[17]Brice L. Martin, *Christ and the Law*, 139. Martin is using the argument of Heikki Räisänen, *Paul and the Law* (Tübingen: Mohr, 1983), 55.

in the Messiah, who was the object of faith offered to sinners during the days of the old covenant.

Nor will it help interpreters to dodge this Torah source for the kind of faith-righteousness that is being advocated here by concluding, as Martin did, that "in Rom 10:6–8 Paul gives a pesher-like Christian interpretation to Deut 30:11–14, an interpretation facilitated by the association of this passage with wisdom in ancient Judaism."[18] The parenthetical material in Romans 10:6–8 was not meant to add an altogether new form of theology to the passage in Deuteronomy, as if Paul were attempting to bring new relevancies into the text that were not part of the ancient meaning. Instead, both Moses and Paul are in basic agreement that the life being offered to Israel, both in those olden days and now in the Christian era, was available and close at hand; in fact, it was so near them that it was in their mouth and in their heart. There is no use trying to make a search of heaven or crossing over the oceans in order to obtain it. Why not confess with their mouths and believe in their hearts in the Messiah?

What is more, note that in Deuteronomy 30:16 there are two commands that must not be confused or reversed in sequence: first, the command to love God, and then the command to keep all his commandments! Thus, in the very context that Paul appeals to, a carefully enunciated line of demarcation is set forth between believing the way God has offered for people to come and choosing death and destruction by turning away in their hearts from God (Deut. 30:6, 15, 17). Paul only makes more explicit what Moses had affirmed and implied.

The main point should not be overlooked: The word that had been as near as the mouth and heart of every Israelite in Moses' day was "the word of faith [Paul was] proclaiming" (Rom 10:8b). How could the connection have been any more clearly indicated? What will it take for modern Christians to see that Moses, in the same way that the apostle Paul advocated, wanted Israel to "believe unto righteousness" (Rom. 10:10; cf. Deut. 30:14). The fact that Moses uses the word "obey" in Deuteronomy 30:14 when he urged: "No, the word is very near you; it is in your mouth and

---

[18]Brice L. Martin, *Christ and the Law*, 140. This view is featured in M. Jack Suggs, "The Word Is Near You: Romans 10:6–10 within the Purpose of the Letter," in *Christian History and Interpretation: Studies Presented to John Knox*, eds. W. R. Farmer, C. F. D. Moule, and R. R. Neibuhr (Cambridge: Cambridge University Press, 1967), 289–319.

in your heart so you may obey it" is no more damaging to our case than is the fact that John 3:36 uses the same word "obey" in parallelism with "believe."

The term *telos* in Romans 10:4 means "goal" or purposeful conclusion. The law cannot be properly understood unless it moves toward the grand goal of pointing the believer toward the Messiah, Christ. The law remains God's law, not Moses' law (Rom. 7:22; 8:7). It still is holy, just, good, and spiritual (Rom. 7:12,14) for the Israelite as well for the believing Gentile.

COMMON MISCONCEPTIONS ABOUT THE LAW

There are some misconceptions concerning the law that are often marshaled in opposition to the Christian use of the law as just described.

The Law as an Individual Unity

That the law must be viewed as a single unity is one of the most common of all objections made against any Christian use of the law.[19] The attempt to claim any distinctions in the law, it is strenuously argued, is wrongheaded and will result in certain error. Thus, if one agrees that Christ set aside the ceremonial law by his substitutionary death and resurrection, then Christians are

---

[19]H. A. W. Meyer wrote: "In *nomos*, however, to think merely of the moral law is erroneous; and the distinction between the ritualistic, civil, and moral law is modern" ("Matthew" in *Commentary on the New Testament* [New York: Funk and Wagnalls, 1884], 1:120). Similarly, A. S. Peake ("Colossians," in *The Expositor's Greek Testament* [Grand Rapids: Eerdmans, 1967], 3:527) commented, "But this distinction between the moral and ceremonial Law has no meaning in Paul. The Law is a unity and is done away as a whole." Cf. similarly A. J. McClain, *Law and Grace* (Chicago: Moody, 1954), 10–12. D. J. Moo (" 'Law,' 'Works of the Law,' and Legalism in Paul," *WTJ* 45 [1983], 84) affirmed that "*nomos* is basically for Paul a single indivisible whole. . . . Paul's argument prohibits a neat distinction of moral and ceremonial law." A year later, however, Moo wrote: "While it is true that a theoretical distinction [between the moral and ceremonial law] . . . was not made, there emerges, for instance in Philo and at Qumran, a *practical* differentiation of this nature. Jesus' appropriation of the prophetic emphasis on the need for *inner* obedience, his comment about 'the weightier matters,' the elevation of the love command . . . all suggest that he may have operated with a similar distinction. . . . It is not illegitimate to find the seeds of this kind of distinction in passages such as Mark 7:1–23" ("Jesus and the Authority of the Mosaic Law," *JSNT* 20 [1984], 15, italics his). See the argument in Walter C. Kaiser, Jr., "God's Promise Plan and His Gracious Law," *JETS* 33 (1990), 289–302.

thereby excused from the entirety of the law, since it is an indivisible unity.

Arguments for this all-or-nothing case usually appeal to three texts: (1) "For whoever keeps the whole law and yet stumbles at just one point is guilty of breaking all of it" (James 2:10); (2) "Again I declare to every man who lets himself be circumcised that he is obligated to obey the whole law" (Gal. 5:3); and (3) "Anyone who breaks one of the least of these commandments and teaches others to do the same will be called least in the kingdom of heaven" (Matt. 5:19). The point usually made for all three of these texts is that "all" means every law, not just the moral, civil, or ceremonial law. Either one observes every precept of the *tôrâ* or none: one must not pick and choose.

But the argument advanced here proves too much—even for its most zealous advocate. The argument that the *tôrâ* is a unity can be used against this position, for the same law of Moses that gave us the legal aspects of that revelation also contains the promise made to the patriarchs. Would this mean that it is impossible to separate out the promise since there is no internal principle noted in the text of the *tôrâ* that advises us how to do this?

Furthermore, why would God want to take this same *tôrâ* and place it on the hearts of all who believe in the new covenant (Jer. 31:33)? If the fulfillment of a part of the law, namely, its ceremonial part, removes the necessity of keeping any other part of it, why resurrect the thing for the new covenant? Surely, it is the same "law" God revealed to Moses that is to be put on the hearts of those in the new covenant. How, then, can it be successfully argued that law has now expired and served its time?

It can be agreed, of course, that the law does exhibit a certain unity and that it functions as a single piece. It is also true that the Bible does not explicitly classify laws according to the scheme of civil, ceremonial, and moral laws. But neither does the Bible categorize itself according to most of our topics in systematic theology. The word "Trinity," for example, never appears in the Bible, yet few would argue that it is thereby an improper conclusion! The question, rather, must be this: Is this categorization fair to the biblical text?

On that point there is a large body of teaching. Assigning priority to the moral aspect of the law over both its civil and ceremonial aspects can be observed in a plethora of passages found in the prophets. One need only consult such texts as 1 Samuel 15:22–23; Isaiah 1:11–17; Jeremiah 7:21–23; Micah 6:8, as well as texts in the Psalter such as Psalms 51:16–17. The moral law of God took precedence over the civil and ceremonial laws in that it was based on the character of God. The civil and ceremonial laws functioned only as further illustrations of the moral law. That is why holiness and love could serve as veritable summaries of all that the law demanded.

The Hypothetical Offer of Eternal Life in the Law

The second misconception is the one that claims that the law hypothetically offered eternal life to all who obeyed it. "Hypothetically," wrote Alva J. McClain, "the law could give [eternal] life if men kept it."[20] This charge has been repeated so often that many have come to adopt it as the gospel-truth. Such a conclusion, however, is in no way fair to the texts themselves. Nor does it match what the New Testament concluded, for Paul taught the reverse in Galatians 3:21—"Is the law, therefore, opposed to the promises of God? Absolutely not! *For if a law had been given that could impart life*, then righteousness would certainly have come by the law" (emphasis ours).

The so-called legalistic "if" of Exodus 19:8 and 23: 3, 7 is no more conditional for salvation than the same conditions and commands given to Abraham, such as: "Leave your country" (Gen.12:1); "Walk before me and be blameless" (17:1); "Keep the way of the LORD by doing what is right and just" (18:19). In fact, such commands are in the same category as those given to contemporary believers, such as: "If you love me [note: the same so-called legalistic 'if'], you will obey what I command" (John 14:15); "If you obey my commands, you will remain in my love" (15:10); and "If you want to enter life, obey the commandments" (Matt. 19:17). Hence, the unconditional covenant offered to Abraham and the gracious salvation offered to us today contain

---

[20]Alva J. McClain, *Law and Grace* (Chicago: Moody, 1954), 17. McClain appealed to Leviticus 18:5; Ezekiel 20:11, 13, 21; Matthew 19:17b; and Romans 10:5 to substantiate this claim. The Scofield Reference Bible (1945), page 20, note 1, contends that Israel spoke "rashly" when they pledged in Exodus 19:8; 24:3, 7 the following: "We will do everything the LORD has said." Scofield taught that Israel moved from "believing" to "doing" as the basis for her spiritual life. He failed to put these verses together with our Lord's assessment of the situation in Deuteronomy 5:28–29: "Oh, that their hearts would be inclined to fear me and to keep my commands always, so that it might go well with them and with their children forever!" That does not sound as if the Lord thought Israel had spoken "rashly" or as if they had gone off a faith standard for their salvation on to a works basis—a sort of divine plan B!!

the same commands and warnings that were found in the Mosaic law!

The conditionality taught in these texts does not relate to the promise of eternal life or salvation taught in either the Old or New Testament. Instead, the conditions relate to the quality of life lived in the promise and the joy of participating in all the benefits of that promise. Surely, Andrew A. Bonar's interpretation of Leviticus 18:5, while being very representative of the kind of misinterpretation that that text has received over the years, was exactly the opposite of what the author's intention was, as judged by that context and a biblical theology of Torah in the Pentateuch. Bonar incorrectly taught:

> But if, as most think, we are to take in this place the words, *"live in them"* as meaning "eternal life to be got by them," the scope of the passage is that so excellent are God's laws, and every special minute detail of these laws, *that if a man were to keep these always and perfectly*, this keeping would be eternal life to him. And the quotations in Rom x. 5, and Gal iii. 12, would seem to determine this to be the true and only sense here.[21]

This view can be faulted on at least three crucial grounds: (1) "these things" (which Israel was to do) in Leviticus 18:5 are the statutes of the Lord placed in contrast to the customs and practices of the Canaanites and the Egyptians; (2) the passage in Leviticus 18 is framed with the theological setting of the first and last verses, addressed to those who know that "I am the LORD your God"; and (3) one of the ways of "doing" the law was to recognize that that same law made provisions for those who failed to keep the law in that it provided for sacrifices and the forgiveness of one's sins.

A much safer guide here for understanding these texts that seem on a prima facia reading to teach a hypothetical offer of salvation by works is that of Patrick Fairbairn:

> Neither Moses nor Ezekiel, it is obvious, meant that the life spoken of, which comprehends whatever is really excellent and good, was to be acquired by means of such conformity to the enactments of heaven; for life in that sense already was theirs. . . . Doing these things, they lived in them; because life

---

[21]Andrew A. Bonar, *A Commentary on Leviticus* (London: Banner of Truth, 1966; reprint of 1846), 329–30 (emphasis his). C. L. Feinberg in *The Prophecy of Ezekiel* (Chicago: Moody, 1969), 110, had a similar conclusion: "Obedience would have brought life physically and spiritually, temporally and eternally."

thus had its due exercise and nourishment and was in a condition to enjoy the manifold privileges and blessings secured in the covenant. And the very same may be said of the precepts and ordinances of the gospel: a man lives after the higher life of faith only insofar as he walks in conformity with these; for though he gets life by a simple act of faith in Christ, he cannot exercise, maintain and enjoy it but in connection with the institutions and requirements of the gospel.[22]

All who believed in the Old Testament trusted in the Man of Promise who was to come. Had this not been the method by which men and women were saved during the Mosaic era, the writer of Hebrews could not have claimed that the same gospel that had been preached to us was the gospel that had also been preached to those who died in the wilderness (Heb. 4:2). The problem with those rebellious Israelites in the desert was not that they had refused to utilize God's hypothetical plan of earning their salvation; no, it was that they had failed to believe the gospel! Their works would only have been the proof of the reality of their claim that they had indeed trusted in the Man of Promise who was to come.

TOWARD A THEOLOGY OF TORAH

The root of all our problems of relating Law to Gospel may be traced back, in large measure, to our rendering Hebrew *tôrâ* by *nomos* in the Greek Septuagint and the New Testament, not to mention English *law*, French *loi*, and German *Gesetz*. Unfortunately, all of these renderings convey the impression that the Pentateuch is that portion of Scripture that contains formal regulations, ritual associations, and strict codes that had to be followed on pain of death! Perhaps it was this incorrect conclusion that led to the misguided inference that legal instruction had now been replaced by the gracious promise of God's gospel.

However, *tôrâ* is much more than mere law.[23] Even the word itself does not indicate static requirements that govern the whole of human experience. Instead, *tôrâ* probably comes from the Hebrew verb *yārâ*, meaning "to throw or shoot." In the Hiphil

---

[22]Patrick Fairbairn, *An Exposition of Ezekiel* (Evansville, Ind.: Sovereign Grace: 1960), 215–16 (emphasis his).

[23]Also see James Tunstead Burtchaell, "Is the Torah Obsolete for Christians?" in *Justice and the Holy: Essays in Honor of Walter Harrelson*, eds. Douglas A. Knight and Peter J. Paris (Atlanta: Scholars Press, 1989), 113–27.

stem, it takes on the meaning of "to teach, to point out [the] direction." Thus, Exodus 24:12 used the noun form of this verb in connection with *tôrâ*: "The LORD said to Moses, 'Come up to me on the mountain and stay here, and I will give you the tables of stone, with the law [*tôrâ*] and commands [*miṣwâ*] I have written for their [teaching, or] instruction [*lehôrotām*, from *yarâ*]." Other passages that clearly indicate that *tôrâ* was not meant merely for legal purposes include: "Act according to the law [*tôrâ*] they teach you [*yôrûkā*] and the decisions they give you. Do not turn aside from what they tell you, to the right or to the left" (Deut. 17:11); "Do exactly as the priests . . . instruct you [*yôrû*]" (Deut. 24:8); and, "In the last days . . . many peoples will come and say, 'Come, let us go up to the mountain of the LORD, to the house of the God of Jacob. He will teach us [*yôrēnû*] his ways, so that we may walk in his paths.' The law [*tôrâ*] will go out of Zion, the word of the LORD from Jerusalem" (Isa. 2:2–3). Especially significant is this last passage, which also links the *tôrâ* with "teaching and instruction" rather than legal hoops and hurdles. But it also pictures the Messianic age as one in which the Mosaic law will be taught and regarded as the word of the Lord. And its purpose will not be mere legal performance, but it will serve as a means of giving direction and guidance to the people so that they may walk according to the will of God. The meaning of *tôrâ*, then, is directional teaching or guidance for walking on the path of life.

The Pentateuch itself cannot be explained away as a legalistic document, for as Hans-Christoph Schmitt has argued in his redactional structuring of the Pentateuch, the most characteristic feature in the redactional seams of this five-volume book is the consistent use of the word for "faith" or "believe" [*he'amên be*] at the critical transitional points between sections within the whole corpus.[24] The key texts of that redaction are: Genesis 15:6, "Abram believed the LORD, and he credited it to him as righteousness"; Exodus 4:5, "so that they may believe that the LORD, the God of their fathers . . . has appeared to you"; Exodus 14:31, "the people

---

[24]Hans-Christoph Schmitt, "Redaktion des Pentateuch im Geiste der Prophetie," *VT* 32 (1982), 170–89. For a slightly different conclusion, based on much the same data as Schmitt raises, see John H. Sailhamer, "The Mosaic Law and the Theology of the Pentateuch," *WTJ* 53 (1991), 241–61. I am indebted to my colleague, John Sailhamer, for calling to my attention Schmitt's article. For one of the most stimulating articles on these matters, see Joseph P. Braswell, " 'The Blessing of Abraham' versus 'The Curse of the Law': Another Look at Gal 3:10–13," *WTJ* 53 (1991), 73–91.

. . . put their trust in [the LORD] and in Moses his servant"; Numbers 14:11, "How long will these people . . . refuse to believe in me?" and Numbers 20:12, "the LORD said to Moses and Aaron, 'Because you did not trust in me. . . .'" One could also add Genesis 45:26 and Deuteronomy 1:32 and 9:23.

The significance of these texts on belief and faith at the crucial seams in the Pentateuch is that believing and faith are at the heart of the *tôrâ*. Even more interesting is the fact that in each of these texts, believing is linked with the concept of *keeping God's tôrâ*. Conversely, where faith and belief are absent, they lead to rebellion against God's law. Therefore, if one does not have faith, even a meticulous observance of all the commandments will avail little—as far as salvation is concerned!

The strategy of the Pentateuch, then, revolves around a crucial hermeneutic. The theology of belief and faith was meant to inform the theology of commands and statutes. To reverse these theologies violates the belief structure that appears to govern the whole organization and flow of the materials in the first five books of the Bible. It leads one to locate the law in another context and causes puzzlement about how or why the Savior would ever want to reintroduce *tôrâ* during the Messianic era of the "last days" or in the times of the new covenant. In summary, law is not the nucleus of the Torah; covenant-faith is the nuclear and guiding concept that must take priority if one is to follow and obey the directions and teachings of the law successfully.

BEGINNING WITH THE WEIGHTIER MATTERS OF THE LAW

It appears that the old stalemate over law and grace is about to break loose. Now that dispensationalism has decided to hold no longer that there are two new covenants, one for Israel and one for the church, it is possible to show that the law has a very definite role to play in the life of the church.[25]

---

[25]As recently as 1953, John F. Walvoord could say, "The concept of two new covenants is a better analysis of the problem" ("The New Covenant with Israel," *BSac* 110 [1953], 204). However, ever since about 1965, that view has quietly been undergoing a change in dispensational circles. Shortly thereafter, Robert L. Saucy boldly asserted, "The Scriptures, however, do not reveal a separate new covenant [for the Church]" (*The Church in God's Program* [Chicago: Moody, 1972], 78). He continued: "Although the Old Testament references to the new covenant were for the nation of Israel, the members of the church also share in its provisions" (p. 80).

But the most amazing results are now possible. For one thing, the new covenant unquestionably includes the Mosaic law as part of God's special work on the hearts of believers. Bruce Waltke said it best:

> Jeremiah unmistakably shows [the new covenant's] continuity with the provisions of the old law. . . . The "law" in view here is unquestionably the Mosaic treaty. It is summarized by the expression, "Know YHWH." . . . In short, the new covenant assumes the content of the old Mosaic treaty. But its [new] form is like that of YHWH's grants to Abraham and David. Unlike the Mosaic treaty that rested on Israel's willingness to keep it [a fact I have disputed already in this chapter], YHWH will unilaterally put his law in Israel's heart.[26]

Therefore, in one way or another, the believing community must face the fact that we are not finished with the *tôrâ* that God gave to Moses. Of course it is true that Christ fulfilled the ceremonial aspects of the law, but it cannot be shown that this has in effect removed the law from any believer's life of obedience, any more than our trust in Christ has freed us from the requirement to keep our Lord's commandments if we love him (John 14:15).

However, the law is not a monolithic unity. All too many Christians unwittingly appeal to Hebrews, to Ephesians 2:15, and to Colossians 2:14–15 in order to defend their view that Christ's fulfillment of the ceremonial law has terminated the need for Christians to keep *any* of it. This process, however, solves the problem by imposing categories and definitions external to the text rather than demonstrating the issue from within the text.

The best authority one could cite for teaching that there was a distinction within the law itself is our Lord. In Matthew 23:23, the Lord taught us to distinguish between the weightier and lighter matters of the law and referred to greater and lesser commandments. If the law were such a monolithic unity, how is our Lord himself able to require of us something that our definitions tell us is impossible?

In arguing for a ranking or weighing of the law, we do not mean to imply that we agree with the view know as "Hierarchial

---

[26]Bruce K. Waltke, "The Phenomenon of Conditionality Within the Unconditional Covenants," in *Israel's Apostasy and Restoration: Essays in Honor of Roland K. Harrison*, ed. A. Gileadi (Grand Rapids: Baker, 1988), 136–37.

Ethics."[27] The major problem with this view is its argument that when a Christian is faced with a genuine moral conflict of two absolutes, it is incumbent on the believer only to follow the higher moral demand; there is an automatic exemption from any responsibility to keep the lower norm. However, as Erwin Lutzer pointed out, the problem with hierarchicalism is that these moral absolutes reflect the character of God. How, for example, could a Christian lie (presuming that this was a lower norm in a life-threatening situation) and thereby reflect the character of God as truth?[28] Hierarchicalism should be advised to follow the critique offered by C. Gordon Olson:

> My first and main contribution to the discussion is to suggest that rather than seeing a continuous graded hierarchy of absolute norms, Geisler would have done better to divide ethical norms into two main categories: absolute norms which are grounded in the character of God, and limited norms, which derive their force from some secondary, indirect basis. It seems to me that all the examples of Geisler's exemption principle have to do with conflict between these two kinds of norms.[29]

Oddly enough, it seems that the unified character of all the laws in the Pentateuch is confidently based on the fact that late Jewish tradition said that the law consisted of 613 statutes: 365 prohibitions (one for each day of the year) and 248 positive commands (one for each member of the body).[30] These 613 laws were further grouped into two sets of twelve different categories: twelve positive families and twelve negative families. The earliest record we have of such distinctions is that of Rabbi Shem'on ben Azzai, who referred to the 365 prohibitions around A.D. 110, and Rabbi Shim'on ben Eleazar, who seems to be the first to refer to

---

[27]This view was set forth by Norman Geisler in his *Ethics: Alternatives and Issues* (Grand Rapids: Zondervan, 1971); *The Christian Ethic of Love* (Grand Rapids: Zondervan, 1973); and *Options in Contemporary Christian Ethics* (Grand Rapids: Baker, 1981).

[28]Erwin W. Lutzer, *The Morality Gap* (Chicago: Moody, 1972).

[29]C. Gordon Olson, "Norman Geisler's Hierarchical Ethics Revisited," *EJ* 4 (1986), 4. See also the unpublished paper by Robert V. Rakestraw, "Graded Absolutism: An Analysis of Norman Geisler's Ethics" (Drew University Research Paper, 1980), and William F. Luck, "Moral Conflicts and Evangelical Ethics: A Second Look at the Salvaging Operations," *GRJ* 8 (1987), 19–34.

[30]See a listing of these in John H. Sailhamer, *The Pentateuch as Narrative* (Grand Rapids: Zondervan, 1992), 481–516.

the number of 613 laws in A.D. 190.[31] Thus, anyone who says that if Christians obey any part of the law, they are obligated to keep all 613 laws, it is clear that they have confused the later Jewish traditional construction of the law with the Mosaic Torah.

The foundation of the law in the Old Testament is that it proceeds from God. Next is the corollary that the basis for all obligation to obey the law is the redemption and deliverance of God for his people. Did not the Decalogue begin in the environment of grace and redemption by saying, "I am the LORD your God, who brought you out of Egypt, out of the land of slavery" (Ex. 20:2)? A third factor is laid in the example of our Lord when he said: "Be holy because I, the LORD your God, am holy" (Lev. 19:2; cf. 11:44–45).

These three facts point to the priority and the precedent-setting nature of the moral law, which stems from the character and nature of God. Since God's character will never change, the moral law based on it is as abiding and as absolute as the very attributes, qualities, and nature of God himself.

The remaining aspects of the Mosaic laws, whether they be civil or ceremonial laws, are but illustrations, applications, or situationally-specific implementations of that same permanent moral law. This point can be seen, for example, in the theological and religious motive clauses that were supplied for most types of law throughout the Old Testament.[32] These clauses plead God's holy character, his nature, and his salvific acts on behalf of his people as a motivation for their observing the law. Indeed, the very structure of the whole book of Deuteronomy follows the contents of the Decalogue, in order, from Deuteronomy 5–26.[33]

This same recognition of the priority of the moral law as an interpretive base for understanding all laws of God can be seen in the former and latter prophets, not to mention the psalmists. In

---

[31]W. Grundmann, "μεγας," *TDNT*, 4.535 (n. 31). Grundmann does go on to add, "but both [Rabbis] assume that they [the 365 and the 613 laws] are already known; cf. Str. -B., I, 900."

[32]First pointed out by B. Gemser, "The Importance of Motive Clauses in the Old Testament," in VTSup 1 (1953), 50–66; especially 57–61.

[33]First pointed out by Stephen A. Kaufman, "The Structure of the Deuteronomic Law," *MAARAV* 1/2 (1978–79), 107. See also Walter C. Kaiser, Jr., "The Law of Deuteronomy," in *Toward Old Testament Ethics* (Grand Rapids: Zondervan, 1983), 127–37. Also see the convenient tables and discussion of James B. Jordan, *The Law of the Covenant* (Tyler, Tex.: Institute for Christian Economics, 1984), 199–206. Jordan also correlates the Ten Commandments with the civil laws of the covenant code of Exodus 21–23.

fact, Micah 6:6–8 introduced the very same question as Deuteronomy 10:12: "And now, Israel, what does the LORD your God ask of you?" The answer was the same: justice, mercy, and a genuine heart relationship—these were God's own prerequisites to obeying his laws. That was what Samuel had to teach Saul in 1 Samuel 15:22 and what David had to learn all over again in Psalm 51:16–19; that is, an obedient heart took precedence over all forms of ritual and offering. Moreover, the prophets never wearied of rebuking their listeners for a religious sterility presented as a substitute for the moral norms that God wished to see as the bases for any further acts of worship and dedication. Many texts demonstrate this principle: Isaiah 1:11–18; Jeremiah 7:21–24; Hosea 6:6; Amos 5:21–24; 7:21–23; and Micah 6:6–8.

CONCLUSION

It is the moral law of God found in the Decalogue and the Holiness Code of Leviticus 18–19 that must act as the absolute norms against which all other commands in God's law are judged, interpreted, and applied to today. The hunger for someone to give the believing community instruction in the proper use of law is so great that one popular seminar since 1968, focusing on Proverbs (a veritable republication of the law of God in proverbial form, as can be seen from the marginal references to Exodus, Numbers, and Deuteronomy), has literally had tens of thousands of people swarming to its sessions in every major city in North America and now all over the world.[34] This is an indictment on the church and its reticence to preach the moral law of God and to apply it to all aspects of life as indicated in Scripture.

The case for a single, monolithic law that refuses to recognize Jesus' ranking the moral law above all other laws as being of greater weight, significance, and importance must now be scrapped. Indeed, the claim that the law of the Lord, in all its parts, has now ceased to be valid because of Christ's perfect fulfillment of the ceremonial part of the law (of what is curiously claimed to be an indivisible law) must itself also be abandoned in light of the teaching of Moses, Jesus, and Paul.

Instead, what is needed now is a reading of and a response to the law of the Lord—just as it was needed in the day of Moses! We must turn to the Lord and ask that the veil over our eyes be lifted (2 Cor. 3:14–16); otherwise, when Moses is read, there will

---

[34]In the Basic Youth Conflicts seminars.

still be a mere "letter" (*gramma*) reading of the law, which, according to Romans 2:27, is a felony before God. However, when the law is read and observed with the proper priorities, there is no more bondage to the "letter," but great liberty in the word of the Lord (2 Cor. 3:17), even the perfect law of liberty (James 1:25; 2:12).[35]

---

[35]For a discussion of *gramma* and an exegesis of 2 Corinthians 3 that goes counter to much popular misunderstanding of these texts, see Walter C. Kaiser, Jr., "The Weightier and Lighter Matters of the Law." For a discussion on how modern readers of the Torah are to apply the ancient text to current questions, see the same author's article, "A Single Biblical Ethic in Business," 84–88. There we discuss the methods of analogy and middle axioms (both of which we reject), and general equity and the method of the ladder of abstraction (both of which we urge as having great benefit for the church).

Response to Walter C. Kaiser, Jr.

Willem A. VanGemeren

The discussion of the place of the law in the Bible is properly broadened by Walter Kaiser. The law is not merely a negative statement or burden. All too many dismiss the law, and while speaking about the freedom of the Christian, invent or submit to a new legalism. The law is God's instruction in righteousness. Its place in Christian growth is vital, but like any support structure it has strengths and weaknesses. Kaiser sensitively and deliberately points out that the weaknesses and the strengths of the law lie in the use and abuse humans make of it. They may use the law for the purpose of obtaining righteousness with God (Gal. 3:21); they may assume that they can merit eternal life by keeping the law; they may keep the law separate from Christ. Any of these three positions misses the point: Christ is the *focus* of the law. He is the object of our faith, the source of all righteousness, and the giver of eternal life (3:4).

I cannot but express my wholehearted accord with Kaiser's conclusion that the law is God's law and that it is just, holy, and spiritual. In the Old Testament, the Lord expected faith in him and love for him as the ground for keeping the law (Deut. 30:16). The Lord Jesus expects no less from his followers.

Kaiser's interpretation of the New Testament data is supported by an exegesis of the Old Testament texts. His attention to the evidence in both Old and New Testaments demonstrates his commitment to *tota Scriptura*. The argument is straightforward. First, the place of the law in the new covenant was prophesied by the prophets and confirmed by the Lord Jesus and his apostles

(John 14:15). Second, the moral law has a priority over the civil and ceremonial laws as it reflects the character of God, is the word of God, and is the proper expression of gratitude for one's salvation. Third, the teaching that no one can please God without faith applies to both the saints before Christ and after his coming. Fourth, the prophets and the Lord Jesus confirm the hermeneutic of "the weightier things" of the law, according to which God gave his law to guide the godly on the way of godliness, even in the application of the ceremonial and civil laws.

In concurring with Kaiser's presentation of the law, I would develop the place of the law in two other directions. First, the Decalogue is a summary of the Father's *will* by which he instructs and disciplines his children. In view of the *anthropocentric perspective* (selfishness, narcissism) of our generation, Christian ethics offers a *theocentric perspective*.[1] The former perspective raises the question of relevance and personal meaning in the pursuit of morality.[2] Salvation in the biblical sense is a corrective to mere morality. By nature people want to be free in choosing principles of morality, but God calls on his children to serve him. Left to themselves, humans fall short of reflecting God's perfections and of doing his will because of their fallen state. In the application of redemption, the Holy Spirit helps them to look at the issues from a theocentric perspective. This opens up a new dimension in Christian ethics, the essence of which has been delicately captured in the Westminster Larger Catechism: "Man's chief and highest end is to glorify God and fully to enjoy him forever" (A. 1).

The Christian is not a lonely pilgrim in this journey. Christ has taught each one to seek God's grace in prayer, such as the Lord's Prayer. This prayer, set in the context of a restatement of God's law (the Sermon on the Mount), captures the tenor of our Lord's relationship to the Father. The Lord Jesus showed constant consideration for the Father's reputation (name), program (kingdom), care for his children, and the full operation of his will in heaven and on earth. So he taught his disciples to do God's will, while trusting him for their daily concerns: "But seek first his kingdom and his righteousness, and all these things will be given to you as well. Therefore do not worry about tomorrow, for

---

[1]In *Interpreting the Prophetic Word* (Grand Rapids: Zondervan, 1989), I argue for eschatological ethics as a way of living in preparation for eternity (pp. 355–68).

[2]This distinction is further developed in my upcoming book, *Double Vision: The Christian Faith and the Pursuit of the American Dream* (publisher still pending).

tomorrow will worry about itself. Each day has enough trouble of its own" (Matt. 6:33–34).

The wise application of the law of God to every situation in life is sanctification. The death and resurrection of Christ assure the follower of the Lord Jesus of a new life. In union with Jesus Christ and by the power of the Holy Spirit, the believer desires to know and to do the *will of the Father.* Concern for God's will alters the source of one's happiness. Instead of being open to divine instruction in some unspecified way, the law of God in the school of Christ is a mirror by which the Christians may receive encouragement and discipline. They receive encouragement from knowing that, like Christ, they are seeking to please the Father. It is also an instrument by which the Lord Jesus corrects his followers, reproving them of sloth and of the sins of omission and commission. In submitting themselves to a standard or norm, they see a change in their approach to life. Gone is the sense of self-satisfaction based on a personal standard of achievement. Their desire is to do God's will and, in so doing, to reflect the perfections of God. In dependence on the grace of the Lord Jesus and on the power from the Holy Spirit, the disciple works out his or her salvation "in fear and trembling" (Phil. 2:12).

Thanks be to God that the Holy Spirit transforms individuals, who love God, but are looking for guidance apart from the whole Bible. Through his illumination and guidance, he brings them to a point where they sweetly comply with the moral law, and thus submit themselves to the Father's will. Through the Ten Commandments the Holy Spirit prods believers to conform to Christ.

Second, God's will demands a response of *obedience.* It is the Father's will that his children conform to his character and learn "obedience." Of course, obedience must come from a believing heart. Nevertheless, I want to stress the word "obedience," because in our modern intoxication with liberty, many evangelicals have lost the art of simply trusting God by being obedient to specific commands. Christian character is not shaped by opportunities for self-enhancement, but by learning to respond rightly to mundane issues. When so trained in the school of obedience, we possibly have a chance to respond to crises. Christ, the master in the school of obedience because of his suffering (Heb. 5:8), has liberated the children of God from the bondage of the law to be obedient slaves of righteousness (Rom. 6:16). The Westminster Larger Catechism expresses this truth in a succinct statement: "The duty which God requireth of man, is obedience to his revealed will" (A. 91).

Let me interject a lesson I learned from a Kenyan Christian. During my tenure at Reformed Theological Seminary, the Lord sent Samuel Maina, a godly pastor from Nairobi, Kenya. He endeared himself to our family by his love for God and people, as well as by his openness to God's Word. Samuel believed that he was obedient to Christ in pursuing further theological training. When I asked him how he could be away from his family for the many months, he answered simply, "As David learned to be obedient in the wilderness, so I have learned to be obedient." This expression of commitment to God was tested when, within a year, his wife came over at the occasion of Samuel's graduation and passed away during surgery. I had the privilege of returning with Samuel to Kenya and of ministering to him and the Christian community during the funeral and the period of mourning. Upon my return, Samuel wrote, "In obedience to the Lord, I married my wife. . . . In obedience to him, I have given her to him." I was struck by Samuel's godly response to a personal crisis. Yes, he had learned obedience.

In conclusion, I do not believe that Kaiser, my friend and colleague, will dispute these two considerations. The pursuit of doing God's *will* and of learning *obedience* will open the Christian heart to the law of God. Christians, too, need a norm and explicit "rules"' for living wisely in a crooked and perverse generation. The often amorphous expressions of love reveal an absence of ultimate standards, of responsibility, and of accountability. If Christ really is the standard, the Christian will obey the law of love, and in so doing will also obey the Decalogue. But if Christ is not in practice the standard, the Christian will not fulfill his or her responsibility. At issue is not whether the Christian is free or bound to the law. All Christians are free from the burden of the law. The real issue is a matter of how we interpret the gospel. Kaiser and I agree that the Christ of the Scriptures invites his followers to listen in stereo. When we consider the words of the Gospels, we hear the words of Jesus who invites us to listen carefully to what the Father has revealed through Moses.

Response to Walter C. Kaiser, Jr.

Greg L. Bahnsen

Dr. Kaiser has, true to form, given us a tremendous article that both gets to the heart of the issue about the law's place today and touches the heart. His love for the Torah, which gives "direction and guidance" to show us the way—the way to Christ and thus the way of life—shines even through his technical discussions. Would that more of God's people thought as clearly and felt as confident as Dr. Kaiser about the goodness and value of the law in the age of the new covenant. His essay displays agreement with the attitude of the apostle Paul, whose testimony was clear: "In my inner being I delight in God's law" (Rom. 7:22). I hope that Dr. Kaiser's study engenders this spirit in its readers, as it has for me. His closing words are on target for those who ask about the continuing usefulness of the Mosaic law in the Christian church: "when the law is read and observed with the proper priorities, there is no more bondage to the 'letter,' but great liberty in the word of the Lord (2 Cor. 3:17), even the perfect law of liberty (James 1:25; 2:12)." This is the same response, says Dr. Kaiser, that was called for and needed in Moses' day. I especially appreciate this highlighting of the unity of God's Word and redemptive work from cover to cover in the Bible, something that reflects the unity, stability, and faithfulness of God himself.

I have enjoyed and learned from the essays by the other contributors to this volume, but of all of them I find myself in closest theological agreement with what Dr. Kaiser has written, as well as with his method (exegetical rigor wedded to conceptual clarity and cogency of reasoning). As will be evident from my analyses and responses to the other essays, I do not believe these are unrelated. The reason why so many evangelical and Reformed theologians come to questionable doctrinal conclusions (not only about the law) is that there is so little cultivation and implementation of clear concepts, logical discipline, and accountability to the whole of scriptural teaching. The opening of Dr. Kaiser's essay observes that certain negative statements in the New Testament about the law "appear to be so definitive for many" that they feel the issue of the law's place in the Christian's life needs no further investigation. (That is precisely why a volume like this one is appropriate and called for, in my opinion.) Such thinking, he says, does not adequately deal with the full witness of the New Testament (much less the Old), being too "atomistic" and "one-sided." As a result, contemporary thinking on the law fails to be systemic and coherent. He quotes C. E. B. Cranfield's sad but accurate remark that "muddled thinking," "unexamined assumptions," and "careless and imprecise statement[s]" encumber even much modern scholarship, not to mention popular opinion, about the Old Testament law.

Dr. Kaiser's handling of the material for consideration was not as extensive or detailed as the other authors in this book, but its methodological strengths led him to theological conclusions that are hard to fault. He argues, even as I would as a theonomist, that "any solution that quickly runs the law out of town certainly cannot look to the Scriptures for any kind of comfort or support." Furthermore with exclamation: "the gracious salvation offered to us today contain[s] the same commands and warnings that were found in the Mosaic law!" In fact, as far as I can tell, I am in principial agreement with nearly everything in the theological position he takes in his essay here—the necessity of distinguishing moral from ceremonial law, seeing Christ as the aim or goal of the law (Rom. 10:4) and the object of faith for Old Testament believers, disallowing the notion that the Old Testament even hypothetically offered legalistic salvation, realizing that Christ's setting aside the ceremonial law by his substitutionary death does not excuse Christians from the entirety of the law, etc. While extensive agreement with another author in the book probably renders me disappointing to the editor as a critical respondent, let me get unnecessarily picky for a few paragraphs, just for the sake of furthering our dialog in this volume.

Dr. Kaiser's interpretation of Romans 9:30–10:13 is right on target in explaining the main thrust of Paul's teaching in that passage, and he is correct in his understanding of most of the premises by which Paul reaches his conclusion. Instead of finding the righteousness that was intended by the law, namely the righteousness of faith with Christ as its object, Israel tried to attain righteousness by works; accordingly, in ignorant zeal, they stumbled at believing in Christ, oblivious to the fact that Christ was the very aim or goal of the law's teaching about righteousness. As Kaiser nicely puts it, Israel wanted a "homemade righteousness." In the process of presenting his interpretation of the passage and the theological conclusions arising from it, however, Kaiser treats Romans 9:31 and the phrase "law of righteousness" in a way that is not necessary (as far as I can see) to his overall interpretation of the passage, and that has not persuaded me (as yet anyway). Kaiser considers this verse one of five "indictments" Paul charges against the Jews, namely that "righteousness was made into a law rather than the Israelites finding the righteousness that God had intended to come from the law of Moses" (thus understanding the crucial phrase as "a law out of righteousness"). Kaiser admits that "most exegetes understand *nomos* in this phrase to refer to the Old Testament law," though, and I do not see any reason to disagree with them here. Paul *describes* Israel's failure in verse 31 and then provides the *explanatory indictment* for that failure in verse 32. Israel quite correctly pursued the "law of righteousness"—the Mosaic law—but did not arrive at what it required (v. 31); indeed "they stumbled" badly (cf. v. 32b). Now then, why is this? Verse 32a answers with only an adverbial expression. It is not what Israel was doing (the verb) that made her stumble and fall short, but rather *the way or manner* in which she attempted it: namely, "not by faith but as it were by works." I may be missing something, but I do not see why Kaiser feels the need to explain the expression *nomos dikaiosynēs* in the way he does ("one of the most critical decisions" to be made in this passage, he claims).

On another point, Dr. Kaiser is true to the biblical testimony, I believe, in maintaining that there is a "moral law" that is distinguished in the Old Testament (e.g., distinguished from the ceremonial law), even though the Bible does not classify laws according to some explicit scheme. (The argument from critics at this point—no literary separation, thus no conceptual distinction—is hopelessly contrived, as Kaiser recognizes.) Nevertheless, he later seems to identify "the moral law" exactly (not simply by example) with "the Decalogue and the Holiness Code of Leviticus 18–19." His position does not require him to do anything like this, much less to be so narrow in selecting what Old

Testament literature is "moral law." The reader does not find any rationale set forth by Kaiser that might justify this particular way of identifying the moral law. It is surely odd on the face of it that what Jesus quoted as "the great and first commandment" (i.e., Deut. 6:5; cf. Matt. 22:37–38) is not included in what Kaiser denotes as the Old Testament's "moral law." For a somewhat broader conception one can consult the way in which theonomic ethics addresses this matter.

Also with respect to the category of "moral law," it is difficult to understand and potentially misleading that Kaiser asserts: "The moral law of God took precedence over the civil. . . in that it was based on the character of God." Both the relational claim and its rationale are in need of clarification. In what sense does the moral law take "precedence" over the civil law, or, of the many conflicting senses in which "precedence" might be used, which did Kaiser intend? (Is the one kind of law expendable? Does it wait to be kept until the other is first obeyed?) What kind of priority or greater importance does he have in mind? Because I am somewhat familiar with other things Kaiser has written in this area, it is a safe guess that the remark in this essay about "precedence" means that the moral law is "weightier" than the civil law (i.e., encompasses more of one's duties to God and provides the purpose and spirit by which the other is to be kept). But the elusive comment becomes unwittingly dangerous as a theological generalization when conjoined to the rationale that the moral law "takes precedence" because "it was based on the character of God." But surely the civil laws of the Old Testament were likewise based on God's justice (Heb. 2:2), were they not? Surely they too stemmed from the wisdom of God (Deut. 4:5–8), did they not? What do the Scriptures say? "*All* his precepts are trustworthy. They are steadfast for ever and ever, done in faithfulness and uprightness" (Ps. 111:7). "*All* your righteous laws are eternal" (119:160). Accordingly Moses exhorted Israel to "be careful to obey *all* these regulations I am giving you . . . because you will be doing what is good and right in the eyes of the LORD your God" (Deut. 12:28) (emphasis added). Clearly the civil laws of the Old Testament were "based on the character of God" as much as any others. Their literary character (narrower, illustrative, applicatory) and their epistemological function (explanatory)[1] may grant

---

[1]Kaiser is much sounder when he takes a different approach elsewhere and distinguishes the moral law from civil laws by saying the latter are "illustrations,

"precedence" to the broader or more general commandments of the law, but *qua* morality and divine grounding, the civil statutes cannot be distinguished or subordinated. They stem from God's character and, as Kaiser elsewhere reasons, they must be "as abiding and as absolute as the very attributes, qualities and nature of God himself." His character "will never change."

Another questionable generalization is Kaiser's claim that "the basis for all obligation to obey the law is the redemption and deliverance of God for his people." The logical inference from that comment would readily be that only those who have been redeemed or delivered by God have any obligation to obey his laws. In that case the indictments uttered by the Old Testament prophets against the pagan nations for violating the moral demands of the law would have been groundless. Isaiah's accusation was that "the earth is defiled" because its inhabitants "have disobeyed the laws [and] violated the statutes" (24:5). Moses viewed all of God's law as a model for the surrounding nations to learn how to do justice (Deut. 4:5–8), and the psalmist was eager to declare those liberating commandments before their kings (Ps. 119:45–47). Paul saw the entire world, Jew and Gentile alike, as accountable to the ordinances of the law (Rom. 1:32; 2:14–15). We must, therefore, take it as a hasty generalization to say that the basis "for all obligation" to the law is God's redemption and deliverance of His people.

Finally, an issue that does not come up for discussion in Kaiser's essay is the use of the Old Testament civil laws in modern society—something which would be of interest and enlightenment to theonomic readers. Actually, all readers might have expected at least a brief explanation about the application of the civil laws since, given Kaiser's endorsement of the continuing validity of the law today, one of the immediate objections raised by people (I hear it all the time) is, "But it would be horrible for our own society to observe those standards of civil justice! So you *must* be wrong about the law." From my reading elsewhere, I believe I have some inkling of the direction of Kaiser's thought on this subject, and with minor variation and slight adjustment, he appears to be on the same wavelength as theonomic ethics.[2] There

---

applications, or situationally-specific implementations" of the moral law, which he then describes as "an interpretative base for understanding all the laws of God."

[2] See my discussion of Kaiser's interface with theonomy in *No Other Standard: Theonomy and Its Critics* (Tyler, Tex.: Institute for Christian Economics, 1991), 159–60, 256ff., where it appears there is no real or significant disagreement between us,

are also possible indications of this in the essay under review here. In his conclusion Kaiser proclaims an "indictment on the church" in our day for "its reticence to preach the moral law of God and to apply it to all aspects of life as indicated in Scripture." He is not a pietist or retreatist, but has a desire that every aspect of human life—presumably even politics—receive the direction of God's moral law. Does this mean that the civil laws of the Old Testament should guide us today? Apparently so since, like theonomists, Kaiser views them as "illustrations, applications, or situationally-specific implementations of that same permanent moral law." Notice that these laws have an "illustrative or applicatory" nature, in which case there may be differences between the "specific" way in which the Old Testament communicates God's will in these statutes and the particular application which would be made in modern culture. That is, along with theonomic ethics, Kaiser urges in his concluding footnote that the concept of "general equity" holds "great benefit for the church" in its responsibility to apply "the ancient text to current questions." All of this is encouraging to hear! Still, it would have been more satisfying to have Kaiser say a bit more, developing the usefulness and validity of the civil laws of the Old Testament in the modern political order. The inconsistency within many a theologian's ethical system is often opened up to full view when it comes to this issue. In Dr. Kaiser's case, please say it is not so.

---

although the question of flexibility within the penal code of the Old Testament calls for further investigation.

Response to Walter C. Kaiser, Jr.

Wayne G. Strickland

Kaiser argues that the moral facet of the Mosaic law is obligatory for the believer today. To him, the Old Testament prioritized aspects of that law, and Christ validated those distinctions by ranking the moral law above both the civil and ceremonial aspects (Matt. 23:23). The moral law should be distinguished from the other aspects because it "stems from the character and nature of God." Whereas Christ fulfilled the ceremonial part of the law, the moral law remains an obligation for the believer. This Kaiser sees confirmed by Jeremiah 31:33: "I will put my law in their minds" (a passage that refers to "this same *tôrâ*"). In other words, the new covenant, which includes application for church-age believers, promises the placement of *Mosaic* law within the hearts of new covenant believers. Finally, Paul's various statements on the law may be properly coordinated based on understanding that his negative statements regarding law treat those individuals who were framing a "homemade" law of righteousness (Rom. 9:30–10:13). In truth, the law of God was always designed for sanctification and never for the attainment of eternal life.

There are commendable elements in Kaiser's treatise on the Mosaic law. Methodologically, he recognizes the crucial nature of the Pauline passages (Galatians and Romans) as definitive contributions to the issue. Likewise, he recognizes the importance of allowing the Old Testament to speak for itself on the distinctions within Mosaic law. He clearly states that this law was not "intended as an alternative method of obtaining salvation." Furthermore, passages such as Leviticus 18:5 should not be understood as being addressed to an unregenerate nation, but rather to a regenerate nation. He correctly asserts that the Mosaic law provided a means of sanctification for those in a covenant relationship with God in the Old Testament.

Kaiser's difficulties begin with his choice of Romans 9:30–10:13 as a "chair passage" on law. Since Romans and Galatians are the two letters in which Paul gives the most extensive discourse on law (these two books use the term *nomos* more frequently than the other Pauline epistles), and since Romans is the most systematic, theological treatise, Kaiser has dubbed Romans 9:30–10:13 a "chair passage." Reportedly, this passage provides "one of the clearest expositions of what Paul meant as he used *nomos*." However, one may easily disagree with the choice of Romans 9:30–10:13 as one of the clearest expositions, especially given the debate over the meaning of "law of righteousness" and *telos*. Would it not be more profitable to choose a passage such as Galatians 3:15–29, in which Paul explicitly *purposes* to discuss the use of the Mosaic law and to correct false views of the law? In fact, Kaiser fails to give sufficient attention to Galatians, the letter that treats law to an even greater extent than Romans.

I also have a fundamental disagreement with Kaiser over Paul's message in Romans 9:30–10:13. The problem as expressed by Paul is not simply that Israel pursued a "law of righteousness." One valid purpose of the law was to express the sin-grace construct (especially via the sacrifices). It was designed in part to impel unbelieving Israel to faith in God. Yet pursuit after the law of righteousness was unsuccessful (9:31b), not because of the law itself, but because of its not being pursued properly; that is, it was pursued by works rather than by faith (9:32). Paul does not say that Israel erred in pursuing the law of righteousness, nor does he disparage the law of righteousness. Rather he argues that Israel did not pursue, strive after, or use the law in the proper manner. Romans 9:32 makes the point that it was not pursued by faith (*ek pisteōs*, genitive construction denoting manner), but by works (*ex ergōn*, genitive construction denoting manner). Neither is there sufficient evidence to suggest that anything other than the Old Testament law is in view in the phrase *nomon dikaiosynes* ("law of righteousness").

The problem was not in the law itself, but in its misuse; according to Paul, it was the *manner* of its use, not the pursuit of a *different* law, that was the issue at stake. The law that Paul is discussing is the Mosaic law, misused by Israel, and he condemns such an errant approach to the application of the law. It is noteworthy that where Paul addresses such concerns, it is not the term itself (*nomos*) that conveys the meaning legalism but rather the description of the way in which the law is used as taken from the immediate context that indicates whether or not legalism is in view. Paul realizes that Israel abused the Mosaic law, thus interfering with her ability to recognize God's saving grace. Therefore, God abrogated the Mosaic covenant by Christ's work on the cross. Not only did the Israelites misuse the Mosaic law, but Paul consequently alerts them that the law has been completely abrogated. This will assist in eliminating any temptation to appeal to the Mosaic law in an erroneous manner for salvation. If part of the law remains in force, confusion may still exist regarding the purpose and use of the Mosaic law. Thus God removed the law in its entirety.

In Romans 10:6–8 Paul gives proof of the abrogation of the Mosaic law. In Moses' day, the law served a role in righteousness in the sense of sanctification. Paul makes a general reference to Moses' statement in Leviticus 18:5 (Rom. 10:5), reminding the audience that the Old Testament saint had been obligated to live by the Mosaic law. Yet Moses himself also spoke of a *future* day when the law would not be binding for righteousness. Paul cites Deuteronomy 30:11–14, which is part of God's promise for the ultimate fulfillment of the command given in the day of Moses to a regenerate audience.[1] Moses anticipated an end to the usefulness of the law of righteousness, and that end has come with Christ.

Kaiser also rejects the cessation view of Romans 10:4, based on the argument that Paul is denouncing the legalistic misuse of the Mosaic law rather than deprecating the Mosaic law itself. Thus *telos* takes on the nuance of goal or purposeful conclusion. He maintains that the term must be understood in context with the accompanying phrase "righteousness by faith." Since the passage as a whole is not teaching cessation, the term *telos* should be taken as "goal." In response, I acknowledge that the meaning of *telos* cannot be completely *settled* on the basis of a word study of Pauline usage, but we must understand that a legitimate option for the sense of *telos* is cessation. Scholars such as D. Fuller have tried to argue that "termination" is not a legitimate option for *telos*

---

[1]For an extended discussion of Deuteronomy 30, see the section in my essay on the dispensational approach that deals with the contribution of Romans 10:5–8.

in Romans 10:4, since it is so rare.[2] He allows for only three New Testament examples where *telos* is seen as termination.[3] Yet there are other clear examples (e.g., Mark 3:24; 1 Pet. 4:7). Furthermore, Paul's use of *telos* in this manner in 2 Corinthians 3:13 confirms that he is aware of this nuance.[4]

Kaiser's association of *nomou Christos eis dikaiōsynēn panti to pisteuonti* (lit., "law of Christ for righteousness to everyone who believes") in Romans 10:4 with the phrases in Romans 10:6 and 10 in order to prove that the *nomos* in verse 4 is not Mosaic law, is misleading, because the term *nomos* is not used in association with the phrases in verses 6 and 10. Paul has consistently used *nomos* in the sense of Mosaic law in this section, so that there must be a difference and contrast between law righteousness (v. 4) and faith righteousness (vv. 6, 10). Further, Paul intends a contrast here, confirmed by the employment of the adversative particle *de* (translated "but" in all major translations of the Bible) that joins the phrases "righteousness of the law" (v. 5) and "righteousness of faith" (v. 6). In other words, there has been a dramatic development in salvation history that has resulted in the termination of Mosaic law righteousness. Thus the "chair passage" does not sustain Kaiser's theological motif that Paul disparages only a homemade law rather than the law itself. Paul is suggesting, instead, that the Mosaic law was designed to be employed by faith, but Israel did not pursue it properly, i.e., through the avenue of personal faith. However, that problem has been completely eradicated with the advent of Christ, who has brought the termination of the law.

Although I agree with Kaiser that there are distinguishable aspects of the Mosaic law, this principle does not give sanction for retaining one part of the law and jettisoning other aspects. Kaiser objects to the idea that law is an indivisible unity: "the argument that the *tôrâ* is a unity can be used against this position, for the same law of Moses that gave us the legal aspects of that revelation also contains the promise made to the patriarchs." What he has overlooked is the fact that the promises found in the Mosaic law

---

[2]Daniel P. Fuller, *Gospel & Law: Contrast or Continuum?* (Grand Rapids: Eerdmans, 1980), 82.

[3]Ibid., 84, note 29.

[4]Fuller admits the termination nuance here (ibid.). Other examples of Pauline usage in the sense of cessation are 1 Corinthians 1:8; 15:24; and Philippians 3:19. See the discussion of Romans 10:4 in my dispensational essay for other arguments favoring the cessation view.

are merely reiterations and expansions of the foundational promises given in the Abrahamic covenant that preceded the Mosaic law. The law came alongside the Abrahamic covenant promises. The promises are rearticulated in the Mosaic covenant, but are not dependent on the Mosaic law. Paul appeals to the Abrahamic covenant to support the promise. Thus the promises are not abrogated by the termination of law, since the Abrahamic covenant has not been terminated. This, then, is Paul's point in Galatians 3: The coming of the Mosaic law did not invalidate the promises of the Abrahamic covenant (3:17). The promises are not based on or dependent on law (v. 18), although neither is the law contrary to the promises of God (v. 21). The inheritance based on promise is not in any way dependent on Mosaic law, according to Paul in verse 29. The promise of blessing is in the Seed; Jesus Christ relates to the Abrahamic covenant. Paul says, "If you belong to Christ, then you are *Abraham's* seed, heirs according to the promise" (v. 29; emphasis added).

Certainly there are core moral and ethical commandments and other sections that apply the principles to concrete situations. In addition, there are sections that illustrate the ethical principles. But these are not easily packaged or easily separable, as even Kaiser admits. No solid case is made for the threefold division: moral, civil, and ceremonial. The passages cited by Kaiser at most suggest a distinction for "ceremonial" aspects, but do not sustain the threefold division accepted by many. No evidence is given of the termination of "civil" law, a major problem for this non-theonomic view. Further, 1 Samuel 15:22–23 (cited by Kaiser) does not distinguish the ceremonial law from moral law, but rather God's command to Saul to utterly destroy the Amalekites from the burnt offerings and sacrifices of Saul. This is not distinguishing the Mosaic "moral" law from the "ceremonial" law. If these are such fundamental distinctions, where is the evidence?

Additional problems with the threefold distinction relate to the fact that penalties were attached to the "moral" law that are not enforced today. The knotty problem of the fifth commandment of the Decalogue (which many argue is the heart of the moral law) with its ceremonial connotations (i.e., life in the land) makes it impossible to neatly carve out such distinctions in the Old Testament (Ex. 20:12). Rather than being faced with picking and choosing certain laws from the Mosaic code to remain in force, the entire code and expression of God's law has been replaced with another law, the law of Christ, built upon the same eternal moral standard. The entire Mosaic law, insofar as they illustrate God's ethical standards and graciousness, are still normative for preaching and teaching.

Jeremiah 31:33 is marshaled as support that "this same *tôrâ*" (Mosaic law) is placed on the hearts of all who believe. Yet does Jeremiah explicitly argue that the Mosaic law is placed on the heart? There is nothing in the context to require that this *tôrâ* is exactly the Mosaic law. Indeed the new covenant is *contrasted* with the old covenant in this passage. Jeremiah could just as well be arguing that the moral standards that form the basis for the entire external Mosaic law will be placed on the hearts of believers. Otherwise one might be forced to understand that the law to be placed on the heart includes the ceremonial and civil aspects. If the ethical principles underlying the Mosaic legislation are understood as in view in Jeremiah 31:33, then this problem dissipates. Abraham, prior to the existence of the Mosaic law, kept God's law (Gen. 26:5); Moses and the Israelites kept the Mosaic law; and the believer today keeps the law of Christ (Gal. 6:2), based on the new covenant promises; but they are all expressions of the same eternal moral standard that reflects the character of God.

Kaiser places great weight on Jesus' testimony regarding distinctions in the law and then allows for the continuation of the authority of the "moral" aspect of the Mosaic law. He interprets Christ himself as teaching the principle of distinction in Matthew 23:23. Yet perhaps Kaiser has read too much into this passage and has committed the very mistake he warns against—solving "the problem by imposing categories and definitions external to the text rather than demonstrating the issue from within the text." First, the issue in Matthew 23 is hypocrisy rather than the divisions within the law; the passage is not designed to teach that there are differing aspects of the law. Furthermore, Jesus and Matthew do not intend to treat the issue of continuity or discontinuity. The Pharisees have been guilty of handling the law in a hypocritical fashion, and Jesus' main concern is the importance of the central issues of justice, mercy, and faithfulness (Mic. 6:8; Zech. 7:9), without at the same time suggesting that other matters are optional. For instance, Christ is not suggesting that for Old Testament saints the tithe was optional or unimportant. In fact, Christ goes on to ensure that there is no misunderstanding by exhorting the submission to weightier matters "without neglecting the former." If anything, Matthew 23:23 would seem to argue that the entire law must be kept. It does not allow for any abrogation at this point.

Kaiser suggests that the moral law should be distinguished and take precedence over the other aspects of Mosaic law because it alone stems from God's nature and character. However, he has not demonstrated that justice, mercy, and faithfulness were intended to represent the moral aspect of the law. Would not these attributes correspond equally to the "civil" law? In addition, it may easily be argued that the entire law is based on God's character. The priority of moral law is based on the fact that it proceeds from God, but has not *all* law proceeded from God?

Moreover, Kaiser argues that Christ fulfilled the ceremonial part of the law in his death on the cross, so that the ceremonial provisions of the law do not remain in force. Yet Christ fulfilled all the Mosaic law, not simply the ceremonial provisions. This is Christ's own testimony in Matthew 5:17. That Christ had in mind the *entire* Mosaic law is confirmed by the correction of abuses immediately following this statement of fulfillment (vv. 21-48). For instance, he corrects abuses dealing with fasting, a regulation that is not part of the so-called moral law.[5]

Matthew 23:23 certainly allows for the principle of more important and less important Mosaic legislation, but could it not also be said that worshiping God is more important than not stealing? Kaiser fails to demonstrate any clear biblical guide for applying the principle. Likewise, Christ differentiates blasphemy of the Holy Spirit and blasphemy of Christ in Matthew 12:31–32, arguing that blasphemy against the Holy Spirit may not be forgiven, but blasphemy against Christ is forgivable. However, does that mean there is exemption from the prohibition of blasphemy against Jesus Christ or that there is a basic unity regarding these sins? Recognizing that Jesus saw distinctions in the Mosaic law does not validate the concept of partial enforcement of the Mosaic code.

In summary, the Kaiser argument fails at several points. His analysis of the principle of differentiation within the Mosaic law fails to recognize that nowhere is there any neat or easy division of the law that allows for the traditional moral, civil, and ceremonial divisions. Christ does not suggest that *any* of the provisions of the law are expendable, only that the gravity of omitting the more central provisions is greater, and he explicitly follows up with the

---

[5]See V. Poythress, *The Shadow of Christ in the Law of Moses* (Brentwood, Tenn.: Wolgemuth and Hyatt, 1991), 256–69, for a helpful discussion of Christ's fulfillment of the Law and Prophets.

statement not to neglect the other matters of the law. Furthermore, although arguing for the priority and precedence of moral law, Kaiser does not give argumentation or justification for the temporary nature of the rest of the law. Nowhere in his essay does he scripturally justify the termination of "civil" or "ceremonial" aspects, which is vital to sustaining his thesis. He merely mentions that Hebrews only allows for the abrogation of the ceremonies and rituals of the old covenant. The burden of proof rests with the one who posits that Paul calls for only partial abrogation of the law, yet Kaiser has barely mentioned evidence for this crucial portion of his thesis.

Although Kaiser attempts to make a plausible case for Romans 9:31–10:13, the understanding of *nomos* in 9:30 as legalism does not stand. In addition, he fails to recognize the full import of the major salvation historical development associated with Christ. In order that there will be no temptation to use the Mosaic law (*nomos*) illicitly, Christ has brought an end or termination to the Mosaic law. This helps to guarantee that there will be no attempt to secure the righteousness of God by law.

Response to Walter C. Kaiser, Jr.

Douglas Moo

A tenacious defense of the continuing importance of the Old Testament in the lives of Christians has been a hallmark of Walter Kaiser's academic ministry. This defense has been, and still is, much needed. Far too many Christians are abysmally ignorant of even the basic content of the Old Testament. Too many pastors avoid the Old Testament or preach only a few of its more famous stories and texts. Evangelical scholars and publishers have perpetuated the problem by producing three or four solid exegetical commentaries on New Testament books for every one on an Old Testament book. I agree wholeheartedly therefore with Kaiser's insistence that no evangelical theology worthy of the name can ignore the Old Testament or its law. And I agree also with his methodology: rooting our theological conclusions firmly in the careful interpretation of one or more key teaching texts. Too many of us are content with a superficial "proof-texting" method that almost insures we will come out of the study of the Bible with whatever views we went into it with.

Nevertheless, while sympathetic to his concerns and supportive of his method, I find that I come out at a different point than he does on the question of Law and Gospel. Properly defined (for which see my essay), I agree with the Lutherans: Law and Gospel are key antithetical concepts that run throughout Scripture. Both are manifestations of God's grace and part of his one great plan for the salvation of the world. But they are different, "Law" comprising that which God demands of us, "Gospel" what he freely gives us to meet our spiritual need. The Mosaic law, while a manifestation of God's grace, must be ranged on the side of "law." But the Mosaic law must also be integrated into the more "horizontal" continuum of salvation history. In this sense, while Christians remain subject to God's "law" in this broad sense, they are no longer, I argue, *directly* subject to the *Mosaic* law. I set out the reasons for this conclusion in my essay; here I must show how I would defend that position vis-à-vis the points that Kaiser makes in his paper. I will organize my comments in three sections, in which I respond, respectively, to (1) miscellaneous issues and text; (2) Kaiser's exegesis of his key text, Romans 9:30–10:13; and (3) the distinction between the "weightier matters" of the law and the rest of the law.

First, some miscellaneous points. Despite Kaiser's criticism, I still think that texts such as Matthew 19:17, Romans 2:13 and 7:10, and (possibly) 10:5 teach that the Mosaic law contains an implicit promise of eternal life to its doer. Paul claims in Galatians 3:21 that it is impossible for any law to confer life, not that it is impossible for any law to offer life. But this restatement of the fundamental theorem of what Reformed theologians call the "covenant of works" does not mean that the Mosaic Law is *advocating* a method of salvation other than faith. Kaiser is surely right here: Whatever we do with individual texts such as Leviticus 18:5, the Mosaic law does not advocate salvation by works. But what I am arguing is that the principle is still enunciated there; and whenever the law is illegitimately separated from its undergirding salvation historical framework of promise and covenant, it can offer its adherents only one means of salvation: works, a means that human sinfulness renders forever incapable of saving.

I therefore concur with Kaiser: The Pentateuch is not a legalistic document; faith is at the heart of its message. But Kaiser's use of the word *tôrâ* at this point raises a critical issue. If by *"tôrâ"* is meant the five books of Moses, I have no objection. But if by *"tôrâ"* we mean what the New Testament authors usually mean when they use the word "law" (Greek *nomos*), then I must disagree. For the New Testament authors generally use "law" to refer to the commandments of the Mosaic law, and their application of the Greek term to this body of commandments is quite accurate. *Tôrâ* in this sense, I would argue, does not teach or demand faith; as Paul said, "The law is not based on faith" (Gal. 3:12a). To apply a distinction we drew earlier: The Pentateuch contains both "Gospel" and Law, promise and demand. But we commit a serious theological mistake by mixing them.

The meaning of the term "law" surfaces elsewhere as a point

of contention between Kaiser and myself. For instance, he interprets the word "law" in Romans 3:21a—"But now the righteousness of God has been manifested apart from the law" (RSV)—in terms of "works of the law" in 3:28, concluding that "'apart from observing the law' had nothing to do with the Torah God had revealed to Moses." By this Kaiser apparently means that the phrase "observing the law" refers to the Jewish legalistic perversion of the law; and this is what "law," then, in 3:21 must also mean. Yet there is strong reason to doubt the "legalistic" interpretation of "observing the law" (see my essay). And quite apart from that, what is the justification for thinking that the word "law" in 3:21 must mean what "works of the law" means in 3:28? Why should we find the clue to the meaning of the word "law" in 3:21 in a different phrase seven verses later rather than in the immediately preceding occurrence of the word in 3:20b: "through the law we become conscious of sin" (NIV)? Or, to introduce another text, why does "law" refer to legalistic misunderstanding in Romans 3:21a but to the *tôrâ* as God gave it in 3:31 (as Kaiser argues it does)? A method of interpretation that uses two different meanings of the same word in the same context without substantiation is unlikely to clear up the "muddled thinking" against which Kaiser is protesting.

Second, disagreement over the meaning of the word "law" in Paul is central also to my response to Kaiser's interpretation of the "chair passage," Romans 9:30–10:13. I would agree that this is among the three most important extended teaching passages on the Mosaic law in the New Testament (I am not sure, however, that I would rank it ahead of Matt. 5:17–48 or Gal. 2:16–4:7). Yet it is also one of the most difficult exegetically. Since I have given my own interpretation of the passage in my essay, I will confine myself here to a response to Kaiser's interpretation.

Kaiser's basic argument is that the contrast in this passage is not between the Mosaic law and Christ, but between the Jewish perversion of the law and Christ—between "works righteousness" and "righteousness by faith." Far from standing opposed in this passage, in fact, the Law and the Gospel stand side by side as witnesses to the truth of righteousness by faith alone. Two exegetical decisions are crucial to Kaiser's interpretation. First is his insistence that the phrase "law of righteousness" (*nomon dikaiosunēs*) in 9:31 "cannot mean 'a law that promises righteousness' or 'a law that results [either truly or falsely] in righteousness'"). Rather, it must refer to the method of righteousness by works adopted by the Jews. Now, as a matter of fact, I think that

Kaiser is right to make the contrast in two kinds of righteousness central in verses 30–32. But I am not sure that we can remove the Mosaic law from the phrase. Kaiser gives no reasons for excluding the interpretation "law that promises righteousness." Since this paraphrase is unobjectionable grammatically, I presume that his objection is theological: that the law simply does not promise righteousness and so Paul could not have meant that. But this is perilously close to assuming what one needs to prove. Moreover, Kaiser fails to deal with the fact that the word *nomos* is the governing word in the phrase. As Cranfield, whom Kaiser quotes approvingly at several points, has shown, it is unlikely that this word order allows the interpretation "righteousness of the law" or "legalistic righteousness." These considerations suggest that Paul is faulting the Jews for focusing too narrowly on the Mosaic law and seeking "on the basis of works" (see the latter part of v. 31) to achieve the law and hence earn righteousness. While faulting the Jews for "works righteousness," Paul also faults them for a preoccupation with the Mosaic law. Some antithesis, then, between the Mosaic law and righteousness by faith is present here.

The second key exegetical buttress to Kaiser's interpretation of the passage is the continuative understanding of *de* in 10:6, thereby bringing into harmony Paul's quotations of Leviticus 18:5 and Deuteronomy 30:12–14, "the righteousness that is by the law" and "the righteousness that is by faith." Kaiser's grammatical argument for this view is that the combination of *gar* (used at the beginning of v. 5) and *de* (used at the beginning of v. 6) means "for . . . and," not "for . . . but." I have two objections to this argument. First, it isolates a construction that does not warrant such isolation. The conjunctions *gar* and *de* do not form a correlative pair in Greek, so there is no justification for treating them as a pair and finding in their combination any kind of consistent meaning. Second, even when considered in this artificial combination, the word *de* does not usually mean "and." For instance, of twenty-four occurrences of *de* in the sequence *gar . . . de* (with no intervening conjunction) in Romans 1–8, three are continuative ("and"), three explanatory ("that is" or "now"), and fifteen contrastive ("but").[1] Belonging to the last category, for

---

[1]Continuative: 4:15; 7:8–9; 8:24; explanatory: 1:11–12; 2:1b-2; 6:7–8; 5:13; contrastive: 2:25; 5:7–8; 5:10–11; 5:16; 6:10; 6:23; 7:2; 7:14; 7:18b; 7:22–23; 8:5; 8:6; 8:13; 8:22–23; 8:24–25.

instance, is Romans 6:23: "For (*gar*) the wages of sin is death, but (*de*) the gift of God is eternal life in Christ Jesus our Lord." These statistics suggest that, if anything, we should expect the *de* in 10:6 to mean "but."

And that it should, in fact, be so translated is clear from other considerations. Paramount among these is the key parallel text of Philippians 3:7–9, the only other place in which Paul uses both phrases, "righteousness . . . that comes from the law" and "righteousness that comes . . . by [or through] faith." In this text, it is clear that these two kinds of righteousness are set in antithesis to one another. Almost equally significant is the context. While Kaiser claims that the phrase "righteousness that is by the law" in Romans 10:5 should not be compared with "law of righteousness" in 9:31, there is every reason for doing so. For we would then have a coherent, thrice-repeated contrast between two kinds of right-eousness: "righteousness that is by faith" versus "law of right-eousness" in 9:30–32; "their own [righteousness]" and "God's righteousness" in 10:2–3; and "the righteousness that is by the law" and "the righteousness that is by faith" in 10:5–8. Kaiser's objection that Paul would not pit one Old Testament text against another against their original meanings assumes his interpretation of Leviticus 18:5—which I have elsewhere contested.

While, then, Kaiser's general conclusion—that Romans 9:30–10:13 focuses on a difference between God's gift of righteousness by faith and a Jewish attempt to secure their own righteousness through works—is accurate, his exclusion of all contrast between the Mosaic law and Christ cannot be accepted. As Kaiser would insist, "law" in 10:4, a pivotal text, refers to the Mosaic law—not to a Jewish perversion of it. As the "outcome" (*telos*) of the law, Christ is the point toward which it has all along been moving (see my essay for defense of this interpretation). The failure of so many Jews was to become so preoccupied with the law that they missed this climax of salvation history and kept seeking righteousness from the Mosaic law. Their attempt to do so is certainly, at least in one sense of the word, "legalism," but the word "law" in itself does not mean "legalism" anywhere in this text. Moreover, while the law after Christ is certainly still "God's law," "holy, righteous and good" and "spiritual" (7:12, 14), its exact relationship to the believer has still not been determined. The coming of Christ as the "purposeful conclusion" of the law does not annul it or remove it from the Bible—but it does dramatically affect its actual function in the lives of believers. No longer are God's people required to obey directly large sections of that law, such as its requirements about sacrifices, festivals, food, and other rituals. If the law remains in any way a direct authority for the believer, one must conclude that certain of its laws are to be put in a different category than these. This is exactly what Kaiser argues, and it is the nub of the difference between us.

Finally, throughout his article, Kaiser attaches different meanings to the word "law." It sometimes refers to the law as God gave it (e.g., Rom. 3:31; 7:12, 14, 25; 8:7; 10:4), at other times to the law as the Jews have perverted it (e.g., Rom. 3:21, 28; 9:31). Even more significant for the issue of this book, however, is his distinction between the moral law on the one hand and the civil and ceremonial law on the other. Thus, for instance, Colossians 2:14–15, Ephesians 2:15, Hebrews, and apparently Matthew 5:17 refer to the ceremonial law; whereas, for instance, James 1:25 and 2:12 refer to the moral law. As with the viewpoints of Bahnsen and VanGemeren in this volume, this distinction is crucial to Kaiser. By utilizing it, he can maintain a continuing direct authority of parts of the Mosaic law (the "moral" law) while admitting that the larger part of the Mosaic law (the ceremonial and civil parts) are no longer a direct source of authority for the believer. To Kaiser's credit, he does not just assume such a division within the law; he argues for it.

He begins with some logical deductions. First, he suggests, those who claim a unity for the law end up proving too much; for the promises, included in the law, would have to be jettisoned along with the commandments if we are no longer bound to the law. The mistake here is a simple misunderstanding of how the advocates of the unity of the law are using the word "law." As I use it, for instance, in claiming that the law is a basic unity, I apply it to the commandments of the Mosaic law—not to the Pentateuch as a whole. The problem here, then, is one I pointed out earlier: a failure to define carefully and use consistently the word "law."

Kaiser's second objection is that a complete removal of the law from the lives of believers contradicts the fact of its being written on the heart of believers through the Spirit under the new covenant. As I argue in my essay, however, what is written on the heart is not the detailed commandments of the Mosaic law, but its basic moral requirements; and it is those commandments as now written on the heart, fulfilled in Christ, and meditated by the Spirit, that guide the believer—not the commandments of the *tôrâ* as such.

I agree that we cannot reject the distinction between moral law and other kinds simply because the Bible nowhere states it.

But I would insist again, as I do repeatedly in this volume, that one must find clear implications of such a division in the Bible if we are to accept it. While Kaiser is right to point out that we have no unambiguous first-century evidence for the enumeration of 613 commandments in the law, it must be pointed out that we have plenty of evidence from that time and before that Jews viewed the *tôrâ* as an essential unity.

Key here is what I mean by "essential unity." By this I do not mean that laws were not sometimes, for various specific purposes, divided into various kinds, or that they were not even graded in importance—usually to make a homiletical point. What I mean is that we have no evidence that first-century Jews divided the *tôrâ* in so basic a way that some parts could be considered "optional" or "temporary."[2] Nor does the Old Testament or New Testament suggest this kind of basic division. To be sure, many prophetic passages highlight the paramount importance of the heart atti-tude. Yet even when these appear to be set in contrast to what we might call "ritual" requirements (e.g., Hos. 6:6), it is clear that the intention of the prophet is not to dismiss the rituals as optional or capable of being ignored. Certainly the Old Testament from beginning to end insists that a heart devoted to God, with its responses of acting justly, loving mercy, and walking humbly with God (see Mic. 6:8), is paramount. Without it all the adherence to ceremonial ritual in the world will avail nothing. But this is not to say that sacrifices were ever considered optional in the Old Testament.

Likewise, our Lord can scold the Jews for focusing on the "trivia" of the law at the expense of its "weightier matters," while still insisting that they do the trivia as well (Matt. 23:23). What I am arguing is that we have insufficient basis in Scripture to apply to the word "law," as a self-evident and well-developed category, the restrictions of "ceremonial law" or "moral law." Any such distinction will have to be demonstrated from the context. I am suggesting, then, that the burden of proof is on those who hold views such as Kaiser's to demonstrate in given texts that a restricted number of Mosaic commandments are intended when the word "law" occurs. Without such evidence, each interpreter

---

[2]This is how I would reconcile the two statements from two different articles of mine that Kaiser quotes in his footnote 19: the law is *basically* a single indivisible whole, while Jesus and others can highlight its more important parts for practical purposes.

will be able to create whatever theology of the Mosaic law he or she wants by simply claiming certain texts refer to one kind of law and others to another kind. I am not denying that sufficient evidence for such a distinction in some texts cannot be found. But what I am arguing is that the key New Testament texts about *both* the value *and* the discontinuity of the "law" refer to the same entity: the Mosaic law as a whole. As a whole, the Mosaic law is *both* "spiritual" (Rom. 7:14) *and* a killing "letter" (Rom. 2:28–29; 7:6; 2 Cor. 3:5–7), *both* valid "until heaven and earth disappear" (Matt. 5:18) *and* "fulfilled" in Christ (Matt. 5:17), *both* "upheld" by the gospel of faith (Rom. 3:31) *and* no longer the "supervisor" of those who have faith (Gal. 3:25). I am forced by the exegetical data to maintain each of these statements. Yet where some find contradiction and others "tension," I find the possibility of a satisfactory theological harmonization (see my essay for a beginning attempt at such a harmonization).

A DISPENSATIONAL VIEW

Wayne G. Strickland

Chapter Four

A DISPENSATIONAL VIEW

Wayne G. Strickland

THE INAUGURATION
OF THE LAW OF CHRIST
WITH THE GOSPEL OF CHRIST:
A DISPENSATIONAL VIEW

Wayne G. Strickland

Throughout much of its existence, the church has sought to gain a clear understanding and exposition of the relationship between Law and Gospel. Is there a legitimate interface between them, or are they antithetical and separate? Perhaps the truth lies somewhere between these extremes? It will be the purpose of this essay to investigate the nature of the relationship between Law and Gospel. Specifically, how should the modern believer, having responded to the Gospel, relate to the Mosaic Law in this church age?

THE IMPORTANCE OF THE ISSUE

The resolution of the Law/Gospel debate is no simple exercise, but neither is it a trivial issue. Among the theological issues raised by Paul, this one has perpetually been regarded as one of great significance.[1]

---

[1]So writes Joseph A. Fitzmyer, *To Advance the Gospel* (New York: Crossroad, 1981), 147. An indicator of the significance of the issue is the large number of book-length treatments in recent years. Following is a sampling of such discussions: E. P. Sanders, *Paul and Palestinian Judaism* (Philadelphia: Fortress, 1977); *Paul, the Law, and the Jewish People* (Philadelphia: Fortress, 1983); Hans Hübner, *Law in Paul's Thought* (Edinburgh: T. and T. Clark, 1984); W. D. Davies, *Jewish and Pauline Studies* (Philadelphia: Fortress, 1984); Robert Badenas, *Christ the End of the Law: Romans 10:4 in Pauline Perspective*, JSNTSup 10 (Sheffield: JSOT, 1985); H. Räisänen, *Paul and the*

Theologically, the issue's importance is threefold. First, one's view of the relationship between Law and Gospel may influence the understanding of the cardinal doctrine of justification. As Berthold Klappert has noted, Luther's discussion of Law and Gospel was centered primarily in the context of justification, using the terms "Law" and "Gospel" as kerygmatic categories.[2] Second, the understanding of the relationship may have a decided impact on sanctification. Does the law have any role in the contemporary believer's lifestyle? Using Luther as an example once more, it is clear that he argued in *Die Thesen gegen die Antinomer* that there was some usefulness for the law in the believer's life, though John Calvin may be regarded as the one who championed the third use of the law (*tertius usus legis*) for the sanctification of the saint.[3]

Third, on a broader and all-encompassing level, the issue has great significance for one's theological system. The differing solutions to the Law-Gospel debate result in diverse theological systems. Daniel Fuller has tried to show how differing perspectives concerning the bond between Law and Gospel have necessarily resulted in divergent theological systems.[4] We may note that the Law/Gospel issue is foundational to the system of theology commonly termed "dispensational." Fuller recognizes this and argues against the legitimacy and viability of dispensational theology, based on his understanding of a Law-Gospel continuum.[5]

Law (Philadelphia: Fortress, 1986); Stephen Westerholm, *Israel's Law and the Church's Faith* (Grand Rapids: Eerdmans, 1988); Brice L. Martin, *Christ and the Law in Paul* (Leiden: Brill, 1989); W. D. Davies, *Jewish and Pauline Studies* (Philadelphia: Fortress, 1984).

[2]B. Klappert, *Promissio und Bund: Gesetz und Evangelium bei Luther und Barth* (Göttingen: Vandenhoeck und Ruprecht, 1976), 127.

[3]For instance, he writes: "Law indeed without our being necessary to it, and even against our will, is there in fact; before justification, at the beginning, middle, and end of it, and after justification." (*WA* 39:1, 353). Calvin and the Reformed theologians stressed this use as the chief function of the law (*Inst.* 2.7.12). See also J. W. Montgomery, "Third Use of the Law," *Present Truth* 2 (March 1973), 14–16.

[4]Daniel P. Fuller in *Gospel & Law: Contrast or Continuum?* (Grand Rapids: Eerdmans, 1980) argues that although different in significant areas, the common understanding of covenant theology and dispensationalism of a contrast between Law and Gospel does not stand. Rather a continuum exists between Law and Gospel, necessitating a consequent rejection of both systems of theology.

[5]Fuller, *Gospel & Law*, 1. He calls dispensationalism a "system for biblical interpretation" and opts for an "obedience of faith" hermeneutic.

THE APPROACH OF THIS ESSAY

In order to understand better the applicability of the Mosaic law to the modern Christian, it is imperative first of all to understand how the ancient Hebrews related to the law. Therefore I will begin with a brief exposition of the concept of the Mosaic law as presented in the Old Testament, paying particular attention to the purpose of the law and its relationship to redemption. Other salient factors such as the nature of the Mosaic covenant and the recipients of the revelation will also be presented. Following this section will be an analysis of the concept of the Mosaic law as presented in the New Testament, and especially as developed by Paul. The purpose and recipients of the law as well as the meaning of phrases like "works of the law" (e.g., Rom. 3:28; Gal. 3:21 NASB) will be studied. At this juncture, the relationship of the Mosaic Law to the Gospel will be investigated. I will then discuss the applicability of the Mosaic law to the modern Christian and follow that up with a treatment of the law of Christ. It should be noted that the model presented will be *a* dispensational model, not *the* dispensational model. It would be presumptuous to try to speak for all dispensationalists, especially since there is substantial development taking place within dispensational circles.[6]

THE MOSAIC LAW AS PRESENTED IN THE OLD TESTAMENT

Before the question of the applicability of the Mosaic Law to modern Christians may be answered, we must first briefly consider its development in the Old Testament. A perusal of treatises on the Mosaic law reveals a striking lack of consensus on this issue. Certain questions that deserve attention surface: Did obedience to the Mosaic law bring spiritual redemption? Did the law have a tripartite nature, i.e., moral, civil, ceremonial? What was the purpose or function of the law for the Old Testament saint?

---

[6]Although there is consensus on many fundamentals of dispensational theology, great differences also exist. This may be observed by examining the proceedings of the Dispensational Study Group over the past few years in conjunction with the annual Evangelical Theological Society meetings. See especially C. Blaising, "Developing Dispensationalism," a paper read at the Evangelical Theological Society Meeting, November 1986, at Atlanta, Georgia.

The Non-Salvific Design of the Mosaic Law

A common assumption among many non-evangelical theologians is that compliance with the law resulted in salvation in the Old Testament. New Testament scholars have especially argued that the Old Testament taught spiritual salvation via obedience to God's law.[7] Indeed, some texts do seem to indicate the law as a way of redemption—e.g., Leviticus 18:5; Deuteronomy 4:1, 8; 27:26; and 28:58–59. In Deuteronomy 4:1, for example, Israel is commanded to obey God's "decrees and laws" in order to live (i.e., obtain spiritual salvation), and verse 8 seems to confirm that obedience to the Mosaic law is in view here.

Furthermore, some have argued that the traditional dispensational view advocates two ways of salvation in the Bible: one based on compliance with the Mosaic law and the second based on faith in Christ.[8] In this scheme, a Hebrew was required to obey the Mosaic law in order to be justified, and for that reason the law was peculiar to that dispensation. The New Testament dispensation, however, provided for a person to place faith in Christ for salvation, terminating the Mosaic law as a means of salvation.

There are several reasons why the interpretation that salvation in the Old Testament is based on obedience to the Mosaic law must be rejected. God never intended his law to provide spiritual redemption for his people. Not only does the New Testament specify that Old Testament saints were saved by faith rather than works (e.g., Rom. 4:3), but the few Old Testament passages that comment on the *way* of salvation confirm that obedience to the Mosaic stipulations is not the requirement for redemption.

Genesis 15:6 is the first passage that provides a clear explanation of the means of salvation in the Old Testament. This passage is doubly significant since it not only is pre-church age, but also pre-Mosaic. The Abrahamic covenant has been revealed

---

[7]See, for example, Rudolf Bultmann, "Christ the End of the Law," in *Essays, Philosophical and Theological* (New York: Macmillan, 1955), 54; and Hans Conzelmann, *An Outline of the Theology of the New Testament* (London: SCM, 1969), who asserts that the law has been terminated as a way of salvation, but not as an ethic. More recently, E. P. Sanders has argued that the customary understanding of Paul's doctrine of the Mosaic law is flawed. Contrary to many, Sanders argues that Paul never thought it impossible to keep the law, nor did he conceive of works-righteousness as legalism (*Paul*, 26–27). However, Sanders does argue convincingly that the law was not regarded as the sole means of salvation (ibid., 426–27).

[8]See Fuller, *Gospel & Law*, 1–64. Klyne Snodgrass has likewise accepted the notion that dispensationalists taught two ways of salvation ("Spheres of Influence: A Possible Solution to the Problem of Paul and the Law," *JSNT* 32 [1988], 94, 108).

(Gen. 12:1–3; 15:1–4), and Moses records Abram's response to that covenant: he "believed the LORD" (15:6).[9] No works of Abram were involved; the gracious work of God was the sole basis. The object of Abraham's faith was expressed as in "the LORD." That works-righteousness was not in view was confirmed by Moses' follow-up statement in this verse, "and he credited it to him as righteousness."

As one studies the Mosaic law, it becomes increasingly clear that its purpose was not to save, for it contains no clear message of salvation or redemption. Furthermore, whatever role the Mosaic law may have had, faith was *not* preempted as the proper response of the individual. The most convincing evidence for this observation is found in Exodus. There God gave his law to an already redeemed or covenant nation (Ex. 20). Salvation came to the Hebrews prior to revelation of the law on Mount Sinai, during their experience in Egypt when they placed blood on the lintels and crossed over the Red Sea. Then we read: "the people feared the LORD and put their trust in him." Such faith rules out the possibility that adherence to the law brought about salvation. Israel acknowledged this spiritual deliverance when they sang with Moses: "In your unfailing love you will lead the people you have redeemed."

Leviticus 18:5 likewise excludes the possibility of law salvation. Since Paul cites Leviticus 18:5 in Romans 10:5, the question arises: Did Moses argue that salvific righteousness results from keeping the law? Furthermore, did Paul understand that the Mosaic law or Torah advocated eternal salvation via obedience or works righteousness? Indeed, Hans Joachim Schoeps has argued that the Jewish epoch centered on righteousness through obedience to the law, but that Paul recognized an abandonment of this way of salvation with the law of Christ.[10] For Schoeps, the coming of the Christ necessitated a revised understanding of the function of the law. D. Fuller, following the lead of John Calvin, argues that Leviticus 18:5 is addressed to an unregenerate audience.[11] Yet

---

[9]Geerhardus Vos, *Biblical Theology* (Grand Rapids: Eerdmans, 1954), 98.

[10]H. J. Schoeps, *Paul* (Philadelphia: Westminster, 1961), 171–78. A similar view is expressed by F. Hahn in "Das Gesetzesverständnis im Römer- und Galaterbrief," *ZNW* 67 (1967), 32, 50.

[11]Fuller, *Gospel & Law*, 67–88. Fuller does not agree totally with Calvin in that while both agree that Leviticus is addressed to an unregenerate audience, Calvin suggests that Deuteronomy 30:11–14 (also cited by Paul in Rom. 10) is addressed to a regenerate audience. See John Calvin, *Commentaries on the Epistle of Paul the Apostle to the Romans* (Grand Rapids: Eerdmans, 1947), 385–92.

several commentators contend that an already regenerate audience was present.[12] As R. K. Harrison notes in his commentary on Leviticus, the address is integrally tied to the Sinai covenant. "A holy, pure and just God has revealed Himself afresh to the Israelites, and has presented them with a covenant formulation, the terms of which have been accepted."[13] In short, God is addressing his laws to a covenant, believing nation, giving no indication that salvation is in view. The law presents Moses and the redeemed people with their responsibilities as a theocratic nation under God;[14] obedience to the commandments will bring physical blessing and long life.

Leviticus 18 itself provides several clues supporting the regenerate state of the nation being addressed. In verses 2–3, God commands Moses to tell the children of Israel, "I am the LORD your God. You shall not do as they do in Egypt, where you used to live. . . ." This statement is best understood in light of Exodus 6:6–7, where God spoke to the pre-Exodus nation prior to their spiritual redemption:

> I will bring you out from under the yoke of the Egyptians. I will free you from being slaves to them, and I will redeem you with an outstretched arm and with mighty acts of judgment. Then I will take you as my own people, and I will be your God. Then you will know that I am the LORD your God, who brought you out from under the yoke of the Egyptians.

Subsequent to this Exodus passage, God became Israel's God— specifically, the covenant Lord of that generation. The admonition not to do what was done in Egypt (Lev. 18:3–5) served to remind the Israelites of the promise in Exodus 6 that he would enter into a covenantal relationship with them. The emphasis on that covenantal relationship begins and ends God's message in Leviticus 18: "I am the LORD your God" (vv. 2, 30). This phrase (or a similar phrase) appears consistently throughout the address, stressing that Israel's salvation has already been secured (18:4, 5, 6, 21).[15]

---

[12]Anne Lawton, "Christ: The End of the Law, A Study of Romans 10:4–8," *TJ* 3 (Spring 1974), 23; S. H. Kellogg, *The Book of Leviticus* (Minneapolis: Klock and Klock, 1978), 380–81; and G. J. Wenham, *The Book of Leviticus*, NICOT (Grand Rapids: Eerdmans, 1979), 31, 253.

[13]R. K. Harrison, *Leviticus*, TOTC (Downers Grove, Ill.: InterVarsity, 1980), 30.

[14]Ibid., 185.

[15]See J. H. Sailhamer, "The Mosaic Law and the Theology of the Pentateuch," *WTJ* 53 (1991), 241–61, for an intriguing study designed in part to argue that the theological purpose of the Pentateuch is to contrast faith and the works of the law through the comparison of the lives of Abraham and Moses.

Further confirmation is found in such passages as Nehemiah 9:8; Psalm 106:12–31; Isaiah 45:25; 54:17; Micah 6:6–8; Habakkuk 2:4. In other words, according to the testimony in the Old Testament, the Mosaic law was never intended to provide salvation. All expositions of the law lack statements that suggest a soteriological purpose. For instance, when Isaiah could have appealed to compliance with the law as the means of salvation, he instead recorded the Lord as saying, "In the LORD all the descendants of Israel will be found righteous and will exult" (Isa. 45:25).

It is important to note that dispensationalists have never advocated the position that there are two ways of salvation: Mosaic law for Old Testament people of God and faith for the New Testament people. Admittedly, isolated statements have been made that might lead one to conclude that dispensationalists hold to two ways of salvation, but these statements have generally been clarified. Despite such clarifications, however, some have persisted in charging dispensationalists with fostering the dual salvation system.[16] In addition, other clear statements made by these same early dispensationalists that present only *one* way of salvation throughout the Scriptures are virtually ignored.[17]

---

[16]One of the most recent examples of the persistence in accusing dispensationalism of two ways of salvation is the severe work of John H. Gerstner, *Wrongly Dividing the Word of Truth: A Critique of Dispensationalism* (Brentwood, Tenn.: Wohlgemuth and Hyatt, 1991), 149–69. Daniel P. Fuller argued in his *Gospel & Law* that older dispensationalists such as C. I. Scofield and L. S. Chafer taught two ways of salvation (pp. 22–33). He raised the problem in connection with *The Scofield Reference Bible* note on John 1:17 and the charges of two ways of salvation lodged against L. S. Chafer by the Southern Presbyterians. He also raised a question about the phrase, "We believe that . . . salvation *in the divine reckoning* [italics mine], is always by grace through faith," in Dallas Theological Seminary's doctrinal statement, wondering "whether or not Dallas Seminary was now really affirming that in all dispensations, the only condition men had to meet in order to be saved was faith in God's gracious promise" (p. 38). See also Klyne Snodgrass, "Spheres of Influence," 94; C. B. Bass, *Backgrounds to Dispensationalism: Its Historical Genesis and Ecclesiastical Implications* (Grand Rapids: Eerdmans, 1960), 313–36; and C. Norman Kraus, *Dispensationalism in America: Its Rise and Development* (Richmond, Va.: John Knox, 1958), 117–18.

[17]John Feinberg examines this persistent view of dispensationalists teaching two ways of salvation, despite the repeated efforts to clarify the issue by more recent dispensationalists and by the revision of unguarded statements in *The Scofield Reference Bible* (see his "Salvation in the Old Testament," in *Tradition and Testament: Essays in Honor of Charles Lee Feinberg*, eds. John S. and Paul D. Feinberg [Chicago: Moody, 1981], 40–44). In truth, *all* dispensationalists have taught only one method of salvation as expressed by Scripture.

Any suggestion of two ways of salvation contradicts the entire teaching of the Bible. Dispensationalists and non-dispensationalists admit that no one (apart from Christ) has ever obeyed, or could ever obey, the law perfectly enough to merit salvation. Moreover, it must be emphasized that the New Testament exposition of the law demonstrates that it would be impossible to be saved even if the law were completely observed (Rom. 3:20; Gal. 2:16).

The Purpose of the Mosaic Law

Demonstration of God's Graciousness

What then was the purpose of the law according to the Old Testament? First, the giving of the law itself demonstrated God's graciousness to Israel. Abraham was called out from among the Gentiles as the father of the nation of Israel because God *chose* to enter into a special relationship with them. They became his "treasured possession" (Ex. 19:5) out of all the other nations of the world.[18] The fact that God had given Israel a set of guidelines for the affairs of life, such as government and worship, constantly reminded them of God's concern for them as his special nation. If Israel ever forgot that God's grace had motivated his giving them the law to show them how to please him, all they had to do was read this humbling message:

> The LORD did not set his affection on you and choose you because you were more numerous than any other peoples, for you were the fewest of all peoples. But it was because the LORD loved you and kept the oath he swore to your forefathers that he brought you out with a mighty hand and redeemed you from the land of slavery, from the power of Pharaoh king of Egypt." (Deut. 7:7–8)[19]

---

[18]Gerhard von Rad records God's gracious activity, proven by the election of Israel, as a theological emphasis in the book of Deuteronomy (*Old Testament Theology* [New York: Harper and Row, 1965], 1.178). W. C. Kaiser, Jr. remarks similarly in *Toward an Old Testament Theology* (Grand Rapids: Zondervan, 1978), 113: "Let it be noted well that even the Sinaitic covenant was initiated by Yahweh's love, mercy, and grace (Deut. 4:37; 7:7–9; 10:15, *passim*)." See also Bruce Kaye and Gordon Wenham, eds., *Law, Morality, and the Bible* (Downers Grove, Ill.: InterVarsity, 1978), 7; and G. F. Oehler, *Theology of the Old Testament*, 4th ed. (New York: Funk and Wagnalls, 1892), 175.

[19]A similar statement is found in Deuteronomy 9:6, 8, where Israel is given the possession of the land not because of their inherent righteousness, since they are stubborn, but rather because of the grace of God.

Israel was reminded by its inauspicious and humble beginning that it was God's gracious activity that even allowed it to continue as a nation.

Furthermore, the blessing that resulted from the law was a reminder of and testimony to the grace of God. Among the blessings through the law were: (1) a homeland that was rich in produce, enabling the nation to live off the land (Deut. 7:13); (2) the prevention of illness due to diseases (v. 15); and (3) victory over their enemies (v. 16).[20]

The land was in a special sense viewed as a blessing from God during the Mosaic era. As the Israelites possessed the land and lived off it, they were repeatedly forced to recall the grace of the God who had given them the land. To Israel blessing was tied to the land *itself*.[21] For this reason, many of the blessings of obedience to the law centered around the enjoyment of the "land flowing with milk and honey" (Ex. 33:3; Lev. 16:13–14). It should be no surprise that the commandment to honor parents was also tied to blessing in the land (Ex. 20:12).

Provision for Approaching God

Second, the Sinaitic covenant was also designed to facilitate the life of faith or the sanctification of God's people. God intended that Israel would become a *holy* nation, a "kingdom of priests" (Ex. 19:6). Thus, the law defined the responsibility of the covenant nation to God, marking out the requirement for fellowship and communion with him. It gave specific instructions to them concerning appropriate behavior within the covenant relationship. The entire life of the Old Testament saint was regulated, including diet and marital relationships. Israel needed such instruction to maintain fellowship with God as his redeemed people.[22] The law

---

[20]C. C. Ryrie, *The Grace of God* (Chicago: Moody, 1963), 103. Gordon Wenham notes that it was God's grace in choosing Israel that should have motivated them to obey God, thus enjoying the promise of blessing (*Leviticus*, 12).

[21]A plethora of Old Testament passages explicitly associate the blessing of God to the land, because it was a good gift (Deut. 1:25; 3:25; 4:21–22; 6:18; 9:6; 11:9, 17; 15:4; 23:20; 27:3; 28:8; 31:20). Martens remarks that theological treatments concerning the land are scarce until recently; he spends several pages explaining that the central message of the Old Testament must include, as part of God's purpose, the land as blessing. He writes: "It may go without saying that a gift from the hand of God to his own people would be a desirable and good gift, a blessing" (*God's Design: A Focus on Old Testament Theology* [Grand Rapids: Baker, 1981], 106).

[22]Kaiser, *Toward an Old Testament Theology*, 44; R. E. Clements, *Abraham and David* (Naperville, Ill.: Alec R. Allenson, 1967), 87–96; E. W. Nicholson, "The

therefore functioned as a means of blessing for those already redeemed. The Psalms likewise confirm that the law provided the saint with the means for living a life in fellowship with God (e.g., Pss. 15; 24).

Disobedience to the law did not remove them from the coveted covenant relationship, for that relationship depended on God's faithfulness. However, disobedience did affect the *enjoyment* of the blessings attendant to salvation.[23] Note, however, that the consequences for disobedience to the law are not stated in terms of eternal condemnation, but rather in terms of physical, temporal punishment (Deut. 28:58–62). This also indicates that the Old Testament law did not have Israel's eternal salvation in view.

Finally, the law included not only a description of the requirement of holiness, but also the provision for forgiveness for Israel's failure to obey through the prescribed sacrifices (e.g., Lev. 1–7). The blood of the sacrifice brought about cleansing, sanctification, and renewed fellowship.[24]

Provision for Worship

It was not only important to be holy, forgiven of sin, and in fellowship with God, but it was also essential to be a worshiping people. The Israelites were obligated to engage in actively declaring the worthiness and glory of God. Worship was in part expressed through the annual cycle of feasts. For example, the Passover (Lev. 23:5–8) reminded them of God's deliverance and resulted in their declaration of God's worth and glory and their recognition of his initiative in providing salvation.

Govern the Theocracy

Israel was unique in that they were a nation ruled by God and set apart by him to mediate his blessing to the remaining nations.[25] This theocratic kingdom was governed by the temporary and

---

Decalogue as the Direct Address of God," *VT* 27 (1977), 425–26; von Rad, *Old Testament Theology*, 1.192.

[23]Eichrodt, *Theology of the Old Testament* (Philadelphia: Westminster, 1967), 2.289.

[24]See Keil, *Biblical Archaeology* (Edinburgh: T. & T. Clark, 1887–88), 1.299.

[25]This is contrary to G. Bahnsen, *Theonomy in Christian Ethics*, Expanded Edition, (Phillipsburg, N.J.: Presbyterian and Reformed, 1984), 430, who argues that Israel was not exclusively a theocracy, since God is declared king over the whole world.

regulatory aspects of the law. For instance, the theocratic constitution provided for securing the land that was promised them (Ex. 23:20–31), including the allotment (Num. 26:52; 27:11; 33:53–36:13) and boundaries of the land (Ex. 23:31; Num. 34:2–12; Deut. 11:24). Even the use of the land was regulated–for example, the plowing and planting (Lev. 25:8–24) and the seventh year of rest (25:1–7). God promised that the land would provide theocratic blessings, such as rain for crops and a bountiful harvest (Deut. 11:10–17), if they obeyed his constitution as found in the law.[26]

Rules were also given for the governing of the people. Some people were excluded from the congregation (Deut. 23:1–8) and others, not racially Israelites, were included because they trusted God (Ex. 12:38). Israelite marriages (Deut. 21:10–14; 22:13–30; 24:1–4; 25:5–10) and civil affairs (Deut. 16:18–17:13) were included in the rules. Even more importantly, the law functioned as a test of whether or not one was part of the theocracy. Deuteronomy 28:1–14 outlined blessings for those in proper relationship to the theocratic Ruler. These individuals believed that God was fulfilling the land promises as well as the promise to set Israel above all the other nations (Deut. 28:1). However, disobedient individuals could expect curses (Deut. 28:15–68) for their refusal to abide by the demands of the theocracy.

Israel's theocracy resulted in a dual consequence for sin, reflecting the saint's twofold relationship to God as Savior and Ruler. Sin was a spiritual offense against God their Savior, but also a governmental offense against him as Ruler.[27] Consequently, the sacrifices were designed not only to restore a relationship of fellowship with the God who had redeemed them, but also to restore a relationship of harmony with government in the theocracy.

THE MOSAIC LAW AS PRESENTED IN THE NEW TESTAMENT

This brief excursus of the Old Testament presentation of the law prepares us for an investigation of the New Testament contribution regarding the law. We will study the purposes of the law and the relationship of the law to legalism in this section. That

---

[26]H. Schultz, *Old Testament Theology* (Edinburgh: T. & T. Clark, 1895), 2.280–85.

[27]J. Feinberg, "Salvation in the Old Testament," 67.

will lead us into the next sections on the relationship of the Law to the Gospel, the question of the applicability of the law to the modern Christian, and an explanation of the law of Christ.

Traditionally, dispensationalists have emphasized the discontinuities between the Law and Gospel, basing their teaching especially on the Pauline contribution to the issue. Although formerly there was greater consensus regarding the discontinuities among "traditional"[28] dispensationalists than currently exists,[29] the contrasts between Law and Gospel remain a major dispensational motif for many.

The Purposes of the Law

We have seen the Old Testament claim that the law was designed to show the graciousness of God, validate his blessing on saved Israel, and explain how to live the life of faith and to please God. In spite of these clear purposes, Paul felt obliged to ask why the law had been given. The major treatise answering this question appears in his letter to the Galatians (Gal. 3:24–4:1), though he provides answers at other points as well.

The Law as Exposing Sin

First, Paul contends that the Mosaic law was intended to reveal and expose sin.[30] Indirectly, this function of the law revealed God's method of salvation, for by demonstrating to Israel that he would deal with sin, God hoped to impel them to faith in him. Paul himself readily admitted that although salvation was not obtained by observing the law, God's method of salvation was given in the law. The sinfulness of humankind was revealed by comparing human behavior to the holiness revealed in the law (see Gal. 3:19). At the same time, God manifested to Israel that

---

[28]By "traditional" dispensationalists I am referring to original formulations of the system by people such as J. N. Darby and C. I. Scofield, as well as subsequent expressions of dispensationalism by L. S. Chafer and C. C. Ryrie.

[29]A significant example of one who presents a dispensationalism with greater emphasis on continuities between law and grace (as well as Israel and the church), is Kenneth L. Barker, "False Dichotomies between the Testaments," *JETS* 25 (March 1982), 3–16.

[30]J. D. Pentecost, "The Purpose of the Law," *BSac* 128 (1971), 229; Mark Karlberg, "Justification in Redemptive History," *WTJ* 43 (1981), 225; "Reformed Interpretation of the Mosaic Covenant," *WTJ* 43 (1980), 1–57; Eichrodt, *Old Testament Theology*, 390–91; Oehler, *Theology of the Old Testament*, 183. This function of the law is also noted by B. S. Childs, *The Book of Exodus: A Critical, Theological Commentary* (Philadelphia: Westminster, 1974), 373.

access to him was possible by his gracious activity and their recognition of a need for his grace.

Paul's discussions of the law's relationship to sin may be grouped under three headings: (1) law as revealing the reality of sin (Rom. 3:20); (2) law as demonstrating the sinfulness of sin (7:7); and (3) law as revealing of the guilt associated with sin (3:19; Gal. 3:22; Col. 2:14).

(1) In Romans 3:20 Paul treats the critical and often misunderstood issue of the relationship between law and justification. In this letter, his most overtly theological writing, Paul presents the thesis that the righteousness of God is obtained solely by faith in him since humans are sinful. After briefly introducing the theme of the righteousness of God (Rom. 1:16–17), Paul's initial objective is to articulate and validate the need of both Jews and Gentiles for the righteousness of God (1:18–3:20). In summing up his argument, Paul argues that the Old Testament teaches that everyone is under sin and in need of God's righteousness (Rom. 3:9–20, where Paul quotes Ps. 5:9; 10:7; 14:1–3; 36:1; 140:3; Isa. 59:7–8 as support). These passages he calls the "law" (nomos), meaning here (and occasionally elsewhere) the entire body of Old Testament literature.[31]

Then Paul shifts in Romans 3:19 naturally from the broader use of nomos to its narrower and more prevalent application, the Mosaic law, arguing that the adherence to the law was not designed to effect personal justification. Its purpose was to inform humankind of their sinfulness: "for through the law we become conscious of sin" (Rom. 3:20b).[32] Paul uses the term epignōsis here; the normal form gnosis has been intensified by adding the prefix epi, in order to convey the idea of the clear knowledge of sin which the law communicates. In fact, it appears that the term epignōsis relates to both the idea of "recognition" as well as to the idea of "advanced or further knowledge."[33] As Cranfield confirms, "the truth is rather that the condition of all men is such that the primary effect of the law in relation to them is to show up their sin

---

[31]The term nomos may refer to the entire Old Testament in Romans 3:19, since Paul previously referred to passages in the Psalms and Isaiah. Similarly, in 1 Corinthians 14:21 Paul makes reference to Isaiah 28:11–12 as from the law.

[32]See Geoffrey J. Paxton, "Law and the Christian," Present Truth 2 (March 1973), 23, who describes one of the purposes of law as exposing sin.

[33]This idea is brought out by William Sanday and Arthur C. Headlam, A Critical and Exegetical Commentary on the Epistle to the Romans, ICC (Edinburgh: T. and T. Clark, 1902), 46.

as sin and themselves as sinners."[34] Thus through the law the Jew became aware of personal sin.

Paul has other passages where he also presents the law's purpose as revealing sin to those in need of righteousness. In 1 Timothy 1:8, he establishes a contemporary applicability of law: The law is good and can in fact be used "lawfully" (NASB). In verse 9, however, he eliminates the suggestion that the law is good for sanctification, because it is not for the righteous but for "the lawbreakers and rebels, the ungodly and sinful. . ." (1:9–10). This use remains true for the church age or dispensation.

(2) The law not only gave knowledge of sin, but also demonstrated the sinfulness of sin (Rom. 7:7–13). Paul writes: "I would not have known what sin was except through the law" (v. 7). Expanding on the proposition that knowledge of sin comes via the law, Paul gives a personal testimony of his own knowledge of sin by the law and concludes that the law exposes sin for what it is—utterly sinful, i.e., open, conscious rebellion against God (v. 13). The law functioned in Paul's own life to force him to come to grips with the ugliness and pervasiveness of sin. It produced not merely a recognition that he was sinning, but accompanying that knowledge was an inner conviction of sin.[35] It forced him to admit his culpability and the gravity of sin as an act contrary to the nature of God.

(3) The final connection between law and sin developed by Paul is that the law reveals the guilt and condemnation associated with sin. Paul clearly believed that the Mosaic law served the purpose of effectively convincing sinners of their accountability before God due to sin (Rom. 3:19). This purpose is indicated by the *hina* clause ("so that"). When the law indicts, no one can return any response. On the contrary, every mouth is silenced and the whole world is "held accountable to God." The word *hypodikos* ("accountable"), when used in conjunction with the dative case,

---

[34]C. E. B. Cranfield, *A Critical and Exegetical Commentary on the Epistle to the Romans,* ICC (Edinburgh: T. and T. Clark, 1975), 1.199. Robert D. Brinsmead adds this comment: "As the law gave occasion for many infractions, so it multiplied sin. This prevented Israel from reverting to a pagan insensibility. By making Israel painfully aware of sin, it helped nourish her Messianic hope" ("Jesus and the Law," *Verdict* 4:6 [1981], 5).

[35]Charles Hodge, *Commentary on the Epistle to the Romans* (Grand Rapids: Eerdmans, 1953), 222. See also Richard N. Longenecker, *The Ministry and Message of Paul* (Grand Rapids: Zondervan), 94; *Paul, Apostle of Liberty* (New York: Harper and Row, 1964), 123–24.

"may denote either the judicial authority in relation to which one is *hupodikos* or—and this is more common—the injured party with a right to satisfaction."[36] Since this word occurs only here in the New Testament, the context favors the picture of a person standing before God as Judge, clearly having been proven guilty and expecting the sentence of condemnation.

Paul makes the same point in Galatians 3:22: "the Scripture declares that the whole world is a prisoner of sin." The "Scripture" in view here is the law as discussed in Galatians 3:10–21; the manner in which the law was able to make humankind a prisoner of sin was by confining everyone under its penalty, thus precluding sin from being the source of life.

We noted in the previous section of this essay that the purpose of the law as portrayed in the Old Testament was to demonstrate the graciousness of God. Paul, however, understands it as connected to sin. Thus, important questions surface: How *was* the Jew justified under the Mosaic economy? Was it by a different method from the New Testament? In answer, we must first of all assert that salvation is based on God's grace and is appropriated through faith; this is true both in the Mosaic economy (Hab. 2:4) and in the church era (Gal. 3:11). Yet the progress of revelation as it applies to justification indicates that the content of faith may differ. As Ryrie has acknowledged; "the *basis* of salvation in every age is faith; the *object* of faith in every age is God; the *content* of faith changes in the various dispensations."[37]

In both Old and New Testament, the basis of salvation and of God's gracious activity is the death of Christ. Leviticus 17:11 discusses the basis of salvation in the time of Moses as blood sacrifice; the blood of a slain animal was applied to the believer, though it was only temporarily efficacious in providing atonement, for it had to be repeated every year. The deeper significance of that sacrificial blood pointed forward to the ultimate basis for salvation, the death of Christ (Heb. 10:10–14). Note too how Isaiah describes the suffering servant, the Messiah, as the Lord's sacrifice (Isa. 53:2–12). Consequently, while the basis for salvation had not yet been fulfilled when the Mosaic economy commenced, the law was nevertheless able to reveal God's gracious provision

---

[36]Cranfield, *Romans*, 1.197.

[37]C. C. Ryrie, *Dispensationalism Today* (Chicago: Moody, 1965), 123. See also S. Toussaint, "A Biblical Defense of Dispensationalism," in *Walvoord: A Tribute*, ed. D. K. Campbell (Chicago: Moody, 1982), 82.

for sin in the "sin-grace" construct by pointing to the basis of justification in the blood of the Lord's sacrifice. Because of Israel's limited perspective and understanding in the Old Testament, no one at that time had a clear perception of the necessity of Christ's death until it was accomplished in history.[38]

One may object that if Israel did not in fact understand the Messianic predictions about the atonement, then the law had a revelatory function in explaining the "sin-grace" construct only after the law had been terminated. In answer, we must realize that lack of understanding does not mean this purpose of the law was not revealed. The fact that prophets recorded it is sufficient to demonstrate that this purpose was there. In keeping with the progressive nature of revelation, God did continually give a clearer picture of the method of justification.[39]

It is this purpose of the law in revealing sin that Paul remarks as being good (Rom. 7:12) and that he depends on to help inform his audience concerning the ongoing role of law in relating sin and grace in justification (5:20–21). The Mosaic law has an abiding or permanent purpose in exposing sin.

The Law as Tutor

The second purpose of the law was that it was designed to act as a "custodian" until the incarnation of Christ (Gal. 3:24 RSV). The Old Testament saint may not have fully realized this, but Paul, reflecting back on the covenant, now clarifies that purpose in Galatians 3:24–4:1. In this section, he explicitly answers the question of the purpose of the law posed earlier in 3:19a. He had just refuted the misunderstanding of the law by the Judaizers and was now presenting a positive exposition of the true purpose of the law, using the word *paidagōgos* ("custodian").[40]

> Now before faith came, we were confined under the law, kept under restraint until faith should be revealed. So that the law was our custodian until Christ came, that we might be justified by faith. But now that faith has come, we are no longer under a custodian. (Gal. 3:23–25 RSV)

---

[38]See J. Feinberg, "Salvation in the Old Testament," 39–77.

[39]See R. C. H. Lenski, *The Interpretation of the Epistles of St. Peter, St. John and St. Jude* (Minneapolis: Augsburg, 1966), 67.

[40]J. H. MacGorman, "The Law as Paidagogos: A Study in Pauline Analogy," in *New Testament Studies: Essays in Honor of Ray Summers in His Sixty-Fifth Year*, eds. Hubert L. Drumwright and Curtis Vaughan (Waco, Tex.: Baylor University Press, 1975), 102.

In the Greek world, a *paidagōgos* was generally a slave who functioned in both a custodial and an educative fashion as a tutor. His responsibility was to supervise the entire lifestyle of the child, giving constant attention to the academic, social, and spiritual nourishment of the child until maturity. In a similar manner, therefore, the Old Testament Jew was a child supervised by the law. The redeemed Jew needed this constant supervision in order to know how to please and worship God. The law had this function until Christ arrived and led believers to himself to be justified by faith in him. Thus the law is regarded by Paul as clearly inferior, in the sense of being *preparatory* to the gospel of Jesus Christ. With the advent of faith in Jesus Christ, however, the law as a pedagogue is no longer necessary.[41] In other words, the law is temporary with regard to this regulatory purpose. "The context makes it clear that the apostle is speaking . . . of the historic succession of one period of revelation upon another and the displacement of the law by Christ."[42]

The Relationship of *Nomos* to Legalism

Expositors such as C. E. B. Cranfield and D. Fuller have attempted to harmonize the "seeming" contradictory statements of Paul regarding the law by arguing that wherever Paul disparages the law, he is actually denouncing legalism.[43] According to this understanding, Paul did not present the Law and Gospel in antithesis, merely the Gospel and the Pharisaic misunderstanding

---

[41]See the following discussions on the law as tutor: MacGorman, "The Law as Paidagogos", 99–111; D. Fürst, "παιδεύω," *NIDNTT*, ed. Colin Brown (Grand Rapids: Zondervan, 1978), 3.779; H. Ridderbos, *The Epistle of Paul to the Churches of Galatia*, NICNT (Grand Rapids: Eerdmans, 1953), 146; G. Howard, *Paul: Crisis in Galatia: A Study in Early Christian Theology* (New York: Cambridge University Press, 1990), 65; K. Stendahl, *Paul Among Jews and Gentiles, and Other Essays* (Philadelphia: Fortress, 1976), 20–21.

[42]E. deWitt Burton, *A Critical and Exegetical Commentary on the Epistle to the Galatians*, ICC (Edinburgh: T. and T. Clark, 1921), 200. See also G. Howard, *Paul: Crisis in Galatia*, 78; and R. D. Brinsmead, "Jesus and the Law," 5.

[43]Fuller, *Gospel & Law*, 97–99; C. E. B. Cranfield, "St. Paul and the Law," *SJT* 17 (1964), 54–55; Fuller gives an extensive argument for the "legalistic" view of *nomos* based on Paul's use of the term in Romans 10:5–8 and Galatians 3:10–12. Others who have presented the same or a similar Pauline construction are Burton, *Galatians*, 458; Charles H.Cosgrove, "The Mosaic Law Preaches Faith: A Study in Galatians," *WTJ* 39 (1976–77), 153–55; Ragnar Bring, "Paul and the Old Testament: A Study of the Ideas of Election, Faith and Law in Paul, with Special Reference to Romans 9:30–10:13," *ST* 25 (1971), 21–60; Hans Hübner, *Law in Paul's Thought*, 137–38.

of the Law. Cranfield attempts to prove this thesis by citing that Paul did not have a separate Greek term available to represent legalism.[44] Consequently, he had to employ the term *nomos* to denote both the Sinaitic legal code and the abuse or legalistic use of the law. Is this a warranted understanding of the term? We must examine briefly how Paul uses the term *nomos* and phrases such as "works of the law" (Gal 3:2 NASB).

The Pauline Usage of "Law"

An analysis of Paul's use of *nomos* reveals that he uses the term in three different ways. First, he uses the term to refer to the Old Testament Scriptures as a whole. In some respects, this use follows the Hebrew term *tôrâ*. As mentioned above, in Romans 3:10–18 Paul quotes as *nomos* (see v. 19) various passages of the Old Testament that are not part of the Mosaic covenant or Pentateuch. *Nomos* here refers to the entire Old Testament Scriptures. Similarly, Isaiah 28:11–12 is labelled *nomos* in 1 Corinthians 14:21.

Paul applies the expression more narrowly to the Pentateuchal portion of the Old Testament. In Romans 3:21b Paul writes: "to which the Law [*nomos*] and the Prophets testify." Clearly Paul restricts *nomos* here to Pentateuch. Another example of this use is found in Galatians 4:21b: "Are you not aware of what the law says?" The entire Pentateuch must be in view here, since the subsequent verses allude to Genesis 16:15 and 21:2, 9.

This application of *nomos* is further restricted to the injunctions of the Mosaic covenant. This is Paul's most frequent meaning of the law—the "legal" sections of the Torah. Examples abound of this usage by Paul (e.g., Acts 13:39; Rom. 5:20; Gal. 5:3; 6:13).

Closely related to this use is a set of Pauline passages where *nomos* describes the epoch or dispensation of Mosaic law. Perhaps the clearest example is found in Romans 6:14–15. In the context, Paul is discussing *sanctification* rather than justification (vv. 12–13), and he sets up a contrast between law and grace. He writes, "because you are *not* under law [*hypo nomon*], but [*alla*] under grace [*hypo charin*]" (v. 14). The identical preposition *hypo* governing each prepositional phrase and the employment of the strongly contrastive particle *alla* demonstrate that Paul's purpose is to set in clear antithesis the ideas of grace and the law of Moses. He is not

---

[44]Cranfield, "St. Paul and the Law," 55.

suggesting that there was no grace under the law, but that in the Mosaic economy, sanctification came via obedience to the demands of the law, and that this economy has now been superseded by the dispensation of grace. Paul repeats this contrast in the next verse (v. 15).

The apostle employs the same phraseology, "under law" (*hypo nomon*) four times in 1 Corinthians 9:20, contrasting it to the obligation of the church saint, who is "in the law of Christ" (*ennomos Christou*). The contrast clearly demonstrates Paul's understanding of a former period dominated by the commands of the Mosaic law (see also Gal. 3:23; 4:4–5). This first category of usage is generally not disputed within Pauline studies.

The second category of Pauline usage regards *nomos* as the general principle of law. Contrary to the contention of Sanday and Headlam, it is not true that Paul intends for the articular *nomos* to refer to the principle of law.[45] Paul seldom uses the term in this way, but Romans 7:21 is a clear example: "So I find this law [principle] at work." In the subsequent phrase he identifies or explains the principle, that whenever a person wishes to do good, evil appears to be close at hand. This "law" is derived from Paul's experience or the experience of others. Other debated passages where Paul may be using *nomos* in the sense of principle are Romans 3:27; 7:23, 25; 8:2; and Galatians 4:21.

The third way that Paul uses *nomos* recognizes the major development in history associated with the Incarnation. Just as Paul occasionally uses *nomos* to refer to the Mosaic dispensation, it is apparent that in spite of changes in the dispensations, there still is law. In Romans 3:27b Paul refers to it as the "law . . . of faith," contrasted to the principle or *nomos* "of works" (RSV) found in the earlier portion of the same verse. Later, Paul describes the law as the "law of the Spirit of life in Christ Jesus" (Rom. 8:2 RSV). Again, this law is clearly different from the former Mosaic law discussed in Romans 8:2–3, for this law liberates from the "law of sin and death." Elsewhere Paul refers to the law of the present period as "the law of Christ" (Gal. 6:12).

As previously mentioned, some would argue that Paul

---

[45]Sanday and Headlam, *Romans*, 58. For a discussion disproving this thesis, see G. E. Howard, "Christ the End of the Law: The Meaning of Rom 10:4ff.," *JBL* 88 (1969), 331 fn. 2; R. Longenecker, *Paul, Apostle of Liberty*, 118–19; Edward Grafe, *Die paulinische Lehre vom Gesetz nach den vier Hauptbriefen* (Freiburg: J. C. B. Mohr, 1884), 5–8; P. P. Bläser, *Das Gesetz bei Paulus* (Munster: Aschendorff, 1941), 1–23; Westerholm, *Israel's Law*, 106.

occasionally uses *nomos* in a fourth manner, meaning legalism or the misuse of the law. It must be admitted that Paul does identify the misuse of the Mosaic law and condemns such an approach to the application of the law. However, it is noteworthy that wherever Paul addresses such concerns, it is not the term itself that conveys the meaning legalism, but the description in the context of the way in which the law is used that indicates that legalism is in view. For example, in Romans 4:13–14 Paul makes it clear that the Mosaic law is misused if it becomes the means of attempting to attain the promise to Abraham. The term *nomos* itself is not designating legalism; rather, it refers to the Mosaic law as revealed to Moses. But the way that the law is used is presented as inappropriate; the ones seeking justification through the law are "the adherents of the law" (RSV; see also Rom. 10:5; Gal. 3:18; 3:21).

If the term *nomos* itself meant legalism, Paul could have merely written "law" rather than "the righteousness that comes by [law]." This explanation about people seeking justification by following the law was only necessary if the audience did not understand "legalism" as part of the semantic range of *nomos*. Likewise, when Jesus refers to those who misunderstand the law, he does not give the term itself the meaning of "misuse of the law." Rather, he understands "law" in its ordinary sense and addresses the corruptions of the law by the Pharisees.

The Contribution of Romans 10:5–8

Regarding Romans 10:5–8, the problem of Paul quoting two passages in the Pentateuch to support opposing modes of righteousness is raised.[46] How can Paul refer to Leviticus 18:5 in support of righteousness based on the law and at the same time quote Deuteronomy 30:12–14 in support of righteousness by faith? Fuller answers this question by adopting the construction of Flückiger, who argues that Paul quotes Deuteronomy 30:11–14 after Leviticus 18:5 in order to combat the Pharisees' idea, that their lifestyle had to be copied in order to be saved; he invokes Deuteronomy 30:11–14 to rebuke the Pharisees for "misconstru-

---

[46]The view that Paul employed a Jewish *midrash* or *pesher* approach to this Deuteronomy passage must be rejected, since Paul did not customarily depart so radically from the original intent of the Old Testament author. This is the view advanced by Robert Badenas in *Christ the End of the Law*, 126–27.

ing the law of Moses."[47] Thus the antithesis in Romans 10:5–8 is not between the Law and Gospel, but between the Pharisaic perversion of the Law and Gospel.

In answer to this, we note first that Paul quotes the last portion of Leviticus 18:5 in Romans 10:5 from the Septuagint: "The man who does these things will live by them." The first half of this verse is Paul's commentary on this phrase, where he explains that Moses was writing about the righteousness of the law. In other words, the person who performs the righteousness of the law will live by it. Paul is evidently making a loose reference to Moses' statement in Leviticus 18:5.[48]

Who then is the audience being addressed in Leviticus 18:5? It seems to be a covenant (believing) nation, *not* an unbelieving people. Israel is being given responsibilities at a time when they are an already redeemed people. In other words, this verse refers not to the justification, but to the sanctification of the Israelites. Yet without discussing the merit of the view, Fuller adopts the proposal that Leviticus 18:5 is addressed to an unregenerate audience. Others, however, suggest a regenerate audience.[49] Walter C. Kaiser, Jr. is surely correct in his two comments supportive of the view that the audience was regenerate:

2. While the customs of these pagans lead to lust and abomination (vss. 3, 30) Israel's happy privilege of keeping God's laws only perpetuated a life already begun by faith.

3. The passage begins and ends (vss. 1, 30) with the theological setting of "I am the LORD your God"; thus law-keeping here is

[47]Fuller, *Gospel & Law*, 70; see Felix Flückiger, "Christus, des Gesetzes *telos*," *TZ* 11 (1955), 155. To Paul righteous deeds are not performed by one's own efforts, but rather through the word which one believes and confesses.

[48]This is the general consensus of commentators on Romans 10:5: e.g., E. H. Gifford, *The Epistle of St. Paul to the Romans: With Notes and Introduction* (Minneapolis: Klock and Klock, 1977), 183; Sanday and Headlam, *Romans*, 285; H. P. Liddon, *Explanatory Analysis of St. Paul's Epistle to the Romans* (1899; reprint: Minneapolis: James and Klock Christian Publishing Co., 1977) , 180; Hodge, *Romans*, 337; and Frederic Louis Godet, *Commentary on St. Paul's Epistle to the Romans* (New York: Funk and Wagnalls, 1883), 377.

[49]Harrison, *Leviticus*, 185. See also Lawton, "Christ: The End of the Law," 23; Kellogg, *The Book of Leviticus*, 380–81; Wenham, *Leviticus*, 31, 253; W. J. Dumbrell, *Covenant and Creation* (Nashville: Nelson, 1984), 123; von Rad, *Theology of the Old Testament*, 2.391.

Israel's sanctification, the grand evidence that the Lord was indeed their God already.[50]

The problem appears to be Deuteronomy 30:11–14, a verse that is also quoted by Paul in Romans 10:6–8 and one that seems to contradict his earlier statement in Romans 10:5. As in Leviticus 18:5, Paul does not borrow Deuteronomy 30:11–14 word for word, but merely utilizes certain phrases from the Old Testament passage. He also changes the force of the passage from an indicative to a prohibition. Paul explicitly writes that Deuteronomy 30:11–14 refers to "righteousness that is by faith." This phrase seemingly disproves what Moses wrote in Leviticus 18:5 and what Paul wrote in Romans 10:5. Yet is that necessarily so?

An examination of Deuteronomy 30 reveals that the situation in that passage is vastly different from the situation of Leviticus 18:5. Leviticus 18:5 reveals the *current* situation of the nation Israel under Moses, whereas Deuteronomy 30 speaks of a *future* situation.[51] In this passage there is a prophetic glance at the ultimate restoration that reveals the Lord's promised grace. God's purpose in the implementation of the curses is revealed as bringing about repentance on the part of Israel and consequent blessing. Past blessings and curses will come to mind, causing a return to the Lord. Israel will listen to God and obey him. Then, according to Deuteronomy 30:3, the Lord will restore, gather, and bring them into the land.[52] It is crucial to note that the commandments for Israel's obedience are given in the day of Moses, whereas the fulfillment of the obedience is at a future time when God circumcises their hearts.[53]

Deuteronomy 30:11–14 goes on to clarify the nature of the decision to be made by Israel at Moab. The commandment was

---

[50]Walter C. Kaiser, Jr., "Leviticus 18:5 and Paul: Do This and You Shall Live (Eternally?)," *JETS* 14 (1971), 14.

[51]Fuller rejects this thesis (*Gospel & Law*, 68), adopting instead the proposal of F. Flückiger ("Christos," 155), who maintains that while Deuteronomy 30:6 speaks of a future regeneration, verses 11–14 speak about what is true at present. He therefore concludes that verses 11–14 speak to unregenerate people. Only then can the meaning in Leviticus 18 correspond to the meaning in Deuteronomy 30. Cranfield appears to adopt a similar stance (*Romans*, 2.522–26).

[52]John Arthur Thompson, *Deuteronomy: An Introduction and Commentary*, TOTC (Downers Grove, Ill.: InterVarsity, 1974), 285.

[53]Von Rad remarks: "From this standpoint the speaker looks to the future and announces a redemptive activity by which God himself creates for his people the prerequisites for complete obedience" (*Deuteronomy* [Philadelphia: Westminster, 1966], 184).

given to them in that day, and it was characterized as not too difficult or impossible, but accessible and realistic. The law was therefore revealed as that to which Israel could and should respond (as in Lev. 18:5). It was a theocratic economy with theocratic responsibilities (not soteric responsibilities), but the perfect fulfillment on the level of an entire generation of saints in Israel was reserved for God's promise of future fulfillment.[54]

The command given in the present but fulfilled in the future (vv. 11–14) is also suggested in v. 8, where obedience to the current command is seen in the future: "You will again obey the LORD and follow all his commands I am giving you today." Fuller regards this verse as belonging to the 30:1–10 unit. Thus, if Deuteronomy 30:1–10 is future and includes the phrase "which I am giving you today," it is equally possible for Deuteronomy 30:11–14 to be further discussion of the future, furnishing the possibility and reason for the future fulfillment of the commands God was giving them.

Leviticus 18:5 was addressed to a regenerate covenant people, outlining the principles necessary for the enjoyment of (eternal) life and the principles necessary to please God during the Mosaic economy. However, unlike this verse, Deuteronomy 30:1–14 addresses a future scene that is not part of the Mosaic economy and takes place when the Mosaic law will no longer be the operative principle. The ultimate fulfillment will be seen in the millennial kingdom as discussed by Jeremiah (Jer. 31:31–34). Leviticus 18:5 refers to the enjoyment of salvation or righteousness that came by the adherence to the Mosaic law. However, the enjoyment of salvation in Deuteronomy 30 comes by the righteousness of faith. There is a law still involved, but it is not the Mosaic law; rather, it is a law engraved on the hearts of the believers (Jer. 31:31–34).

It does appear that Deuteronomy 30 is addressed to a regenerate audience. This audience, like the Leviticus 18 audience, has entered into a covenant with God. In fact, in Deuteronomy 27:9 Moses addresses them as a people for the Lord God. The occasion for the book of Deuteronomy is the renewal of the covenant, where the nation of Israel formally declared their

---

[54]S. R. Driver notes that verses 11–14 are loosely connected with verses 1–10, although he also suggests that it is unlikely that verses 11–20 were originally the sequel to verses 1–10 (*Critical and Exegetical Commentary on Deuteronomy*, ICC [New York: Charles Scribners, 1895], 331).

faithfulness to the Lord and promised obedience.[55] Therefore Deuteronomy 30 must be viewed in its entirety as a promise of God for the ultimate fulfillment of the command given in the day of Moses to a regenerate audience. It is during this ultimate fulfillment that the righteousness of faith empowered by God's initiative is illustrated.

This understanding eliminates both the necessity of reading into Romans 10:5–8 a correction of the Pharisaic misinterpretation of the law and the idea of Paul quoting Old Testament passages as negative support. Paul merely gives clarity to the revelation of God to Moses that the righteousness of the law was operable during Moses' life, but that a future time would see righteousness based on faith. It is plausible to suggest that Paul utilizes the principle found in Deuteronomy 30:11–14 and extends its meaning beyond the normal historical sense in the original text, but not contrary to its original sense. Specifically, in Romans 10:8 he draws out the principle found in Deuteronomy 30:11–14 and applies it to the situation in the church by suggesting that his day was the time of the righteousness based on faith. This natural understanding of Romans 10:4–8 indicates that Paul had in mind a contrast between the righteousness based on law and the righteousness based on faith. The end of the law of righteousness came with Christ; with its cessation was the clear description of faith righteousness from the preaching of the word of faith.

Finally, Paul's discussions on the law were necessitated not by the problem of Pharisaic misunderstandings of the law, but rather by the application of the law, whether misunderstood or not, on the part of Christians. If the law principle was ended, it would be natural for Paul to be concerned about any suggestion that Christians were obligated to obey the law (whether Jewish Christians or Gentile Christians). The major problem of Galatians was the fact that some Jewish Christians were indeed teaching the necessity of works after salvation in order to please God. This was the problem that the Council of Jerusalem had addressed; this is also the reason Paul confronted Peter and told him that a person is not justified by observing the law, but rather through faith in Christ (Gal. 2:11–16). In Galatians 3:3 Paul shows that these

---

[55]P. C. Craigie, *The Book of Deuteronomy*, NICOT (Grand Rapids: Eerdmans, 1976), 31–32. See also Georg Braulik, "Law as Gospel: Justification and Pardon According to the Deuteronomic Torah," *Int* 38 (January 1984), 5–14, who argues for a redeemed audience in Deuteronomy.

Galatians had already placed faith in Christ, but were now resorting back to the obedience of the law in order to please God: "Are you so foolish? After beginning with the Spirit, are you now trying to attain your goal by human effort?"

Paul's View of the Law in Galatians 3:10–12

The use of *nomos* by Paul to convey legalism is also argued from Galatians 3:10–12. Specifically, some maintain that Paul occasionally employed *nomos* to "represent the Jewish legalistic *mis*interpretation of the law," so that the contrast in Galatians 3:10–12 is between the legalistic practice and the Gospel.[56] Since this is crucial to the advocacy of a continuum between Law and Gospel, we must also examine this passage.

The Use of Deuteronomy 27:26 in Galatians 3:10. Paul uses Deuteronomy 27:26 in this passage. In Deuteronomy, Moses enjoins obedience to the entire body of law, while Paul states that those people bound by the law are under a curse.[57] Paul's repeated use of Old Testament quotations in order to refute Judaizers presents a problem. It is suggested that if Paul attached to the phrase "works of the law" the meaning "works which are the result of the observance or performance of the law," as Strack and Billerbeck suggest,[58] then the quotation of Deuteronomy 27:26 at the end of Galatians 3:10 is not suitable to sustain the first part of this verse ("All who rely on observing the law are under a curse"). Deuteronomy would then be suggesting that "a curse rests on those who do *not* comply with the law's commands. . . . Only if Paul used the term 'works of law' as representing something sinful and deserving of a curse, would his use of Deuteronomy 27:26 be a proof that the two halves of Galatians 3:10 constitute a coherent argument."[59]

One option utilized to solve the problem is to insert an explanatory proposition between the two halves of the verse, such as, "Nobody can keep the law perfectly." Charles Ellicott writes, "With regard to the argument, it is only necessary to observe that the whole obviously rests on the admission, which it was

---

[56]C. F. D. Moule, "Obligation in the Ethic of Paul," in *Christian History and Interpretation: Studies Presented to John Knox*, eds. W. R. Farmer and C. F. D. Moule (Cambridge: Cambridge University Press, 1967), 392.

[57]R. Bring, *Commentary on Galatians* (Philadephia: Muhlenberg, 1961), 120.

[58]H. Strack and P. Billerbeck, *Kommentar zum neuen Testament* (München: C. H. Beck'sche, 1979), 3.160–61.

[59]Fuller, *Gospel & Law*, 90.

impossible not to make, that no one of *nomos* can fulfill all the requisitions of the law."[60] The consequent thought would be that the nature of the curse of the law is in the failure to continually obey *all* of the law *perfectly*. Fuller, however, rejects this option, suggesting that the Judaizers would have denied the validity of such an insertion. He maintains that "a curse does not fall so much on the one who disobeys a precept of the law as on one whose conduct and attitude undermines the integrity of the law."[61]

The scene in Deuteronomy 27 is that of the renewal of the covenant with Israel. Verses 15–26 detail the twelve curses (the Dodecalogue). The twelfth curse (Deut. 27:26) acts as a summary curse inclusive of all previous curses. It is significant to note that Paul quotes from the Septuagint (LXX) in order to make his case, for the Masoretic text of Deuteronomy reads as follows: "Cursed be the one who does not execute the words of this law to do them." However, the LXX reads: "Cursed is every man who does not continue in *all* the words of this law to do them." Guided by the Holy Spirit in his writing of Galatians 3:10, Paul utilized the LXX in order to emphasize that unless the entire law is executed and abided by, the curse of God is invoked. In doing so, he was suggesting that the "reach of the law is so all-pervasive that man cannot claim justification before God on the basis of 'works of the law.'"[62] Even H. Hübner, who accepts the idea of *nomos* as referring to the legalistic misinterpretation of the law in Romans 10:4,[63] recognizes the import of the reference to the LXX translation of the passage.[64]

Thus, commentators are justified in inserting an explanatory proposition in Galatians 3:10 that focuses on the "all" of Deuteronomy 27:26: "No one can keep the law perfectly." For this reason also Paul goes on to add that Christ redeemed them from the curse of the law, since the law was not able to save any human beings from the curse. There is no merit to support Fuller's statement that "a curse does not fall so much on the one who disobeys a precept of the law as one whose conduct and attitude undermines the

---

[60]C. Ellicott, *The Epistle to the Romans*, Laymen's Handy Commentary (Grand Rapids: Zondervan, 1957), 71.

[61]Fuller, *Gospel & Law*, 92.

[62]P. C. Craigie, *Deuteronomy*, 334.

[63]Hübner, *Law in Paul's Thought*, 138.

[64]Ibid., 18–19.

integrity of the law."[65] Paul was not speaking of revolt against God when referring to "works of the law," but rather compliance with the commands of the law. His point to the Judaizers was that any attempt to gain merit or salvation by compliance with the law would result in failure and curse, because no one was able to comply with *all* the law on the procurement of salvation. While the law is holy, good, and spiritual (Rom. 7:12, 14), humans cannot conform to its standards in a perfect manner.

The Significance of the Use of Leviticus 18:5. The meaning of *nomos* in Galatians 3:11–12 is likewise in harmony with its meaning in the previous verse, for there is nothing in the context to cause a shift in understanding from legalistic misunderstanding to revelatory law. Some exegetes observe that "law" in verse 12 must refer to the objective law itself because Paul quotes Leviticus 18:5, part of the objective law. This is indeed a strong argument, one that leads to the rejection of the idea that *nomos* has the sense of legalistic distortion. Fuller, however, attempts to argue that the legalists liked to quote Leviticus 18:5 and that the Pharisaic understanding is likewise utilized in Psalms of Solomon 14:1–2.[66]

There are two problems with this understanding. First, it is a serious matter to suggest that Paul would allow himself to succumb to the temptation to follow the example of a legalist and misinterpret or abuse a passage of Scripture, without making it clear that he was showing how Judaizers abused the passage. It was not Paul's practice to fall into the same trap of not rightly dividing the Word of God, but rather to expose the error. In addition, merely because Moses is not cited as the author of the passage does not mean that Paul intends a different meaning. In the previous verse (Gal. 3:11), Paul does not mention that Habakkuk is the author of the quotation, yet there is no hint that he intends to convey a different meaning.

The Significance of the Context Following Galatians 3:12. The most damaging evidence leading to the rejection of the thesis that the law in Galatians 3 refers to the legalistic misunderstanding of the law is found in the verses immediately following Galatians 3:10–12. Cranfield insists that the law in Galatians 3:15–18 is properly understood not as "law in the fullness and wholeness of its true character, but the law as seen apart from Christ."[67] In other

---

words, the theme of the misuse of law continues in the verses following verse 12. Yet, verses 17–18 clearly speak of the revelatory law. The Mosaic law came 430 years after the Abrahamic promise, and the inheritance based on law is contrasted with the one based on promise. Certainly, it was not the legalistic perversion of the law that was given to Israel! Furthermore, verses 19–29 detail the purpose of the revelatory law, the Mosaic law, not the misunderstanding of the law. As discussed earlier, the law in the sense of Sinaitic legislation was a standard of God's holiness and never intended to impart life.

Critics respond that the Judaizers would never have accepted Paul's contention that the Mosaic covenant was antithetical to the Abrahamic promise. That may be true, but Paul did not expect the Judaizers to agree with him; rather, he was addressing the believers in Galatia who were not as hardened as the Judaizers. Paul contrasted the Mosaic law and the Abrahamic covenant in order to educate and inform them of the true purpose of the law. Whether the Judaizers accepted the truth or not was of no consequence to Paul. He was never one to refrain from stating the truth merely because an adversary would not agree.[68]

The conclusion, therefore, that Galatians 3:10–12 indicates that "all God's soteric promises are fulfilled on the basis of satisfying the condition which the Scripture calls 'the obedience of faith' (Rom. 1:5; 16:26)" cannot stand. Paul spends a great deal of time contrasting the Mosaic law to faith, and in his exposition of the purpose of law he discounts the soteric possibility of the law. When the Mosaic code was given, it was addressed to a covenant nation—not for salvation but for sanctification and blessing. To suggest otherwise is to confuse the purpose of the law for theocratic righteousness with the righteousness of salvation that has always been based on faith.

THE MOSAIC LAW AND THE CHRISTIAN

The question still remains: "How should the Christian life be affected by the Mosaic law? Is the believer bound to or obliged to keep the law?"

Passages Presented as Advocating Continuity

Regardless of whether or not one believes that Paul used *nomos* to refer to the Pharisaic misunderstanding of the Mosaic

---

[68]For further discussion of Galatians 3 see Westerholm, *Israel's Law*, 109–115.

law, there are many who believe that the Bible contains clear passages advocating continuity between the Mosaic moral law and the church-age believer. Passages such as Matthew 5:17–19; Mark 7:1–23; Romans 7:12, 14, 22; and 1 Timothy 1:8 are marshaled in evidence of the continuity. We must therefore briefly treat selected passages presented in support of continuity.

Matthew 5:17–19

Matthew 5:17–19 is one of the key passages that some claim proves the sustained applicability of the Mosaic law during the church period. In fact, this passage provides the major justification for theonomy and reconstructionism.[69] According to its advocates, Christ himself taught that the entire law abides forever (i.e., "until heaven and earth disappear").[70] Bahnsen further contends that "Jesus binds us to all the commandments of God forever."[71] To him, the Matthean passage teaches that Christ confirmed or established the law rather than merely fulfilled it. In order to sustain this thesis, the critical word *plērōsai* must be understood as meaning "confirmed" or "ratified" rather than "fulfilled"; Christ is in fact arguing that he establishes or ratifies the law of Moses.[72]

The reconstructionist continuum model, however, is based on an erroneous understanding of *plērōsai* in this passage. It is, of course, lexically possible to adopt the meaning "to confirm" for *plērōsai*, since it takes this nuance in a few passages of the LXX and Apocrypha as well as three New Testament passages (Rom. 15:19; 2 Cor. 10:6; James 2:23). Yet the customary usage of this word is "to fulfill," especially in reference to the realization of prophecies.[73] One would expect to find the word *histēmi* if the nuance were "to confirm or establish." The contrasting idea in the verse of "*abolishing* the Law and the Prophets" also suggests the meaning of "fulfillment" for *plērōsai* rather than "confirmation." Furthermore, this meaning for *plērōsai* harmonizes with Matthew's use elsewhere in his gospel (e.g., 1:22; 2:15, 17, 23; 3:15; 4:14; 8:17), where it expresses the fulfillment of Old Testament prophecy.

---

[69]G. Bahnsen, *Theonomy*, 52.

[70]Ibid., 83.

[71]Ibid.

[72]Ibid., 67–70.

[73]G. Delling, "πληρόω," *TDNT* 6.293. See also V. Poythress, *The Shadow of Christ in the Law of Moses* (Brentwood, Tenn.: Wohlgemuth and Hyatt, 1991), 363–77.

In Matthew, the phrase "the Law and the Prophets" refers not simply to the Mosaic law, but to the entire Old Testament (cf. 7:12; 11:13; 22:40). Thus the term "law" in the following verse is an abbreviated way of referring to the same Old Testament. It should also be noted that the explicit reference to "Prophets" indicates that the author is speaking of prophecy. That fulfillment of the prophecies of the Old Testament is in view is signaled by the phrase "until everything is accomplished" in verse 18. Some argue that this phrase should be translated "until the end of all things" (i.e., until the end of the world), further emphasizing the previous phrase "until heaven and earth disappear." The link to prophetic statements, however, seems to argue against this understanding. Finally, the reconstructionist appeal to 5:17–19 actually leads to a contradiction within their system, since an absolute confirmation of the law would not allow for *any* abrogation of *any* portion of the Mosaic law.[74]

Though Christ rejects the thesis that the Old Testament Scriptures can be abolished, he does say that they must be fulfilled. The prophetic statements of Scripture can be abolished only when they are fulfilled, and Christ in fact perfectly fulfills the prophecies of the Old Testament. As long as this world exists, there will be no repeal of the Law and Prophets apart from fulfillment. Since Matthew 5:17–19 must be interpreted along a "fulfillment/abolishment" continuum, it may not be used, as theonomists do, to support the abiding validity of the Mosaic law for the church-age believer.

Romans 7

Another passage purported to support the notion of continuity is Romans 7:12, 14, 22. Based on his remarks in verse 4, it is clear that Paul intends to set some sort of a contrast between the believer in Christ and the law. Union with Christ means dying to the law—the major thesis of Paul in the chapter. There is freedom from bondage of the Mosaic law through salvation in Christ Jesus. Just as the death of one spouse brings the severance of the

---

[74]For further discussions of Bahnsen's treatment of Matthew 5:17–19, see R. L. Harris, "Theonomy in Christian Ethics: A Review of Greg L. Bahnsen's Book," *Presbyterion: Covenant Seminary Review* 5 (Spring 1979), 2–16; G. Aiken Taylor, "Theonomy Revisited," *Presbyterian Journal* 37 (Dec 6, 1978), 12–22; and V. Poythress, *The Shadow*, 251–86. Please note that Stanley Toussaint seems to agree with the understanding that *plérósai* means "to confirm" or "establish" in Matthew 5:17–19 (*Behold the King* [Portland, Ore.: Multnomah Press, 1980], 99).

marriage relationship (vv. 1–3), so also death to the law, brought about by union with Christ, severs our relationship to the Mosaic law. The importance of this truth is highlighted by Paul's virtual repetition of this idea in verse 6. He does not appear to be speaking merely of freedom from the perversion of the law or freedom from the condemnation of the law, as Cranfield suggests.[75] The comparison to the legitimate marriage relationship severed by death makes this interpretation unlikely.

Commentators like Calvin, wishing to preserve the idea that the law is still binding on the believer for the purposes of sanctification, argue that a Christian's freedom is from the condemnation of the law. It seems, however, that Paul is speaking of much more than deliverance from condemnation. He is suggesting a wholesale shift in jurisdictions, from a period where the law had jurisdiction to a new period where the Spirit reigns. The age of the church has rendered the law inoperative. Paul significantly employs such phrases as "body of Christ" (v. 4) to highlight the contrast between the church age and the old age under the law. The notion that sanctification takes place apart from the Mosaic law is also implied by the reference to bearing "fruit to God" through our relationship in Christ instead of through our relationship to the law. Likewise in verse 6, Paul argues that sanctification is facilitated by freedom from the law so that "we serve in the new way of the Spirit, and not in the old way of the written code." The church age, characterized by the Spirit, has replaced the Mosaic era.

This leads to Paul's discussion on the positive value of the Mosaic law. The believer in Christ might be tempted to ask whether the law is therefore sin. Paul quickly dispels that notion by arguing that the law functioned to reveal and expose sin. He indicates how in his own life, the law forced him to come to grips with the ugliness and pervasiveness of sin. It was not so much that he recognized he was sinning, but felt convicted of sin. Hodge has captured Paul's meaning: "The kind of knowledge of which the apostle speaks is not mere intellectual cognition, but also conviction. It includes the consciousness of guilt and pollution. The law awakened in him the knowledge of his own state

---

[75]Cranfield (*Romans*, 1.332) suggests that Paul is only speaking of freedom from bondage to the perversion of the law or the illegitimate use of the law.

and character."[76] In other words, Paul's point is not the mere proof of the fact of sin, but the adequate discernment of its culpability.[77] The law enabled Paul to understand the gravity of sin as an act contrary to the nature of God. Nevertheless, it was not the law that became the cause of death, but the sin revealed by the law. Thus "the law is holy . . . righteous and good" (v. 12), not in the sense that one must obey the law for sanctification, but in the sense that it originated from a holy, righteous, and good God; it reflects the moral perfection of its Giver.[78]

Merely noting that the character of the law is in accord with its origin does not validate holiness as a legitimate function of the law. Perhaps the testimony of Peter gives a clue regarding why the law was given to Israel. He seems to suggest that the Mosaic law was given to Israel to reveal the holiness of God (1 Pet. 1:15–16). He reminds his readers that the law given to Israel included explicit testimony to the holiness and morally perfect character of the God who had entered into the covenant with them.

1 Timothy 1:8

Finally 1 Timothy 1:8 is often cited as support that Paul thought of a continuity between Law and Gospel. There Paul is addressing Timothy, stating that the law is good if employed properly. Does that mean that the law is perhaps useful to the church-age saint for sanctification?

Paul clarifies his meaning in verses 9–10. He argues that the law was intended to be used after the manner of Galatians 3. The law is *not* made for the righteous or saved person in this church age; it is made for the unrighteous. In particular, Paul claims that the so-called moral law, the Decalogue, is designed to be used by the unbeliever rather than the believer. That is, it was made for those who commit offenses against God (e.g., "lawbreakers and rebels") and against their fellow humans (e.g., "those who kill their fathers and mothers . . . adulterers and perverts"). The next verse also implies that the law is no longer binding on the church-age saint.

---

[76]Hodge, *Romans*, 222. See also Longenecker, *The Ministry and Message of Paul*, 94; *Paul, Apostle of Liberty*, 123–24.

[77]Godet, *Romans*, 272.

[78]Brinsmead, "Jesus and the Law," 6; F. F. Bruce, "Paul and the Law of Moses," *BJRL* 57 (1975), 276; H. H. Esser, "νόμος," *NIDNTT*, 2.445.

The Role of Distinctions

Advocates of the third use of the law for believers generally base the appeal for the abiding validity of the moral law on the distinctions in the law itself. The customary classification differentiates between the moral, civil, and ceremonial aspects of the law.[79] Kaiser argues for the abiding validity of the moral law based on the distinctions between "light" and "heavy" commandments within the law (see Jesus' statements in Matt. 23:23).[80] But this classification system is not clearly defined in Scripture. Christ was not suggesting that any of the laws were expendable to the Pharisees. Rather, he was challenging their teaching that they could keep the dictates of the law that were easier to follow but ignore its heart.

There are various terms applied to the aspects of the Old Testament law, some of which may refer to differing parts of the Mosaic law. The term translated "words" refers to the Decalogue. "Commandments" likewise refers to dictates given by God in the form of apodictic legislation (Ex. 15:26; Deut. 6:1–2). The term "statute" refers in Leviticus to an ordinance that is ceremonial in nature, but elsewhere it refers to any regulation. "Judgment" may refer to judicial decisions or case legislation (Deut. 16:18–19), often called civil legislation. In other places, however, the various terms are used interchangeably or synonymously.[81] We conclude that any clear biblical testimony to a threefold division is lacking.[82]

Israel had no option to ignore a category of law (Lev. 26:14–15; Deut. 11:1). Moses provided no hierarchy of laws as justification for selective obedience, even during a later period. In

---

[79]Another classification divides the law into *apodictic* and *casuistic* categories.

[80]Walter C. Kaiser, Jr., "The Weightier and Lighter Matters of the Law: Moses, Jesus and Paul," in *Current Issues in Biblical and Patristic Interpretation*, ed. Gerald Hawthorne (Grand Rapids: Eerdmans, 1975), 176–92.

[81]Craigie, *Deuteronomy*, 129. For more detailed discussions of the various terms employed to describe the portions of the law, see R. K. Harrison, "Law in the Old Testament," *ISBE*, ed. Geoffrey W. Bromiley, rev. ed. (Grand Rapids: Eerdmans, 1986), 3.76–85; M. Noth, *The Laws in the Pentateuch and Other Studies* (Edinburgh: Oliver and Boyd, 1966).

[82]Vern Poythress argues for a "rough" distinction between the moral and ceremonial aspects of the law, based on the inclusion of the Ten Commandments in Deuteronomy 5 and the "commands, decrees, and laws," in Deuteronomy 6–31. The reason for the designation "rough" is that "some obviously moral commands are included in the later chapters" (*The Shadow*, 100). Poythress suggests that the undue focus on the distinctions betrays the unity intended by God.

several Old Testament contexts, the purported moral and ceremonial aspects seemed inextricably intertwined (e.g., Ex. 23; Lev. 19; Deut. 22–23). G. J. Wenham has correctly noted: "The arbitrariness of the distinction between moral and civil law is reinforced by the arrangement of the material in Leviticus. Love of neighbor immediately precedes a prohibition on mixed breeding; the holiness motto comes just before the law on executing unruly children (19:18–19; 20:7–9)."[83]

Furthermore, the New Testament treats the entire Mosaic law in an epochal or dispensational sense as a unit. Paul does so in Galatians 5:3, arguing that the believer is to walk by the Spirit, not try to live by the law, since that would require one to "obey the whole law." He never furnishes guidelines to provide a framework for distinguishing between the law's temporal and permanent aspects. James likewise warns against breaking any part of the law (James 2:8–10); if one tries to live by the law, one must live by the entire law.

Arguments for Discontinuity

There are compelling reasons to understand a basic discontinuity between Old and New Testaments. The justification stems from the entrance into the new covenant and various New Testament passages where the discontinuity is clearly presented.

The New Covenant

The death and resurrection of Christ, inaugurating a new work organically related to Christ (i.e., the body of Christ), certainly creates the logical possibility of a major change in relationship to the Mosaic law. The new covenant has rendered the old covenant inoperative. Just as there was no Mosaic law during the dispensation from Adam to Moses, so also there is a period following the Mosaic era in which the law is no longer the operative principle.

The author of Hebrews states plainly that a drastic change has occurred because a different priesthood has been placed into operation. Jesus is a priest, but not according to the Mosaic law (Heb. 7:12). Many other differences have been inaugurated by the new covenant, such as greater glory, greater power, and greater finality; these call into question the continuity between Old and New Testaments. The question is often asked whether the guiding

---

[83]Wenham, *Leviticus*, 34.

hermeneutic should be to hold the Mosaic principles as legally binding unless explicitly repealed in the New Testament or to treat the Mosaic law as non-binding unless repeated in the New Testament. Actually, this choice is a moot issue, since in fact the old covenant has been explicitly abrogated (Heb. 8:8–9, 13).

Passages Advocating Discontinuity

The clearest evidence for the discontinuity position derives from many passages in the New Testament that suggest the cessation of the Mosaic law as binding for the church-age saint: Romans 3:21–31; 4:5, 13–25; 5:13; 6:14–15; 7:6; 10:4; 1 Corinthians 9:19–23; 2 Corinthians 3:3, 6–18; Galatians 2:19; 3:1–5, 10–29; 4:8–11, 21–5:1; 5:3, 18; Philippians 3:1–11; Colossians 2:14; Hebrews 7:11–28; 8:4–6, 13; 9:8; 10:1–18; James 2:8–10. Several passages have already been at least briefly treated (Gal. 3:10–12; James 2:8–10), and several other key passages will be examined to uncover the contribution made to the resolution of the issue.

Romans 6:14–15. One passage that clearly presents a contrast between law and grace is Romans 6:14–15. Paul's development of God's righteousness in Romans commenced with an exposition of the theme (1:16–17) and its need (1:18–20). He explained that righteousness is imputed; one is justified by faith alone (3:21–5:21). Throughout his argument, Paul claimed that such righteousness was never designed to be gained via the Mosaic law. In this he confirmed the testimony of the Old Testament that law was for sanctification, not justification. Paul felt obliged to discuss the law only because it was the major revelation of the Mosaic dispensation that dominated the period just ended. In 3:20–28 he reminded his audience that justification is not earned by observing the law; subsequently he presented a series of contrasts between faith and law (4:13–25). The benefits of justification were surveyed in chapter 5, including the statement: "The law was added so that the trespass might increase" (v. 20). It is significant that Paul employed the term "come in beside" (*pareiserchomai*), because he portrayed the law period as a new one, but not one that was intended to replace grace or was designed as a new means to provide redemption. Rather, the law period was designed to be a complementary revelation to bring about greater awareness of violations of God's standard (cf. 3:20).[84]

---

[84]The question may be asked: In what sense does the law increase the transgression? For a discussions of the three major options, see Räisänen, *Paul and the Law*, 141.

After explaining the basis of attaining righteousness as justification by faith and the role of the law as exposing the transgression, Paul proceeded to discuss the topic of sanctification for those having already received God's redemption (Rom. 6–8). He referred to this audience as those who have "died to sin" (6:2), "were baptized into Christ Jesus" (v. 3), and "have become united with him . . . in his death" (v. 5). Clearly the issue has shifted from justification to sanctification.

Paul's point is that the believers in Christ do not need to let sin reign over them (6:12–14). Sanctified Christians must avoid sin (v. 13) and not be mastered by it (v. 14). Instead, they must present themselves to God in holy living as a consequence of justification.[85]

Romans 6:14 is a transitional statement that prepares us for the discussion of the relationship of the law to sanctification in Romans 7:1–25. Paul has been developing the thesis that the benefit of God's imputation of righteousness is the elimination of the necessity of the lordship of sin. Having been united with Christ, sin must not become lord over the believer (v. 14a). Paul, however, does not follow this up by stating, "for you are not under sin, but under grace"—as might be expected if he intended to speak of the condemnation of the law (cf. 3:8; 5:16, 18; 8:1). Instead, he articulates a contrast between law itself and grace. In Paul's mind, the righteousness provided by the work of Christ on the cross is closely aligned with and inseparable from the change in eras which has recently taken place. The advent of the grace dispensation has signaled the cessation of the law dispensation, a transition that provides validation of the impotence of sin. The law served to increase sin and has now been dealt with in such a manner as to render it ineffective. Under grace the believer may focus on the positive principle of living in union with Christ.

It seems clear that the term *nomos* here refers to the Mosaic law. J. Murray has argued against this view, stating that many "who were under the Mosaic economy were the recipients of grace"[86]; instead, law should be understood in the more general sense as commandment.[87] It is argued that the lack of a definite

---

[85]This should not be understood as eschatological. The future tense merely highlights the certainty and gives assurance of its possibility. See J. D. G. Dunn, *Romans*, WBC (Waco, Tex.: Word, 1988), 1.299.

[86]Murray, *The Epistle of Paul to the Romans*, NICNT (Grand Rapids: Eerdmans, 1960), 1.228.

[87]Ibid., 229.

article before the term "law" demonstrates that the principle of law is in view, not the Mosaic law. But there is nothing in the context that warrants a shift in understanding from the previous meaning in Romans 5:20. Likewise, the following context regards the law as the Mosaic law (7:4–14). In addition, general law does not provide a sufficient contrast to grace, because there is law in this sense in grace too—see Paul's reference to "the law of Christ" in Galatians 6:2. It makes sense only if we understand Paul as contrasting two periods, one characterized by the Mosaic law and the other characterized by grace.

Westerholm has noted studies of *nomos* which show that Paul used *nomos* with and without the article with no "change in nuance or meaning."[88] Of the eight places where he employs the term "law" with the preposition "under," the article is never found, nor are there any other examples in Scripture where the noun in the accusative case is found with an article. Only in James 2:9 is the preposition found with the articular noun "law," and there it is in the genitive case. Note also that H. Hübner's contention that Paul refers to the termination of the "Lordship of the perverted law" is to be rejected as without support, since there is no discussion of the perversion of the law in the immediate context.[89]

Paul argues in Romans 6:14 that the authority of the law has been replaced by a different authority, grace. The two phrases "under law" (*hypo nomon*) and "under grace" (*hypo charin*) are set in contrast to each other. The phrase "under law" occurs several times in Pauline literature (e.g., 1 Cor. 9:20; Gal. 3:23) and clearly refers to the Mosaic economy. In 1 Corinthians 9:20 (where the phrase occurs four times), it clearly designates the Mosaic law. Paul states in Galatians that Christ was born under the law (Gal. 4:4); that is, he was born during the Mosaic or law dispensation, when the law was operative and authoritative. The same contrast between the present dispensation and the previous law period is presented in Galatians 5:18, where the work of the Holy Spirit, placing believers into the body of Christ and guiding them, shows that the law period has been preempted. As E. P. Sanders remarks: "Paul views all Christians, whether Jew or Gentile, as having died to the law. It is part of the old world order, just as are

---

[88]Westerholm, *Israel's Law*, 106.
[89]H. Hübner, *Law in Paul's Thought*, 115.

sin and the flesh, and it must be escaped."[90] With the inauguration of a new epoch, our relationship to law has changed. Whereas the law formerly dominated and controlled, it now has no authority over the life of the saint.

This clear articulation that the law is no longer the dominant authority leads to a new discussion launched by Paul that the believer is now obligated to obey Christ as his slave (Rom. 6:15–23). There again Paul makes his case for a dispensational change. The former state was characterized as being "under law" (i.e., under the dominion of law), but since we are now under the authority of grace we must obey as slaves of righteousness. While one might be tempted to engage in sin since the law has been terminated, Paul makes it clear that this termination gives no such warrant, for with the change in dispensations has come a union with Christ that results in believers now being slaves to righteousness.

Romans 10:4. Another passage advocating discontinuity between law and grace is Romans 10:4. (The contribution of 10:5–8 has previously been presented.) The key to understanding Paul's message is to understand *telos* (translated either "end" or "goal"). This passage has been the focus of much attention in recent years. H. Hübner, for example, using the meaning "end," claims that Paul is teaching cessation of the "misuse of the law."[91] Thus he detects an argument based on cessation, but cessation only of the misuse of law rather than law itself. Likewise, H. Räisänen, E. P. Sanders, and John Murray reject *telos* as meaning "goal."[92]

C. E. B. Cranfield, however, has popularized the idea that *telos* should be translated "goal."[93] He contends that "for Paul, the law is not abrogated by Christ,"[94] and further notes:

> This thesis is stated in full awareness of the widespread tendency today observable not only in popular writing, but also in serious works of scholarship, to regard it as an assured result that Paul believed that the law had been abrogated by Christ.[95]

---

[90]Sanders, *Paul, the Law, and the Jewish People*, 83.

[91]H. Hübner, *Law in Paul's Thought*, 138. It is important to keep in mind that Hübner believes that Paul contradicts himself in the various discussions of the law.

[92]Räisänen, *Paul and the Law*, 53–56; Sanders, *Paul, the Law, and the Jewish People*, 38–39; and Murray, *Romans*, 2.49–50.

[93]Cranfield, *Romans*, 2.515–20.

[94]Ibid., 852.

[95]Ibid.

Dan G. McCartney submits that "theonomists as well as most Reformed Christians are quite right in pointing out that this [Romans 10:4] does not mean that Christ is the termination of the law but that he is its goal."[96] Badenas contends that etymological studies of *telos* confirm that the notion of "termination" is secondary and "the notion of 'abolition' is completely alien to the semantic content of *telos* and other words of its same root."[97] In a footnote, Fuller also rejects the possibility of the understanding of "termination," since it is only used in that sense three times (according to his reading of Arndt and Gingrich, *BAGD*).[98]

Yet a closer examination of *BAGD* reveals that perhaps their testimony against this understanding of *telos* is not as certain as suggested. First, the word group *telos* has one of two major meanings: (1) "end" and (2) "rest or remainder."[99] Under the major heading "end" *BAGD* place both options suggested by Fuller as to the meaning of *telos* in Romans 10:4. The reason why "goal" is placed under the major heading "end" is that once the goal has been reached, it is understood that there is a cessation or termination. Therefore *telos* when understood as "goal" *may* mean simply a directional or purposeful result leading to termination. Note too that the authors of *BAGD* are indecisive regarding the categorization of *telos* as used in Romans 10:4. They admit the possibility of understanding it as a "*goal* toward which a movement is being directed, *outcome*."[100] However, they also place this verse under the category "*end . . . in the sense of termination, cessation*." They specifically state: "Perh. this is the place for Ro 10:4, in the sense that Christ is the goal and the termination of the law at the same time, somewhat in the sense of Gal. 3:24f."[101] In other words, *BAGD* can hardly be used as solid support denying the validity of *telos* as "termination" in Romans 10:4. They establish that no matter what category of use is suggested, the idea of termination is involved.

---

[96]Dan G. McCartney, "The New Testament Use of the Pentateuch: Implications for the Theonomic Movement," in *Theonomy: A Reformed Critique*, eds. W. S. Barker and W. R. Godfrey (Grand Rapids: Zondervan, 1990), 130.

[97]Badenas, *Christ the End of the Law*, 44.

[98]Fuller, *Gospel & Law*, 84 n. 29.

[99]*BAGD*, 811.

[100]Ibid.

[101]Ibid.

Furthermore, both Gerhard Delling[102] and R. Schippers[103] list Romans 10:4 as an example of *telos* signifying "cessation." F. F. Bruce also suggests that *telos* as utilized by Paul in Romans 10:4 has the nuance of "cessation." He writes: "It is plain that Paul believed and taught that the law had been in a major sense abrogated by Christ. 'Christ is the end of the law,' he wrote, 'that everyone who has faith may be justified' (Rom. x 4)."[104] Later in the same article he adds:

> The affirmation that "Christ is the end of the law" has been variously understood. The word "end" (*telos*) can mean "goal" or "terminus," and here it probably means both. Christ, for Paul, was the goal of the law in the sense that the law was a temporary provision introduced by God until the coming of Abraham's offspring in whom the promise made to Abraham was consummated; the law, in other words, "was our custodian until Christ came, that we might be justified by faith" (Gal. iii.19, 24). But Christ was also, for that reason, the terminus of the law; if, as Paul says, the law was a temporary provision, the coming of Christ meant that the period of its validity was now at an end.[105]

Badenas's argument that a temporal end is better conveyed by the Greek term *eschaton* or *teleutē* (when referring to one's end or death) fails to recognize that there are clear examples in the New Testament of the use of *telos* in the sense of cessation or termination (see 1 Cor. 1:8; 10:11; 15:24; 2 Cor. 1:13; 3:13; 11:15; 1 Thess. 2:16; Phil. 3:19). In addition, it could just as easily be asserted that if goal or fulfillment had been intended, Paul would have used *teleiōsis* or *plērōma*.[106]

The idea of the end of the law in the sense of termination is clearly suggested by the fact that in Romans 10:2 Paul does not say the Jews "*had* a zeal," but that "they *have* a zeal" (RSV). He is not addressing the situation that existed before the gospel was clearly articulated by Christ, but the contemporary situation after the new era has been inaugurated. In other words, even though the

---

[102]Gerhard Delling, "τέλος," *TDNT*, 8.56.

[103]R. Schippers, "télow," *NIDNTT*, 2.61.

[104]Bruce, "Paul and the Law of Moses," 262.

[105]Ibid., 264.

[106]Sanday/Headlam, *Romans*, 285; Murray, *Romans*, 2.49; O. Michael, *Der Brief an die Römer: Kritisch-exegetischer Kommentar über neue Testament* (Göttingen: Vandenhoeck and Ruprecht, 1963), 224.

dispensation of law has been terminated, the Jews still maintain their zeal for the law.

Another argument raised in support of understanding Romans 10:4 as signifying goal or completion is the use of the particle *gar* ("for"). Fuller suggests this term "signifies that what follows provides an argument in support of what precedes."[107] His understanding of verse 3 is that the Jews repudiated God's righteousness both in the rejection of the Mosaic law and Christ, which are "in such a continuum that to repudiate one is to repudiate the other."[108]

It is certainly true that the *gar* of verse 4 offers some form of explanation of the situation in verse 3. However, the validity of Fuller's argument depends upon his understanding of the content of verse 3. He has made a quantum leap in assuming that merely because Israel rejected the law and Christ, they must be in continuum. This verse suggests that there is a contrast between God's righteousness and the Jews' righteousness. As early as 1:17 Paul reveals his main theme that God's righteousness is by faith. Throughout the book he consistently associates God's righteousness with faith (e.g., 3:22, 25); thus it is natural to understand the phrase "God's righteousness" in 10:3 in the same fashion. Even Cranfield, who adopts a similar view to Fuller for these verses, admits that the natural understanding of "God's righteousness" as used by Paul implies faith righteousness.[109]

The best understanding of *gar* in Romans 10:4, therefore, is to see it as explanatory. It explains why in seeking their own righteousness the Jews failed to subject themselves to God's righteousness. The righteousness they pursued was a law righteousness (9:31), but law righteousness was not sufficient because Christ ended its era. Furthermore, the cessation of law righteousness applies to everyone who believes. In other words, those who rely on faith righteousness understand that Christ is the end of the law righteousness pursuit. Paul then goes on to explain the contrast between the futile law righteousness and faith righteousness (vv. 5–8). The righteousness that Israel failed to achieve by the works of the law has been replaced by righteousness made possible by Christ's coming. Now it is possible to achieve God's righteousness by faith.

---

[107]Ibid.

[108]Ibid., 85.

[109]Cranfield, *Romans*, 28.

Finally, the understanding of *telos* as "termination" or "cessation" best harmonizes with Paul in other passages. In Romans 7:4, Paul contrasts the law and grace or faith. They are not described as a continuum because the law has ended. Rather, those who place faith in Christ, thus being joined to the body of Christ, are made to die to the law. In 7:6, Paul further claims that the believer has been released from the law. Once again, the cessation of law is in view.

In conclusion, "termination" or "cessation" is probably the best understanding of Romans 10:4. The term *telos* perhaps had a dual significance for Paul and therefore was the ideal term to use. There was a sense in which Christ was the fulfillment or goal of the law because the law was a temporary custodian for the Jews until Christ came; it revealed to them God's standards of righteousness. However, when Christ arrived on the scene, the usefulness of the law ceased and was no longer necessary. With the meaning of "cessation" for *telos*, Paul is contrasting the law righteousness with faith righteousness. The coming of Christ to the human scene brought an end to the law, making an appeal to Romans 10:4 in support of a continuum unjustified.

2 Corinthians 3:3, 6–18. In many senses, Paul's discussion of the law in 2 Corinthians 3 is clearer and easier to define than most other Pauline discussions of the law. This is due in part to the fact that this passage is not designed to describe or explain the purpose of the Mosaic law. It is not as easy to posit that a contrast does not exist, or that the contrast is between legalism and grace rather than the Mosaic law and grace. Paul clearly articulates a discontinuity here, a strong contrast.[110] Note that H. Hübner barely mentions this passage and D. Fuller fails to discuss the contribution of this passage to the law issue at all.

In 2 Corinthians, Paul defends his ministry against charges that he was not genuinely God's minister. This leads him to argue that the Corinthians themselves are his "letter of recommendation," his proof of a genuinely valid ministry. He follows this with a contrast to the old covenant ministry.

This section is replete with contrasts between the Mosaic and church periods. These contrasts are designed to convey the supremacy of new covenant ministry over against the old covenant. The first series of contrasts are presented in verse 3. New covenant believers are the letter written with the Holy Spirit as opposed to the old covenant written with ink (see v. 6). The

---

[110]Räisänen, *Paul and the Law*, 233.

new covenant writing is on human hearts as tablets while the old covenant writing is on tablets of stone (see also v. 7). The contrast clearly involves the very center of the Mosaic law, the Ten Commandments (Ex. 19–20).

In 2 Corinthians 3:6 Paul continues the contrast by noting that he is a minister of this "new covenant," implying that the other is the old covenant. Later, Paul explicitly refers to the "old covenant" by name (v. 14). According to him, the old covenant, a ministry characterized by death (v. 7) and condemnation (v. 9), kills; whereas the new covenant, a ministry characterized as one of the Spirit (v. 8) and righteousness (v. 9), gives life. Finally, the old covenant is described as having faded away while the new covenant ministry remains (v. 11). To summarize, it is a contrast between Israel, Moses, the Mosaic law, and the letter on the one hand, and the church, Paul, the Holy Spirit, and the new covenant on the other hand.

Despite the clear articulation of contrasts, there is some discussion regarding the nature of the contrast. First, is the contrast between two covenants or merely two ministries? Cranfield contends: "the key to the true understanding of this whole passage [2 Cor. 3:7–11] is to recognize that it is really the two ministries which are being contrasted rather than the two covenants themselves; when this is recognized the connection between verses 7–11 and verses 4–6 and 1–3 becomes clear."[111] He supports this understanding by the fact that Paul is discussing his ministry in the preceding and subsequent sections of 2 Corinthians.

Yet the contrast in ministries can be sustained in part only because of the contrasts between the covenants themselves. It is not the ministry that was written in stone with ink (3:3, 7), but the old covenant. Furthermore, the ministries flow out of and are made possible by the respective covenants. Paul would never say that his ministry flows out of the old covenant.

Another issue regards the nature of the law written on the tablets of human hearts. Kaiser contends that "God would write the *same* law (for he has no other law) on their hearts."[112] Yet Paul does not say that the *same* law is written on their hearts, nor does he say *any* law is written on their hearts. The letter of Christ is written on their hearts. Although he does not cite these passages,

---

111Cranfield, "St. Paul and the Law," 58.

112W. C. Kaiser, Jr., "Weightier and Lighter Matters," 186.

Paul is clearly alluding to Jeremiah 31:33 and Ezekiel 11:19; 36:26. To suggest that this must refer to the same law begs the question. The law of Christ that embodies the same moral standard as the law of Moses could easily be what is written on the human heart, regenerated by the Spirit of God. Furthermore, law existed *before* the Mosaic law. God's moral standards do not change, but the concrete expressions of it may change.

It may be objected that the contrast is between legalism or the perversion of the law and the new covenant. Cranfield, an example of this approach, bases it on the use of the term *gramma* ("letter"). He contends that *gramma* refers to Jewish legalism.[113] However, as Räisänen notes, the word cannot realistically refer to Jewish legalism because of the reference to Moses and the original giving of the law (3:7) and the assessment that the giving of the Mosaic law came with splendor.[114] In addition, the passage gives no hint of any misinterpretation or misapplication by Pharisees or any other group.

It is further argued that Paul's use of *gramma* rather than *graphē* ("writing") is significant (3:6); he is not suggesting that the *graphē* of the old covenant has faded, but rather the *gramma*, (i.e., the improper use of the law based on mere outward adherence; cf. Rom. 2:29). However, it may be that Paul employs *gramma* instead of *graphē* since he has earlier used the term in a positive way in describing the new covenant ministry. In verse 3 Paul remarks that the Corinthians were written (using *graphō*) with the Spirit and that this is in stark contrast to the old covenant *gramma* (v. 6). Paul may also have chosen to use *gramma* to highlight or emphasize that the old covenant was in ink, written on stone tablets. The letter or written code of the old covenant kills in the sense that it has the power to condemn sinfulness (vv. 8–11).

Whether Paul is actually arguing for cessation of the old covenant depends in part on the meaning of *katargeō* ("fades away"). Paul clearly intends to contrast the covenants by presenting the old covenant as fading or coming to an end (3:11). This is the normal or customary meaning of *katargeō*. Specifically, the glory on Moses' face was fading, and Paul uses this phenomenon to illustrate the temporary and inferior nature of the old covenant. Just as the glory of Moses ended, so also the old covenant has

---

[113]Cranfield, "St. Paul and the Law," 57; *Romans*, 854.

[114]For a discussion of the problem with this view, see Räisänen, *Paul and the Law*, 44–46, 57.

been terminated. In fact, Paul confirms the idea of cessation by his use of *telos*, meaning "cessation" or "termination" in verse 13.

The identity of the referent of the fading may contribute to the proper understanding of the passage. If that which has faded is the old covenant, then it is clear that the covenant itself was temporary, transitory, and inferior. It has been postulated that the referent of the fading is the glory or external shine on the face of Moses (3:7) rather than the covenant itself. As mentioned earlier, however, Paul is using the glory on Moses' face as an illustration of the temporary old covenant. Further, although "glory" (*doxa*) is grammatically feminine in gender, the participle translated "that which fades" is neuter. Thus it does not specifically or exclusively refer to glory, but more generally to the fading of the old covenant as exemplified by the glory on Moses' face. That the fading refers to the Mosaic dispensation is validated by the similar use of neuter gender participles (*katargoumenon* and *menon*) in verses 10 and 11.

One final issue to be resolved is the consequent charge that if Paul is referring to the cessation of the old covenant, he is disparaging the revelation of God. This charge against Paul is unwarranted, for he gives a balanced assessment of the old covenant. On a positive note he presents the law as having glory (3:7, 9, 11), but asserts that period has now passed. It was historically conditioned, and the function of the old covenant has now been replaced by the new covenant. This change coincides with the incarnational ministry of Christ.

In summary, the ministry of righteousness in Christ remains, and the ministry of death and condemnation in the law has ended. If the Mosaic Law has faded or come to an end, it is no longer binding on the church-age believer for sanctification.

Philippians 3:7–9. Finally, we must discuss the antithesis between Law and the Gospel of Jesus Christ in this passage. Most agree that there is an antithesis here. The feminine article in the accusative case (referring to "righteousness") prefaces both prepositional phrases "from the law" and "through faith." Paul clearly intends to contrast these two. Even Fuller admits that this passage supports the antithetical use of the terms "righteousness of the law" and "righteousness of faith."[115] E. P. Sanders notes that the distinction is clearer in this passage than Romans 10:4.[116] In other words, Paul is addressing two different types of righteousness:

---

[115]Fuller, *Gospel & Law*, 86.
[116]Sanders, *Paul, the Law, and the Jewish People*, 43.

one obtained by the adherence to the Mosaic law and the other obtained by faith.

However, some object that Philippians 3:9 may not be embraced to argue for the cessation of the Mosaic law because Paul is contrasting not law and faith righteousness, but the erroneous use of the law leading to self-righteousness and the righteousness of faith.[117] Note J. J. Muller's comment on this verse: "no longer a righteousness which consisted in the strict outward fulfillment of the obligations of the law and was based on the works of the law, no longer the law-observing Pharisaic righteousness which characterized [Paul's] previous life, but instead a righteousness 'through faith in Christ'. . . ."[118] Furthermore, it is argued that "law" here was used to denote the common misinterpretation of Moses by the Jews in rebellion against God.[119] This view is based on the articulation by Paul that the righteousness was "his own" (3:9).

There are several false assumptions that create difficulties for this view. First, the earlier reference to Paul as a Pharisee is given as evidence that Paul's use of the law was the typically Pharisaic misunderstanding of the law. In other words, if he was a Pharisee, he had to misuse the law. This is guilt by association and is not sustained by the text. Paul does not even hint that he sinned or misused the law; he never condemns his actions. Second, as E. P. Sanders has pointed out, this view depends on reading Romans 3:27 and 4:2 into this passage by suggesting that Paul's reference to "righteousness of my own" is an articulation of a boastful and prideful attitude. Nowhere can this be drawn from the Philippians 3:9 text.

In fact, Paul modifies the first type of righteousness as that which is based on the Mosaic law. The phrase "that comes from the law" is designed to modify or explain "a righteousness of my own," implying that the law was the source of the righteousness. It is designed to point the reader back to Paul's earlier discussion in verses 4–6. Paul has just contrasted his former life and his present life. He was a Jew of Jews, "as to righteousness under the law, blameless" (3:6 RSV). Paul does not suggest that he misused

---

[117]See, for example, Bultmann, *Theology of the New Testament* (New York: Scribner, 1951), 266–67.

[118]J. J. Muller, *The Epistles of Paul to the Philippians and to Philemon*, NICNT (Grand Rapids: Eerdmans, 1980), 114.

[119]Fuller, *Gospel & Law*, 87.

the law, since he was found blameless. Note that he does not flinch or hesitate to use the term "blameless" (i.e., "without fault"). Paul does not say he was "so-to-speak blameless," or that he only appeared to be or thought he was blameless. The adjectival and adverbial forms of this word are found seven times in the New Testament, all but two being Pauline usages. Not a single example can be given of "blameless" or "blamelessly" referring to misplaced or false blamelessness. In fact, Luke 1:6 refers to the assessment of blamelessness of Zechariah and Elizabeth in evaluation of their obedience to the commandments and ordinances of the Lord.

However, in verse 9 Paul states that his former life was his own righteousness, and more importantly, it was derived from the law. He did not misuse the law, but rather derived his righteousness from the law. The righteousness was his own personal righteousness, but based on the law. This thought of Paul is parallel to that of Romans 10:5–8.

Confirmation of the idea that Paul viewed his behavior regarding the law as "blameless" is found in Acts 22:3, where he explains that he was taught according to the perfect manner of the law under Gamaliel and that he was zealous toward God in his understanding of the law. It is thus unwarranted to argue that Paul was emphasizing a contrast to be between faith righteousness and *legalistic* law righteousness.

Paul's former way of life and motivation—the righteousness based on law—he formerly considered to be gain, but he now counts them loss for Christ (3:7). What precipitated this change in attitude toward law righteousness is the dispensational change inaugurated by Christ. This change is a permanent change, as demonstrated by his use of the perfect tense in *hēgēmai* ("I counted as loss"). This tense designates a past action with continuing results; it is a lasting condition or state. In the next verse, Paul uses the same term in the present tense (*hēgoumai*) to confirm that it is his present attitude as well. The appeal to righteousness based on the law will never again be a method or approach. Establishing or attaining righteousness based on the law is futile because of the fact that Christ has revealed a righteousness based on faith in him. Thus, Philippians 3:9 provides yet another confirmation that Paul viewed the law as temporary and invalid because of the work of Christ, who has now established a righteousness independent of the Mosaic law.

THE CONTEMPORARY CHRISTIAN AND LAW

Thus far I have argued that the regulatory purpose designed as the rule of life for Israel was clearly a temporary arrangement, not binding on the church saint. Does this then leave no rule of life binding on the New Testament saint? To this question we now turn our attention.

Moral Standards

A discussion of the role of law for the Christian begins with the moral law (to be distinguished from that aspect of the Mosaic law that is also commonly termed "moral law"). This is the law of God expressing his will that is not written externally, but on the heart of the rational creature. This intuition of God and his moral will stem from the *imago dei*.[120] In Romans 1:18–19 Paul claims that God has revealed himself to humans and that this includes his "righteous decree" (Rom. 1:32). In 2:14–15, he argues that Gentiles without the Mosaic law still stand under condemnation, because the unwritten law is implanted within their soul. Though the Jew had the written law, there is a sense in which all in fact possess law (2:14). This idea of the moral law written within a human being is repeated by Paul in verse 15 to confirm the guilt of the Gentiles. It is this moral law of God inscribed intuitively on human hearts that furnishes the foundation for the Mosaic law, where it has clear expression in an explicit codified form. In addition, as I will now demonstrate, this moral law is expressed in the "law of Christ" for New Testament believers.

Mosaic Law/Law of Christ Parallel

The Mosaic law naturally ended when God suspended his program with Israel (Rom. 9–11) and inaugurated his program with the church. God's moral law in and of itself does not change, but its specific application and structure in the Mosaic code ended with the repeated violations of the Mosaic covenant and the beginning of the church dispensation. Yet Paul considered himself

---

[120]Helpful discussions of the moral standard of God may be found in A. H. Strong, *Systematic Theology: A Compendium and Commonplace Book for the Use of Students* (Philadelphia: Griffith and Rowland, 1907), 537; M. Erickson, *Christian Theology* (Grand Rapids: Baker, 1983–86), 1.168–73; B. Demarest, *General Revelation* (Grand Rapids: Zondervan, 1982), 63–64; A. W. Pink, *The Doctrine of Revelation* (Grand Rapids: Baker, 1975), 41–45; Burton, *Galatians*, 450; F. Stagg, "The Plight of Jew and Gentile in Sin, Romans 1:18–3:20," *RevExp* 73 (1976), 407–9.

faithful to the law of God, though not bound by the law of Moses (1 Cor. 9:20). How could he make such a statement? The key appears to be a proper understanding of the interface between "the law of Christ" and the Mosaic law. Specifically, the law of Christ is the new covenant counterpart to the Mosaic law. Just as the Mosaic law was normative for the Jew, the law of Christ is binding for the Christian. Both are specific applications of God's eternal moral standard.

This law of Christ is discussed both by Paul (Rom. 13:8–10; Gal. 5:14; 6:2; 1 Cor. 9:21) and by James (James 1:25; 2:8, 12). It is no mere rephrasing of the Mosaic law, for it consists not of a concrete corpus of demands, but rather of basic principles, for each believer is promised permanent indwelling by the Holy Spirit. Since the Holy Spirit ministers in the life of the New Testament believer on behalf of Jesus Christ, there is no need for any lengthy, detailed, codified, external means of restraint as in the Mosaic law.[121]

Paul appealed to the Galatians to love each other as the fulfillment of the law's requirement, remarking that the whole law was fulfilled in the command to love our neighbors (Gal. 5:14). This law Paul later describes as "the law of Christ" (6:2), because Christ articulated this principle in his earthly ministry (Matt. 22:37–40). Yet Paul only mentions love toward neighbor and not love for God. How is it that the entire law is fulfilled when only one part of the law of Christ is mentioned? Probably Paul considered love for God as prerequisite to a proper love for neighbors.

Finally, just as the Mosaic law had a revelatory aspect and regulatory aspect, so also the law of Christ seems to have both aspects. For instance, the revelatory aspect of the law of Christ manifests God as a God of love. This is borne out in the foot-washing incident of Christ, where he demonstrated love for others (John 13:34). On this basis the regulatory aspect is raised by Paul in the command for husbands to love wives (Eph. 5:25).

To summarize then, the moral law expressed in the Mosaic law under the old covenant has its parallel in the law of Christ under the new covenant, so that the believer today may know God's moral will. In addition, the principle expressed in a Mosaic statute may still be preached in the church in the same sense as

---

[121]B. Wintle, "Paul's Conception of the Law of Christ and Its Relation to the Law of Moses," *RTR* 38 (1979), 43.

the fulfillment of the law of Christ furnishes fulfillment of the essence of the Mosaic law.

CONCLUSION

The revelatory function of the law was in mind when Paul discussed the merits of the law. He was accurate in his assessment of the law as far from being evil (Rom. 7:7–14). He was equally discerning when he suggested that the law is holy (v. 12). Paul did not say that the law formerly was holy, but that the law *is* holy, righteous, good (v. 12), and spiritual (v. 14). In this regard, the law has abiding application to the life of a believer even in the church age. The nature of the law has not changed, so its revelatory purpose transcends the Mosaic economy and remains valid in the church dispensation. In fact, the law as it functions in a revelatory manner acts to preserve the unity between the two eras. Since God's character is immutable, it stands to reason that insofar as the law reveals God's character, it remains valid. In revealing the "sin-grace" construct, the law provides abiding and powerful testimony to human sinfulness and God's gracious provision of justification. The method of justification in the Mosaic era is identical to the current method: grace. This is the sole method ever used by God. Likewise the "sin-grace" construct in the Mosaic era revealed that the basis of justification was and still is blood atonement.

Nonetheless, as has been discovered, there is an aspect of the law that has ceased in its validity and applicability. The regulatory purpose recognizes that the Mosaic law was given specifically to the nation Israel in order to provide guidelines for their relationship to God. This regulatory purpose provided the requirement and means of fellowship, including the provision for the worship of God. The Mosaic law also served to govern Israel as a theocracy with a unique relationship to God. However, when Israel failed in its stewardship responsibilities under the Mosaic dispensation, the law in its regulatory function ceased in validity. Paul is equally clear that the law functioned in a temporary fashion as a tutor until the advent of Christ (Gal. 3:24), whereupon it ceased as a means of righteousness (Rom. 10:4). The Mosaic law, described as a ministry of death (2 Cor. 3:7), faded and no longer remains (v. 11), leaving the hope that is found in the person of Jesus Christ. Instead, the New Testament believer is governed by the law of Christ, a law that is fulfilled by loving one's neighbor (Gal. 5:14; 6:2).

Armed with this understanding of the twofold purpose of the law, the seemingly contradictory assertions of Paul concerning the law may be understood in a harmonious manner. With this understanding it is no longer necessary to propose a construct where obedience is the defining element of faith and where Gospel and Law are in absolute continuum. The law is properly understood to reveal the problem of sin and the necessity of grace in redemption, but the law is not seen as binding for the church saint. Rather, the law prefigures the redemption wrapped up in the person of Jesus Christ. The regulatory aspect of the law, binding on the Mosaic believer, dealt with sanctification and not justification, and it has been terminated with regard to the regulatory aspect. As with Paul, the church-age believer may rejoice that "now that faith has come, we are no longer under the supervision of the law" (Gal. 3:25).

With the recognition of the antithesis between Gospel and Law, it is no longer necessary to reject the basic Israel-church distinction, a distinction that rests on the sure foundation of sound historico-grammatical hermeneutics.[122] This results in God working with more than one people in redemptive history; the Abrahamic covenant will find its fulfillment literally in the future with the nation Israel rather than the church, although the church participates in the blessings of the covenant. Scripture reveals the future fulfillment of the program for Israel in the Messianic millennial kingdom when Christ, the greater Son of David, will rule. At that time the nation Israel will finally recognize Jesus Christ as the Messiah, the ultimate content of their saving faith in common with the church. Then Jesus will have been recognized not only in his role as the suffering Messiah, but also as the reigning Messiah. Such is the importance of understanding that the Mosaic Law is antithetical to the Gospel and has no part of it. Law and grace as methods of justification must not be allowed to mix, or else grace has been lost.

---

[122]This distinction may not be pressed in the eternal state, when it can be said that there is one people of God.

Response to Wayne G. Strickland

Willem A. VanGemeren

For Strickland the tension between Law and Gospel is strictly a systemic issue. It defines the dispensational system and hermeneutic from rival theological systems. The contrast of Law and Gospel, together with the related issue of Israel and the church, may well be the sine qua non of dispensationalism.

Strickland defines the relationship between the Law and the Gospel by differentiating the revelatory and regulatory functions of each. The *revelatory* function of the law includes the revelation both of God's character and of human sinfulness. The law reveals God's holiness, justice, and righteousness. As God is holy, just, and righteous, so is the law. It witnesses beyond itself to God's nature and to his authority in decreeing how he wants his people to respond to him in worship and in life. Second, the law reveals human sinfulness, the knowledge of sin, the sinfulness of sin, and the guilt of sin. Third, the law opened the vista of faith to God's grace in providing atonement by blood sacrifice, which pointed ultimately to the necessity of the death of his Son.

The *regulatory* function of the law governed Israel's worship (sacrifices, temple), theocratic kingdom, and ethics. For its time, it was a gracious expression of God's commitment to Israel, of his expectations, and of the basis upon which the Lord bestowed blessings on the theocratic nation. It was also a curse, for obedience to God's law was the basis for their inheritance. This negative aspect explains why the regulatory function of the law was temporary. It was only a " 'custodian' until the incarnation of

Christ." With his coming, the regulatory purpose of the law ceased to be meaningful.

Strickland defines the word "Law" as an era in salvation history (a dispensation) when sanctification was based on *law-keeping*. In contrast, the word "Gospel" connotes the era in salvation history when sanctification is based on *faith*. With the revelation in Jesus Christ, the era of the law has come to an end (Rom.10:4; cf. 2 Cor. 3:3, 6–18; Phil. 3:7–9). Notwithstanding several positive endorsements of the Law (Matt. 5:17–19; Mark 7:1–23; Rom. 7:12, 14, 22; 1 Tim. 1:8), Strickland concludes that Christ's coming marks the "end" of the law and consequently that the regulatory function of the Law is abrogated. The revelatory function of the Law continues as a testimony to God's goodness and holiness (Matt. 5:17–19), as a reminder of the bondage of the era of the law (Rom. 7:12, 14, 22), and as a witness to human sinfulness (1 Tim. 1:8). Replacing the authority and bondage of the law (Rom. 6:14–15) is Christ's revelation as the basis for sanctification.

What is the place of law in Christian ethics? Strickland's answer is unambiguous. God's standard for all people is the moral law, but this law is not to be equated with the Mosaic law. Instead, the Mosaic law, while it was a reflection of the moral law, was only a *temporary* application of that law. The passing of the old era has opened up a new revelation of God's moral law. In the present dispensation, Christ's teaching is the relevant application of God's moral law for the church. It is not a summary of the Mosaic law or a stricter interpretation of the Decalogue. Instead, the "scattered principles" found throughout the New Testament provide the new framework for a distinctive Christian ethic.

Strickland's argument is clear, but not without problems. I applaud his affirmation that God's standard is absolute and that the moral law is for all ages. I applaud his emphasis on the one way of salvation. But I censor his confusion of the Law/Gospel distinction by introducing the contrast between Israel and the church as the two peoples of God. Here we stand at the crossroads of dispensational and Reformed theology. Reformed theology as a system of continuity seeks the correlation of Law and Gospel, Israel and the church, whereas dispensationalism, at least the position represented by Strickland, allows the distinctions to multiply to the point that they affect the relevance and practical use of the Old Testament in the church.

Let us focus in on Strickland's discussion of Romans 10:5–8. He rejects the view that Paul's negative view of *nomos* should be understood in the context of the Jewish abuse of the law (legalism). Many scholars have sought to explain Paul's complex view of the law in the context of Jewish legalistic abuses (e.g., Fuller, Dunn, Silva). According to their interpretation, the apostle denounced the misuse of the Law—not unlike the Gospels, according to which Jesus censured the Pharisees for having made many and minute regulations, but held his contemporaries responsible for not listening to Moses and the prophets.

In support of his position, Strickland deduces from Romans 10:5–8 (cf. Gal. 3:10–12) that the Mosaic law and Christianity have little in common. They represent two kinds of righteousness: a righteousness based on the law and a righteousness based on faith. The former focuses on Moses and is without Christ, whereas the latter focuses on Jesus as the Christ. If this is what Paul is saying, then I must submit to my brother in the Lord and repent from my Reformed view of the law. I cannot, however, for three reasons. First, there is the nagging question of the meaning of "law" (is it legalism or the Mosaic law?). Second, the tension of Law and Gospel is not a simple historical progression from Law to Gospel, but is to be seen in terms of the tension of the *now* (the present state of redemptive history) and the *not yet* (the realization of the divine promises). Whenever God reveals his will to humans, the "now" of the Lord calls for a human response to his promises of a future prepared by him for all the saints. Hence, the Lord commends the faithful for living with the hope in the "city with foundations, whose architect and builder is God" (Heb. 11:10).

Third, the apostolic citations from the Old Testament (Lev. 18:5; Deut. 30:13–14) need be understood from the vantage point of their original context (what did Moses really say?) and of the apostolic meaning (was Paul interpreting the text, or did he make a rhetorical use of it?). Since the Father commissioned Moses to prepare the way for the Son, his message cannot be so radically different from the New Testament interpretation. The Gospel is found in the Law. The Gospel is the proclamation that God seeks sinners and justifies them. Set within its context, Leviticus 18:5 is the essence of the Gospel. As the light of the candle anticipates the brightness of the morning sun, so Leviticus 18:5 was God's revelation that, in principle, has all the essential aspects of the Gospel. The text is properly framed between a statement of the Lord's self-identification: "I am the LORD your God. Keep my decrees and laws, for the man who obeys them will live by them. I am the LORD" (vv. 4b-5). Hereby, the demand of obedience is set within the context of the proclamation that the Lord is God, that he is the God of his people, and that he is their redeemer and sustainer. Blessed are the people whose God is the Lord.

After all, there are two mutually exclusive ways: the *religion* of this world (the Egyptians and Canaanites, vv. 2–3) and the *revelation* from the Lord.[1] The one is the horizontal way whereby people learn from others. This path leads to syncretism, to acculturation, and ultimately to complete adaptation to the manners and customs of this world. The way of *religion* is the broad road that entices so many to define and worship a higher power and to cultivate a network of relations (structures) for the purpose of giving people a sense of ultimate meaning in life. The way of *revelation* is vertical in that God comes down to humans, speaks to them, and demonstrates his grace in acts of deliverance. He holds them accountable for their response to his revelation, rewarding all who come to him in faith and demonstrate their faith by loving him, listening to him, keeping his law, and by depending on him for life. This is the most difficult road because it requires of all who enter onto it to repent from their stubborn autonomy, to love a transcendent deity, to grow in faith, and to learn to please him *regardless of what he may require.* The essence of the gospel of Jesus Christ is thus found in the gospel of Moses.

With this background in mind, I understand that Moses called God's covenant people to pay attention to the radical nature of the gospel. The good news calls people away from trusting humans and challenges them to trust in deity for life, for happiness, and for blessing. The primary focus of the text is on the radical claims of God on his people; after all he is the Lord: "Do not follow their practices. You must obey my laws and be careful to follow my decrees. I am the LORD your God" (vv. 3b-4). In its context, the next verse—"Keep my decrees and laws, for the man who obeys them will live by them. I am the LORD"—is a summary statement of what the Lord has already declared to Moses in the first four verses. It serves to remind Israel that the Lord is the giver of all good gifts. He brought them out of Egypt and gave them the promised land. He is the object of their worship, love, and submission.

Paul's citation from Moses (Lev. 18:5) is an illustration of how the Jews had mistakenly argued that justification came by keeping

---

[1]This distinction is further developed in my book *Double Vision: The Christian Faith and the Pursuit of the American Dream* (publisher not yet defined).

the law (v. 5). The gospel of Moses called on people to place their faith in the Lord, in his redemption, and in God's new ways in the progress of redemption. Again and again Israel refused to open themselves to a true understanding of God's way. They substituted religion for revelation, syncretism for uniqueness, and rigidity for openness to God. The prophets, our Lord, and the apostles faced the same problem. In citing this text, Paul took a prophetic stand against the perversion of true religion to mere religion. While the Jews were zealous for maintaining their structures of religion and society, they were resistant to God's new way of revelation in Jesus Christ. They substituted the true way of righteousness by faith with a righteousness that comes from the law: "Since they did not know the righteousness that comes from God and sought to establish their own, they did not submit to God's righteousness" (Rom. 10:3).

Strickland's approach to the Old Testament raises several related issues. He holds that righteousness was based on law-keeping in the Old Testament and that it is now based on faith. The author carefully qualifies himself lest he be misunderstood. He affirms the evangelical position that salvation is always by grace and never by works, including the period of the Mosaic covenant. He rightly rejects the position that there are two ways of salvation: law in the Mosaic era and faith in the era of the Church. On the surface, it appears that he follows Paul's distinction between the kind of righteousness defined in Leviticus 18:5 and the righteousness defined in Deuteronomy 30:13–14. A closer analysis confirms that the gospel of Leviticus 18:1–5 is the same as what Moses proclaimed in Deuteronomy 30:1–21:

(1) God has always demanded that his children *love* him wholeheartedly: "obey him with all your heart and with all your soul according to everything I command you today" (Deut. 30:2; cf. 6:5).

(2) Only the Lord can so dispose our wicked hearts by the *grace* of regeneration: "The Lord your God will circumcise your hearts and the hearts of your descendants, so that you may love him with all your heart and with all your soul, and live" (v. 6).

(3) While love for God is always the prerequisite for *obedience* (law), the earnest desire to know and to do God's will is the concomitant and the expression of true love for him (v. 20).

(4) The *law* in Deuteronomy 30:1–15 is none other than what Moses had already given Israel: "You will again obey the Lord and follow all his commands I am giving you today" (v. 8); "if you obey the Lord your God and keep his commands and decrees that

are written in this Book of the Law and turn to the LORD your God with all your heart and with all your soul" (v. 10).

(5) This law was already *internalized* in some of God's people who were listening to Moses: "Now what I am commanding you today is not too difficult for you or beyond your reach. It is not up in heaven, so that you have to ask, 'Who will ascend into heaven to get it and proclaim it to us so we may obey it?' Nor is it beyond the sea, so that you have to ask, 'Who will cross the sea to get it and proclaim it to us so we may obey it?' No, the word is very near you; it is in your mouth and in your heart so you may obey it" (vv. 11–14).

(6) The *promise of life* (righteousness) is always to be seen in relationship to faith. When Moses spoke of blessing, goodness, and life (vv. 15–21), he made it clear that the people had to look in faith to the Lord, even as their father Abraham had: "For the LORD is your life, and he will give you many years in the land he swore to give to your fathers, Abraham, Isaac and Jacob" (v. 20).

(7) The *reality of life* (righteousness), blessing, and goodness is in Jesus Christ. In him all the promises of God find their confirmation (2 Cor. 1:20). All who are in Christ, Jews or Gentiles, are *new creatures*. In their newness of life, they share in the promises and in the responsibilities of the one people of God (Gal. 3:29).

Strickland's hermeneutic approach also raises questions regarding the place of the *tôrâ* in the new covenant. After all, Jeremiah's *tôrâ* in the promise of internalization—"I will put my law in their minds and write it on their hearts" (Jer. 31:33)—is the Mosaic law. The phrase "my law" occurs elsewhere in Jeremiah's speeches of judgment: "Hear, O earth: I am bringing disaster on this people, the fruit of their schemes, because they have not listened to my words and have rejected my law" (6:19); "It is because they have forsaken my law, which I set before them; they have not obeyed me or followed my law" (9:12); and "'It is because your fathers forsook me,' declares the LORD, 'and followed other gods and served and worshiped them. They forsook me and did not keep my law'" (16:11). Even though the word *tôrâ* may have a broader designation (instruction), the earlier linkage of the *tôrâ* with the priests defines it as a body of known laws and regulations (2:8).[2] Why was the internalization so

---

[2]William Holladay, *Jeremiah One*, Hermeneia (Philadelphia: Fortress, 1986), 88–89.

important in Jeremiah's vision of restoration? Because he had encountered stubborn people (9:14; cf. 3:17; 7:24; 11:8; 13:10; 16:12; 18:12; 23:17) who refused to trust the Lord and expressed it by their utter disregard for the law of Moses. However, the prophet consoled them with the promise that the Lord would renew the covenant, change their hearts, and help them to do his will *after the exilic experience*.[3]

The difference between Israel and the Church cannot be defined in terms of righteousness (works vs. faith), in the distinction of the divine administration (law vs. grace) or motivation (law vs. the Spirit). Dispensational and Reformed theologians and exegetes may each cite texts in favor of their position, but the crux is Jesus' place in the whole of redemptive history. Since the revelation of God is in the Old Testament, the Old must be understood in the light of the gospel of Jesus Christ. The opposite is also true. Since the gospel of Christ is found in the Old Testament, the New Testament books must be seen in the light of the Old.

There is another dimension. Both Old and New witness to the promise that Jesus will come to accomplish all things written of him in the sixty-six books of Scripture. In the fullness of time, God sent his Son as the agent of restoration, and the Father and the Son have sent the Holy Spirit to assure the people of God of, and keeps them longing for, the restoration-to-come.[4] As long as the "whole" (the "perfect") is not yet here, they still await the fulfillment of the divine promises. However, in awaiting the coming of Jesus Christ and his kingdom, they must exercise caution and humility in interpreting the Word in the light of the whole.

Eschatology colors Strickland's interpretation when he applies the promise of restoration to the Millennium. Moses prophetically envisages Israel's apostasy, exile, and restoration in his messages, collected in our book of Deuteronomy. The story of their apostasy is given in the pre-exilic prophets—in the historical books ("the Former Prophets": Joshua, Judges, Samuel, Kings) and in the prophetic books proper ("the Latter Prophets"). The reality of God's judgment in exile is also explicitly dealt with in the Old Testament, as is the fulfillment of the promise of restoration.

---

[3]William Holladay, *Jeremiah Two*, Hermeneia (Minneapolis: Augsburg Fortress, 1989), 198.

[4]Willem A. VanGemeren, "The Spirit of Restoration," *WTJ* 50 (1988), 81–102.

Moses' promise of restoration finds its initial fulfillment in the restoration of the Jews from exile under Zerubbabel in 538 B.C. (see my comments in response to Moo). The renewal of the covenant, too, had already some reality in the post-exilic era. I believe that while Jeremiah's prophecy of the new covenant (Jer. 31:31) has its realization in the eternal state, the fulfillment is progressive. After the exile, God's people began to enjoy the benefits of restoration, including the experience of internalization of God's law (cf. Hag. 1:14; 2:4).[5] The members of the church of Jesus Christ enjoy even greater benefits as the Holy Spirit applies God's word to their hearts. Nevertheless, they still await the fullness of the new covenant when every tear will be wiped away and sorrow will be no more.

Christians are slaves, associates, and exiles. Believers, who are regenerated by the Holy Spirit, united in the Lord's death and resurrection, and indwelt by the Holy Spirit, understand things spiritually. They walk in the Spirit. They are new creatures, and as such they have been transformed to be slaves unto righteousness, "But thanks be to God that, though you used to be slaves to sin, you wholeheartedly obeyed the form of teaching to which you were entrusted. You have been set free from sin and have become slaves to righteousness" (Rom. 6:17–18).

In Christ, believers are slaves of righteousness, but as exiles they await the fullness of redemption (1 Pet. 2:11–12). They still need a road map or basis for understanding what true righteousness is like. The norm of righteousness is the law of God, as qualified and interpreted by the Lord of history, Jesus Christ. The essence of the moral law is found in the Decalogue, but even the Ten Commandments can be abridged: "And what does the LORD require of you? To act justly and to love mercy and to walk humbly with your God" (Mic. 6:8). How shall we know what it means to love one another, to act justly, and to walk humbly? The Reformed answer to this question is clear. We still need the Ten Commandments as the revealed summary of God's will. Even as the ungodly need the law to be reminded of their sinfulness, so the law mirrors God's perfect righteousness and reveals any latent and obvious want of conformity to the Lord Jesus Christ. In this light, we read 1 Timothy 1:8–10 and apply it to our hearts:

---

[5]For a brief statement of this approach to the Bible, see W. A. VanGemeren, *Interpreting the Prophetic Word* (Grand Rapids: Zondervan, 1989), 90–99, 376–83.

We know that the law is good if one uses it properly. We also know that law is made not for the righteous but for lawbreakers and rebels, the ungodly and sinful, the unholy and irreligious; for those who kill their fathers or mothers, for murderers, for adulterers and perverts, for slave traders and liars and perjurers—and for whatever else is contrary to the sound doctrine.

By grace are we saved, but as long as we are in the body, we need God's grace to keep us on the path of righteousness. When we look back on this path, we see Moses and his law. Ahead of us is Jesus Christ, the perfect standard of righteousness. Between Moses, who makes us realize how our present beings are still so much a part of this world, and Jesus Christ, who assures us of the victory, we experience the struggle of the apostle Paul, who said,

> When I want to do good, evil is right there with me. For in my inner being I delight in God's law; but I see another law at work in the members of my body, waging war against the law of my mind and making me a prisoner of the law of sin at work within my members. What a wretched man I am! Who will rescue me from this body of death? Thanks be to God—through Jesus Christ our Lord!
>
> So then, I myself in my mind am a slave to God's law, but in the sinful nature a slave to the law of sin. (Rom. 7:21–25)

Jesus has not only summarized this law in his command to love God and to love humankind; he has also assured us of a new and better relationship. We are his *associates*, if we are obedient to his royal ethics:

> You are my friends if you do what I command. I no longer call you servants, because a servant does not know his master's business. Instead, I have called you friends, for everything that I learned from my Father I have made known to you. You did not choose me, but I chose you and appointed you to go and bear fruit—fruit that will last. Then the Father will give you whatever you ask in my name. This is my command: Love each other. (John 15:14–17)

I end on a personal note. Desiring to be a close associate of the Lord Jesus, I long to be a slave of righteousness when sin has no more power over me. The reality of perfection (the *not yet*) is not yet. By grace I am a citizen of the kingdom of God. By grace I live as an exile in this world. In this tension, the moral law of God, as summarized in the Decalogue and as interpreted and applied by the Lord Jesus, helps me to see myself for what I am, to look for the grace of my God and Savior, to serve both God and people in the spirit of the Lord Jesus and by the power of the Spirit, and to prepare myself for the coming of the Lord Jesus. The challenge of the apostle Peter is still as relevant today as it was in the first century:

> Therefore, prepare your minds for action; be self-controlled; set your hope fully on the grace to be given you when Jesus Christ is revealed. As obedient children, do not conform to the evil desires you had when you lived in ignorance. But just as he who called you is holy, so be holy in all you do; for it is written: "Be holy, because I am holy." (1 Pet. 1:13–16)

These last words—a citation from the Old Testament (Lev. 11:44, 45; 19:2; 20:7)—confirm the relevance of the law. They open believers to God's holiness, instruct them to be holy, and encourage them to prepare themselves for the new order in which everything and everyone will be holy and righteous. Thanks be to God for the grace of his revelation in the Law and in the Gospel.

Response to Wayne G. Strickland

Greg L. Bahnsen

The essay by Dr. Strickland will be an encouragement and model to any believer who is committed to dealing point by point with the biblical texts in order to draw sound and faithful doctrinal conclusions. I commend his diligence and, with him, praise God for the infallibility of his blessed word in the Scriptures of the Old and New Testaments, by which we can be confident of "being equipped for every good work" (2 Tim. 3:16–17). He is also to be commended for his humility and teachability: he acknowledges that his is only "a" dispensational approach to the subject of the Mosaic law today, and he also allows that dispensationalism is changing. And what changes! As a Reformed and covenantal theologian, I was just amazed to read my dispensational brother, Dr. Strickland, write these words:

> The law has abiding application to the life of a believer even in the church age. . . . its revelatory purpose transcends the Mosaic economy and remains valid in the church dispensation. In fact, the law as it functions in a revelatory manner acts to preserve the unity between the two eras. Since God's character is immutable, it stands to reason that insofar as the law reveals God's character, it remains valid.

I had to pinch myself! What a marvelous step toward a unified outlook.

But then I should know better than to get too excited before pursuing fuller investigation and analysis! As good as this may be as a start toward concord, there is plenty of work yet to be done.

After all, one begins to get theologically nervous when Strickland writes: "the Mosaic Law is antithetical to the Gospel and has no part of it"—*no part*! Comparing this categorical assertion with the quotation above, one's logical nerves might get rattled as well.

Looking at the details of Dr. Strickland's essay, a sampling of incidental criticisms might come to a respondent's mind. The author speaks of "the sin-grace construct," but never explains what the expression denotes. Although God is "the authority" in both old and new covenants, Strickland uses the expression "the authority of grace" as though it had some clear sense and as though whatever it might mean could *not* apply to the Old Testament (cf. Rom. 6:14). He reasons fallaciously about linguistics, saying that a concept (like "legalism") could not be "part of the semantic range" of a *single* word ("*nomos*") if the concept is also sometimes expressed by means of a *phrase* using the same word (e.g., "righteousness based on the law"). But then the concept of the Old Testament Scriptures as a whole could not, on Strickland's rule, ever be denoted by the single word "law" because it is also sometimes denoted by a phrase containing that same word ("the law and the prophets")! Strickland seems to miss the logic of the biblical writer at times, as when he suggests that in Romans 5:13–14, the law is not eternal (the very *opposite* of the unspoken premise necessary to complete Paul's argument). Likewise, Strickland claims that the word "law" in Galatians 3:17 has the sense of "revelatory law," whereas the text of that verse plainly treats "the law" which came 430 years after as the counterpart to a previously ratified "covenant"—thus denoting by the word "law" a covenant within history (the Mosaic covenant).

Strickland mistakenly treats "covenant nation" as identical with "believing nation"—contrary to so much taught throughout the sweep of Old Testament history and theology—and says "the covenantal relationship" stresses "that Israel's salvation has already been secured." In fact, however, individuals could be under God's covenant and still be unsaved (e.g., those who perished for not looking upon the serpent on the pole, those who were swallowed up in the rebellion of Korah, those called upon to circumcise their hearts, those not numbered among the seven thousand who had not bowed the knee, those excluded in God's reckoning from the righteous remnant, etc., etc.). To use Paul's expression: "not all who are descended from Israel are Israel" (Rom. 9:6) and "a man is not a Jew if he is only one outwardly" (i.e., circumcised, the covenant sign; Rom. 2:28). Strickland repudiates the distinction of "ceremonial law," declaring that the law must be treated "as a unit." But then he later unwittingly reintroduces that very same conceptual distinction and declines to treat the law as an unbreakable unit when, having said that although the law continues to reveal sin, he adds that "the law prefigures the redemption wrapped up in the person of Jesus Christ" and as such no longer binds today! It seems then, that Strickland needs to think through some of his premises and biblical interpretations a bit more clearly and consistently.[1]

At some points he treats the blessings/curses of Deuteronomy 28 as theocratic or national (corporate) blessings/curses, but at other points he erroneously treats them as blessings/curses to individuals (contrary to v.1, "set you high above all the nations on earth"; v. 36, "the king you set over you," etc.). He claims the Mosaic civil law was for Israel (only?) a standard of "theocratic" sanctification, maintaining fellowship with God, or blessing in the land—which is acceptable enough as long as he does not conceive of this as denying that the law was also the standard of justice for the surrounding nations as well (Deut. 4:5–8). He makes the odd remark that "the law functioned as a test of whether or not one was part of the theocracy," which on a surface reading certainly seems false since people continually broke the Mosaic law and were still part of the theocratic nation. However, Strickland proceeds to define not being part of the theocracy as "refusal to abide by the demands of the theocracy" (not under God's rule). That is, his statement dissolves into a trivial tautology: the theocratic law's demands functioned as a test of whether one was part of the theocracy—that is, whether one was obedient to the demands of the theocracy. The reader suspects Strickland is saying something less significant than he thinks he is. Yet he can also indulge overstatement, as when he says "it makes sense only if we understand Paul as contrasting two periods [of time]" in Romans 6:14—even though he simply neglects to treat the possibility that Paul's contrast is between being "under [the resources of] law" and "under [the resources of] grace," which

---

[1]This is especially evident throughout the second half of his essay when he surveys "Passages Advocating Discontinuity," but editorial limitations require that I forego elaboration. Rebuttal interpretations of the passages surveyed by Strickland may be found in my essay in this volume and/or related books (listed in fn. 5).

exactly fits the context. But such detail-criticisms of his essay as we have considered here would be of subordinate importance.

Looking at the overall position that Dr. Strickland's essay develops, the thing that stands out prominently—and for which the author apparently offers no resolution—is the inherent contradiction at the heart of things. Stand back from the details of his discussion (many of which are good and helpful) and scan the pattern of the entire landscape for a moment. As Strickland attempts to synthesize his particulars into generalized conclusions, among the judgments to which he comes about the Mosaic law in the life of the New Testament Christian are two that simply cannot be harmonized. Upon analysis, they openly contradict each other. Let me try to show how this is.

On the one hand, true to his dispensationalism, Strickland asserts that "in the Mosaic economy, sanctification came via obedience to the demands of the law, and . . . this economy has now been superseded by the dispensation of grace." Later he writes: "There is freedom from bondage to the Mosaic law through salvation in Christ Jesus," by which "bondage" he means more than the Jewish perversions of the law or the condemnation issued by the law itself. Chiding Calvin for holding that the law "is still binding on the believer for the purposes of sanctification," Strickland teaches that the church age "has rendered the [Mosaic] law inoperative."

In the author's conception of things, the "redeemed Jew" of the Old Testament was "like a child supervised by the law . . . in order to know how to please and worship God." But with the advent of Christ, says Strickland, "this regulatory purpose" is no longer necessary. The believer no longer gains a knowledge of how to please God by means of the Mosaic law. To be sure, "in spite of changes in the dispensations, there still is law," but Strickland wants to make very sure to tell the reader "this law is clearly different from the former Mosaic law." Although such a claim is left undefined and undefended—and is wide open to theological refutation (has the intrinsic righteousness of the immutable God changed from one dispensation to another?)—my only point is to indicate what Strickland claims to be the case. He says the Old Testament looks ahead to a future day "when the Mosaic law will no longer be the operative principle," although "there is a law still involved." Strickland goes on to say that according to Jeremiah 31:31, this law will be engraved on the hearts of believers. This to me is a bewildering misreading of Jeremiah's words, through which God promised to write, *not a new law*, but rather "my law" on the heart of his people [31:33]. What well-known law, associated with the Exodus [v. 31], would any Old Testament Jew think of when God speaks of "my law" except the Mosaic law?[2]

In an unargued assertion that Strickland takes for granted, he says "Paul's discussions on the law were necessitated not by the problem of Pharisaic misunderstandings of the law [how can this square with Gal. 2:19; Phil. 3:5–6; etc.?], but rather the application of the law, whether misunderstood or not, on the part of Christians." He concludes that Paul opposed "any suggestion that Christians were obligated to obey the law." On the contrary, it seems Paul himself not only suggested but mandated without apology that "keeping God's command is what counts" (1 Cor. 7:19). Alluding to 1 Peter 1:15–16, Strickland says the apostle merely notes that the law's character "is in accord with its origin"; this does not make sanctification "a legitimate function of the law." The author is shortsighted in his reading here. Peter not only notes as a matter of fact the holiness of God; he also exhorts believers to be "obedient children" (v. 14), who strive to be holy "just as he who called you is holy." Moreover, Peter makes God's holiness their standard of sanctification by quoting the Mosaic law and requiring New Testament believers to follow it!

It seems to me that Strickland's treatment of the evidence is heavy laden with exegetical and logical mistakes, but nonetheless the main thing to be observed is his theological inference that the New Testament advocates sanctification apart from the Mosaic law. He argues that whatever positive may be said about the Mosaic law, it may not be upheld in any "sense that one must obey the law for sanctification."

Nevertheless—and this is where the essay's incoherence manifests itself—Strickland still wants to speak of "the positive value of the Mosaic law," and adduces the fact that it "functioned to expose sin." He writes that "Paul contends that the purpose of the Mosaic law was intended to reveal and expose sin. . . . The sinfulness of humankind was revealed by comparing human behavior to the holiness revealed in the law." This claim, which is

---

[2]Another awkward aspect of Strickland's interpretation, presented as it is in the framework of dispensationalism, is his claim that Deuteronomy 30:1–14, whose ultimate fulfillment he finds discussed in Jeremiah 31:31–32, looks ahead to the millennial kingdom. Yet he must admit, given the use of Deuteronomy 30 in Romans 10:6–8, that "[Paul's] day was the time" to which it applies—"the situation in the church."

demonstrably biblical in character, indicates that the Mosaic law with its statues on human behavior reveals what people ought and ought not to do; it reveals what divine holiness is, by which one is to compare one's own behavior (by contrast) and gain knowledge of one's sin. Strickland admits that the Mosaic law "is a reflection of the moral perfection of its Giver." And the reader should note very well that the law "forced [Paul] to admit . . . the gravity of sin as an act contrary to the nature of God." According to Strickland, Romans 3:20 proves that "Paul presents the law's purpose as revealing sin to those in need of righteousness"; indeed, for Strickland, it points up the universal need for salvation created by law-breaking, for Paul argues that everyone, Jew and Gentile, is under sin. Strickland later grants that the "moral law inscribed on human hearts . . . furnishes the foundation for the Mosaic law, where it has clear expression in an explicit codified form." Following Romans 3:19, Strickland recognizes the scope of the law's work to reveal sin, "that every mouth may be silenced." So then, he writes that the Mosaic law was intended to give not only "knowledge of sin" but also demonstrate the "sinfulness of sin" (as well as to bring personal conviction of the depth of one's departure from God's holiness). Furthermore, this purpose of the law in revealing human righteousness, Strickland maintains, is true of the church age or dispensation. In his essay's conclusion he states "the law has abiding application to the life of a believer even in the church age."

Now then, if the Mosaic law continues to reveal to all people today God's moral perfection and holiness, explaining to them what sin is—an act contrary to the nature of God—then the conclusion is inescapable that the Mosaic law informs us of the divine and universal standard of right and wrong. Strickland concedes that the Mosaic law shows us what sin is. He recognizes that sin is that which humans ought not to do. Therefore, the Mosaic law shows us today what we ought not to do—which is just to say that the law regulates (communicates the moral standards for) our conduct as New Testament Christians. Sanctification is to follow holiness (which Strickland says is revealed in the Mosaic law) and in my attitudes and conduct to put away sin (which is revealed by means of the Mosaic law, as Strickland again says). When, for instance, I read in the Old Testament law, "Do not accept a bribe" (Ex. 23:8) or "Do not defraud your neighbor" (Lev. 19:13), God has communicated to me what he requires my behavior to be. He does not have a double standard of morality, as though unbelievers are forbidden to do so, but believers may take bribes and defraud others! (Disgracefully, some professing Christians act that way in the name of "grace"!) The Mosaic law does not reveal what sin is to us that we might go on sinning! Surely Strickland would say the same (cf. Rom. 6:1–2). We must say, if we are consistent with the premises of Strickland's essay then, that the Mosaic law reveals a standard of sanctification to New Testament believers—which is diametrically *contrary* to what we previously saw Strickland asserting.

The devastating self-inflicted wound at the heart of Strickland's essay is the incoherent attempt to say *both* that the Mosaic law is not a "regulatory" standard of Christian sanctification and living, *and yet* that the Mosaic law continues to "reveal" the standard of holy behavior for all people (by which they know their sin). The two poles of the dialectic are set side by side when Strickland writes, "the Mosaic law naturally ended when God suspended his program with Israel," and then makes his very next sentence: "Certainly God's moral law in and of itself does not change"![3] Moreover, he grants that "the principle" (or "essence") expressed in a Mosaic statute "may still be preached in the

---

[3]Strickland's alleged distinction between a "revelatory" and "regulative" function of the Mosaic law (his "twofold purpose of the law") does not relieve the internal discord because both its exegetical warrant and conceptual clarity are impeachable. It just restates in new linguistic garb the old distinction between the "second use" and "third use" of the law (cf. Formula of Concord), confusedly wedded to a popular distinction between the law's authority in guiding individual piety over against guiding socio-political affairs in "the theocracy." Nothing is proved by tinkering with vocabulary.

For a discussion of the imprecision and muddled character of another kind of dispensational distinction used at this point—between the culturally defined "Mosaic code" and God's eternal "moral law"—see my book (with Kenneth L. Gentry, Jr.), *House Divided: The Break-up of Dispensational Theology* (Tyler, Tex.: Institute for Christian Economics, 1989), 90ff. Strickland writes that "the law of Moses" and "the law of Christ" are both "specific applications of God's eternal moral standard"—in which case, they would have to lead to the same conclusions or applied judgments in response to practical ethical questions. If not, they do not express the same "eternal moral standard" after all. (This observation especially needs to be made when we read Strickland treat "the law of Christ" not as concrete demands, but "scattered principles" applied by the internal leading of the Holy Spirit!) Thus Strickland's pitting of one against the other is conceptually clouded. He says the law of Christ "is no mere rephrasing of the Mosaic law," and there are senses in which I would want to say the same. But one cannot overlook the fact that one of the "laws" laid down by Christ is precisely that we conform to "the smallest letter . . . the least stroke of a pen" of the Mosaic law (Matt. 5:18–19) or else suffer the sanction of demotion within his kingdom. The law of Christ contains the law of Moses, both conceptually and by dominical decree.

church" because fulfilling the law of Christ simultaneously "furnishes fulfillment" of the law of Moses! This contradiction, I believe, unravels the logical and theological cogency of Strickland's overall position and renders it unacceptable as an evangelical approach to the issue of the Mosaic law. He has not presented a coherent option.

Before ending this analysis, we must examine further one of the conflicting sides of the theological incongruity in Strickland's theological position: namely, that aspect of his discussion that negates (rather than upholds) the moral authority of the Old Testament. My book *Theonomy* argues that our guiding hermeneutical assumption should be that the principles of the Mosaic law continue to bind unless repealed in the New Testament, which if true would destroy Strickland's opposite guiding principle of discontinuity. At one point in a cavalier manner he waves this off as "a moot issue," but he knows better. In his essay Strickland wants to address the theonomic position, and indeed needs to offer a rebuttal to it, in order to sanction his rejection of the continuing validity of the Mosaic law's moral demands for New Testament believers.[4]

He makes a weak effort in this direction under his discussion of "The Mosaic Law and the Christian," starting off with a misbegotten attempt to reduce how much effort would be needed for the task. First, Strickland tries to reduce the theonomic position to Matthew 5:17–19 (calling it "the major justification for theonomy"), and then second, he tries to reduce the theonomic argument from that passage to the single word *plērōsai*, saying that "in order to sustain" the theonomic thesis, this term "must be understood as 'confirmed' or 'ratified' rather than 'fulfilled.' " Ah, would that it were so easy! The fundamental operating premises of theonomic ethics could be—indeed, in my books,[5] are—readily

---

[4]Space restrictions prevent me from elaborating on Strickland's misrepresentation of theonomic ethics as denying that Israel was uniquely a nation with God as its supreme ruler and that she was set apart by God or guided by him in a special way. Years ago Meredith Kline courageously tackled the same straw man. In my reply, I offered massive testimony from my book *Theonomy* to show that theonomic ethics maintains a view quite contrary to portrayal given here (see "M. G. Kline on Theonomic Politics: An Evaluation of His Reply," *Journal of Christian Reconstruction* 6 [Winter, 1979–80]: 195–221).

[5]*Theonomy in Christian Ethics* (Nutley, N.J.: The Craig Press, 1977, 1984); *By This Standard: The Authority of God's Law Today* (Tyler, Tex.: Institute for Christian Economics, 1985); *House Divided: The Break-up of Dispensational Theology*, with Kenneth L. Gentry, Jr. For a reply to challenges, taking in extensive discussion of

proven from any number of New Testament passages, only one of which is Matthew 5:17–19. Because it is such an explicit and important text and has often been made the center of discussion, *Theonomy* gives it detailed discussion. But the theonomic thesis could be demonstrated without any reference to this text at all. Moreover, even if linguistic scholarship fully negated my semantic understanding of the one word *plērōsai* in Matthew 5:17 (which it does not, for even critics like Strickland grant its possibility), the theonomic view of the passage as a whole would still stand.

Strickland's debate with theonomy is encumbered with misrepresentation. He claims that according to *Theonomy*, "*plērōsai cannot* be understood as meaning 'fulfilled'"; I translate it "to confirm," he alleges, "*rather than* 'fulfilled'" (emphasis added). This is utterly false. I have no problem with translating *plērōsai* as "to fulfill" in Matthew 5:17—and when referring to the text, that is often the very word I utilize. But as anybody who is party to exegetical and theological debates centering on this text realizes, the word "fulfill" can be taken in a host of different (even conflicting) ways. For that reason it is necessary to go further, as I undertook to do in *Theonomy*, and ask *in what sense* Christ claimed to fulfill the law—to find the precise meaning to be given the term in this particular context. I offered "to confirm" as the intended meaning as an explanation of "to fulfill," *not* "rather than" the translation of "to fulfill." Strickland has badly misread the issue.

And what is Strickland's argument against understanding the word as "to confirm"? He says this is not "the customary usage" nor the way Matthew most often uses the term. That cannot be meant as a serious linguistic argument, certainly not a relevant or decisive one in attempting to determine a word's meaning in a particular context. The axiom assumed and wielded by him in this criticism—namely, in each and every text a particular word necessarily means whatever the author most often means by it in other texts—has not been thought out carefully. By applying it consistently in conjunction with a bit of statistical analysis, we could thin out our Greek lexicons considerably! Indeed Strickland's assumption would reduce every word to one and only one single meaning, since every usage outside of the statistical majority usage would, *ipso facto*, be disqualified as not the way it is

the exegesis of Matthew 5, including each critic cited by Strickland, see *No Other Standard: Theonomy and Its Critics* (Tyler, Tex.: Institute for Christian Economics, 1991).

most often used. To prove that a particular word in Matthew 5:17 does not in fact carry the specific sense suggested by another author, Strickland needs much more than a passing reference to a statistical generalization. There is good reason to believe, as I show in *Theonomy*, that *in this particular textual setting* the word "fulfill" most likely takes the precise sense of "confirming the law in full measure." Notice the syntactic opposition to "abolish" in the same phrase, the explanatory upholding of the law's authority in the very next verse, and Christ's illustrative assault on the current diminishing of the law's demand in vv. 20–48.

But the theonomic interpretation of Matthew 5:17–19 cannot be correct, reasons Strickland, because it "would not allow for *any* abrogation of *any* portion of the Mosaic law." Once again, however, he has badly misread. As a matter of linguistic and exegetical fact, Christ does not offer any qualifications to his absolutistic endorsement of the law's validity specifically in Matthew 5; however, as a matter of theological relevance, Matthew 5 is not the only text where Christ or the New Testament authors speak about the law. The theonomic view has always been, accordingly, that the absolutistic declarations of Christ in Matthew 5:17–19 provide the Christian's first-line, operating assumption—the generalization within which one begins his or her approach to the Old Testament law. We must *presume* that every Old Testament commandment (even the least, v. 19) continues to bind us *unless* teaching from Christ or the apostles elsewhere qualifies or alters that presumption. If this interpretation of the teaching of Christ is mistaken, Strickland has yet to demonstrate so. He has not even begun with an accurate understanding of the view he sets out to refute.

In my opinion, Matthew 5:17–19 clearly and obviously presents Jesus as endorsing the ethical instruction of the Old Testament law. What is Strickland's own understanding of this passage? It is nothing short of remarkable. According to him, what Jesus was talking about in verses 17–18 was not the moral demands ("law, commandments") of the Old Testament, but rather its *prophecies*. The passage teaches, he claims, that "the prophetic statements of Scripture can be abolished only when they are fulfilled." But the alert reader must cry out: "Where is there *any* mention or discussion of Old Testament prophecies in this passage or its local context?" The fact is that there is not so much as a word about Old Testament prophecies to be found. Strickland fabricates that this is the subject under discussion and then imports it into the passage from outside. Any reader can see that

Christ is not discussing prophecy but ethics, at this particular point—indeed, extending to the end of the sermon.

Leading up to verses 17–18, Jesus discusses attitudes and "good works." Then in verses 17–18, says Strickland, Jesus emphatically denied that the Old Testament *prophecies* could go unfulfilled. Why would that be relevant to what the Lord has just been teaching? Furthermore, the problem with Strickland's view is not simply that it is arbitrary; it also makes nonsense of the text in question. Notice that the word "therefore" (*oun* in the Greek text; cf. NRSV) connects verses 18 and 19. Verse 19 is presented as an inference or application of the premise provided in verse 18. On the Strickland hypothesis, then, we have Jesus declaring that, because Old Testament *prophecies* must be fulfilled, anybody who breaks one of *"these commandments"* will be demoted in God's kingdom. This renders the word "therefore" unintelligible, moving from a premise about prophecies to a conclusion about commandments! And Strickland's interpretation suppresses and ignores the demonstrative pronoun "these" in verse 19: "Anyone who breaks one of the least of *these* commandments." Here Jesus refers back to the subject of his statement in verse 18: "not the smallest letter, not the least stroke of a pen, will . . . disappear from the law." "These" are *not* the prophecies of the Old Testament, as Strickland strains to maintain, but rather the commandments. In my opinion Strickland simply foists on Matthew 5:17–19 a preconceived theological scheme—his dispensationalism; he must resort to this type of reasoning in order to avoid saying that the moral instruction of the Mosaic law continues to be a standard of sanctification for the New Testament Christian. From the heart I write to you as brothers and friends: heed the words of your Lord. "Anyone who breaks one of the least of these commandments and *teaches others to do the same* will be called least in the kingdom of heaven."

There are other, equally inadmissible, interpretations of biblical texts to which Strickland's dispensationalism forces him. For instance, he says that Paul eliminated the idea that the law "is good for sanctification." When Paul declares the conspicuous goodness of the law in 1 Timothy 1:8–9, he does not, according to Strickland, intend for it to be used by Christians, but only by unbelievers: "the Decalogue is designed to be used by the unbeliever *rather than* the believer" (emphasis added); "the law is *not* made for the righteous or saved person in this church age." Actually, contrary to Strickland, the referent of "the law" in this passage unquestionably ranges beyond the Decalogue to such things in the Mosaic case laws as kidnapping, homosexuality, etc. Also contrary to Strickland, Paul is not here using the substantive adjective "a just one" as a synonym for "a justified one," as would be required by Strickland interpreting the word to point to "the saved man."

For Paul, even the justified or saved need to be called to "pursue righteousness" (1 Tim. 6:11)—which indisputably characterizes the Mosaic commandments (cf. Rom. 7:12). In Paul's outlook, the saved are not viewed in themselves as fully and consistently just. They still need ethical guidance and restraint, making them among those for whom the Mosaic law is applicable (cf. Rom. 8:4, 7–9). But Strickland claims that this guidance needed by the Christian *may not* come from the Mosaic law. Why not? Is there something defective or wrong about its moral directions? Strickland is on the horns of a dilemma regardless of how he answers that question. It is noteworthy that Paul says in this very passage that the things that are condemned by the law are the very same things that are contrary to the teaching of the gospel (vv. 10–11). The interpretation of 1 Timothy 1:8–9 offered by Strickland also implicates him in self-contradiction. According to Strickland, Paul was referring to the Mosaic law, and Paul denied that this law was enacted for those who are saved. Yet earlier in his essay Strickland had labored extensively to demonstrate, to the contrary, that the Mosaic law was revealed to a redeemed (saved) people!

Despite good intentions, dispensational systems of interpretation, it seems to me, always end up entangled in incoherence like this.

Response to Wayne G. Strickland

Walter C. Kaiser, Jr.

The dispensational solution to the Law/Gospel tension observed in the biblical text desires to make the "law of Christ" a new law that now serves as the counterpart to the Mosaic law in the new covenant. This solution sounds similar to one proposed some years ago for the new covenant itself, i.e., two new covenants were invented in order to give one to Israel and one to the church. It is a pleasure to report that this solution of two new covenants has now been rejected, and almost everyone today agrees that there is only one new covenant—since about 1965!

It would be another source of relief in the body of Christ to realize as a result of these essays on the Law and the Gospel that any distinction between the law originally issued by our Trinitarian Lord and the law of Christ would be dropped as well! The tendency to relegate the Old Testament law to Moses rather than to the divine source from which it came is all too noticeable—especially in those passages where the interpreter would wish to place a temporal ceiling or cultural handicap on the Mosaic law.

Even when Christ or the apostles explicitly cite the Old Testament and they say they are repeating what is found in the "Scripture" or the "Law and the Prophets" (Matt. 22:37–40; Rom. 13:8–10; Gal. 5:14; James 2:8–12), the position Strickland adopts in his essay flatly denies it! Instead, he writes that this allegedly new law of Christ "is no mere rephrasing of Mosaic law, for it consists not of a concrete corpus of demands, but rather of basic principles [wherein] . . . the Holy Spirit ministers in the life of the New Testament believer . . . [so that] there is no need for any lengthy, detailed, codified, external means of restraint as in the Mosaic law." To compound this error, we are then told that love to our neighbor is the fulfilling of the law's demands (Gal. 5:14), which in turn is identified as the "law of Christ" in Galatians 6:2.

Everything in this extremely important theological and exegetical move awaits any proof from the Scriptures. In fact, rather than exhibiting the fact that Christ and the apostles rejected the Old Testament form and substance of the commands they cited, the evidence is overwhelmingly in the opposite direction. What is more, an excellent case can be made for the fact that the whole book of James is itself a series of expositions on every verse in Leviticus 19:12–18 (except v. 14). As proof we cite:

Lev. 19:12	James 5:12
Lev. 19:13	James 5:4
Lev. 19:15	James 2:1, 9
Lev. 19:16	James 4:11
Lev. 19:17b	James 5:20
Lev. 19:18a	James 5:9

James called the same law that Paul is alleged to have called the "law of Christ" the "royal law found in Scripture" (James 2: 8). I am afraid it is going to prove to be just as impossible to show that the law of Christ (or the royal law) was a separate and different law from the law the Father revealed to Moses as it was to prove that there were two new covenants.

Moreover, love cannot be the new substitute for the old law in that the old law required the same love. Furthermore, love is not a "what?" word, but only a "how?" word. Love will never tell us *what* we are to do in order to live and behave as God wants us to do. It will tell us, however, *how* it is we are to act when we do what it is that we should be doing.

This solution to our problem is a new type of replacement theology. Just as covenant theology has incorrectly replaced Israel with the church, this solution would replace the revelation of the character of God in his law with the character of Christ. How can this house stand if it is divided against itself?

But there is more. Four other problems need to be addressed. It is alleged that: (1) the *tôrâ* of the new covenant is not the same law given to Moses, but is the law of Christ; (2) the *tôrâ* is "just, holy, good, and spiritual" with regard to its source, but not with regard to its substance; (3) there are no distinctions to be made in God's one unified law; and 4) Pharisaic legalism is the same thing as the righteousness of law commended by Scripture. Each of these assertions are wide of the biblical mark and must call for vigorous comment.

The New Covenant *Tôrâ* is the Same as the Mosaic Law

Clearly, Jeremiah 31:33; Ezekiel 11:20; 36:27, make it plain that in the new covenant God will place his *tôrâ* ("law") "in their minds and write it on their hearts," so that his people would be able to follow *ḥuqqây* or *ḥuqqotây* ("my statute" or "my decrees") and *mišpātây* ("my laws" or "my judgments"). The burden of proof is not on those who say this is the same law as the one that God gave to Moses; rather, it is squarely on those who have some other law in mind than the one to which these words ordinarily point in this document. Even the attempt to drive some type of wedge between the moral law that existed before Moses and the moral standards that God gave to Moses will not work. What sense does it make to say, "God's moral standards do not change, but the concrete expressions of it may change"? If the first part of that statement is correct, as it is, must the second part mean that the concrete expressions change also the substance of the morality that they embody? And if the substance is not changed, then why all the fuss and protest against the Mosaic form, which carries the same substance that existed *before* the Mosaic law as exists *after* the Mosaic law? Do you see why it is unnecessary to posit two (or more) different laws? It is indeed the same expedient that has been tried so often in the history of this theological formulation: The tendency has been to slice terms into separate meaning packages where the terms were merely functioning as synonyms for one another, e.g., the kingdom of God and the kingdom of heaven, the three or four different types of "gospels," the day of Christ and the day of the Lord, and the new covenant (for the church) and the new covenant (for Israel).

Some of the other essays have pointed to the eschatological function of the law of God; therefore there is no need to repeat that material here. But the point must not be missed: If the *tôrâ* that God will write on our hearts is in any way connected with his ancient law given to Moses, we will certainly be wide of the mark in urging the church to have nothing to do with that law! In fact, to break the least of those laws and *to teach others to do the same* will earn those interpreters the dubious honor of being "called the least in the kingdom of heaven" (Matt. 5:19). I do not say this on my own authority, nor on that of some other jaundiced position, but on the authority of the Lord of Glory himself!

The Law is Holy, Righteous, and Good in
Its Source and Substance

So captivated is this position with the fact that "the Mosaic Law is antithetical to the Gospel and has no part in it" that even when the text says the reverse, it must explain it away, as if it never claimed otherwise. Surely one must acknowledge that Paul clearly teaches that "the law is holy, and the commandment is holy, righteous and good" (Rom. 7:12). In fact, Paul adds, "We know that the law is spiritual" (v. 14). So how can this holy, righteous, good, and spiritual law be antithetical to the gospel and be given no part in it? Something that is so holy, good, and spiritual, much less righteous, would seem to be an aid to the gospel and our living the life of faith! Especially since Paul on at least two occasions flatly, squarely, and unequivocally contradicts this thesis of antithesis and abolishment of the law of God: "Do we, then, nullify the law by this faith? Not at all! Rather, we uphold the law" (3:31). Again: "Is the law, therefore, opposed to the promises of God? Absolutely not!" (Gal. 3:21a).

How can anyone possibly wiggle out of this direct teaching? The position advocated in the essay we are evaluating argued: " 'The law is holy . . . righteous and good' (v. 12), not in the sense that one must obey the law for sanctification, but in the sense that it originated from a holy, righteous, and good God . . . . Merely noting that the character of the law is in accord with its origin does not validate holiness as a legitimate function of the law." Surely it is a most curious and astounding form of argumentation to agree to the fact that the law is holy, in that "it reflects of the moral perfection of its Giver," but then to disagree that it can function in a way consistent with those perfections to reveal the holiness of God!! In fact, the law was not only given to Israel to instruct them in holiness (as Lev. 19:2 and numerous other verses taught), but it was to that same holiness that God called the church (1 Pet. 1:15–16). What could be plainer?

The One Law of God Exhibits Distinctions Within It

The argument that the law is such a unified whole that any fulfillment or completion of any portion of it thereby precludes all further use of it in the future cannot be consistently held without contradicting itself. First of all, the law, or better still, the Torah, includes all of the five books of Moses—Genesis to Deuteronomy. If no distinctions can be made within Torah, then Christians, when they jettison the law as having been fulfilled, must be ready also to jettison the promise given to Abraham, Isaac, and Jacob! It too is part of the "law." Obviously, few, if any, are willing to pay such a high price. If it is argued, as it surely will be, "But by the 'Law' I only meant the legal portions of Torah," then our advocate for a unified law has already made a distinction that is extra-biblical—and one that that type of advocate usually denies to others! Moreover, it is difficult to show that the biblically preferred term of *tôrâ* can be equated or even limited to the Sinaitic legislation—are we to delete the promises of Genesis 12–50 from the *tôrâ*? But even if the law were limited to the Sinaitic legislation, even there the promise made to the fathers Abraham, Isaac, and Jacob would shine through. Therefore the very principle that was supposed to segment out the legal materials from the promise will not allow us to do so unless we resort to our English, French, or German meanings for the word "law" instead of the Hebrew concept of *tôrâ*.

But there is more. Did not the earlier and latter prophets teach us that there were priorities and rankings even within the one law of God? Does not the word of 1 Samuel 15:22b urge: "To obey is better than sacrifice, and to heed is better than the fat of rams"? Did not David (Ps. 51:16–19), Isaiah (Isa. 1:11–20), Hosea (Hos. 6:6), Jeremiah (Jer. 7:21–24), Micah (Mic. 6:6–8), and many others distinguish between that which was spiritually prior and the performance of certain acts urged by that same law? If this law of God were all of one piece on a single level with no ranking or assigning of priorities, why do these prophets all insist on elevating the moral and spiritual aspects of *tôrâ* above the rest of *tôrâ*? That, in fact, is what Jesus taught when his listeners stumbled over finding no distinctions within the law. He advised them to go home and reflect on what Hosea 6:6 and Micah 6:8 were teaching (Matt. 9:13; 12:7; 23:23). What blind guides the religious leaders of that day were, Jesus complained, if they would strain at the minutiae of the law and yet neglect the "more important matters of the law" (Matt. 23:23). If our generation finds it difficult to make any such distinctions in the one law, our Lord and Master does not. All who claim to follow our Lord should take his example seriously.

The rejoinder to such straightforward teaching on the legitimacy of distinctions in the law is to say that Jesus was still in the dispensation of the law during the time he uttered those words. Otherwise, Jesus would also teach that we should tithe "mint, dill and cumin" (Matt. 23:23).

Not withstanding the validity of the times in which Jesus

made this statement, nothing will gainsay the fact that there *are* distinctions to be made in the law itself. For Jesus to have also taught that there were such distinctions in the law in the days when the Sinaitic covenant was still in force is to agree that they can be made now as well as then. That is what the argument is all about. And if these distinctions exist, and they do give pride of place to the internal, moral, ethical, spiritual, and holy, then why does my generation persist in saying that no such distinctions exist and none must be made in our day? We could be in deep trouble with our holy Lord for perverting his holy law.

The Righteousness of the Law Is Opposed to Pharisaic Legalism

Failure to understand that Paul contrasted faith righteousness with legalistic righteousness (a move the article we are reviewing claims is "unwarranted") will lead to all sorts of exegetical and theological problems. It almost seems as if Paul did not need to have faith in Christ (according to the argument of the chapter we are evaluating), since he pronounced himself "blameless" in Phil. 3:6 with regard to his observance of the law. Even when it is acknowledged that the accrued righteousness was "a righteousness of my own" (3:9), advocates of the position set forth by Strickland are unwilling to call this a misuse of the law. To their way of thinking, this was normative and expected until the dispensational change inaugurated by Christ's coming precipitated a change in attitude toward law righteousness.

But abuse it is! And an abuse gigantic enough to land Israel in the wilderness or in a Babylonian exile—and to land the church in who knows what sort of serious consequence nationally. Was not the same gospel preached to those carcasses that fell in the wilderness as it was to us (Heb. 3:17; 4:2)? What was the problem with the preaching that was offered to that wilderness crowd? Was it a failure to do the deeds of the law? No, it was a failure, first of all, to believe and to set any deeds of the law in the prior context of faith. How then can this position legitimately conclude (after protesting so vigorously that it never has taught that there are two ways of salvation in the Bible) that "establishing or attaining righteousness based on the law is futile because of the fact that Christ has [now?] revealed a righteousness based on faith in him" (pp. 45–46)? Paul's experience with the law was not just B.C.; it was B.F. (*Before Faith*). In no sense whatsoever can such a use of law ever be said in any time or place to be biblical in its description or practice. Given such an unbiblical distinction, is it any wonder that a veil is still over the eyes of many as they read the Old Testament, even to this very day? And can this not be the reason why so many of the contemporary scholars fail to understand the key contrasts Paul is making in Rom. 9:30—10:11, much less many of the other Pauline statements on the law?

Conclusion

The law did not originate with Moses; it came from the mouth of God (Ps. 119:13, 71). God's "laws endure to this day" (v. 91), are "eternal . . . in the heavens" (vv. 89, 160), and "are forever right" (v. 143). Moreover, God's "law is true" (vv. 142, 151), his "commands are righteous" (vv. 75, 172), and his "ancient laws . . . [give] comfort" (v. 52) and allow us to "walk about in freedom" (v. 45). Even though God's "commands are boundless" (v. 96), they "are the joy of my heart" (v. 111), and these "statutes are forever right" (v. 144). "Great peace have they who love your law, and nothing can make them stumble" (v. 165).

Response to Wayne G. Strickland

Douglas Moo

I read Wayne Strickland's dispensational analysis of the Law/Gospel issue with the feelings of one listening to a familiar symphony slightly off key. Everything sounds *just about* right. Thus I *generally* agree with almost all of Strickland's broad theological conclusions as well as with most of his specific exegetical and theological arguments. But I am uncomfortable with the tone of these conclusions, and I disagree with some of the exegetical decisions that contribute to this tone. Let me begin with areas of agreement.

First, with respect to some specifics. I appreciate Strickland's emphasis on the sanctifying purpose of the Mosaic law. As he points out, dispensationalism (sometimes unfairly) has been accused of teaching that the law was a means of salvation in the Old Testament. Clearly this is not the case. As "covenant" law, the Mosaic stipulations were given to people already in covenant relationship with the Lord. Clarification of the dispensational perspective on this point is helpful. I think Strickland is right in arguing that major dispensational theologians in the past did not truly teach this, and it is certainly important to note that contemporary dispensationalists have generally been quite careful to distance themselves from any such idea. (Nevertheless, as I will suggest below, there may be more of a connection between "law" and salvation than Strickland acknowledges.)

I also commend Strickland's refusal to dissolve the Law/Gospel contrast by turning it into a "legalism"/gospel contrast. As I have argued in my own paper, the case for understanding the word *nomos* to denote a legalistic misunderstanding of the Mosaic law is weak. We cannot by this means "tone down" key Pauline texts that stress the discontinuity between the law of Moses and the Christian (e.g., Rom. 6:14; 7:4–6; Gal. 3:15–25). Strickland gives full weight to these texts. He rightly argues that "under the law" denotes being under the law's jurisdiction, a situation that has changed for God's people with the coming of Christ. On target also, I think, is Strickland's suggestion that *nomos* sometimes moves from its specific meaning "Mosaic law" to the Mosaic era, or dispensation, of which it was the central feature. Thus, he reads the latter part of Galatians 3, rightly I think, as a description of the function of the law in the life of Israel. But this "regulative" function of the law is ended, as this passage makes clear, with the coming of Christ.

Strickland and I, in opposition to the other contributors to this volume, are skeptical about the traditional tripartite division of the law and its application to the question of continuity. We also agree in arguing that Jeremiah's new covenant prediction about the law being "written on the heart" need not mean that the Mosaic law *as such* is now the internal moral guide for the Christian. Welcome also is his insistence that Galatians 3:10 assumes that the law cannot be fulfilled; it is, then, for this reason that the curse comes on those who seek justification by doing the law.

I could mention many other specific points of agreement. The result of so many agreements on the details is a natural one: agreement on the general teaching of the Bible about the applicability of the Mosaic law to the Christian. Both Strickland and I argue that the Mosaic law is not a *direct* guide for the conduct of the Christian. As I have suggested, however, there are some points of disagreement between us. I will mention some specifics first, before concluding with a discussion of the major difference between us.

I concurred above with Strickland's conclusion that the Mosaic law was not given as a means of salvation to Israel. Nevertheless, I think that there is more suggestion of a relationship between the law and salvation than Strickland allows. First, I am not as sure as Strickland that "disobedience to the law did not remove [the Israelites] from the coveted covenant relationship, for that relationship depended on God's faithfulness." For instance, Leviticus 18:29 warns, "Everyone who does any of these detestable things—such persons must be cut off from their people." Deuteronomy 29:19–20 presents the same truth more starkly:

When such a person hears the words of this oath, he invokes a blessing on himself and therefore thinks, "I will be safe, even though I persist in going my own way." This will bring disaster on the watered land as well as the dry. The LORD will never be willing to forgive him; his wrath and zeal will burn against that man. All the curses written in this book will fall upon him, and the LORD will blot out his name from under heaven.

While God promises continuing faithfulness to the people of Israel even in the face of persistent sin (cf. Lev. 26:14–45), the individual Israelite could, it seems, be cut off from the covenant for flagrant disregard of the law of God. True, the Old Testament does not clearly promise eternal punishment for disobedience of the law. But what must be kept in mind is that the Old Testament, and especially the Mosaic law, rarely speaks in terms of "eternal" life and punishment. To some degree, the Mosaic covenant's promises and warnings in terms of this life become typologically significant of eternal matters.

Second, unlike Strickland, I think that texts such as Matthew 19:17; Romans 2:13b; and 7:10 imply that perfect obedience of the law would, in fact, procure one's salvation. While the Scriptures make clear that salvation by such doing is forever excluded by the fact of sin, they also suggest that obedience to the law is set forth as a *theoretical* means of salvation. What I am suggesting in both these points, then, is that we cannot neatly remove the Mosaic law from the salvific framework in the Old Testament. The law was not given to bring the nation of Israel, or any individual Israelite, into salvation; but failure to do it on the part of an individual could mean exclusion from salvation in the end.

The issue of the law's role in the life of Israel surfaces at another point where I disagree with Strickland. He seeks to unravel the admittedly tangled hermeneutical problem of the quotation of Deuteronomy 30:12–14 in Romans 10:6–8 by arguing that Deuteronomy 30:11–14 is a promise about the righteousness that God would bring to his people in the future. This is most unlikely. True, Deuteronomy 30:1–9 envisages a situation in the future when the people of Israel, after a time of disobedience, will return to the Lord and experience his blessing again. But verse 11 returns to the situation that Moses is immediately addressing: "Now what I am commanding you today. . . ." Strickland suggests that this phrase no more requires that verses 11–14 refer to Moses' time than does the comparable expression in verse 8: "You will again obey the LORD and follow all his commands I am giving you today." But in verse 8 the phrase "I am giving you today" simply modifies the "commands" only; the main verb in the verse has a future time orientation (perfect with *waw* conversive). There is no such verb in verse 11, requiring that the "you" addressed in the verse remain the same throughout: the people standing before Moses as he speaks ("what I am commanding *you* today is not too difficult for *you* or beyond *your* reach").

We cannot therefore solve the tension between Paul's quotation of Leviticus 18:5 in Romans 10:5 and Deuteronomy 30:12–14 in 10:6–8 by applying one to the old covenant and the other to the new. In their original contexts, each text applies to the Mosaic law, the one summarizing the promise of "life" held out to the Israelite within the law and the other taking away any excuse the Israelite might have to the effect that he or she had "never heard" that law. Paul extends the original sense of these passages as he uses them to summarize two contrasting approaches to righteousness. He applies the Deuteronomy text to the gospel, which offers a righteousness based on what God in Christ had already done for sinners. He uses Leviticus 18:5 as a convenient and perhaps customary summary of the focus of the Mosaic law: human doing. Divorced from the fulfillment of the promise in Christ, a continuing preoccupation with the law as the focus of God's work means that one is restricted to such human "works" as the only means of attaining righteousness. This, Paul is arguing, is just the mistake that many of his fellow Jews were making.

In contrast to Strickland, then, I think that Paul's contrast between "the righteousness that is by the law" and "the righteousness that is by faith" (Rom. 10:5–8; cf. also 9:30–32; 10:2–3) is a contrast between God's way of making people righteous and a Jewish misinterpretation that elevated the law into a means of salvation. Strickland appears to deny that Paul's reference to "law righteousness" has anything to do with a Jewish misuse of the law. And he is even clearer in his discussion of the parallel expression in Philippians 3:9: Paul's former "law righteousness" was a legitimate point of pride for him. What makes it wrong at the present is simply the "dispensational change." Christ has come to bring the law to its end, and any further pursuit of law righteousness is futile and wrong-headed. While he is not entirely clear, then, Strickland seems to suggest that the law righteousness that Paul speaks of in Romans 9:30–10:8 and Philippians 3:6–9 is not a means of salvation but simply a matter of conformity to the demands of the law—"theocratic righteousness." What is wrong with "law righteousness" is not that it involves a legalistic perversion of the law into a means of salvation but simply that it has now been outmoded by the advance in salvation history.

Strickland's emphasis on salvation history at this point is similar to that of E. P. Sanders, whom he cites favorably. Yet there are problems with this way of viewing the matter. First, the phrase "the righteousness that is by faith," with which "the righteousness that is by the law" is contrasted (cf. Rom. 10:5–6; 9:31–32), is clearly a salvific righteousness. And this, of course, is the issue that Paul is addressing at this point in Romans: why Gentiles are being saved while so many Jews are not (see 9:30; 10:1, 9–13). His explanation is that Jews have falsely pursued a relationship with God based on works (9:32) and the law (9:31). Failure to understand the shift in salvation history is certainly part of the problem (10:4). But this cannot be the entire problem, since, as Strickland himself insists, righteousness had always been by faith. This was not something new with the coming of Christ, as Abraham and David attest (Rom. 4:1–8). Criticism of the Jews for misusing the law as means of righteousness cannot therefore be removed from Paul's discussion of "law righteousness." I agree with Strickland—the word "law" itself does not indicate legalism. But, as he also indicates, the combination of the word "law" with other terms can denote a legalistic attitude in Paul; and here, I think, is a case in point.

My disagreements with Strickland on the points treated thus far are rather insignificant, in that they do not affect the final theological conclusion. More serious, in this sense, are some points I now want to raise. As I said earlier, I am in general agreement with Strickland's theological "bottom line": the law of Moses, being one "codification" of the law of God (one that was intended for the people of Israel under the Mosaic covenant), is no longer directly binding on the people of God who now live under a new covenant inaugurated by Christ. But Strickland goes on to imply that only indirect continuity between the law of Moses and the "law of Christ" exists, both reflecting ultimately God's eternal moral law. My quarrel with this conclusion is that it does not, perhaps, do justice to the points of continuity between the law of Moses and "the law of Christ" that are emphasized in the New Testament. Differences between Strickland and myself in the interpretation of three passages serve to point up this difference.

Strickland understands Matthew 5:17 as a statement primarily (perhaps exclusively) about Christ's fulfillment of Old Testament prophecies. I think that this skews not only the meaning of this passage but one's general theological synthesis. Strickland bases his interpretation mainly on the fact that Jesus here claims to fulfill "the Law and the Prophets," a phrase that in Matthew refers to the entire Old Testament. In fact, however, the phrase in Matthew plainly focuses not on the prophecies of the Old Testament but on the legal, or commanding, aspects of the Old Testament. In both the other texts where Matthew uses the phrase (contra Strickland, this exact *phrase* does not occur in 11:13), it is compared with Jesus' *teaching* or commands: Jesus' "golden rule" of Christian behavior sums up "the Law and the Prophets" (7:12); "all the Law and the Prophets hang on" the commands to love God and love the neighbor (22:40).

These references make sense only if the focus of the phrase "the Law and the Prophets" is on what the Old Testament commands people to do, as a comparison (or contrast) with what Jesus is commanding. The verse following Matthew 5:17 also favors this interpretation of the phrase. Strickland suggests that the general sense of "the Law and the Prophets" in verse 17 spills over into the meaning of word "law" in verse 18. But it is more likely that the reverse is the case, especially since verse 19, in continuity with verse 18, goes on to speak of "commandments." These references, along with the exclusive focus on Old Testament commandments in the following passage (5:21–48), show that "the Law and the Prophets" in verse 17 must have primary reference to the commandments of the Old Testament.

This difference in interpretation affects the tone of one's theological conclusions. Because Strickland denies, in effect, that this passage is referring to the Mosaic law, he does not integrate its notes of continuity into his final theological synthesis. When we do so, however, we cannot avoid concluding that Jesus sees his own teaching as organically connected in salvation history to the law of Moses. As the fulfillment of the law, his teaching stands in continuity with it, a continuity that may, in fact, involve the incorporation of Mosaic commands into his own "law" (cf. v. 19).

A similar difference surfaces in the interpretation of Romans 10:4. Strickland and I are in general agreement on the meaning of the controversial word *telos*: it includes reference to both "cessation" and "goal." Strickland focuses on the former idea, suggesting that the primary meaning is that Christ has ended Israel's futile quest for law righteousness. Yet this conclusion does not fit very well with Strickland's own interpretation of "law righteousness" (see above), nor does he justify the move from Paul's reference to Christ as the end of the *law* to Christ as the end to *law righteousness*. Moreover, I question whether it is fair to stress "cessation" as the meaning of the term *telos*. I would argue that Paul has purposely chosen a term with a "teleological" focus, wanting to draw our attention to the continuity between the law and Christ. To be sure, this continuity involves a certain cessation in the law's reign, just as reaching the finish line in a race means an "end" to the race. But "cessation," while therefore implied, is not the main point. And once again, I would suggest, Strickland's exegetical decision at this point contributes to an undervaluing of the elements of continuity between the law and Christ.

I mention one final exegetical point at which Strickland's focus on discontinuity is perhaps too pronounced. He suggests that James's references to the law in 1:25; 2:8; and 2:12 are to "the law of Christ." Now, as I argue in my essay, I think this is basically correct: James's linking of the "perfect law that gives freedom" to the life-giving word (compare 1:25 with 1:18, 22) and his reference to the "royal" law (2:8) point toward a distinctly "new covenant" concept of law. But it is impossible, considering the date of James (probably before 50), his background, and his audience, to eliminate reference to the Mosaic law entirely. Here again, I would argue, we see Mosaic commandments taken up into and made part of the "law of Christ."

I therefore disagree with the balance in Strickland's theological perspective. While I heartily endorse his stress on the basic discontinuity between the law of Moses and the New Testament Christian, I miss what I think are some necessary perspectives on the continuity between the two. Yes, Christ "ends" the reign of the law, imposing his own law "in place of" the law of Moses. But in doing so, the New Testament stresses, he both brings that law to its intended conclusion and goal and also takes up within his own teaching and reapplies to his followers portions of that law. Strickland's focus on discontinuity at this point is, of course, a product of his overall dispensational perspective, as becomes clear when, for instance, he says that "the Mosaic law naturally ended when God suspended his program with Israel (Rom. 9–11) and inaugurated his program with the church." It is just at this point that I disagree. I think that God pursues one program throughout salvation history. The church is today the recipient not only of the blessings, but of the true fulfillment of both the Abrahamic covenant and of the Mosaic covenant. Consequently, while the law of Moses may no longer be a *direct and immediate* authority for the Christian, its teaching remains indirectly applicable to us through the "fulfillment" of that law in Christ and his law.

Chapter Five

A MODIFIED
LUTHERAN VIEW

Douglas J. Moo

THE LAW OF CHRIST AS
THE FULFILLMENT OF
THE LAW OF MOSES:
A MODIFIED LUTHERAN VIEW

Douglas J. Moo

Christians disagree about the place of the Mosaic law in the life of the believer because the New Testament itself contains statements that appear to support opposite conclusions. Our Lord's endorsement of the eternal validity of even the "smallest letter" and "least stroke of a pen" in the law is followed by a warning that breaking even "one of the least of these commandments" will mean demotion in the kingdom of heaven (Matt. 5:18–19). Similar apparently unequivocal assertions of the law's continuing validity are found throughout the New Testament: e.g., "we uphold the law" (Rom. 3:31); "the law is holy, and the commandment is holy, righteous and good" (Rom. 7:12); "the man who looks intently into the perfect law that gives freedom, and continues to do this, not forgetting what he has heard, but doing it—he will be blessed in what he does" (James 1:25). At the other extreme, however, are apparently equally clear assertions of the law's complete cessation for the believer: "Christ is the end of the law" (Rom. 10:4a); "you are not under law" (Rom. 6:14; cf. v. 15); "when there is a change of the priesthood, there must also be a change of the law" (Heb. 7:12).

Such diverse statements about the Mosaic law have both fascinated and frustrated theologians since the inception of the church. And at no time has this been more the case than in the last two decades, which have witnessed a remarkable resurgence of interest in the theology of the Mosaic law.[1] A deluge of books and articles has examined virtually every bit of evidence and from almost every conceivable perspective. Yet nothing even approaching a consensus has emerged. Several factors account for the radically different conclusions reached by biblical scholars and theologians, the most important of which is the diverse theological and hermeneutical frameworks that are used to order and arrange the various texts. Theological and confessional allegiances—Lutheran, Reformed, dispensational, etc.—thus dictate which texts are given precedence and used to interpret others.

I am not criticizing the use of such general theological frameworks, for responsible biblical theology cannot be carried out without some structure to organize the exegetical evidence. The question becomes, then, which structure most accurately captures the pattern of biblical revelation? Or, to limit the issue to the task at hand: Can we find a framework that is capable of organizing into a coherent picture the various texts about the Mosaic law *without* imposing forced and unnatural meanings on those texts? Each of the contributors to this volume will argue that his approach is best able to accomplish this task of integration. In this essay, I will try to show that the exegetical evidence points to what I am calling a modified form of the traditional Lutheran perspective. Luther himself saw Law and Gospel as discontinuous and

---

[1]Stimulating this resurgence has been the new understanding of Judaism advocated by E. P. Sanders (see especially his *Paul and Palestinian Judaism* [Philadelphia: Fortress, 1977]) and adopted by a large number of scholars. Some of the most significant books are: Robert Banks, *Jesus and the Law in the Synoptic Tradition* (Cambridge: Cambridge University Press, 1975); Klaus Berger, *Die Gesetzesauslegung Jesu: Ihr historischer Hintergrund im Judentum und im alten Testament* (Neukirchen/Vluyn: Neukirchener, 1972); Ragnar Bring, *Christus und das Gesetz* (Leiden: Brill, 1969); A. van Dülmen, *Die Theologie des Gesetzes bei Paulus* (Stuttgart: Katholisches, 1968); Daniel Fuller, *Gospel & Law: Contrast or Continuum?* (Grand Rapids: Eerdmans, 1980); Hans Hübner, *Law in Paul's Thought* (Edinburgh: T. & T. Clark, 1984); Brice L. Martin, *Christ and the Law in Paul's Thought* (Leiden: Brill, 1989); Heikki Räisänen, *Paul and the Law* (Tübingen: Mohr, 1983); E. P. Sanders, *Paul, the Law and the Jewish People* (Philadelphia: Fortress, 1983); Frank Thielmann, *From Plight to Solution: A Jewish Framework for Understanding Paul's View of the Law in Galatians and Romans* (Leiden: Brill, 1989); Peter J. Tomson, *Paul and the Jewish Law* (Philadelphia: Fortress, 1991); Stephen Westerholm, *Israel's Law and the Church's Faith: Paul and His Recent Interpreters* (Grand Rapids: Eerdmans, 1988); S. Westerholm, *Jesus and Scribal Authority* (Lund: Gleerup, 1978); S. G. Wilson, *Luke and the Law* (Cambridge: Cambridge University Press, 1983). For a survey of the literature on Paul and the law from 1977–86, see my "Paul and the Law in the Last Ten Years," *SJT* 40 (1987), 287–307.

made the distinction between these two basic to his theology. This distinction has continued to be central to Lutheran theology, and I think that it is both biblical and important. But I also think that the traditional approach needs to be modified by greater attention to the salvation-historical perspective of the Scriptures.

Theologians have used the phrase "salvation history" and its equivalent, "redemptive history," to denote a considerable number of concepts.[2] I am using the phrase in a rather untechnical manner to denote a conceptual framework that is basic to the biblical revelation, a framework with two decisive characteristics. The first characteristic is *historical periodization*. By this I mean that the biblical writers understand salvation as the culmination of a historical process that features several distinct periods of time. At the "center" of history, and forming the decisive turning point, is Christ's death and resurrection. All that came before funnels into this decisive moment, and all that will come after flows from it. Basic, then, to biblical revelation is the contrast between "before" and "after" Christ, a contrast between two "ages" or "eras." Salvation history finds a discontinuity between the time before and the time after Christ at the core of the Scriptures. This is not, of course, to deny the continuity of salvation history—a continuity rooted in one God, carrying out one plan, in one people. But it is to insist that this one continous and eternal plan unfolds in successive and distinct stages.

I will argue that the New Testament writers view the Mosaic law within this salvation-historical framework and relegate it basically to the period of time before the coming of Christ. And it is necessary to stress at this point that the New Testament teaching about the law is first, and most basically, teaching about the *Mosaic* law. This is in contrast to the situation in some theological systems—and this is particularly true of Lutheran theology and a point at which it requires modification—where "law" denotes a general theological category, namely, God's word in its commanding aspect.[3] In this sense, the Sermon on the

---

[2]Works that come closest to my use of the salvation-historical concept are Oscar Cullmann, *Christ and Time* (Philadelphia: Westminster, 1950), and *Salvation in History* (New York: Harper & Row, 1967); Leonhard Goppelt, *Theology of the New Testament*, 2 vols. (Grand Rapids: Eerdmans, 1981, 1982), especially 1:251–81 and 2:37–63; Herman Ridderbos, *Paul: An Outline of His Theology* (Grand Rapids: Eerdmans, 1974), especially 44–86.

[3]Law, says Luther at one point, is "what we are to do and give to God," while Gospel is "what has been given us by God" ("How Christians Should Regard the Law of Moses," *Luther's Works*, vol. 35 [Philadelphia: Fortress, 1960], 162).

Mount is "law" just as much as the Ten Commandments. But the New Testament use of the word "law" (*nomos*) is decisively conditioned by the Old Testament background and the Jewish milieu in which it was written. The word therefore almost always denotes not "law" in general, but the Mosaic law, the *Torah* (*tôrâ*).[4] As a result, the New Testament Law-"Gospel"[5] tension is not, as in Luther, primarily static and theological, but historical. "Law" (*tôrâ*) came into history at a specific point in time (430 years after the promise, according to Gal. 3:17). In the New Testament, therefore, Law and "Gospel" primarily denote, not two constant aspects of God's word to us, but two successive eras in salvation history.[6]

A second element in the salvation-historical approach is a recognition of the frequent *corporate focus* of the biblical writers. This is a natural corollary of the first characteristic. Since the dividing point in the salvation history conception is the death and resurrection of Christ, the contrast between "before" and "after" has to do not with the experience of the individual but with the experience of the world or of God's people. This is not to deny, of course, that the transition from the "old era" to the new effected by Christ in history has its completion and partial parallel in the life of the believer and that the biblical writers often describe this transition in the life of the individual. But it is to place more importance than many theological and hermeneutical approaches have on the significance and frequency of the corporate perspective.

This perspective, as we will see, is central to some of the key New Testament passages on the Mosaic law. I will seek to show in what follows that the salvation-historical approach is able successfully to explain and integrate the various New Testament data about the Mosaic law and the Christian. Specifically, I will argue that the Mosaic law is *basically* confined to the old era that has

---

[4]For a survey of the Pauline use of *nomos*, see my " 'Law,' 'Works of the Law,' and Legalism in Paul," *WTJ* 43 (1983), 73–100.

[5]Quotation marks must be put around the word "Gospel" because the New Testament never, in fact, directly contrasts the word Law with the word Gospel. But the concept denoted by the word Gospel is certainly contrasted with the Law at many points.

[6]On this point, see Otto Weber, *Foundations of Dogmatics*, 2 vols. (Grand Rapids: Eerdmans, 1981, 1983), especially 2.363–64; Gerhard Ebeling, "On the Doctrine of the *Triplex Usus Legis* in the Theology of the Reformers," in *Word and Faith* (Philadelphia: Fortress, 1963), 260–61.

come to its fulfillment in Christ. It is no longer, therefore, *directly* applicable to believers who live in the new era. To establish these points, I will proceed in two stages. First, I will look at the evidence from the Scriptures about the purpose of the law. This step is necessary both to secure a general perspective from which to look more specifically at the question of the applicability of the law to Christians and to see if this evidence implies anything about the law's permanence. Second, I will investigate the teaching about the law in the new age of salvation.

Most of my evidence will come from the teaching of Jesus in Matthew and, especially, from the letters of Paul. We will not ignore other New Testament authors, but they have far less to say on the issues concerning us than do Matthew and Paul. Whatever the exact situation is that Matthew addresses—and Matthean scholars continue to debate the point—it is clear that he is concerned that his Christian audience understand the relationship between the church and Israel and, by extension, between the teaching of Jesus and the Mosaic law. But important as the teaching of Jesus is for the issue of the Christian and the law, it is overshadowed by the evidence from Paul's letters. This is partially because we cannot always be sure whether Jesus was addressing the situation that would prevail after his redemptive acts had opened the new era of salvation or the situation during his earthly ministry when the old covenant was still in effect. Furthermore, Paul's evidence is decisive simply because the issue of the Mosaic law and the Christian was one that Paul had much greater need to address. As the "apostle to the Gentiles," he was used by God to open the doors of the Christian church to Gentiles who had never had any relationship with the Mosaic law. Questions about what relationship, if any, these Gentile converts should have to the Mosaic law were bound to arise. Paul deals with these questions at length in both Galatians and Romans. The former is more polemical in orientation, as Paul must counter a false, "Judaizing," teaching that had quickly arisen in the churches of South Galatia.[7] Romans, on the other hand, was a treatise-style letter

---

[7] I think that Galatians was written just before the Apostolic Council (Acts 15) to the churches founded by Paul on the first missionary journey (the "South Galatian" hypothesis). In defense of this supposition, see F. F. Bruce, *Paul: Apostle of the Heart Set Free* (Grand Rapids: Eerdmans, 1977), 178–83.

sent to a church that Paul had neither founded nor visited and takes a more evenly balanced approach to the issue of the law.[8]

Regarding the witness of the Old Testament, it is necessary to recognize two things: (1) it has relatively little to say directly about the issues of this article; (2) what it does say must always be interpreted in terms of the New Testament witness before it can be integrated theologically. This is simply to recognize—as all Christians do, to one degree or another—that the Old Testament is not the final word on these matters. I will not ignore what it says or argue that the New Testament contradicts or cancels out what it says. But we must take seriously the fact of salvation history and the progressive nature of God's revelation, in which the New illuminates the Old and has the final word on the ultimate structure and meaning of God's word to us.

THE PURPOSE OF THE MOSAIC LAW

In this section, I want to show first, negatively, that the Mosaic law, while implicitly holding out the promise of salvation to those who would do it, was never intended to be, and could never in fact be, a means of salvation. Second, positively, I will argue that God gave the law (1) to reveal his character to the people of Israel and demand that the people conform to it, (2) to supervise Israel in the time before Christ, and (3) to imprison Israel and, by extension, all people under sin.

The Law Does Not Procure Salvation

The law holds out the promise of salvation, but because of human sinfulness, it cannot confer salvation.

The Law's Promise of Life

Old Testament scholars generally agree that God did not give Israel the law so that the people could attain eternal life by it. He gave it to a people whom he had already made his own by his sovereign and gracious act of calling them out of Egypt. Nevertheless, the New Testament teaches that the law of Moses does hold out an inherent promise of life for those who do it. Jesus responded to the rich young man who asked him how he could

---

[8]On the differences between Galatians and Romans on the law, see especially John Drane, *Paul: Libertine or Legalistic?* (London: SPCK, 1975); Ulrich Wilckens, "Zur Entwicklung des paulinischen Gesetzesverständnis," *NTS* 28 (1982): 154–90.

get eternal life, "If you want to enter life, obey the command-ments" (Matt. 19:17; cf. Mark 10:17–18; Luke 18:18–19). This is, of course, not representative of Jesus' teaching on how one may attain eternal life; in this case Jesus wanted to awaken this rather arrogant young man to his need of what Jesus offered in the gospel. But there is no reason on this account to think that Jesus does not view the promise as at least theoretically valid. Paul likewise claims that "it is those who obey the law who will be declared righteous" (Rom. 2:13b) and that the "commandment [representing the Mosaic law] was intended to bring life" (*eis zōēn*; Rom. 7:10).

Romans 10:5 and Galatians 3:12, often quoted as further witnesses to the salvific promise of the law, are not as clear. Both quote Leviticus 18:5: "Keep my decrees and laws, for the man who obeys them will live by them." This verse may mean no more than that the pious Israelite should "live out life" in the sphere of the law.[9] But the use of the language of "life" elsewhere in the Pentateuch to denote the reward God gives for obedience to the law (e.g., Deut. 30:15, 19) makes it more likely that "will live" in Lev. 18:5 is a promise of reward for obedience.[10] Later in Leviticus 18, for instance, disobedience of the law is said to bring expulsion from the land for the nation (v. 28) and from the people of God for the individual (v. 29). This "life," as defined elsewhere in the Pentateuch, involves material prosperity, deliverance from ene-mies, peace in the land that God will give his people, and "long life" (e.g., Lev. 26:3–13; Deut. 28:1–14). Since, however, Israel has already, in a sense, entered into the sphere of these blessings by virtue of God's gracious election, the promise of life must be seen as the promise for the continuation of life. Israel's "life" in this sense is dependent on its faithful observance of the law. This is a constant refrain in Deuteronomy (see, e.g., 4:1–2, 40; 5:33; 6:1–3; 7:12–16; 8:1) and is reiterated in the prophets as well (e.g., Ezek. 33:15: "the decrees that give life"). By contrast, failure to reverence God by obeying his commandments will bring destruc-tion and "death" to Israel.

Leviticus 18:5 is not, then, a promise that the doer of the law

---

[9]See Walter C. Kaiser, Jr., "Leviticus and Paul: 'Do This and You Shall Live' (Eternally?)," *JETS* 14 (1971), 19–28.

[10]See, R. K. Harrison, *Leviticus* (Grand Rapids: Eerdmans, 1980), 185; Gordon Wenham, *A Commentary on Leviticus*, NICOT (Grand Rapids: Eerdmans, 1979), 253; C. F. Keil and F. Delitzsch, *Biblical Commentary on the Old Testament*, vol. 2 (reprint, Grand Rapids: Eerdmans, n.d.), 412.

will attain eternal life. On the other hand, one can make a good case for thinking that Paul, like later Jewish writers (cf. the Onkelos and Pseudo-Jon. Targums) understood Leviticus 18:5 to be promising eternal life for the doer.[11] For in both Romans 10 and Galatians 3, Paul sets Leviticus 18:5 in contrast to statements that righteousness and eternal life come only through faith (cf. Gal. 3:11 and Rom. 10:6–8).[12] Paul's point would then be that life comes only through faith and not through doing the law, as Leviticus 18:5 promised. Paul's application of this verse may, however, be more nuanced and more in keeping with the original sense of the verse. The words Paul quotes from Leviticus 18:5 seem to have become almost a "slogan" to express the conditional character of the Mosaic covenant (see, e.g., Neh. 9:29; Ezek. 20:13, 21; CD 3:14–16; b. Sanh. 59b). Following this tradition, Paul may cite the verse as a succinct summary of the essence of the Mosaic covenant: that blessing is contingent on obedience.[13] On this

---

[11]This is the interpretation that becomes virtually standard in the Reformed and Lutheran traditions. On Rom. 10:5, see Calvin, *Commentary on the Epistle of Paul the Apostle to the Romans* (1540; reprint, Grand Rapids: Eerdmans, 1947); Charles Hodge, *Commentary on the Epistle to the Romans* (1866; reprint, Grand Rapids: Eerdmans, 1950); Robert Haldane, *Exposition of the Epistle to the Romans* (1839; reprint, London: Banner of Truth, 1958). See also Wilckens, "Gesetzesverständnis," 165–72; Westerholm, *Israel's Law*, 134–35; Robert H. Gundry, "Grace, Works and Staying Saved in Paul," *Bib* 66 (1985), 24–25; Hübner, *Law in Paul's Thought*, 19–20 (on Gal. 3:12); Ridderbos, *Paul*, 134. The "christological" interpretation of Rom. 10:5, which takes "the doer" to be Jesus, is most unlikely (contra Karl Barth, *The Epistle to the Romans* [London: Oxford, 1933], 376–77; C. E. B. Cranfield, *A Critical and Exegetical Commentary on the Epistle to the Romans*, 2 vols. [Edinburgh: T. & T. Clark, 1975, 1979], 2.521–22; Andrew Bandstra, *The Law and the Elements of the World* [Kampen: Kok, 1964], 103–5).

[12]A few scholars have argued that Rom. 10:5 ("the righteousness that is by the law") is in continuity with 10:6–8 ("the righteousness that is by faith"): see Cranfield, *Romans*, 2:521–22; Felix Flückiger, "Christus, des Gesetzes *telos*," *TZ* 11 (1955), 153–57; Fuller, *Gospel & Law*, 66–88; Ragnar Bring, "Das Gesetz und die Gerechtigkeit Gottes: Eine Studie zur Frage nach der Auslegung des Ausdruckes *telos nomou* in Röm. 10:4," *SJT* 20 (1966), 19–23. But this interpretation fails to take seriously Paul's manifest contrast between these two kinds of righteousness in Phil. 3:6–9 and misunderstands the context. See almost all the commentaries on Romans.

[13]On the conditional character of the Mosaic covenant, see R. E. Clements, *Old Testament Theology: A New Approach* (Atlanta: Knox, 1978), 101–3; 116–19; David Noel Freedman, "Divine Commitment and Human Obligation: The Covenant Theme," *Int* 18 (1964), 419–31. Many think that a greater emphasis on the conditionality of the covenant, with a consequent absolutizing of the law, took place in the later stages of the Old Testament and in early Judaism (see Ernst Würthwein, "Der Sinn des Gesetzes im Alten Testament," *ZTK* 55 [1958], 255–70).

reading, Paul is warning Jews and Judaizing Christians who are insisting on adherence to the law as essential to justification that they must live with the consequences and find their relationship with God through that means that the law itself recognizes: doing the commandments.[14] Paul may not be claiming, then, that Leviticus 18:5 promises eternal life to the doer. But he is insisting that whatever "life" one tries to find through the law can be found only by doing—a doing that, because of human sin, can never achieve that goal of life.

The reader may think that I have just affirmed contradictory points: that God did not give the law to save his people, and that the law promises salvation if it is kept. But these two statements are not incompatible. By the latter, I mean simply that the law, in stating God's demand of his people Israel, promises them also that successfully meeting that demand would bring them salvation. But this is not to say that the law could ever in fact be obeyed so fully by sinful human beings that it *would* save anyone; and God, knowing this, never intended the law to save anyone. It would be as if I were to give a basketball to my son for the first time in his life and tell him: "Here: if you make 100 free throws in a row, you will not have to practice and train to become a basketball player." So God, in the law he gave to Israel, implied that perfect obedience would bring eternal blessing and salvation; but he never gave the law with that purpose, knowing the impossibility of fulfilling it. To use the terminology of covenant theology, the law expresses a "hypothetical covenant of works."[15] In the law God says in effect: "Here is who I am, and here is what you must be if you want to stand before me." In seeing the impossibility of ever achieving by works the holiness that God demands, the pious Israelite would, as God intended, flee in faith to the mercy of God, wherein can be found the only means of righteousness actually available to sinful humanity.

But there is no good reason to think that the basic conception of the covenant changes within the Old Testament.

[14]For this general approach, see Thomas Edward McComiskey, *The Covenants of Promise: A Theology of the Old Testament Covenants* (Grand Rapids: Baker, 1982), 121–27; Andreas Lindemann, "Die Gerechtigkeit aus dem Gesetz. Erwägungen zur Auglegung und zur Testgeschichte von Römer 10.5," *ZNW* 73 (1982), 244–46; Hans-Joachim Eckstein, " 'Nahe ist dir das Wort.' Exegetische Erwägungen zu Röm 10.8," *ZNW* 79 (1988), 204–6.

[15]On this point and in agreement with our conclusions, see Roger T. Beckwith, "The Unity and Diversity of God's Covenants," *TynBul* 38 (1987), 112–13; cf. also Westerholm, *Israel's Law*, 144–50.

The Law Cannot Confer Salvation

The implicit promise of the law to save those who obey it can never be fulfilled. While by no means an innovation, this principle was a staple of Reformation teaching and has been a consistent characteristic of orthodox Protestant theology. Among the Reformers it was Luther who pursued this principle most vigorously, elevating into a hermeneutical principle the opposition of Law and Gospel. He insisted that the Law, whether Mosaic or otherwise, can only tell us what God expects of us and, because of our inability to do what he demands, drive us sinners to despair and to the sweet relief of the Gospel.[16] The Law, because its nature is to demand works, can never be the agent of liberation in any way. This strict contrast between Law and Gospel, with its corollary opposition of works and faith, was not maintained by all the Reformers (Zwingli, for instance, softened the opposition considerably[17]) and has been challenged in a variety of ways by contemporary scholars. Nevertheless, Luther on this point was right: the Mosaic law can never become an agent of liberation from sin, for its nature is to demand works that can never be done sufficiently by sinful humans so as to gain approval before God.

The inability of the law to save is plainly taught in the New Testament. Luke records Paul telling the synagogue audience in Pisidian Antioch that through Christ, "everyone who believes is justified from everything you could not be justified from by the law of Moses" (Acts 13:39). The author to the Hebrews shows that the law, only a "shadow of the good things that are coming," could never secure ultimate forgiveness or holiness (Heb. 10:1–14). Paul claims in Galatians that "if righteousness could be gained through the law, Christ died for nothing" (Gal. 2:21b), and that "if a law had been given that could impart life, then righteousness would certainly have come by the law" (3:21b). Further substantiation of this inability of the law to save comes in Paul's assertion that "works of the law" (ta erga tou nomou) cannot justify, confer the Spirit, or work miracles (2:16; 3:2, 5, 10; cf. Rom. 3:20, 28).

To be sure, opposition to this interpretation came already in the early church, with Origen and others suggesting that "works

---

[16]"The Law shows up sin and makes man guilty and sick; indeed proves him worthy of being damned. . . . The Gospel offers grace and remits sin and cures the sickness unto salvation" ("Scholium" on Rom. 10:15, in *Lectures on Romans, Luther's Works*, vol. 25 [Saint Louis: Concordia, 1972]).

[17]See W. P. Stephens, *The Theology of Huldrych Zwingli* (Oxford, Clarendon, 1986), 164–69.

of the law" denoted only ceremonial observances.[18] Recent interpreters suggest that the phrase may indicate works done in a legalistic spirit[19] or "Jewish identity markers," namely, Sabbath, circumcision, and food laws.[20] The acceptance of such restrictive meanings to the phrase would mean that the texts just mentioned would not be denying that justification comes through works done in obedience to the law, but only through certain kinds of works or through works done in the wrong spirit. While most of those advocating this interpretation would not go so far, it does open the door to making the law, if done in the right way or in the right spirit, a means of salvation.

However, this revisionist interpretation of "works of the law" is not acceptable. The equivalent Hebrew phrase is rare but refers generally to *anything* done in obedience to the law.[21] Because of the Jewish milieu in which Paul was writing, "works of the law" is his way of referring to those things done by human beings in obedience to the law of Moses. These particular works represent what we might call "good works" generally; see, in this regard, the obvious connections between "the works of the law" in Romans 3:20, 28 and Abraham's "works" in 4:2–5, as well as the "works" of Jacob and Esau in 9:11–12. "Works of the law," then, is a subset of the more general category "works." The Reformers and their heirs were quite right to use these verses to deny that human beings could be justified before God by anything that they might do.[22]

As we noted above, Luther's insistence on a rigid distinction between the Law and the Gospel was rooted in a fixed association

---

[18]See Maurice Wiles, *The Divine Apostle: The Interpretation of St. Paul's Epistles in the Early Church* (Cambridge: Cambridge University Press, 1967), 67–69; Karl Hermann Schelkle, *Paulus, Lehrer der Väter. Die altkirkliche Auslegung von Römer 1–11* (Düsseldorf: Patmos, 1956), on Rom. 3:20.

[19]Fuller, *Gospel & Law*, 90–98.

[20]See especially James D. G. Dunn, "The New Perspective on Paul," *BJRL* 65 (1983), 107–11; "Works of the Law and the Curse of the Law (Galatians 3:10–14)," *NTS* 31 (1985), 528–29; *Romans 1–8*, WBC (Waco, Tex.: Word, 1989), 158–60.

[21]See 4QFlor 1:7; 1QS 5:21, 6:18. The phrase also apparently occurs in a letter found at Qumran (according to Tomson, *Paul and the Jewish Law*, 66). See also the phrase "works of the commandments" (2 *Baruch* 57:2) and the rabbinic use of the words "works" (*ma'aśîm*) and "commandments" (*miṣwôt*).

[22]For further substantiation of this interpretation of the evidence, see Moo, " 'Law,' 'Works of the Law' and Legalism in Paul," 73–100; Moo, *Romans 1–8*, WEC (Chicago: Moody, 1991), 208–211, 212–18; Westerholm, *Israel's Law*, 116–21.

of the Law with doing and the Gospel with believing. The logic could be stated in this way:

1. Salvation comes only by believing.
2. The law is associated with doing and not with believing.
3. Therefore, the law cannot bring salvation.

Some contemporary scholars, however, would deny this conclusion—not because they want to argue that salvation can come by works (i.e., denying point 1), but because they think that the law can be associated with believing (i.e., denying point 2). There is no doubt that the word *nomos* can mean something other than the Mosaic law. It sometimes has a "canonical" sense, that which is central in the Jewish estimation of Scripture, standing for the Pentateuch (1 Cor. 9:8, 9; 14:21, 34; Gal. 4:21b) or for the whole Old Testament (John 10:34; 12:34; 15:25; Rom. 3:19a); note, also, the combinations "Law and Prophets" (Matt. 5:17; 7:12; 11:13; Luke 16:16; John 1:45; Acts 13:15; 24:14; Rom. 3:21b) and "Law of Moses, the Prophets and the Psalms" (Luke 24:44). It would indeed be appropriate to speak of believing the "law" whenever the word has this sense (although, in fact, this connection is never made in the Scriptures). Calvin, in this regard, argues that the law can have both a narrow sense—the commands in and of themselves—and a broader sense—the commands as part of the encompassing framework of the covenant of grace (*Inst.* 2.7.2). But what we have here are two different meanings of the word "law"; it reflects no softening of the crucial distinction between faith and works or between Law (in the sense of "the commandments") and the Gospel.

When the New Testament uses *nomos* to depict the body of commandments given to Israel through Moses, the word is never connected with faith or said to have salvific power. Those who dispute this assertion point especially to three expressions in Paul: "law . . . of faith" (Rom. 3:27), "law of the Spirit" (8:2), and "law of righteousness" (9:31).[23] In the first two instances, however, it is unlikely that Paul is referring to the Mosaic law at all, for both contexts feature a contrast between two "laws." In 3:27, Paul

---

[23]See especially Klyne Snodgrass, "Spheres of Influence: A Possible Solution to the Problem of Paul and the Law," *JSNT* 32 (1988), 93–113; Eduard Lohse, *Theological Ethics of the New Testament* (Minneapolis: Augsburg/Fortress, 1991), 157–65; Cranfield, *Romans*, 1.219–20; Dunn, *Romans 1–8*, 185–87, 416–17; and *Romans 9–16*, WBC (Waco, Tex.: Word, 1988), 581–83; Gerhard Friedrich, "Das Gesetz des Glaubens. Römer 3,27," in *Auf das Wort kommt es an. Gesammelte Aufsätze*, ed. J. H. Friedrich (Göttingen: Vandenhoeck & Ruprecht, 1978), 107–22.

argues that it is the law of faith, not the law of works, that excludes all boasting before God. That the law of works is the Mosaic law is clear from the context (see "observing the law" in 3:28; lit. "works of the law"). It is then argued that the law "of faith" is also the Mosaic law, viewed not from the standpoint of the works it demands, but from the standpoint of the faith that it also demands or bears witness to. But the emphasis on faith *apart from the law* in both 3:21–22 and 3:28 makes this interpretation unlikely. Rather, Paul is utilizing a more general meaning of the word *nomos* ("principle"; cf. NIV) to create a rhetorical contrast between the law of Moses that demands works and the "law" (or principle) of the new covenant (inherent already, of course, in the old; cf. Rom. 4). This "law" Paul identifies in 3:28: "We maintain that a man is justified by faith apart from observing the law."[24]

A similar more general use of *nomos* is almost surely to be found in Romans 8:2; it would render Paul's argument almost senseless were he affirming the ability of the law of Moses to deliver from the power of sin (v. 2), for he goes on immediately (v. 3) to deny to the law precisely this power. Probably neither occurrence of *nomos* in Rom. 8:2 refers to the Mosaic law but to two opposing "principles" or "powers," as if Paul were saying: "the power of the life-giving Spirit in Christ Jesus has set you free from the power of sin and death" (cf. "law of sin" in 7:23).[25]

In Romans 9:31, on the other hand, "law of righteousness" almost certainly refers to the Mosaic law, the genitive *dikaiosynēs* indicating the object of the law: "the law that demands righteousness."[26] Yet Paul faults the Jews for pursuing this law through works (*hōs ex ergōn*) rather than through faith (v. 32a). Some argue

---

[24]For this interpretation of 3:27, see especially Heikki Räisänen, "Das 'Gesetz des Glaubens' (Röm. 3,27) und das 'Gesetz des Geistes' (Röm. 8,2)," NTS 26 (1979–80), 101–17. See also Moo, *Romans 1–8*, 251–53. For substantiation of this meaning of *nomos*, see Räisänen, "Sprachliches zum Spiel des Paulus mit NOMOS," in *The Torah and Christ* (Helsinki: Kirjapaino Raamattutalu, 1986), 119–47.

[25]See, again, Räisänen, "Das 'Gesetz des Glaubens' "; and Moo, *Romans 1–8*, 504–8; see also Leander E. Keck, "The Law and 'The Law of Sin and Death' (Rom. 8:1–4). Reflections on The Spirit and Ethics in Paul," in *The Divine Helmsman: Studies on God's Control of Human Events, Presented to Lev. H. Silberman*, ed. James L. Crenshaw and Samuel Sandmel (New York: KTAV, 1980), 41–57.

[26]Against this interpretation see Calvin, who views the phrase as a *hypallage* and translates it "righteousness of the law" (*Romans*, 378), and William Sanday and Arthur C. Headlam, who think that *nomos* here means "rule" (*A Critical and Exegetical Commentary on the Epistle to the Romans* [Edinburgh: T. & T. Clark, 1902], 279).

that here Paul saw the law broadly as something to be believed and not just done.[27] Again, however, the context makes this interpretation unlikely. Paul's careful contrast between Gentiles and Jews in vv. 30–31 makes it necessary to attribute to both the same goal of pursuit: righteousness. Moreover, v. 31 finds clear parallels in 10:3, 5, where the issue again is righteousness. We must, then, place the emphasis in 9:31 on righteousness: it was "the law in terms of its demand for righteousness" that Israel pursued and never attained (v. 31), for righteousness is based on faith and not on works (v. 32a).[28]

These texts raise a broader issue in Paul's use of *nomos* that we might consider here. Many who think that "law of faith" and "law of the Spirit" refer to the Mosaic law viewed improperly think also that the contrasting phrases, "law of works" and "law of sin," refer to the Mosaic law as misunderstood or misused by human beings. In fact, scholars since the beginning of the church have pursued this line of interpretation, to the point that many of Paul's negative statements about the law are interpreted as directed not toward the law as God gave it, but only to the law as people have perverted it.[29] The word *nomos* in these texts, they argue, means "legalism," or it refers to the ceremonial law only or to the law falsely used as a national charter of exclusivism for Israel. By such an interpretation, these scholars are able, they claim, to resolve the tension between Paul's negative and positive statements about the law.[30]

But this whole approach to Paul's teaching on the law must be rejected. First, there is no good evidence that Paul ever uses the word *nomos* to refer to "legalism" or to a misunderstood law. When he wants to denote a legalistic conception, he uses phrases such as "seeking to be justified by the law, or by works of the law." Second, most of the negative statements Paul makes about the law come in contexts in which he has unambiguously

---

[27]See Fuller, *Gospel and Law*, 66–88; Cranfield, *Romans*, 2.509.

[28]See John Ziesler, *Paul's Letter to the Romans* (London: SCM, 1989), 253–54; Tom Schreiner, "Israel's Failure to Attain Righteousness in Romans 9:30–10:3," *TJ* 12 (1991), 211–20; Martin, *Christ and the Law*, 136–38; Sanders, *Paul, the Law and the Jewish People*, 42; Westerholm, *Israel's Law*, 126–30.

[29]This development in the early church was stimulated by the problem of answering Marcion. See Wiles, *Divine Apostle*, 50–52.

[30]Important examples of such an approach are: C. E. B. Cranfield, "St. Paul and the Law," *SJT* 17 (1964), 43–68 (see a revised form of this material in his *Romans*, 2.845–62); Fuller, *Gospel & Law*, 66–105.

identified the law as the law given by God (see Rom. 3:19–20; the passive verb in 5:20; 7:7; Gal. 3:15–18). Third, Paul views God's work of redemption in Christ as the answer to the problem posed by the negative effects of the law (Rom. 3:21–26; 7:4–6; 8:2–4; Gal. 3:13–14; 4:7). Sending Christ to die on the cross implies that the situation from which we had to be rescued was not the subjective one of misunderstanding or misusing the law, but the objective one of being imprisoned under its sin-revealing and sin-provoking powers. Solving the apparent tension between Paul's positive and negative statements about the law by attributing a different meaning to the word in each set of statements must, therefore, be rejected as on overly simplistic alternative.[31]

I return now to the main point: Paul, by definition, understands the Mosaic law to call for works and not for faith. Indeed, he clearly affirms just this in Gal. 3:12a: "The law is not based on faith"; i.e., "the law is not a matter of believing" (*ek pisteōs*). A similar definition is assumed by Eph. 2:15: "the law with its commandments and regulations." This perspective is maintained throughout the New Testament. The Mosaic law, by its nature, demands works. But since salvation can be achieved only by faith, the Mosaic law can have nothing to do with securing salvation.

The Law Cannot Save Because of Sin

The Mosaic law holds out the promise of life for those who do it. But no one can ever achieve life through the law, because it is impossible to do it. This principle is made evident in several New Testament texts. Peter speaks of the law as "a yoke that neither we nor our fathers have been able to bear" (Acts 15:10; see the reference to salvation in v. 11). But it is again in Paul that the most important and most debated texts are found. In Galatians 3:10–12, Paul argues that justification can come only by faith and not by the works of the law because a curse rests on "all who rely on observing the law . . . for it is written: 'Cursed is everyone who does not continue to do everything written in the Book of the Law' [Deut. 27:26]" (Gal. 3:10). While it has been contested in recent years,[32] the point that Paul is making here is that a curse, rather than salvation, comes by reliance on the law because no one can

---

[31]For detailed argument, see my " 'Law,' 'Works of the Law' and Legalism," 73–100. Cf. also Westerholm, *Israel's Law*, 130–36.

[32]See especially Sanders, *Paul, the Law and the Jewish People*, 20–22.

"continue to do everything" that it demands.[33] The same logic is even more evident in Romans. The explanation for why the promise that doers of the law will be justified (Rom. 2:13) can never come to fruition (3:20) is given in 3:9b: "Jews and Gentiles alike are all under sin." Human inability to fulfill the law is why it can never be the means of salvation.

Paul makes this same point later, in Romans 7:7–8:4. The "later" (post-Pelagian) Augustine, most of the Reformers, and a large number of expositors to this day argue that Paul in the latter part of Romans 7 is describing his own experience as a Christian.[34] But this is unlikely. The person depicted in these verses is "sold as a slave to sin" (7:14) and "a prisoner of the law of sin" (7:23). Both descriptions conflict squarely with what Paul affirms to be the experience of all Christians in Romans 6 (no longer "slaves of sin" [see vv. 6, 16–17, 18, 20, 22]) and Romans 8 (set free from "the law of sin and death" [see v. 2]). Romans 7 is Paul's description of his own life, and that of other Jews, under the law of Moses.[35] The giving of the law to Israel, Paul affirms, has meant not life (as some Jews believed) but death (vv. 7–12); for the law is given to human beings who are already "under sin" (3:9) and who cannot therefore obey the good and holy law that God gives them (vv. 14–25). Thus, as Paul summarizes in 8:3, the law cannot rescue from the power of sin because the law is "weakened by the flesh [sarx; NIV 'sinful nature']." Here again, then, Paul describes human sinfulness as the reason why the law cannot bring salvation.

I have devoted most of my attention in this section to the New Testament, simply because the most decisive and clear biblical statements on these issues are found there. Nevertheless, I should note that, although not a great deal is said about these matters in the Old Testament, there are indications that it teaches the same

---

[33]See Hübner, Law in Paul's Thought, 18–19; and especially Thomas Schreiner, "Is Perfect Obedience to the Law Possible? A Re-examination of Galatians 3:10," JETS 27 (1984), 151–60; and "Paul and Perfect Obedience to the Law: An Evaluation of the View of E. P. Sanders," WJ 47 (1985), 245–78.

[34]Recent important defenses of this view are: Anders Nygren, Commentary on Romans (Philadelphia: Augsburg, 1949), 284–97; Cranfield, Romans, 1.344–47; Dunn, Romans 1–8, 387–89; 403–12; J. I. Packer, "The 'Wretched Man' in Romans 7," SE 2, 621–27.

[35]See my Romans 1–8, 469–96, for a detailed defense of this view. In agreement, see also most of the church fathers and W. G. Kümmel, Römer 7 und die Bekehrung des Paulus (Leipzig: Hinrichs, 1929); Ernst Käsemann, Commentary on Romans (Grand Rapids: Eerdmans, 1980), 199–212; Brice L. Martin, "Some Reflections on the Identity of ego in Rom. 7:14–25," SJT 34 (1979), 39–47.

truths. As we have seen, the Old Testament holds out the promise of "life"—in the sense we have defined it—for those who do the law. But the Pentateuch itself, when seen as a whole, takes a decidedly pessimistic viewpoint on the ability of Israel to fulfill its covenant obligations.[36] In his concluding words to Moses, God predicts that the people of Israel "will turn to other gods and worship them, rejecting me and breaking my covenant" (Deut. 31:20). It is this rebellion that the prophets observe, both predicting and reflecting on the exile as God's judgment on his unfaithful people and at the same time announcing the good news that God will yet remain faithful to his promise to Abraham and provide a "new covenant," to be established on the grounds of God's transforming work in the hearts of his people (see Jer. 31:31–34). The law's failure to deliver because of human sin is one of the clearest and most persistent themes of the Old Testament. Faith in the God of the promises, not obedience to the law, is seen to be the way to ultimate blessing.

The Law Reveals the Character of God

As we noted above, God did not give the law of Moses to Israel to save the people. Rather, it was God's gracious revelation of his character, and it demanded that those who were now his people become like him in character. "I am the LORD who brought you up out of Egypt to be your God; therefore be holy, because I am holy" (Lev. 11:45) is a repeated refrain that states a central purpose of the law. God's character is the implied basis for the entire law; in different ways, its various commandments and prohibitions spell out implications of his character for his people Israel. This purpose of the law is so plain that we need say little about it. But we should note two aspects particularly relevant to our purposes. First, the Mosaic law is not *simply* revelation of God's character; it is a demand for conformity to that character and contains threats of punishment for disobedience. What we are insisting on here is that the Mosaic law is, indeed, *law*.[37] The

---

[36]In agreement with this conclusion, although argued on different premises, see John Sailhamer, "The Mosaic Law and the Theology of the Pentateuch," *WTJ* 53:2 (Fall 1991), 241–61.

[37]As Walther Zimmerli has correctly argued, the Mosaic law included the threat of judgment for failure to comply with it from the beginning (*The Law and the Prophets: A Study of the Meaning of the Old Testament* [Oxford: Blackwell, 1965], 51–65). He is arguing against, *inter alia*, Martin Noth ("The Laws in the Pentateuch: Their Assumptions and Meaning" in *The Laws in the Pentateuch and Other Essays*

Septuagint translators were, therefore, correct to translate *tôrâ* by *nomos*.[38] Second, the law points to the character of God in different ways. Some laws rather directly relate human behavior to the character of God: for example, we are not to murder because God reverences and sanctifies human life. Others do so in an indirect way: the Israelites are not to eat certain kinds of food because God is holy and the people must be taught that there are "unholy" things from which they must separate themselves. The sacrificial laws teach still another truth about God, that he cannot tolerate sin without some kind of shedding of blood to compensate for that sin.[39]

Hallowed theological tradition suggests at this point that we distinguish among the various laws by allocating them to one of three categories: moral, ceremonial, and civil.[40] The "moral" commandments, it is assumed, are eternally binding in the form in which they were originally given, while the ceremonial and the civil ones, finding their fulfillment in Christ, cease to act as immediate guides to Christian behavior. In fact, this distinction is vital to many approaches to the law in the New Testament; statements about the law's continuity are regarded as statements about the moral law, while assertions of the law's cessation are applied only to the civil and ceremonial law. But this distinction does not hold up under close scrutiny. The structure of the Mosaic law certainly suggests that the Decalogue holds pride of place;[41]

[Philadelphia: Fortress, 1966], 95–102) and Gerhard von Rad (*Old Testament Theology*, 2 vols. [New York: Harper & Row, 1962, 1965], 1.194–202). I will not deal in this essay with the higher-critical hypotheses of the origin of the law and its relationship to the prophets. I will assume that the chronological order now found in the Old Testament is the order in which the relevant events actually occurred.

[38]The validity of this translation has been doubted by some, who think that the Greek *nomos* introduces a harder, more "legal," element than is present in the Hebrew *tôrâ* (see C. H. Dodd, *The Bible and the Greeks* [London: Hodder and Stoughton, 1954], 25–41). But what I have said above, along with other reasons, shows that the lexical overlap in the two words is large (see Stephen Westerholm, "Torah, Nomos, and Law: A Question of Meaning," *Studies in Religion/Sciences Religieuses* 15 [1986], 327–36).

[39]On the various ways in which the law teaches eternal principles, see especially Vern S. Poythress, *The Shadow of Christ in the Law of Moses* (Brentwood, Tenn.: Wolgemuth and Hyatt, 1991).

[40]The distinction is still widely used; see Walter C. Kaiser, Jr., *Toward an Old Testament Theology* (Grand Rapids: Zondervan, 1978), 114–16.

[41]See Gordon Wenham, "Law and the Legal System in the Old Testament," in *Law, Morality and the Bible*, ed. Bruce Kaye and Gordon Wenham (Downers Grove, Ill.: InterVarsity, 1978), 28.

but it is not easy even within the Ten Commandments to distinguish clearly between what is "moral"—and therefore, it is assumed, eternal—and what is not. For instance, the promise attached to the fifth commandment ("Honor your father and your mother") is "so that you may live long in the land the LORD your God is giving you" (Ex. 20:12). Significantly, when Paul "reapplies" this commandment to his Christian readers (Eph. 6:2–3), he "universalizes" the promise: "that it may go well with you and that you may enjoy long life on the earth." An even thornier problem for those who would elevate the Decalogue to the status of eternal moral law is presented by the Sabbath commandment. Thus, in general, it is notoriously difficult to know from the Old Testament itself which commandments should be placed in the category of "moral" and therefore eternally binding *in the form in which they were first given.*

Jews in Jesus' and Paul's day certainly did not divide up the law into categories; on the contrary, there was a strong insistence that the law was a unity and could not be obeyed in parts.[42] This being the case, we would require strong evidence from within the New Testament to think that the word "law" in certain texts can apply only to one part of the law. Jesus recognized that some requirements within the law were more important than others (Matt. 23:23); but he also insists in this very context that all the requirements must be obeyed. Likewise, Paul reminds the Galatians that they cannot pick and choose which commandments of the law they are going to obey: "I declare to every man who lets himself be circumcised that he is obligated to obey the whole law" (Gal. 5:3). And James asserts that "whoever keeps the whole law and yet stumbles at just one point is guilty of breaking all of it" (James 2:10). These points suffice to show that the continuity of the law in the new covenant cannot be founded on such a distinction among the different "kinds" of laws.[43]

The Law Supervised the People of Israel

Old Testament scholars have long noted how many of the laws given to the people of Israel served to preserve and give

---

[42]While there was some debate among Jews about how much of the law was required to be obeyed by a proselyte, the view that the law was fundamentally a unity was basic. See *m. 'Abot* 4.2; *b. Shabb.* 31a, and the discussion in E. E. Urbach, *The Sages: Their Concepts and Beliefs,* 2 vols. (Jerusalem, Magnes, 1979), 1.360–65.

[43]See also Richard N. Longenecker, *Paul, Apostle of Liberty* (reprint; Grand Rapids: Baker, 1976), 119; Bruce, *Paul,* 192–93; van Dülmen, *Theologie des Gesetzes,* 132–33.

cohesion to the nation. By forcing distinctiveness on the people in terms of diet and other areas of lifestyle, they would be kept intact as a nation and "set apart" for God's special purposes in and through them. The New Testament recognizes something like this purpose of the law, teaching that the law was given by God to supervise and safeguard the people of Israel until Christ should come.

The key text is Galatians 3:24: "The law was put in charge to lead us to Christ" (*ho nomos paidagōgos hēmōn gegonen eis Christon*). The NIV (quoted here) suggests that the text is teaching what is known as the second, or "theological," use of the law: that the law was given to show people their need of God and so lead them to Christ. But this application of the text is certainly wrong, and for two reasons. First, a salvation-historical perspective dominates Galatians 3–4, and especially 3:15–4:7. Paul is not speaking of the experience of individuals with the law, but of the purpose of the law in the history of the people of Israel. Consequently, the first person plural ("us") probably refers to Paul and his fellow Jews, not Paul and his fellow Christians.[44] Second, the telic interpretation of the NIV, "to lead us to Christ," is not justified. Temporal statements surround v. 24: "before faith came" (v. 23); "now that faith has come" (v. 25). These make it likely that *eis* in v. 24 also has a temporal meaning: "the law was our custodian *until* Christ came" (RSV; italics mine).[45] In a similar vein, the key word *paidagōgos* does not suggest the notion of instruction that leads to Christ (cf. KJV "our schoolmaster to bring us unto Christ"). The word denoted a person, usually a servant, who had charge over young children. The ancient "pedagogue" was not a teacher but a babysitter.[46] Galatians 3:24, then, is asserting that the Mosaic law functioned among the people of Israel to direct their behavior until the time of their maturity, when the promised Messiah would be revealed (cf. Gal. 4:1–7).

---

[44] See Bandstra, *Law and Elements of the World*, 59–60; Brendan Byrne, *"Sons of God"—"Seed of Abraham." A Study of the Idea of Sonship of God of All Christians in Paul Against the Jewish Background* (Rome: Biblical Institute, 1979), 178–82; Richard N. Longenecker, *Galatians* (Dallas: Word, 1990), 145, 164.

[45] F. F. Bruce, *The Epistle to the Galatians* (Grand Rapids: Eerdmans, 1982), 183; Longenecker, *Galatians*, 148–49; Hans Dieter Betz, *Galatians*, Hermeneia (Philadelphia: Fortress, 1979), 178.

[46] See especially the excellent survey of the evidence by Richard Longenecker, "The Pedagogical Nature of the Law in Galatians 3:19–4:7," *JETS* 25 (1982), 53–61.

The Law Imprisoned Israel (and All People) Under Sin

We have seen that both Old and New Testaments teach that the law could not free people from the power of sin. But the Scriptures go further: the law has actually had the effect of revealing and stimulating sin and of locking up the people of Israel—and, by extrapolation, all people—under the condemning power of sin.

The Law Reveals Sin

In revealing to Israel the character of God, the law at the same time makes clear that any deviation from conformity to that character is sin. Therefore, as Paul puts it, the law brings "knowledge" of sin (Rom. 3:19–20; 7:7–12). By this Paul means not simply that the law has "defined" sin, in the way that the "laws" of golf define throwing a golf ball as illegal. As so often in Scripture, "knowing" in these contexts means to enter into intimate relationship.[47] Israel came to "know" sin through the law by personal and factual experience of their inability to do what the law demanded of them. Using "I," perhaps to represent himself in solidarity with the people of Israel,[48] Paul can say that "I would not have known sin except through the law" (Rom. 7:7b; my own translation), i.e., I would not have known sin to have the power that it really has (see v. 13). Here again, Paul's perspective is salvation-historical, for he describes the negative effect of the giving of the law on Israel. The author to the Hebrews makes a similar point with reference to the Mosaic laws of sacrifice: they acted as a "reminder of sins" (10:3).

The salvation-historical context of these statements makes it unlikely that we can apply them to the function of the Mosaic law for people generally. Indeed, the popular notion that the Mosaic law should be preached as a preparation for the gospel, revealing sin and one's need of salvation, has slim biblical support.[49] None of the examples of evangelistic preaching in the New Testament uses the law in this way. The closest is Jesus' encounter with the rich young man, cited earlier (Matt. 19:16–22 and par.). Here

---

[47]See, for instance, Cranfield, *Romans*, 1.198–99; Ulrich Luz, *Das Geschichtsverständnis des Paulus* (Munich: Kaiser, 1968), 187.

[48]See my "Israel and Paul in Romans 7.7–12," *NTS* 32 (1986), 122–35.

[49]Luther insisted on the continuing use of the law as a means to prod repentance among both unbelievers and Christians. He was opposed, however, by Agricola. See the discussion in Steffen Kjeldgaard-Pedersen, *Gesetz, Evangelium und Busse* (Leiden: Brill, 1983).

Jesus' citations of the commandments may have the purpose of revealing to this man his need of the gospel. However, it was not the commandments of the Mosaic law, but Jesus' "gospel" demand to follow him that drove the young man to despair. Moreover, Jesus cited the Mosaic law because he could assume the applicability of that law to this Jewish man. We must reiterate at this point the importance of keeping the New Testament salvation-historical perspective in view and of exercising caution in elevating what was true for Jews under old covenant with its Mosaic law to the status of a general theological principle.

The Law "Increases" Sin

Paul goes further: He argues that the law has had the effect of multiplying sins: "The law was added so that the trespass might increase" (Rom. 5:20). This increase probably has both a quantitative and a qualitative dimension. Quantitatively, the law has increased the number of sins, both by defining a greater number of things that displease God and by stimulating rebellion against God by its very prohibitions (the principle of "forbidden fruits" being the sweetest). But Paul's emphasis is on the qualitative increase in sin that the law has brought. As he makes clear elsewhere (Rom. 4:15; 5:13–14), the law makes sin a more serious matter by spelling out in detail the will of God. Before the law was given, sin certainly existed, for people knew from nature and conscience (see Rom. 1:19–22, 32; 2:14–15) what God was like and some of what he wanted from his creatures. But the Mosaic law specified in detail God's will for his people Israel, thereby increasing their responsibility and the seriousness of the matter when they failed to meet that responsibility. Jesus indicated the same principle of greater responsibility because of greater knowledge when he warned that it would go easier in the Day of Judgment for the people of Sodom and Gomorrah than for those people in Galilee who had heard but rejected Jesus (Matt. 10:15). Moreover, since the passive verb in Romans 5:20 must have God as its agent—"the law was added [by God]"—it is clear that God intended this effect of the law when he gave it.[50]

Paul is probably making a similar point in Gal. 3:19 with the phrase *tōn parabaseōn charin*. This may mean that the law was

---

[50]On Rom. 5:20, see my *Romans 1–8*, 360–62; and J. C. Beker, *Paul the Apostle: The Triumph of God in Life and Thought* (Philadelphia: Fortress, 1980), 243–45; Luz, *Geschichtsverständnis*, 202–3; Cranfield, *Romans*, 1.292–93.

added "because it was necessary to curb transgressions" or "in order to reveal transgressions," but the use of the word *parabasis*, which Paul always views as the *result* of the giving of the law (Rom. 2:23; 4:15; 5:14; 1 Tim. 2:14), suggests rather the translation "in order to produce transgressions," i.e., to transform sin into transgression.[51]

The Law Imprisons Under Sin

Because the law reveals and increases sin, it has had, in itself, the negative effect of imprisoning Israel under sin's power and thereby bringing condemnation. The Mosaic law, Paul claims, has brought wrath, for it has revealed sin to be transgression against God's good and holy law. It has thus increased Israel's responsibility (Rom. 4:15). Life under the law has led to enslavement to the "the law [or power] or sin" (Rom. 7:23), a slavery from which only Christ and his Spirit can set us free (8:2–3). "The curse of the law" stands over all who are outside of faith in Christ, for the only means of attaining righteousness apart from Christ is through perfect obedience to God's law, a feat impossible for sinful humans to accomplish (cf. Gal. 3:10, 13). Therefore, the law is like an unfulfilled and unfulfillable "IOU" standing against sinful human beings (Col. 2:14). Paul summarizes all this in Galatians 3:22: "The Scripture declares that the whole world is a prisoner of sin" (cf. also Rom. 3:19–20). The law's manifest inability to rescue God's people Israel from sin's power shows, ipso facto, that all people are in a similar situation. As Paul often does, he here argues from the situation of Israel to the situation of all people, viewing Israel's experience with the law as paradigmatic of the experience of all people with God's "law" in its various forms.[52]

In arguing this point, we must again keep in mind that Paul is referring to the effect of the Mosaic law *in itself* on the people of Israel. He is not claiming that every Israelite was finally condemned under sin, but that every Israelite, in terms of the Mosaic covenant in and of itself, was so condemned. For throughout the Mosaic dispensation, as Paul makes clear in Galatians 3:6–9, 15–18, the prior Abrahamic promise arrangement, by which God

---

[51]Hübner, *Law in Paul's Thought*, 26; Ridderbos, *Paul*, 150; Luz, *Geschichtsverständnis*, 186–87.

[52]See Gerhard Ebeling, "Reflections on the Doctrine of the Law," in *Word and Faith*, 275–80; T. L. Donaldson, "The 'Curse of the Law' and the Inclusion of the Gentiles: Galatians 3:13–14," *NTS* 32 (1986), 104–6; Westerholm, *Israel's Law*, 192–95.

justified sinners through their faith, continued in effect. The promise and the law, Paul suggests, operate on different levels. The Mosaic law was given to supervise Israel as a people and to reveal their sinfulness, and those who sought their "life" in its terms were doomed to condemnation and death (3:10, 12–13). The promissory arrangement with Abraham, fulfilled in Christ, on the other hand, functions to save people from the imprisonment under sin produced by the Mosaic law.

At this point the salvation-historical conception that so dominates Paul's discussion of the law must be carefully nuanced. His strict demarcation of two "eras" can lead to the conclusion that all who lived before Christ were necessarily doomed, while all those who live after Christ are, by definition, saved. But this is not, of course, what Paul intends to say. His application of the salvation-historical contrast of "before" and "after" operates on two levels: the level of world history and the level of individual history.[53] In Galatians 3–4, a passage central to our purposes, the former is clearly dominant, as Paul divides history into three stages: before the law (when the promise was given to Abraham), under the law, and after the law (when the promise to Abraham was fulfilled). Until that promise was fulfilled and "faith in Christ" came, the curse reigned. But in so conceptualizing the situation, Paul does not intend to deny the presence of people before Christ who were genuinely saved from the curse (see 3:6–9). These individuals, by God's grace and in anticipation of the perfect sacrifice of Christ (cf. Rom. 3:25–26), could be delivered from the condemnatory aspects of their life under the law of Moses.

Conclusion

Our survey of the purposes of the Mosaic law has produced a rather negative picture. To some extent this is due to the fact that so much of our evidence comes from Paul, who was dealing with those who were placing too much weight on the law. But while this factor may affect the number of references, it does not materially affect the overall perspective. For while Galatians is certainly polemically oriented, Romans is not; and we have just as strong a negative evaluation of the purpose and effects of the law in Romans as we do in Galatians. Furthermore, the picture found

---

[53]On this, see especially Beker, *Paul the Apostle*, 135–81; Kurt Stalder, *Das Werk des Geistes in des Heiligung bei Paulus* (Zurich: EVZ, 1962), 240–48; Luz, *Geschichtsverständnis*, 193.

in Paul is not materially different than that found in other New Testament books (e.g., Hebrews) or in the Old Testament itself. Throughout the Scriptures, while the essential goodness of the law is tenaciously guarded, its failure to rescue humans from the predicament of sin is made clear. The fault is not God's, nor is the law that he gave to blame; it is our fault, who are so under sin's power that we are not only unable to fulfill his good law, but are stimulated by it to rebel even further against our rightful Lord and so make our condition even worse than before. Typical to the salvation-historical conception, these points are made with respect to the experience of the people of Israel with the Mosaic law, but it is clear that what applies to Israel under its law applies at the same time to all people, confronted with God's law in its various forms (see, e.g., Rom. 2:14–15).

THE MOSAIC LAW IN THE NEW COVENANT

Those purposes of the law that are given most attention in the New Testament—guardianship of Israel; revelation of sin—are limited to the time before the coming of Christ. But we must now look more closely at the law as a revelation of God's character and will for his people. In what sense, if any, does the law continue to exercise this function in the new covenant period? Simple, neat answers to this question—e.g., the law has no role anymore; the whole law, or at least the "moral" law continues in force—are easy to give. But I am convinced that they are too neat and miss some of the nuances found within the New Testament. At the risk of committing the same mistake, I will state at this point the position for which I will argue: The entire Mosaic law comes to fulfillment in Christ, and this fulfillment means that this law is no longer a *direct and immediate* source of, or judge of, the conduct of God's people. Christian behavior, rather, is now guided directly by "the law of Christ." This "law" does not consist of legal prescriptions and ordinances, but of the teaching and example of Jesus and the apostles, the central demand of love, and the guiding influence of the indwelling Holy Spirit.

I will try to substantiate this basic thesis by showing that it is compatible with Old Testament teaching, is taught in key New Testament texts (particularly in Matthew and Paul), and is nowhere contradicted within the New Testament. The nature of the material to be surveyed warrants our abandoning the topical outline of the first section in favor of a canonical outline.

The Old Testament

The Old Testament claims the commandments given to Moses are eternally valid (e.g., Lev. 16:24; 24:8). But these texts cannot be used to demonstrate the eternal applicability of the Mosaic commandments in their original form to the people of God. For one thing, the English words "eternal" and "everlasting" translate Hebrew words that mean "lasting for an age" ('ôlām). Thus, for example, the Levitical priesthood is said to be "eternal" (Ex. 40:15), but Hebrews claims explicitly that it has been done away with under the new covenant. For another, the strict application of this logic would mean that every detail of the Mosaic legislation would remain authoritative in the new covenant era, including the sacrificial law. Again, since Hebrews and other New Testament books demonstrate clearly that at least these laws are no longer to be carried out by new covenant Christians, it is clear that we cannot press these Old Testament texts to prove the eternal applicability of the Mosaic commandments. In fact, two other points within the Old Testament itself suggest that the Mosaic law, considered as an integrated regime, was to have only temporary reign.

The first factor is the very nature of the Mosaic law as *covenant* law. The form of the Sinaitic covenant closely resembles second millennium B.C. Hittite "suzerainty" treaties, through which a king entered into a solemn agreement to provide certain benefits for his vassals, contingent on their abiding by the covenant stipulations (see particularly Ex. 19–24 and the Book of Deuteronomy).[54] The point here is simply that the Mosaic law fits squarely into the framework of this kind of covenant "document," and that we should therefore expect the duration of that law to be bound up with the duration of the covenant of which it is a part. "The law is a temporary framework that prescribed the terms of obedience for the people of God in the Mosaic era."[55] Yet the later Old Testament books make clear that the continuation of the Sinaitic covenant is in jeopardy because of Israel's repeated disobedience of the covenant stipulations (e.g., Dan. 9:7–14; Hos. 6:7; 8:1). God does not, therefore, abandon his people; on the

---

[54]See Meredith G. Kline, *Treaty of the Great King* (Grand Rapids: Eerdmans, 1963), especially 27–44; Dennis J. McCarthy, *Treaty and Covenant* (Rome: Pontifical Biblical Institute, 1963); George E. Mendenhall, *Law and Covenant in Israel and the Ancient Near East* (Pittsburgh: The Biblical Colloquium, 1955).

[55]McComiskey, *Covenants of Promise*, 73.

contrary, in an act of sheer grace, he promises to "recreate" a people for himself through a new covenant.

Secondly, this promised eschatological act is based not on the Mosaic covenant, but on God's inviolable promises to the patriarchs. This pattern is replicated in the New Testament, where Paul bases the future salvation of Israel not on God's continuing maintenance of, or restoration of, the Sinaitic covenant, but on the faithfulness of God to his calling of the people Israel and his promises to the patriarchs (see Rom. 11:16, 28–29). Hope for a new covenant that would arise out of the ashes of the old surfaces repeatedly in the prophets (Isa. 24:5; 42:6; 49:8; 54:10; 55:3; 59:21; 61:8; Jer. 31:31–34; 32:37–41; 50:5; Ezek. 16:60–63; 34:25; 37:15–28 [26]; Hos. 2:18). This covenant is no simple renewal of the Mosaic covenant, but a *new* arrangement, "not . . . like the covenant I made with their forefathers" (Jer. 31:32); in it God, by his Spirit (Ezek. 36:24–28), insures that his law is obeyed (Jer. 31:33–34 [the word *tôrâ* is used]; Ezek. 37:24; cf. also 11:20; 36:27 [the words *ḥuqqōt*, "statutes," and *mispōt*, "judgments," are used]).[56] It is precisely this reference to the law of God that draws our attention to the question of the place of the Mosaic law in this new covenant. Since, especially in Ezekiel, the promised new covenant is connected with a return to the land, we might think that the focus is on the return from exile in the sixth century B.C. But, while perhaps including this return, the prophecies clearly go beyond that period of time. Traditional dispensationalism has confined the true fulfillment of these prophecies to the people of Israel in the millennial era, arguing for a renewal of the Mosaic law in all its details at that time. But the New Testament demonstrates that these new covenant prophecies have been fulfilled through Christ and in the Spirit-endowed church (e.g., Luke 22:20; 1 Cor. 11:25; 2 Cor. 3:6; Heb. 8:7–13).[57] Is the Mosaic law, then, to be a constitutive part of the new covenant also?

---

[56]It is true, in a sense, that "Jeremiah found no fault with the Sinaitic covenant," for its failure was due neither to God nor to the covenant arrangement as such (cf. Kaiser, *Old Testament Theology*, 232). Yet fail it did, as Jeremiah and the other prophets make clear, requiring a new and different arrangement. Kaiser himself notes the discontinuity between the Sinaitic and new covenants, affirming that the new covenant is in direct line with the promises to Abraham and David (see pp. 232–34). This continuity with the Abrahamic and Davidic covenants does not, however, justify speaking of this covenant as a "renewed" covenant (contra Kaiser, p. 234; correctly, McComiskey, *Covenants of Promise*, 163–68), for it brings to fulfillment what was only promised in those earlier covenants.

[57]On this, see McComiskey, *Covenants of Promise*, 155–61.

Many argue that this is what the texts we have mentioned require: The new covenant promises the internalization of the same law given by God at Sinai.[58] But there is reason for caution. First, if Jeremiah and Ezekiel are thinking of the Mosaic law, there is no basis to confine the reference to only part of the law (e.g., the so-called moral law). Yet it is evident that the totality of the Mosaic law has *not* been reinstituted as an authoritative source of life in the new covenant—its laws pertaining to food, sacrifices, festivals, and civic matters are not binding on Christians (Mark 7:19; Acts 10:9–16; Hebrews, passim). Those who argue, then, that the Mosaic law continues intact in the new covenant must recognize that it does not continue without variation and modification. The writing of the law on the heart (Jer. 31:33) may indeed involve transformation of the actual content of the Mosaic law. Second, there are references in the prophets to a *tôrâ* that will be established in the last days and that probably does not refer to the Mosaic law as such (Isa. 2:3; 42:4; 51:4, 7; Mic. 4:2). This "Zion torah," perhaps to be understood as a fresh publication of God's will for his people, in continuity with but not identical to the "Sinai torah," may be what is envisaged in Jeremiah 31:33–34 and the Ezekiel texts.[59] Another possibility is that the concept of "law" has here come to have almost a "formal" sense, denoting generally God's will for his people.[60] The point of Jeremiah, then, is that God would ensure that his will—not the Mosaic law as such, in its totality—would be carried out in the new covenant. In any case, there are solid grounds for thinking that Jeremiah's "law written on the heart" is not simply a reissue of the Mosaic law.

Within the manifest continuity of God's plan for his people, then, there are also in the Old Testament clear indications of the discontinuity between the Sinaitic covenant and the way in which God's promises are finally to be fulfilled in the "last days." All Christian interpreters agree that this discontinuity embraces the Mosaic law in some sense. The question then becomes: How much is continued and how do we know what is continued and what is

---

[58]Kaiser, *Old Testament Theology*, 233.

[59]The distinction between the "Sinai torah" and the "Zion torah" has been promulgated particularly by Hartmut Gese (see "The Law," in *Essays on Biblical Theology* [Minneapolis: Augsburg, 1981] 60–92). See also, on Isaiah, R. Ridderbos, *Isaiah* (Grand Rapids: Zondervan, 1985), 54.

[60]O. Palmer Robertson argues that Jeremiah uses *tôrâ* broadly, to mean the "whole of the Lord's teaching" (*The Christ of the Covenants* [Grand Rapids: Baker, 1980] 282, n. 13).

not? The prophetic focus on a new covenant suggests that in the revelation of that new covenant arrangement we will learn just what it means to have God's law "written on the heart." I turn now, then, to the New Testament to find answers to these questions.

Jesus

Much of our evidence in this section will come from Matthew, for he is the evangelist who passes on to us most of Jesus' explicit teaching about the law.

Fulfillment

Particularly significant is Matthew 5:17–48. This passage has two parts. In vv. 17–19, Jesus defends himself against the charge that he is urging the abrogation of the law. Quite the contrary, Jesus claims in what is a justly famous theological summary, "I have come . . . to fulfill [the Law and the Prophets]." He then builds on this claim to continuity with the Old Testament by solemnly asserting the enduring validity of the law (v. 18) and by urging the teaching of its commandments (v. 19). The second part of this passage (vv. 21–48) examines six facets of the superior, "kingdom" righteousness that Jesus requires of his followers (cf. v. 20, a transitional statement). He enunciates these components of kingdom righteousness by comparing his demand with the commandments of the Mosaic law. Since it will be easier to understand the "theory" of Jesus' relationship to the law expressed in vv. 17–19 after looking at the practical examples in vv. 21–48, I will begin with this latter text.[61]

The six comparisons between traditional teaching and Jesus' teaching found here are usually called the "antitheses," because of the formula used to introduce them: "You have heard that it was said to the people long ago . . . but I tell you" (vv. 21–22, 33–34; vv. 27–28, vv. 31–32, vv. 38–39, and vv. 43–44 abbreviate the same formula). This formula suggests that Jesus is comparing his teaching with the teaching that his Jewish listeners have heard in the synagogue. Whether this teaching represents fairly the teaching of the Old Testament itself is not clear; for Jewish

---

[61]For a more detailed study of Matt. 5:17–48, with more argument and citation of views and sources, see my "Jesus and the Authority of the Mosaic law," *JSNT* 20 (1984), 17–28. (The article has been reprinted, with minor revisions, in *The Best in Theology*, ed. J. I. Packer [Carol Stream, Ill.: Christianity Today Institute, 1987].)

synagogue audiences would often hear the Old Testament read in "targumized" or paraphrased form, and these paraphrases often shifted the meaning of the original.[62] This issue is important in assessing the stance of Jesus vis-à-vis the Old Testament commands in this passage. One influential interpretation, for instance, holds that Jesus is simply reasserting the meaning of the original Old Testament commandment over against Jewish misinterpretations of his day.[63] A second popular viewpoint, however, holds that Jesus generally quotes the Old Testament in its original meaning, but in his own teaching he goes beyond that original meaning, promulgating a "deeper" or "more radical" form of the law for the new kingdom age.[64] A quick study of each of the antitheses will reveal, however, that neither of these options is adequate as an overall summary of Jesus' stance on the law in this passage.

The first two antitheses are similar: Jesus quotes a prohibition from the Decalogue and then adds a condemnation of the heart attitude to which the action prohibited in the commandment can be traced. Despite the popularity of the viewpoint, fostered by its prominence in Reformation catechisms, it is unlikely that Jesus is asserting the "true" meaning of the original prohibitions. Nothing in the Old Testament suggests that anger and lust were included in the prohibitions of, respectively, murder and adultery. A good

---

[62]Since most Jews believed that these additions, part of the oral law, or "the traditions of the elders," were handed down at Sinai (cf. *m. 'Abot* 1:1–2), Jesus could well be including them in what was given "to the people long ago" (taking the dative *tois archaiois* as a "pure dative").

[63]This view was held by most of the Reformers (cf. Harvey K. McArthur, *Understanding the Sermon on the Mount* [London: Epworth, 1960], 36) and probably by a majority of contemporary evangelical scholars. See Carl F. H. Henry, *Christian Personal Ethics* (Grand Rapids: Zondervan, 1957), 300–307; John Murray, *Principles of Conduct* (Grand Rapids: Eerdmans, 1957), 158; Greg L. Bahnsen, *Theonomy in Christian Ethics* (Nutley, N.J.: Craig, 1977), 90; Hermann Ridderbos, *The Coming of the Kingdom* (Philadelphia: Presbyterian and Reformed, 1962), 299; Ned B. Stonehouse, *The Witness of the Synoptic Gospels to Christ* (reprint; Grand Rapids: Baker, 1979), 197–211.

[64]A form of this view was the most popular among the fathers of the church (see McArthur, *Sermon on the Mount*, 26–32), and it is the view most widely supported in modern scholarship. See Martin Dibelius, *The Sermon on the Mount* (New York: Scribner's, 1940), 69–71; W. D. Davies, *The Setting of the Sermon on the Mount* (Cambridge: Cambridge University Press, 1963), 101–2; Jacques Dupont, *Les Béatitudes*, vol. 1: Le problème littéraire—Les deux versions du Sermon sur la Montagne et des Béatitudes, 3d ed. (Bruges: Abbaye de Saint-André, 1958), 146–58; Wolfgang Schrage, *Ethik des Neuen Testaments* (Göttingen: Vandenhoeck & Ruprecht, 1982), 63–69.

case can be therefore made here for the second viewpoint: Jesus is "deepening" the law by extending its prohibitions from the sphere of action to that of the thought life. Yet not even this is clear, for Jesus demonstrates no intention, here or in any of the antitheses, of "doing" something to the law, whether it be expounding it or radicalizing it. What the antithetical formula suggests, rather, is that Jesus is placing his own authoritative demand alongside that of the law. It is the "*I* say to you" of the Messiah and Son of God, not the Mosaic law in any sense, that is the basis of the new kingdom demand.

The relationship between the Mosaic law and Jesus' teaching in the third antithesis is even more indirect than in the first two. In quoting Deuteronomy 24:1, Jesus is probably alluding to the broad grounds for the attaining of a bill of divorce that were available to Jewish men who followed, as most of them naturally would, the liberal teaching of Hillel. Jesus' prohibition of divorce and remarriage on any grounds except that of unchastity counters this liberal tendency, agrees generally with that of Shammai, another prominent rabbi of the day, and is generally in accord with what the Old Testament text itself implies.[65] One could, of course, argue that Jesus is simply reasserting the original meaning of the Mosaic law on this point. Nevertheless, Jesus is much more forthright than is the law at any point in branding second marriages after improper divorces adulterous, and his teaching can hardly be said to grow directly out of the Old Testament.

The fourth "thesis" (v. 33) cited by Jesus accurately summarizes several Old Testament texts that demand the faithful performance of vows (e.g., Lev. 19:12; Num. 30:3; Deut. 23:21). Since the Old Testament never commands that a vow be taken, Jesus' prohibition of vows is no abrogation of the law. On the other hand, Jesus does deny, or perhaps restricts, the acceptance of vows implicit in the Old Testament teaching. Once more, we see how inadequate is the notion that Jesus is simply expounding the Mosaic law, for he simply sweeps away the whole system of vows and oaths that was described and regulated in the Old Testament. On the other hand, it is not clear what Old Testament commandment Jesus might be "deepening," unless we apply the idea to the law in general.

In the fifth antithesis (vv. 38–42), Jesus juxtaposes the Old

---

[65]I am here assuming the authenticity of the "exception" clause and that it states a real exception to the condemnation of a second marriage.

Testament law of "equivalent compensation" (see Exod. 21:24; Lev. 24:20; Deut. 19:21) with his own demand, "Do not resist an evil person." Complicating the situation here is the difficulty in deciding exactly what Jesus intends by this prohibition. If he is in fact forbidding the practice of using this law as a rationale for private retaliation, then Jesus is once again neither abrogating nor expounding the law. The law quoted demands that Israel's judges render decisions fairly and make the punishment fit the crime. By prohibiting the application of the commandment in this way, Jesus does not match nor interpret any particular commandment of the law.

The mixture of Old Testament law and popular interpretation is most evident in the final antithesis (vv. 43–47). Nowhere does the Old Testament command that a person hate his or her enemy, nor is this a fair extrapolation from Old Testament teaching generally.[66] Again, however, Jesus' demand that his disciples love their enemies goes beyond anything required in the Old Testament.[67]

When the antitheses as a group are considered, it becomes clear that no single interpretive method explains all of them. In some it could be argued that Jesus is expounding the law (the third), and in others that he is "deepening" the law (the first and second). But a larger category is needed to explain the overall relationship between the Mosaic commandments cited and Jesus' own teaching. What does consistently emerge from the antitheses is Jesus' radical insistence on what *he* says as binding on his followers. He taught "as one who had authority, and not as their teachers of the law" (Matt. 7:29). This independence from both Jewish tradition and from the Mosaic law itself gives us an important indicator for our interpretation of vv. 17–19.

Jesus' insistence that he had come not to "abolish" (*kataluō*) but to "fulfill" (*plēroō*) the law and the prophets (v. 17) deserves to be ranked among the most important New Testament pronouncements on the significance of the Law of Moses for the new Christian era. Matthean usage shows that the phrase "the Law and the Prophets" refers to the commanding aspect of the Old

---

[66] Jesus' quotation may reflect the attitude inculcated among the sectaries at Qumran, who were encouraged to hate "the sons of darkness" (see 1QS 1:3, 9–10; 2:4–9; and Victor Paul Furnish, *The Love Command in the New Testament* [Nashville: Abingdon, 1972], 42–47).

[67] Lev. 19:18 commands the Israelites to love the "fellow Israelite" (r').

Testament (cf. 7:12; 22:40) rather than to the Old Testament generally.[68] That this is the focus in v. 17 is confirmed by the shift to "Law" in v. 18 and "commandment" in v. 19. Some interpreters think that Jesus' fulfillment of the law involves his personal observance of the demands of the law,[69] but the focus throughout this passage on Jesus' teaching rather than on his actions renders this view unlikely. Arguing that "fulfill" must be an exact antonym of "abolish," others think that Jesus is here expressing his intention fully to establish the law by restoring its true meaning.[70] But there is no reason to think that "fulfill" must express the exact opposite of "abolish."

More seriously, such an interpretation overlooks the manifestly eschatological and salvation-historical dimensions of the term "fulfill" (*plēroō*) in Matthew. Matthew uses it fifteen times (compared with two in Mark and nine in Luke), ten of these occurring in the introductions to Matthew's distinctive "formula quotations" (1:22; 2:15, 17, 23; 4:14; 8:17; 12:17; 13:35; 21:4; 27:9). In these quotations Matthew shows how Jesus has "filled up" the entire Old Testament, not only by accomplishing what it predicted but also by reenacting climactically Old Testament historical events (e.g., 2:15). Particularly suggestive of Matthew's viewpoint is 11:13, in which Jesus declares that "all the Prophets *and the Law* prophesied until John" (italics mine). Integral to Matthew's gospel, then, is a scheme of salvation history that pictures the entire Old Testament as anticipating and pointing forward to Jesus.[71]

This background, coupled with the way in which Jesus goes beyond the law in his teaching in vv. 21–47, makes it unlikely that he is affirming in v. 17 his intention simply to establish the Mosaic law as it already exists. Other interpreters, then, view v. 17 as Jesus' claim to be "filling out" the law by extending or radicalizing its demands.[72] But we have already seen that this perspective is

---

[68]See Wolfgang Trilling, *Das wahre Israel: Studien zur Theologie des Matthäus-Evangeliums* (Munich: Kosel, 1964), 173–74.

[69]T. W. Manson, *Ethics and the Gospel* (London: SCM, 1960), 53–54; Theodor Zahn, *Das Evangelium des Matthäus*, 4th ed. (Leipzig: Deichert, 1922), 212–13; Henrik Ljungman, *Das Gesetz erfüllen: Matth. 5,17ff. und 3,15 untersucht* (Lund: Gleerup, 1954), 58–61.

[70]See especially Bahnsen, *Theonomy*, 64–69.

[71]On the fulfillment theme in Matthew, see especially R. T. France, *Matthew: Evangelist and Teacher* (Grand Rapids: Zondervan, 1989), 106–205.

[72]See Dupont, *Béatitudes*, 138–44; W. D. Davies, "Matthew 5.17, 18," in *Christian Origins and Judaism* (Philadelphia: Westminster, 1962), 33–45; Trilling, *Das wahre Israel*, 174–79.

unable to account for all the ways in which Jesus compares his teaching with that of the law in the antitheses that follow. The best interpretation, then, is to give to *plēroō* in v. 17 essentially the same meaning that it has in Matthew's fulfillment formulas: accomplishing that to which the Old Testament looked forward. In Matthew's bold perspective, *all* parts of the Old Testament "prophesy" about Jesus and the age of salvation. Thus, as Jesus "fulfills" Old Testament prophecies by doing what they predicted and "fulfills" Old Testament history by reenacting its events, so he "fulfills" the Old Testament law by making demands to which the law pointed forward. Jesus rejects any notion that his claim to dictate God's will to his followers involves a radical departure from the law or from its intentions. Rather, he is claiming that his teaching brings the eschatological fullness of God's will to which the Mosaic law looked forward. Jesus "fulfills" the law not by explaining it or by extending it, but by proclaiming the standards of kingdom righteousness that were anticipated in the law.[73]

But can this interpretation be squared with what Jesus says about the law in vv. 18–19? These verses appear to give a ringing endorsement to the law's eternal validity (v. 18) and applicability (v. 19). However, few Christians would want to take the verses in just this way,[74] for they would then demand that Christians practice *every* commandment in the law, including commandments relating to the cult that the author to the Hebrews explicitly says are invalidated for Christians. Some have sought to evade this implication by arguing or assuming that Jesus is referring here only to the "moral" law. But we have seen above that these distinctions cannot be read into the New Testament, and particularly not in a text that focuses on the details of every part of the

---

[73]For this general approach, see especially Banks, *Jesus and the Law*, 207–10; J. P. Meier, *Law and History in Matthew's Gospel* (Rome: Biblical Institute, 1976), 75–85; Ben F. Meyer, *The Aims of Jesus* (London: SCM, 1979), 143–53; Robert Guelich, *The Sermon on the Mount* (Waco, Tex.: Word, 1982), 137–38, 163; D. A. Carson, "Matthew," in *The Expositor's Bible Commentary*, vol. 8 (Grand Rapids: Zondervan, 1984), 142–45; France, *Matthew*, 194–95; W. D. Davies and Dale C. Allison, *A Critical and Exegetical Commentary on the Gospel According to Saint Matthew*, vol. 1 (Edinburgh: T. & T. Clark, 1988), 485–87; Poythress, *The Shadow of Christ in the Law of Moses*, 263–67.

[74]The strength of these endorsements has given rise to various theories about Matthew's sources for vv. 18 (with its parallel in Luke 16:17) and 19. For discussion of various theories, see R. G. Hamerton-Kelly, "Attitudes to the Law in Matthew's Gospel," *BR* 17 (1972), 19–32.

law and in a Jewish context. Jesus' teaching about the law in vv. 18–19 must apply to the whole law.

How, then, can Jesus' teaching in these verses be integrated with the New Testament perspective generally? Some think that one, or both, of the "until" clauses in v. 18 sets up a temporal limitation on the validity of the law. The disappearance of heaven and earth and the accomplishment of all things will take place when Jesus completes the work of redemption on the cross and in his resurrection (see Matt. 24:34–35).[75] But there is insufficient evidence to support this limitation. Others argue that v. 19 refers to the commandments that Jesus is teaching (vv. 21ff.) rather than to the commandments of the law (v. 18).[76] But this is not the most obvious interpretation. Probably, then, we should understand v. 18 to be an endorsement of the continuing "usefulness" or authority of the law. Jesus is no Marcionite; and even if his followers are no longer bound by the commandments of the law, they are still to read and profit from it. In v. 19, then, the continuing practice of the commandments of the law must be viewed in light of their fulfillment by Jesus. It is the law *as fulfilled by Jesus* that must be done, not the law in its original form.[77]

Love and the Law

Jesus' insistence that love be the touchstone of all that his disciples do is well known. What relationship does his focus on love bear to the continuing applicability of the Mosaic commandments? Three interpretations are popular: (1) love replaces the law (love in place of the law); (2) love is the criterion by which the meaning and application of the Mosaic commandments are to be evaluated (love over the law); or (3) love is the central demand of the law, without which the fulfillment of the rest of the law is meaningless (love as central to the law). I will argue that elements of both the second and third perspectives are found in Jesus' teaching.[78]

The most direct evidence comes from Jesus' singling out love

---

[75]See Davies, "Matthew 5.17, 18," 44–63; Meier, *Law and History*, 62–64; Guelich, *Sermon on the Mount*, 145–48.

[76]Banks, *Jesus and the Law*, 221–23.

[77]See especially France, *Matthew*, 195–96.

[78]On these points, again see my article "Jesus and the Authority of the Mosaic Law," 6–11; and also the slight revision of the position I take there in "Law," in *Dictionary of Jesus and the Gospels*, ed. I. H. Marshall, S. McKnight, and J. Green (Downers Grove: InterVarsity, 1992).

for God (Deut. 6:5) and love for one's neighbor (Lev. 19:18) as constituting, together, the greatest commandment in the law (Matt. 22:34–40; Mark 12:28–34; cf. Luke 10:25–28). On these two commandments, Jesus claims, "all the Law and the Prophets hang [*krematai*]." As we have seen, "the Law and the Prophets" is an expression Matthew uses to denote the commanding aspect of the Old Testament. Jesus' language here suggests that the two great commandments are to the rest of the commandments as hinges are to a door; without them, the other commandments fall to the ground.[79] Obeying all the commandments in the law without manifesting love for God and love for one's neighbor is useless and unprofitable. Jesus, therefore, does not suggest that love is to replace the law, but that love is central and vital to the law. Similar is Jesus' rebuke of the Jews for paying scrupulous attention to the minutiae of the tithing laws, while neglecting "the more important matters of the law—justice, mercy and faithfulness" (Matt. 23:23, probably alluding to Mic. 6:8). Again, his point is not that the Jews should replace the laws of tithing with these demands, but that they should have focused on the greater demands "without neglecting the former."

Nevertheless, Jesus makes love so central to his understanding and interpretation of the law that it becomes the power of interpreting and applying God's will as revealed in the law.[80] On at least three occasions, Jesus pronounced love for others, or "mercy," to be more important than sacrifices (Matt. 9:13; 12:7 [both quoting Hos. 6:6]; Mark 12:32–34). In keeping with the prophetic tradition, Jesus may simply be insisting on the priority of love within the commandments. But the application of the principle to the Sabbath law (Matt. 12:7) suggests that Jesus goes further. On at least six different occasions (Matt. 12:1–8 = Mark 2:23–28 = Luke 6:1–5; Matt. 2:9–14 = Mark 3:1–6 = Luke 6:6–11; Luke 13:10–17; 14:1–6; John 5:1–15; 9:1–12), Jesus or his disciples violate the accepted Jewish teaching about appropriate behavior on the Sabbath. While none of these actions clearly infringes the written law, the non-emergency healings of Jesus certainly "stretch" it. More important, however, are Jesus' responses to Jewish criticism of his and his disciples' action. It is as

---

[79]Ceslaus Spicq, *Agape in the New Testament*, vol. 1: *Agape in the Synoptic Gospels* (St. Louis/London: Herder, 1963), 30.

[80]Jesus differed fundamentally with the Jewish teachers of his day at this point; see especially Westerholm, *Jesus and Scribal Authority*.

this point that Jesus' citation of Hosea 6:6 (Matt. 12:7) becomes important, for in the Markan parallel, Jesus claims that "the Sabbath was made for man, not man for the Sabbath" (Mark 2:27).[81] He thereby suggests that concern for the welfare of one's fellow human beings plays a role in interpreting the intention and regulating the observance of the Sabbath command.[82]

But Jesus' main justification for his and his disciples' Sabbath activities is Christological. This is clear from the great discourse in John 5 as well as from several details in the synoptic accounts. Jesus justifies his disciples' plucking of grain on the Sabbath by citing the parallel of David, who illegally ate the Bread of the Presence when he and his followers were in need (Matt. 12:3–4 = Mark 2:25–26 = Luke 6:3–4; cf. 1 Sam. 21:1–6). He may thereby be suggesting the principle that human need takes precedence over obedience to details of the law. But the main point runs in a different direction. As Matthew's example of the temple and the priests immediately following (12:5–6) suggests, the main point is a Christological one: As priests who serve the temple are innocent of breaking the law by working on the Sabbath, as David's followers are innocent when they eat consecrated bread, so also the disciples are innocent of Sabbath-breaking, for they are serving and following one who is greater than the temple and greater than David.[83]

This Christological focus is strongly reasserted in the climax of this incident in all three Gospels: "The Son of Man is Lord [even] of the Sabbath." As we have noted, this saying further confirms what we have discovered above: that Jesus was not so much concerned with adjudicating the exact meaning and application of the Mosaic law as he was in asserting *his* claim to bring that which

---

[81]Scholars persist in suggesting that the text be emended to "The Sabbath was made for the Son of Man" (cf. v. 28); a mistranslation of the Aramaic is usually suggested: see F. W. Beare, " 'The Sabbath was made for Man,' " *JBL* 79 (1960), 134. But the emendation is not to be accepted (cf. C. E. B. Cranfield, *The Gospel according to St. Mark* [Cambridge: Cambridge University Press, 1966], 117–18).

[82]The formal similarity between Jesus' statement and the rabbinic claim that "The Sabbath is delivered over for your sake, but you are not delivered over to the Sabbath" (*Mek. Exod.* 31:13) should not blind us to the fact that they are making different kinds of claims. The Rabbi (Simeon b. Menasya) is arguing only that human life can be preserved on the Sabbath; Jesus, however, is justifying a wide variety of non-life-threatening activities (see Joachim Gnilka, *Das Evangelium nach Markus*, 2 vols. [Neukirchen-Vluyn: Neukirchener, 1978, 1979], 1.123).

[83]R. T. France, *Jesus and the Old Testament* (London: Tyndale, 1971), 46–47; Rudolf Pesch, *Das Markusevangelium*, 2 vols. (Freiburg: Herder, 1977), 1.181–82.

was both greater than, and the fulfillment of, that law. While he does not clearly teach the abrogation of the Sabbath command, he redirects attention from the law to himself, the Lord of the Sabbath, and thereby sets in place the principle on which the later church would justify its departure from Sabbath observance.

Jesus, then, both makes love the center of the law and moves slightly in the direction of using love as a criterion to interpret and explain the law. Never, however, does he clearly take the step of using love as the basis for the abrogation of a commandment in the law.

The Mosaic law and the Commandments of Jesus

Our cursory survey of Matthew 5:17–47 shows that Jesus made his own teaching the norm for life in the kingdom. This teaching is neither a repetition nor an expansion of the law, nor is it based on the law. Nevertheless, it stands in salvation-historical continuity with that law. This perspective is reflected throughout the Gospels. True, Jesus does sometimes base his teaching on the Mosaic law and applies that law to his followers and to fellow Jews. But at this point, we must remind ourselves of the importance of recognizing the salvation-historical context in which Jesus is teaching. He himself apparently scrupulously observed all the details of the Mosaic law, and generally addressed both his disciples and his opponents within the context of the Mosaic covenant that was still then in force. His personal obedience of the law and his teaching of such obedience to others cannot, then, be automatically viewed as expressing his belief about what should be the case after his death and resurrection had brought the new era of salvation into existence.

Indeed, we find numerous more or less clear indications that Jesus did not expect the Mosaic law to continue in unabated force. He suggests that the Mosaic law, in allowing for human sinfulness, does not always express God's "perfect will" (Matt. 19:3–12 and par.). Clearest is his teaching that nothing going into a person from outside can make that person "unclean" (Matt. 15:1–20; Mark 7:1–23). Mark, in a parenthetical remark to his readers, brings out the revolutionary implications of such teaching: "In saying this, Jesus declared all foods 'clean'" (Mark 7:19b). Here Jesus announces the abrogation of a significant part of the Mosaic law, acting on the far-ranging implications of his claim to be "Lord of the Sabbath." Significantly, after his death and resurrection, Jesus urges his disciples to teach "all that I have commanded you"

(Matt. 28:19–20, italics mine). What emerges from Jesus' teaching is a shift of focus from the law to Jesus himself as the criterion for what it means to be obedient to God.

Conclusion

The picture we gain of Jesus' teaching about the law, while not crystal clear in all its details, suggests a strong element of discontinuity within the overall continuity of God's plan and purposes. Jesus tells his disciples to look to himself as the fulfiller of the law for guidance in the way they are to live. The Mosaic law, it is suggested, no longer functions as the ultimate and immediate standard of conduct for God's people. It must always be viewed through the lens of Jesus' ministry and teaching.

Paul

I will now try to show that Paul shares this same perspective on the Mosaic law and the Christian. Specifically, I will argue that Paul teaches that Christians should not look directly to the Mosaic law as their authoritative code of conduct but to "the law of Christ." This "law" is not a set of rules but a set of principles drawn from the life and teaching of Jesus, with love for others as its heart and the indwelling Spirit as its directive force. I will follow the same outline that we used to survey the teaching of Jesus, treating in order Paul's teaching about the fulfillment of the law, love and the law, and the locus of authority for believers.

Fulfillment

Paul uses the word *plēroō* with reference to the law of Moses four times (Rom. 8:4; 13:8, 10; Gal. 5:14), but these all refer to concepts that are better discussed under other headings below. Here we want to look at another verse which, although not using the word *plēroō*, expresses a concept similar to that found in Matthew 5:17; this verse is Romans 10:4: "Christ is the end of the law [*telos nomou*], so that [*eis*] there may be righteousness for everyone who believes."

Paul's statement here has almost become a slogan to summarize his attitude toward the Mosaic law. Unfortunately, the exact meaning of the pronouncement is not clear, with the debate centering on the meaning of the three Greek words indicated above. The word *nomos*, as we noted above, is sometimes taken to denote legalism, and this meaning has been applied by some to the word in this verse.[84] As I argued, however, this meaning is unattested in Paul; normally he uses *nomos* to refer to the Mosaic law as such. A second issue is whether the phrase that *eis* introduces depends on *nomos* alone—i.e., "the law which is for righteousness [or] which would confer righteousness"—or on the entire first phrase, as the NIV translation suggests. A comparison of similar constructions in Paul points to the second alternative.[85]

The third and most debated point is the meaning to be given to *telos*. The word has several meanings, the most likely in this verse being "end" (in the sense of "termination") and "goal." If we accept the first meaning, Paul would be asserting a strong discontinuity between the law and Christ, implying perhaps that the law has no more function for those who have come to know Christ and to experience his righteousness.[86] The second meaning, on the other hand, suggests a much more continuous sense, according to which the law may well be understood to remain in full force for believers.[87] However, we do not need to choose between these two options in their extreme forms. Paul's use of *telos* points to a meaning that is perhaps best translated in English as "culmination," combining the ideas of both goal and end.[88] In

---

[84]C. F. D. Moule, "Obligation in the Ethic of Paul," in *Christian History and Interpretation: Studies Presented to John Knox*, ed. W. R. Farmer, C. F. D. Moule, and R. R. Niebuhr (Cambridge: Cambridge University Press, 1967), 402.

[85]See Mark A. Seifrid, "Paul's Approach to the Old Testament in Rom. 10:6–8," *TJ* 6 (1985), 8–9.

[86]See van Dülmen, *Theologie*, 126; Luz, *Geschichtsverständnis*, 139–57.

[87]See Bring, "Gesetz," 1–36; Cranfield, *Romans*, 2.516–19; Fuller, *Gospel & Law*, 82–85.

[88]The word probably means "end" in 2 Cor. 3:13 and 1 Thess. 2:16 and combines the ideas of "end" and "goal" in the sense of destiny, outcome, or culmination in Rom. 6:21, 22; 1 Cor. 1:8; 10:11; 15:24; 2 Cor. 1:13; 11:15; Phil. 3:19; 1 Tim. 1:5. The technical meaning "tax" or "customs payment" is found in its two occurrences in Rom. 13:7. Among others who combine the ideas of "end" and "goal" in their interpretation of the word are Bandstra, *Law and Elements of the World*, 105–6; F. Godet, *Commentary on Romans* (reprint; Grand Rapids: Kregel, 1977), 376; Dunn, *Romans 9–16*, 589–91; Campbell, "Christ the End of the Law," 73–77; Seifrid, "Paul's Approach," 6–10; Drane, *Paul*, 133. Markus N. A. Bockmuehl suggests the meaning "prophetic fulfillment" or "consummation," based on several extra-biblical texts (*Revelation and Mystery in Ancient Judaism and Pauline Christianity* [Tübingen: Mohr, 1990], 150–53). The objection of Robert Badenas (who has made the strongest case for taking *telos* to mean "goal") that such a double meaning should not, except as a last resort, be adopted (*Christ the End of the Law: Romans 10:4 in Pauline Perspective*, JSNTSup 10 [Sheffield: JSOT, 1985], 147) is not to the point. I am not arguing that the word has a double

other words, Paul is saying that Christ is the one to whom the law has all along been pointing—its goal. But now that goal has been reached, the regime of the law is ended, just as a race is ended once the finish line, its goal, has been attained. This does not mean, of course, that the law ceases to exist or even that it has no more relevance to believers. What is suggested, rather, is that the law has ceased to have a central and determinative role in God's plan and among his people. Interpreted in this sense, Romans 10:4 makes a claim that is similar to Matthew 5:17: the Mosaic law points to Christ and is dethroned from its position of significance in mediating God's will to his people with the coming of Christ.

Love and the Law

Two key texts in which Paul applies the language of fulfillment to the Mosaic law are Galatians 5:14 and Romans 13:8–10, in both of which love for one's fellow human being is presented as the "fulfillment" of the law. What implications does this fulfillment have for the application of the law to believers? Many answer that it means only that Paul considers love to be so central to the law that one is not really obeying the law if love is not present. Paul highlights love not to displace the law in any sense, but to point to its true meaning and essence.[89]

But the texts suggest that Paul does, indeed, see love as in some sense displacing the commandments of the Mosaic law. Paul's claim that the commandment "Love your neighbor as yourself" sums up (*anakephalaioō*) all the other commandments (Rom. 13:9) surely points in this direction. If love for others "sums up" the commandments, the implication is that the one who truly loves will have no need of these commandments.[90] Paul's use of fulfillment language in these contexts suggests a similar conclusion. Vital to understanding Paul's perspective on the law is to recognize a principial distinction in his writings between "doing" and "fulfilling" the law. Nowhere does Paul say that Christians are to "do" the law, and nowhere does he suggest that any but Christians can "fulfill" the law. "Doing" the law refers to that daily obedience to all the commandments that was required of the

---

meaning, but that we require two words in English to get at the single meaning for the Greek word used here.

[89]See Ridderbos, *Paul*, 282.

[90]See C.K. Barrett, *A Commentary on the Epistle to the Romans* (New York: Harper & Row, 1957), 251; Dunn, *Romans 9–16*, 778–81; Longenecker, *Galatians*, 241–44; Westerholm, *Israel's Law*, 204–5.

Israelite. "Fulfilling" the law, on the other hand, denotes that complete satisfaction of the law's demands that comes only through Christians' identification with Christ (Rom. 8:4; see below) and their submission to that commandment that Christ put at the heart of his new covenant teaching: love (Gal. 5:14; Rom. 13:8, 10). It is the love of others, first made possible by Christ (hence the "new" commandment [John 13:34]), that completely satisfies the demand of the law.[91]

Two possible objections to this interpretation may be raised. First, is not that demand that Paul claims to fulfill the law part of the law itself (see Lev. 19:18)? Certainly the words are derived ultimately from Leviticus 19:18. But Paul's citation of the verse is due to the fact that Jesus had already singled it out as central to his demand. Paul cites the text, then, not as an Old Testament commandment, but as an Old Testament commandment already transformed into the demand of Christ. A second objection is that loving one's neighbor hardly seems able to encompass within it all that the law prescribes of people, particularly those duties owed to God rather than to other people. But Paul's focus in both texts is obviously restricted to what we might call the "horizontal" relationship (note the commandments cited in Rom. 13:9). He is not necessarily claiming that consistent love for one's neighbor exhausts all that the Christian must do, but that love for the neighbor includes within it all that the law demands of Christians in their relationship with other people.

Finally, the question must be asked: What is the status of the law for those—including all Christians more or less often—who do not consistently and perfectly love their neighbors? Does the law become, as Luther suggested, a means to reveal our failure and judge us for it? To answer this question, we must look more broadly at the place Paul gives to the law of Moses within the new covenant and at the locus of authority he establishes for Christians.

The Law of Moses and the Law of Christ

I will move in this section from the negative to the positive, arguing first that Christians are not, according to Paul, bound to the law of Moses but, secondly, are bound to those principles

---

[91]See especially Westerholm, *Israel's Law*, 201–5; A. Feuillet, "Loi de Dieu, Loi du Christ et Loi de l'esprit d'après les epîtres pauliniennes," *NovT* 22 (1980), 53–54.

established by Christ in his life and teaching—principles mediated and motivated by the Spirit and focused on love; this constitutes "the law of Christ."

No longer "under the law." Paul uses the phrase "under [the] law" (*hypo nomon*) eleven times (Rom. 6:14, 15; 1 Cor. 9:20 [four occurrences]; Gal. 3:23; 4:4, 5, 21; 5:18). The omission of the article in each instance does not indicate that Paul is thinking of divine "law" in general or of law as a principle (as some older commentators thought); the "law" in question is so well known that there is no need to make the word *nomos* definite. As the context in each case makes clear, the law to which Paul refers is the Mosaic law, the *tôrâ*. To understand what Paul means by the phrase and thereby to evaluate accurately the significance of Paul's claim that believers are *not* "under the law" (Gal. 5:18; Rom. 6:14–15; 1 Cor. 9:20), we will examine each occurrence in its chronological sequence. We do not presume that "under the law" must connote the same idea in each of its occurrences, although the stereotypical flavor of the phrase may point in this direction. Three general meanings of the phrase are popular: (1) under the condemnation pronounced by the law; (2) under a legalistic perversion of the law; and (3) under the law as a regime or power, in a general sense. I will argue that it is only the third interpretation that can do justice to the evidence, that the second meaning is not present at all, and that the first may be included, along with the third, in some places.

The first three occurrences in Galatians come within Paul's rehearsal of the role of the law in salvation history (Gal. 3:15–4:7). Paul is trying to convince the Gentile Christians in Galatia of the foolishness of adopting Jewish practices by showing that the time when those practices were necessary has now passed. To accomplish this aim, Paul pictures the law as something of a parenthesis within salvation history; it was "added" well after the promise to Abraham (3:17, 19) and was in effect "until the Seed to whom the promise referred had come" (3:19). It was, then, "before this faith [probably 'faith in Jesus Christ'; cf. v. 22] came" that "we were confined under the law" (v. 23; my own translation; NIV paraphrases). While we cannot be certain, it is likely that the "we" refers to Paul and other Jews. "Under the law," in fact, is only one of several phrases that Paul uses to depict the situation of the Jews in the old covenant in this context; others are "under a *paidagōgos*" (3:25; cf. v. 24), children under "guardians and trustees" (4:1–2), "under the basic principles of the world" (4:3), and "under sin" (3:22; NIV again paraphrases).

If "under the law" is exactly parallel to "under sin," then to be "under the law" could denote being subject to the curse of the law. An additional reason for this interpretation comes in 4:5, where those whom Jesus needs to redeem are those "under law."[92] But other evidence points in a different direction. First, the assertion of v. 22 about being under sin is something of an anomaly in the flow of this context, speaking of "Scripture" (rather than "the law") and of "the whole world" (rather than just the Jews). The identification of the law with the *paidagōgos* in v. 24, however, shows that it is the reference to being "under the *paidagōgos*" that is parallel to being "under the law." And this phrase, as we have seen, denotes not the cursing effect of the law but its custodianship of the people of Israel during the time of their "minority."

A second reason for preferring this broader interpretation of the phrase is Paul's assertion in 4:4 that Jesus was himself "born under [the] law." Since Jesus was not *born* subject to the curse (although he later voluntarily and vicariously took it upon himself; cf. 3:13), the phrase here cannot mean "under the curse of the law." Jesus, Paul is stressing, was a Jew and lived as one who was subject to the requirements of the Mosaic law that had been given to oversee the Jewish people. Like most of the other phrases about bondage in the context, then, "under the law" refers to a status of close supervision and custodial care, a situation that eventually gives way to a time of maturity and freedom.[93]

As we noted above, Paul's salvation-historical conception can allow him to associate this pre-Christian, objective situation of guardianship and immaturity with subjection to the curse and wrath of God. Hence the phrase can occasionally include within it (as in 4:5) nuances of condemnation. But this is a nuance and not the basic meaning of the phrase. And while not stated, Paul's logic implies that the coming of Christ removes the situation during which Israel must be held "under the law." In summary, the context of Galatians 3:15–4:7 shows that "under the law" depicts the situation of Jews before the coming of Christ, when they were subject to the authority and supervision of the Mosaic law.

By submitting to circumcision (cf. 5:2) and to the observance

---

[92]See Thielmann, *From Plight to Solution*, 77–78.

[93]See especially Linda Belleville, " 'Under Law.' Structural Analysis and the Pauline Concept of Law in Galatians 3:21–4:11," *JSNT* 26 (1986), 53–78; Longenecker, *Galatians*, 145–49, 171.

of Jewish festivals (cf. 4:10), the Gentile Christians in Galatia would, in effect, be putting themselves in this same situation. Their acceptance of such old covenant practices, Paul says, shows that they "want to be under the law" (Gal. 4:21), for one cannot pick and choose which commandments of the law to observe (5:3). Paul's Judaizing opponents in Galatia were apparently teaching that Christians needed to observe some of the commandments of the law without taking on themselves the burden of the whole. Paul makes clear in this verse that this is impossible: God's law is a unity, and one cannot pick and choose which commandments to place oneself under (the same point is made in Jas. 2:11–13). This makes it clear that, for Paul, subjection to the law of Moses was an all-or-nothing proposition: Either one was under that law and bound to obey all its commandments, or one was free from that law and free from all its commandments. Thus, acknowledging that a commandment such as circumcision is necessary if one is to belong to the people of God in the new era of salvation entails acknowledging the authority of that entire Mosaic law of which the commandment is a part. This is why Paul is so upset with the Galatians: for them to submit to circumcision is to recognize the continuing supervisory role of the Mosaic law and thereby tacitly to deny that the promised seed, who ends the rule of the law, had come (see 3:19). Paul can therefore warn them that "you who are trying to be justified by law have been alienated from Christ; you have fallen away from grace" (5:4).

This verse, along with many others in Galatians, makes clear that the issue concerned justification rather than sanctification. It could be argued, then, that Paul is denying any role for the law in making people Christians but is not contesting the authority of the law in guiding people who already are Christians. But this interpretation falters on two counts. First, as we have seen, being "under the law," the condition to which the Galatians would in effect go back to if they accepted the Judaizers' program (4:21), does not involve the use of the law for salvation. It denotes the supervisory role of the law. Paul argues, in effect, that accepting the law as a means of justification involves accepting its general supervisory authority (being "under the law"), a role that is now clearly ended with the coming of the promised one.

A second reason for rejecting the view that Paul is limiting his critique of the law to the issue of justification only is Paul's assertion in Galatians 5:18 that "if you are led by the Spirit, you are not under [the] law." This verse comes in the section of the letter (5:13–6:10) in which Paul stresses that Christians, though "free" in Christ (5:1, 13), are nevertheless bound by certain moral imperatives: specifically, to love one another (5:13–15) and to manifest the fruit of the Spirit (5:22–26). By following these, they will fulfill "the law of Christ" (6:2). Now, in 5:18, Paul may mean that it is only those Christians who are fully submitting to the guidance of the Spirit who are in no need of the directives of the law; but those Christians who are not so led are still "under the law." But this interpretation would require that the phrase "under the law" means something different here from what it did earlier, where it denoted the situation that the Galatian Christians would be under if they submitted to circumcision and other Old Testament requirements (cf. 4:21). Therefore, it is more likely that "being led by the Spirit" is a way of designating all Christians, who have come under the dominating influence of the Spirit (cf. also Rom. 8:14, where "being led by the Spirit" confers divine sonship, a status enjoyed by all believers).[94] "Being led by the Spirit," then, parallels "living by the Spirit" (v. 25). Not being "under the law" applies to all Christians and refers not to entrance into the Christian life, but to the living out of Christian existence.

The phrase "under the law" occurs again four times in 1 Corinthians 9:20. In this chapter, Paul cites his own willingness to forego apostolic "rights" for the sake of others. As an example of this attitude, he mentions his flexibility with respect to his manner of life:

> To the Jews I became like a Jew, to win the Jews. To those under the law I became like one under the law (though I myself am not under the law), so as to win those under the law. To those not having the law I became like one not having the law (though I am not free from God's law but am under Christ's law [*ennomos Christou*]), so as to win those not having the law. (9:20–21)

In this passage, it is clear that "under the law" cannot denote being subject to the curse of the law or to a legalistic perversion of the law. Being "under the law" is not contrasted to the situation of Christians, in which case the phrase might mean "under the curse," but to the situation of the Gentiles, those "not having the law." It must refer, then, to that which is peculiar to the Jewish people—and that can only be their subjection to the rule and authority of the Mosaic law. Paul's point, then, is that he as a Christian is not subject to the authority of the Mosaic law, but he

---

[94]See Betz, *Galatians*, 281.

willingly gives up that freedom and conforms to that law when evangelizing Jews.[95]

Finally, in Romans 6:14–15, Paul contrasts being "under [the] law" with being "under grace." These assertions are closely related in Paul's train of thought to Romans 7:4, in which he claims that Christians have "died to the law." Traditional Reformed (and especially Puritan) exegesis has emphasized that the contrast here is between justification and condemnation. Christians are free from the law's condemnation, for their status "under grace" has delivered them from the law as a "covenant of works," in which every infraction had to receive its penalty. But, these exegetes insist, Paul is not asserting that Christians are free from the law "as a rule of life."[96] Other scholars add to this condemnatory sense a nuance of legalism, suggesting that Christians' freedom from *nomos* here involves also freedom from the perverted misuse of the law as a means of salvation.[97]

The idea that Paul is claiming here that Christians are delivered from legalism is particularly unlikely. As we have argued before, Paul does not use the word *nomos* to denote this idea; and here again, release from the bondage of the law takes place through the redeeming work of Christ ("through the body of Christ," 7:4). As Heikki Räisänen says, "It is hard to understand why a method as drastic as the *death* both of Christ and of the Christians would have been necessary to get rid of a mere misunderstanding about the law. A new revelation about its true meaning would have sufficed."[98] That freedom from the law's condemnation is included is probable. But it is questionable whether this is all that Paul means. The issue in Romans 6 is not freedom from the *penalty* of sin, but from the *power* of sin. If sin is not to rule over believers (6:14a), more than forgiveness (i.e., freedom from the law's curse) is necessary. After all, justification in itself could be understood simply as freeing the believer to sin with impunity—which is precisely the objection in 6:1 (cf. v. 15a). In the context, then, "not being under the law" must involve more than freedom from the law's condemnation.

---

[95]For this general interpretation, see Gordon D. Fee, *The First Epistle to the Corinthians*, NICNT (Grand Rapids: Eerdmans, 1987), 429–30.

[96]See Calvin, *Romans*, 233–34; Cranfield, *Romans*, 1.319–20; Patrick Fairbairn, *The Revelation of Law in Scripture* (Edinburgh: T. & T. Clark, 1869), 429–30; Murray, *Principles of Conduct*, 187–88.

[97]Cf. Cranfield, *Romans*, 1.319; Moule, "Obligation," 394–95.

[98]Räisänen, *Paul and the Law*, 46.

Two other contextual factors support a broader interpretation. The last reference to the law before 6:14 comes in 5:20a, where Paul describes the law as an instigator of sin: "The law was added so that the trespass might increase." We would expect Paul's assertion in 6:14 to be the answer to this problem and include, therefore, freedom from the law's sin-inducing function. A second contextual factor is the nature of the argument in 6:15ff. Significantly, Paul's response to the question "Shall we sin because we are not under law but under grace?" does not include a reminder that Christians are still under the law's regulative power. While this is an argument from silence, it has real weight. For if not being under the law was confined only to freedom from its condemnation, we would have expected Paul to have made clear this restriction when this question came up.

I think, then, that not being under the law means not living under the regime or power of the law.[99] Such a concept fits naturally into Romans 5–8, where Paul employs the metaphors of slavery, freedom, and transfer from one regime or power to another to denote the new status of the believer. Christians die to sin and are joined to Christ (6:1–11); are set free from sin and enslaved to God and righteousness (6:15–23); die to the law (7:4), being set free from it (7:6), so as to be joined to Christ (7:4); are released from the sphere of the flesh (7:5; 8:9) and placed within the sphere of the Spirit (7:6; 8:9). That Paul would designate another such transfer from one regime to another by speaking of Christians as no longer under law but grace makes good sense. His point, then, is that the Christian lives in a new regime, no longer dominated by the law with its sin-producing and condemning power, but by Christ and the Spirit. We conclude that as in Galatians 3–4 and 1 Corinthians 9, "under the law" in Romans 6 refers broadly to being under the dominating influence or binding authority of the Mosaic law. The condemnation incurred by failing to obey that law may be included, but it is not the only or even the basic idea. Christians, Paul is asserting and implying in these texts, are no longer subject to the Mosaic law in the most general possible sense.

Several other Pauline texts confirm this exegesis. "The law is

---

[99]See my *Romans 1–8*, 405–8. For similar emphases, see Ridderbos, *Paul*, 148; F. F. Bruce, *The Epistle to the Romans*, 2d ed. (Grand Rapids: Eerdmans, 1985), 132–35; Stephen Westerholm, "Letter and Spirit: The Foundation of Pauline Ethics," *NTS* 30 (1984), 242–43.

not laid on [keitai] the righteous person [dikaiō]" (1 Tim. 1:9; my own translation) probably means that the law is not binding on Christians, on those who have been made righteous by Christ.[100] Similarly, Paul can claim in Ephesians 2:15 that Christ has abolished "in his flesh the law with its commandments and regulations [dogmasin]." Many take this to mean that only the ceremonial provisions of the law—those ordinances that separated Jews and Gentiles (cf. vv. 14, 15b-18)—have been abolished.[101] But a wider reference to the law in general is certainly possible, and perhaps probable, since Paul may well be alluding here to Jewish teaching about the tôrâ as a whole.[102] "Abolish" (katargeō) could then not mean that the law ceases to exist or has no more relevance at all to the Christian, but that it has been "rendered powerless," that is, ceases to stand as an immediate authority for God's people. Somewhat parallel is Colossians 2:14, where Paul speaks of Christ "having canceled the written code [cheirographon], with its regulations [dogmasin], that was against us and that stood opposed to us." The reference is probably to the Mosaic law,[103] and although Paul's primary concern here is clearly the believer's release from condemnation, allusion to the power of the law generally over believers might be included.

Bound to "the law of Christ." Many label the approach that I have outlined in the last section "antinomian." In a sense, of course, this is fair, for I have argued that Paul is "against the law" as a continuing binding authority for Christians. But, as I have repeatedly emphasized, the law from which Paul claims Christians are set free is the Mosaic law, the tôrâ. Nothing that I have said justifies the conclusion that Paul, or any other New Testament writer, denied the applicability of all "law" to the Christian. In fact, one of the texts examined earlier makes clear that Christians are still obliged to "God's law." Paul's claim not to be "under the

---

[100]See particularly Stephen Westerholm, "The Law and the 'Just Man' (1 Tim 1,3–11)," ST 36 (1982), 79–95.

[101]See Walter C. Kaiser, Jr., Toward Old Testament Ethics (Grand Rapids: Zondervan, 1983), 311–12; Knox Chamblin, "The Law of Moses and the Law of Christ," in Continuity and Discontinuity: Perspectives on the Relationship between the Old and New Testaments, ed. John S. Feinberg (Westchester, Ill.: Crossway, 1988), 361.

[102]See Epistle of Aristeas, 139: "Our lawgiver . . . fenced us about with impenetrable palisades and with walls of iron to the end that we should mingle in no way with any of the other nations. . . ." On this verse generally, see Andrew T. Lincoln, Ephesians, WBC (Dallas: Word, 1990), 141–43.

[103]See Peter T. O'Brien, Colossians, Philemon, WBC (Waco, Tex.: Word, 1982), 124–26.

[Mosaic] law" in 1 Corinthians 9:21 is followed immediately by his reminder that he is not, therefore, "free from God's law" but is, in fact, "under Christ's law" (*ennomos Christou*; lit. "in-lawed to Christ").

This is perhaps the clearest Pauline statement of the situation of the Christian with respect to God's law. As we have emphasized, the Scriptures present the law of Moses as a specific codification of God's will for a specific situation: Israel under the Sinaitic covenant. Paul asserts that from this law Christians, who live under the new covenant inaugurated by Christ, have been set free. But Christians are now subject to God's law in another of its manifestations: the law of Christ.[104] I will argue that this "law of Christ," the new covenant form of God's law, is not a code or series of commandments and prohibitions, but is composed of the teachings of Christ and the apostles and the directing influence of the Holy Spirit. Love is central to this law, and there is strong continuity with the law of Moses, for many specifically Mosaic commandments are taken up and included within this "law of Christ."

Justification for understanding of the law of Christ in this manner comes particularly from the context of the only biblical occurrence of this phrase: Galatians 6:2. In light of Paul's insistence that believers are not "under the [Mosaic] law" (see the discussion above), it is impossible to maintain that he means by this phrase the Mosaic law in a "Christianized" form.[105] Rather, as a safeguard against some who might think that Christians, being no longer bound to the law of Moses, have no authority at all to direct their conduct (see 5:13), Paul insists that Christians are still obligated to a "law."

In what does this "law" consist? Since Paul has only a few verses earlier (5:14) highlighted love as the fulfillment of the law, we must certainly include the demand for love as a central component of this "law of Christ." But it is unlikely that Paul confines the law to this demand alone,[106] for also prominent in the

---

[104]On the relationship of God's law to the Mosaic law and "the law of Christ," see especially Feuillet, "Loi de Dieu," 29–65.

[105]Contra, see Herman Ridderbos, *The Epistle of Paul to the Churches in Galatia*, NICNT (Grand Rapids: Eerdmans, 1953), 213; Wilckens, "Gesetzesverständnis," 175.

[106]As many expositors do. See, for example, Ernest de Witt Burton, *A Critical and Exegetical Commentary on the Epistle to the Galatians* (Edinburgh: T. & T. Clark, 1921), 329; Victor Paul Furnish, *Theology and Ethics in Paul* (Nashville: Abingdon, 1968), 60–64.

context (5:16–26) is the fruit-producing ministry of the Holy Spirit. Coupled with the centrality of the Spirit in Paul's teaching about what it means to live as a Christian, this strongly suggests that the directing influence of the Spirit is an important part of this law of Christ. And this, indeed, is foreshadowed in the Old Testament itself, where there is a close thematic relationship between Jeremiah's prophecy about the law written on the heart in the new covenant (Jer. 31:31–34) and Ezekiel's prophecy about the work of the Spirit in transforming the human heart, rendering it able to obey God's will (Ezek. 36:26–27).

It is more difficult to determine whether the law of Christ includes specific teachings and principles. Many deny that this is the case, but their reasons for doing so often betray a bias against finding any specific demands as binding on Christians. The work of Schrage and others has shown that Paul and the other apostles were quite willing to impose specific commandments on their charges;[107] and these commandments were, in fact, often drawn from, or reflective of, Jesus' own teachings. For these reasons, I think it highly probable that Paul thought of the law of Christ as including within it the teachings of Jesus and the apostolic witness, based on his life and teaching, about what it means to reverence God in daily life. This is not, however, to deny the importance of love or the direction of the Spirit. The "law of Christ," Paul's shorthand expression for that form of God's law applicable to new covenant believers,[108] includes all these. Longenecker's succinct summary says it well: The law of Christ "stands in Paul's thought for those 'prescriptive principles stemming from the heart of the gospel (usually embodied in the example and teachings of Jesus), which are meant to be applied to specific situations by the direction and enablement of the Holy Spirit, being always motivated and conditioned by love.'"[109]

This teaching and witness, as we have noted, is built on and

---

[107]Wolfgang Schrage, *Die konkreten Einzelgebote in der paulinischen Paränese* (Gütersloh: Mohn, 1961); T. J. Deidun, *New Covenant Morality in Paul* (Rome: Biblical Institute, 1981), see his summary on 208–10.

[108]See Friedrich Lang, "Gesetz und Bund bei Paulus," *Rechtfertigung: Festschrift für Ernst Käsemann zum 70. Geburtstag*, ed. Johannes Friedrich, Wolfgang Pöhlmann, and Peter Stuhlmacher (Tübingen: Mohr, 1976), 318.

[109]Longenecker, *Galatians*, 275–76 (he is quoting from a previous book of his). See also Longenecker, *Paul*, 184–90; for this general approach, see W. D. Davies, *Paul and Rabbinic Judaism*, 4th ed. (Philadelphia: Fortress, 1980), 111–46; Bruce, *Galatians*, 261; Deidun, *New Covenant Morality*, 210.

incorporates within it many provisions of the Mosaic law. Indeed, we can confidently expect that everything within the Mosaic law that reflected God's "eternal moral will" for his people is caught up into and repeated in the "law of Christ." Having recognized the place within "the law of Christ" of specific commandments, however, I want to insist that they must not be given too much prominence. The basic directive power of "new covenant law" lies in the renewed heart of the Christian (Rom. 12:1–2), a heart in the process of being transformed by God's Spirit into a perfect refractor and performer of God's will. Commandments, even with the work of the Spirit, are still necessary, for our hearts are not yet, and in this life will never be, in perfect conformity with God's will. But Paul would protest against their being given a position of supremacy within new covenant ethics.[110]

Conclusion

Before leaving Paul, I want to look briefly at four texts that could be cited as evidence against the position I am advocating. In Ephesians 6:2–3, Paul cites the fifth commandment of the Decalogue (Exod. 20:12) as evidence for what is "right" for Christians to do. This is one example, I would argue, of the way in which the "law of Christ" incorporates within it teachings from the Mosaic law.[111] It should also be noted (as mentioned above) that Paul significantly changes the promise attached to this commandment, reflecting the transformation the commandment undergoes in being taken up within the law of Christ.

Secondly, Paul's insistence in 1 Corinthians 7:19 that "keeping God's commandments is what counts" has been cited as evidence that he teaches the reapplication of the Mosaic law to Christians. But, particularly in a context where an argument against the necessity of circumcision is featured (vv. 18–19a), it is unlikely that the commandments to which Paul refers are Mosaic commandments.[112] Paul is claiming nothing more than that those commandments that are applicable to Christians should be carefully observed.

---

[110]See Drane, *Paul*, 55–58.

[111]Douglas de Lacey argues that Paul does not give to the Mosaic commandment authority in its own right ("The Sabbath/Sunday Question and the Law in the Pauline Corpus," in *From Sabbath to Lord's Day*, ed. D. A. Carson [Grand Rapids: Zondervan, 1982], 178).

[112]De Lacey, "Sabbath/Sunday Question," 176–77; contra, see Wilckens, "Gesetzesverständnis," 159.

The last two texts, Romans 3:31 and 8:4, can be considered together, because they interpret each other. Paul's claim to "uphold the law" (3:31) has been taken to mean that he upholds the law as a continuing source of authority for Christian conduct.[113] But those who support such a view would have to qualify the verse to mean "uphold *part* of the law," or "uphold the *moral* law," for nowhere does Paul maintain that the law as a whole has a continuing direct authority for Christians. As we have seen, however, there is no reason to limit *nomos* in Paul to part of the law. Others think that Paul is claiming in Romans 3:31 to be upholding the law's function in condemning sinners (cf. 3:19–20),[114] or in witnessing to the righteousness by faith that he is teaching (cf. v. 21 and chap. 4).[115] But since Paul has been thinking of the Mosaic law in its commanding role in the immediate context (cf. vv. 27–28), it is more likely that he is claiming to uphold the law's demands. But in what does Paul's doctrine of justification by faith uphold them?

Romans 8:4 suggests the answer. Here again, many expositors think that Paul is asserting that the Spirit-led walk enables believers to obey the Mosaic provisions, implying the continuing authority of the Mosaic law over believers.[116] But it is significant that the apostle Paul speaks of the demand of the law in the singular: "righteous requirement" (*dikaiōma*; NIV unaccountably translates this word with the plural, "requirements"). This requirement, in light of 13:8–10, might be the love of the neighbor.[117] But the passive form of the verb *plēroō* ("might be fulfilled") points away from any activity on the part of human beings. What Paul must mean in the context, where he is showing how God in Christ has provided for that which sinful humans could not accomplish (v. 3), is that believers who are "in Christ"

---

[113]John Murray, *The Epistle to the Romans*, 2 vols. (Grand Rapids: Eerdmans, 1959, 1965), 1.124–26.

[114]Bandstra, *Law and Elements of the World*, 99–100; W. Grundmann, "στηκω," *TDNT*, 10 vols. (Grand Rapids: Eerdmans, 1964–76), 7.649.

[115]This view is especially popular. See the thorough defense by Thomas C. Rhyne, *Faith Establishes the Law* (Chico, Calif.: Scholars, 1981).

[116]See Cranfield, *Romans*, 1.383–85; Murray, *Romans*, 1.283–84; Thomas R. Schreiner, "The Abolition and the Fulfillment of the Law in Paul," *JSNT* 35 (1989), 60–61.

[117]S. Lyonnet, "Le Nouveau Testament à lumière de l'Ancien. À propos de Rom 8,2–4," *Nouvelle Revue de Theologie* 87 (1965), 582–84; R. W. Thompson, "How Is the Law Fulfilled in Us? An Interpretation of Rom. 8:4," *Louvain Studies* 11 (1986), 32–33.

and led by the Spirit fully meet the demand of God's law by having it met for them in Christ. As Calvin recognized, only such a vicarious fullfilling of the law on our behalf by Christ meets God's demand that the law be fully and completely obeyed.[118] I would suggest, therefore, that in this sense Paul's teaching of justification by faith "upholds the law" (3:31). Justification takes full account of the law, providing for its complete satisfaction in believers through their incorporation into Christ.[119] Neither text in Romans suggests the continuing direct application of the Mosaic law to believers.

Other New Testament Writers

I have been referring in this essay to Jesus' teaching and especially to Paul's letters. As I explained above, this is simply because these are the two main sources for the New Testament teaching about the Mosaic law (143 of the 194 New Testament occurrences of *nomos* are on Jesus' lips and in Paul's letters). Nevertheless, several other authors also contribute to our subject, and I want now to look briefly at this evidence.

John

John is responsible for one of the most famous New Testament statements about the law: "For the law was given through Moses; grace and truth came through Jesus Christ" (1:17). This statement follows and explains ("for") John's assertion that "we have received grace in place of [*anti*] grace" (my translation of v. 16). If we give the preposition *anti* its normal "substitionary" sense, this statement will mean that the grace by which the law was given has been displaced and superseded by the fuller measure of grace that has now come in Christ.[120] John is not, therefore, denying the presence of grace in and with the old covenant. But he is implying a strong disjunction between the era

---

[118]Calvin, *Romans*, 383; see also Nygren, *Romans*, 316–20; Byrne, *Sons of God*, 93–94; Deidun, *New Covenant Morality*, 72–75; Beker, *Paul the Apostle*, 105–7.

[119]Augustine comments on 3:31: "But how ought the Law be affirmed, if not by righteousness? a righteousness, moreover, that exists through faith, for those things which could not be fulfilled through the Law were fulfilled through faith." ("Propositions from the Epistle to the Romans," 13.1–2). See also Luther, "Preface to Romans"; Luz, *Geschichtsverständnis*, 171–72; W. Gutbrod, "νομος," TDNT (1967), 4.1076–77.

[120]See D. A. Carson, *The Gospel According to John* (Grand Rapids: Eerdmans, 1991), 131–33.

of Moses and the era of Christ; the grace by which believers now live comes in Christ "in place of" that grace that accompanied the Mosaic law. The same note of discontinuity is sounded repeatedly throughout John's gospel in his "replacement theme": the presentation of Christ and his work as that which takes the place of and "fulfills" old covenant institutions (e.g., the Feast of Tabernacles [cf. chaps. 7–8]; the Passover [1:29; 19:36]; the manna in the wilderness [chap. 6]; even Israel itself [chap. 15]). While John says nothing explictly in this respect about the law, his appropriation of imagery usually associated with the law (e.g., "light," "bread of life," "living water") may suggest that he includes the law in this replacement scheme.[121]

Luke (-Acts)

Scholars have recently shown considerable interest in the teaching of Luke-Acts on the law, and they have come to remarkably different conclusions. Some think that Luke is a strong defender of the law, teaching that Jewish Christians should be obedient to all its precepts and Gentile Christians to those that particularly relate to Gentiles.[122] But those who see a more "discontinuous" view of the law in Luke–Acts are surely correct.[123] Salvation-history is strong in Luke's writings, and he clearly presents the transition from the "torah piety" observed by Zechariah, Elizabeth, Joseph, and Mary (Luke 1:6; 2:22–24, 27, 39), and by Paul in his youth (Acts 22:3, 12; 23:3) to the situation within the early church, in which the apostolic council declines to force Gentile Christians to observe the law (Acts 15). Nor is it at all clear that the requirements imposed by the council on Gentile Christians are based on the law or were anything more than a temporary accommodation measure. What stands out above all in Luke is his stress on the law as a witness to the events that have taken place in Christ and in the early church (Luke 24:44; Acts 28:23).

---

[121]See S. Pancaro, *The Law in the Fourth Gospel* (Leiden: Brill, 1975).

[122]See particularly Jacob Jervell, "The Law in Luke-Acts," in *Luke and the People of God* (Minneapolis: Augsburg, 1972), 133–51.

[123]Wilson, *Luke and the Law*; Craig L. Blomberg, "The Law in Luke-Acts," *JNST* 22 (1984), 53–80; M. A. Seifrid, "Jesus and the Law in Acts," *JNST* 30 (1987), 39–57.

Hebrews

That the author to the Hebrews views "the law" as outmoded and inapplicable to Christians is obvious; it was "only a shadow of the good things that are coming" (10:1) and can never bring people to that perfection that God demands of his people (7:19; 10:2). Christians who put themselves under the law therefore put in danger their relationship with God. However, the "law" that Hebrews addresses is almost always the sacrificial and priestly law, and it is questionable whether the author would want to extend his critique of these laws to the Mosaic law generally. Evidence that he might want to do so comes from two texts. Heb. 7:11 is a puzzling text, claiming that the law was given to the people of Israel "on the basis of" (*epi*) the Levitical priesthood. This text may suggest that in the mind of the author the law as a whole is bound up with the priesthood. If this is so, he may then be thinking of the Mosaic law generally when he claims in v. 12 that "when there is a change of the priesthood, there must also be a change of the law."[124] A second passage that may point in the same direction is the citation of the new covenant prophecy in 8:7–13. The author argues that the prophecy itself implies the need for "another"covenant (v. 7) to take the place of the Mosaic covenant. Now, in Christ, the old covenant has been rendered "obsolete" (v. 13). But the new covenant (see Jer. 31:31–34, the passage quoted here) carries with it the promise of the law written on the hearts. It is probable that the author sees in this law written on the heart more than the ceremonial parts of the law and that he implies, therefore, a significant transformation in its nature.

James

James's letter to Jewish Christians contains perhaps the strongest evidence against the case that I have been arguing. In keeping with his reputation—greatly exaggerated, it is important to note—as a strict Jewish-Christian conservative, James appears to impose the Mosaic law on his readers.[125] He demands that Christians continue to do "the perfect law that gives freedom" (1:25), reminds us that breaking one part of that law means to break it all (2:10), and warns that we will be judged by the "law

---

[124]See James Moffat, *A Critical and Exegetical Commentary on the Epistle to the Hebrews* (Edinburgh: T. & T. Clark, 1924), 95–96; F.F . Bruce, *The Epistle to the Hebrews*, NICNT (Grand Rapids: Eerdmans, 1964), 145–46.

[125]See O. J. F. Seitz, "James and the Law," *SE* 2 (1964), 472–86.

that gives freedom" (2:12). Certainly, given James's background and readership, the law of which he speaks must have some reference to the Law of Moses. But there are good reasons for thinking that he is not speaking of the law of Moses simply and directly. James's qualifications of this law as "perfect" and "giving freedom" could, in light of Jewish parallels, refer simply to the Mosaic law, but his description of it in 2:8 as "the royal law" goes further. In a context that refers to the "kingdom" (v. 5) and to the commandment that Jesus singled out as central to his own demand (Lev. 19:18; cf. v. 8b), the "royal law" is almost certainly that law or body of commands that Christ made applicable to the kingdom.

That this interpretation is on the right track is suggested also by the flow of thought in 1:18–25. The "perfect law that gives freedom" is clearly the same as that "word" that Christians are to do and not merely listen to (v. 22). But this "word," in turn, must include the message of the gospel, for it is the instrument of new spiritual birth (v. 18). Here also, then, James suggests that the law he has in mind is more than the Mosaic law; it is that body of teaching generally to which Christians are obliged.[126] James's strong dependence on the words of Jesus throughout his letter suggests that Jesus' own teaching is a prominent part of this "law." This is not to say, however, that Mosaic commandments are excluded from James's purview. But it is to say that James is not simply applying the Mosaic law, in totality or without interpretation, to his readers. The allusions to Jesus' teaching and its connection with the gospel message suggest that for James as well, the Mosaic law is applicable to Christians only as part of the larger phenomenon of "the law of Christ," "the royal law."

CONCLUSION

I have tried to show that a salvation-historical approach in which the Mosaic law is tied firmly to the Sinaitic covenant, now abrogated in Christ, is best able to explain the varied data of Scripture. Under such an approach, the Mosaic law is not a *direct* and *immediate* source of guidance to the new covenant believer. How, then, should the Christian read the law of Moses? In what

---

[126]For more detailed argument, see my *The Epistle of James*, NICNT (Grand Rapids: Eerdmans, 1985), 48–50, 83–84, 93–94; cf. also Rudolf Schnackenburg, *The Moral Teaching of the New Testament* (New York: Seabury, 1965), 349–53; Ralph Martin, *James*, WBC (Waco, Tex.: Word, 1988), 51, 67–68.

way is it "profitable" to us (cf. 2 Tim. 3:16)? In at least three ways, I would suggest.

First, as I have stressed, to say that the Mosaic law in itself is no longer binding on the Christian is not to say that individual commandments within that law may not be. In fact, as we have seen, New Testament authors explicitly "reapply" several Mosaic commandments to the Christian (cf. Gal. 5:14; Eph. 6:2; Jas. 2:8–12). The content of all but one of the Ten Commandments is taken up into "the law of Christ," for which we are responsible. (The exception is the Sabbath commandment, one that Heb. 3–4 suggests is fulfilled in the new age as a whole.[127]) I am not, then, suggesting that the essential "moral" *content* of the Mosaic law is not applicable to believers. On the "bottom line" question of what Christians are actually to *do*, I could well find myself in complete agreement with, say, a colleague who takes a traditional Reformed approach to the Mosaic law. The difference would lie not in what Christians are to do but in how it is to be discovered. While my Reformed colleague might argue that we are bound to whatever in the Mosaic law has not been clearly overturned by New Testament teaching,[128] I argue that we are bound only to that which is clearly repeated within New Testament teaching.

A second continuing function of the Mosaic law is its "filling out" and explaining certain basic concepts within both old and new covenant law. For instance, a Christian reading the laws about personal injury in Exodus 21 might well conclude—rightly, I think—that the killing of an unborn baby falls into the category of those takings of human life that are prohibited by both the Decalogue and by the New Testament. The detailed stipulations of the Mosaic law often reveal principles that are part of God's word to his people in both covenants,[129] and believers continue to profit from what the law teaches in this respect.

Finally, as many New Testament authors emphasize, the Christian should read the law as a witness to the fulfillment of God's plan in Christ. Its authority therefore continues—I am no Marcionite. But its authority is not, in the era of the new covenant, the authority of "law" but the authority of a prophetic witness.

---

[127]See D. A. Carson, ed., *From Sabbath to Lord's Day.*

[128]Although not in the traditional Reformed camp, Kaiser takes essentially this view; see *Toward Old Testament Ethics,* 310–14.

[129]See particularly the fine, detailed application of such laws by Poythress, *The Shadow of Christ in the Law of Moses.*

Response to Douglas Moo

Willem A. VanGemeren

I applaud Moo's use of a salvation-historical approach to the issue of Law and Gospel. In *The Progress of Redemption*,[1] I have set forth such an approach in an attempt to update and develop G. Vos's approach to biblical theology.[2] He defined the salvation-historical approach as the study of God's revelation in Scripture that carefully distinguishes the stages in the historical progress of the revelatory process, defines the organic relations in those stages, and promotes godliness.[3] At this point, Moo and I are still in agreement, but it will become clear to the reader that Moo's definition on the relationship between the two stages in redemptive history (Law and Gospel) differs greatly from mine.

The stages in redemptive history are successive and progressive, but also organically related to one another. What then is the relationship of the Old Testament to the New Testament or the Law to the Gospel? While it is in vogue to assume that whatever is old is antiquated and irrelevant and that whatever is new is up-to-date and relevant, the Hebraic usage of "new" rather signifies confirmation or restoration.[4] The new revelation in Jesus Christ

---

[1]Willem A. VanGemeren, *The Progress of Redemption: The Story of Salvation from Creation to the New Jerusalem* (Grand Rapids: Zondervan, 1988).

[2]Geerhardus Vos, *Biblical Theology: Old and New Testaments* (Grand Rapids: Eerdmans, 1948).

[3] Ibid., 13–17.

[4]Pieter A. Verhoef, "*hdš*, New," in *The New International Dictionary of Old Testament Theology*, ed. Willem A. VanGemeren (Grand Rapids: Zondervan, forthcoming).

confirms and restores the revelation of God through Moses. He brings in a greater realization of God's plan. It is not that the era of Moses was a failure, but rather that the Father was pleased to confirm his covenant in his Son and thereby to reconcile all things through his Son.

The coming of Jesus Christ at the "mid" point in salvation history could well distinguish "two successive eras in salvation history." The differentiation between old and new is appropriate as long as the distinctions are not radicalized. God has one plan of salvation, and the two stages (B.C. and A.D.) reveal a continuity. The relationship between B.C. and A.D. is not simply the exchange of Gospel in the place of Law, as Moo rightly admits. There is continuity and progression as one goes from B.C. to A.D. What God has done before the coming of Christ is an anticipation of and has an organic bearing on what God is doing after the incarnation of his Son. All of God's acts and words in salvation history—B.C. or A.D.—have their coherence in Jesus Christ.[5]

I appreciate Moo's admission that the study of the evidence in the New Testament has not brought about a consensus. He implies that this is so because of the theological frameworks that exegetes bring to the exegetical data. I wonder whether it is possible to posit a neutral approach and method to this complex theological issue. Reflection on the issue of Law and Gospel during the last two millennia suggests that it is nearly impossible to remain objective and to provide a synthesis without being affected by the existing syntheses.

Moo admits that he, too, is operating from a theological perspective, one that is close to the Lutheran Law-Gospel distinction.[6] It is no surprise to me that Moo's use of the salvation-historical approach leads to opposite conclusions from mine. Moo concludes that Jesus is the fulfillment of the law and that the Mosaic law is no longer applicable to the Christian. He qualifies this conclusion with three provisos: (1) individual commandments may still be applicable; (2) principles of the law may be useful in the construction of a Christian ethic; and (3) the Mosaic law is an authoritative witness to Jesus Christ. In contrast, I conclude that God's will has not changed and that the moral law

---

[5]See Willem A. VanGemeren, *Interpreting the Prophetic Word* (Grand Rapids: Zondervan, 1990), 90–91.

[6]His position is virtually the same as that of S. Westerholm, *Israel's Law and the Church's Faith* (Grand Rapids: Eerdmans, 1988), 107–9.

(the Decalogue) is a summary of his will. The moral law, or the constitution of God's kingdom, is still in force. The various and sundry laws have been abrogated in favor of a simpler system of ethics. Yet, the civil law is useful because its regulations exemplify concretely the qualities of godliness with which God is pleased.

I agree that the "hallowed theological" traditional distinctions in the Mosaic law (moral, ceremonial, civil) do not derive from the law itself. The various legal collections in the Old Testament are complex in nature. Yet, the position of the Decalogue as preface to the Book of the Covenant (Ex. 20:22–23:19), its prominent place before the more detailed regulations in Deuteronomy (Deut. 5:6–21) and its designation as the "Ten Commandments" (4:13; 10:4) are so distinctive that it may be called the charter. It is foundational because this summary of the moral law defines the relationship of humans to God and to one another. This charter has distinctive qualities on account of its origin. Yahweh, the great King, has defined the ground rules within which his covenant people are set apart from the other nations. From the moment he revealed his law at Mount Sinai, the Lord has looked for children who love him and seek to do his will.

All the detailed regulations of the law have their coherence in the framework of the Ten Commandments as the succinct summary of God's will. The Law and the Prophets, as I have argued in my chapter, make a clear distinction between the spirit of the law and the corpus of the law. The spirit of the Law has been well captured by Micah's summary of the Law of Moses: "To act justly (*mišpāṭ*) and to love mercy (*hesed*) and to walk humbly with your God" (6:8b). Our Lord and the apostles likewise spoke prophetically as they denounced the legalists for substituting rules for relationships and for not understanding Moses and the prophets.

As to the uses or purposes of the Mosaic law, I agree with Moo that the law was never a means of salvation (God forbid!) and that it reveals God's character, condemns the offender, and serves as a custodian till the coming of Jesus Christ. Essentially, he agrees with Calvin's first and second use of the law. The third use of the law, however, is negatively stated as God's *demand* that his people conform to the law. Moo resolves the tension in Paul's theology by the disjunction of the Gospel from the Law.

I believe that the era of promise, given to Abraham, was superior to the law. Recently, Meredith G. Kline has defended this position in his interpretation of Romans 5:13–14, according to which grace was "the principle of kingdom blessing in the

Abrahamic covenant" and works was "the operating principle" of the Mosaic covenant.[7] The era of the law was not an end in itself, but had an eschatological dimension in that it called forth hope in fulfillment and perfection. The law was a burden in that it reminded the godly continually of their inabilities and sinfulness. When they rejoiced in the law of God, their happiness was really in trusting the God who had given his law. Faith in the Old Testament was eschatological as the saints renewed their hope in God, "but those who hope in the LORD will renew their strength. They will soar on wings like eagles; they will run and not grow weary, they will walk and not be faint" (Isa. 40:31). The expressions of hope and of promise find their focus in the coming of Jesus Christ. The apostles witness to the impact of Christ's coming on the promises, on salvation history, and on the canon of the Old Testament. Everything that was associated with the Old Testament was transformed by the coming of Jesus Christ. At this point, Moo and I are in agreement.

Nevertheless, I must express my reservations. First, the continuity between the era of promise (patriarchs) and the fulfillment of the promise in the new covenant may suggest that the Mosaic era—as an administration of law—was a parenthesis. This parenthesis is said to be characterized by law and works and consequently by disobedience and death. Is this portrayal of the Old Testament not a simplification of the complex exegetical data? From the perspective of the coming of Jesus Christ, the distinction is appropriate (Gal. 3:26–4:7), but from the perspective of the eschatological hope in the second coming of Jesus Christ, the distinction oversimplifies the experience of the Old Testament saints as living in between two ages (promise and fulfillment) and that of the Christian, who also lives in between two ages: the now and the not yet. The Old Testament saint received much grace— witness the testimony of the psalmists[8]; the Christian receives more grace. Both are in need of an even greater grace that will be theirs when Jesus comes to renew everything.

Second, Moo and I part company in the exegesis of Paul's experience in Romans 7. I need not go over the arguments of the various positions as they are found in commentaries. I find the

---

[7]Meredith G. Kline, "Gospel until the Law: Rom 5:13–14 and the Old Covenant," *JETS* 34 (1991), 438.

[8]Willem A. VanGemeren, "Psalms: Commentary," in *ECB* (Grand Rapids: Zondervan, 1991), 5:763–68.

treatment in the commentaries of John Murray and James D. G. Dunn helpful and persuasive. Paul's experience as a Christian is that of a man in between the two ages: the age of the flesh and the age of the Spirit. As long as we are in the body, we share in the law of the flesh, but the Spirit of God is calling on us to live by the Spirit. Far from rejecting the law in its comprehensiveness, Paul laments the reality of the old nature.

Is it any wonder that Moo fails to appreciate the place of God's word to Moses in the new covenant? Certainly, the law was part and parcel of the old covenant structure. It tended to obscure the gracious dimension of the covenant relationship by all the negative aspects enumerated by Moo (supervision, imprisonment, revelation of sin, etc.). The prophets, however, did not speak of the new covenant era as a release from the law, but as a spiritual change within the people. The law was to be internalized by God's gracious work within the people. By the work of the Holy Spirit, they would discern the "spirit" of the law from the harshness of the law. When law or *tôrâ* is defined as the oral or written instruction in God's will, we come closer to the biblical usage and are reminded that the source of the law is God himself. Hence, the association of law with "legal" begs the issue that is the subject of this book.

The prophets witness to the continuity of the law in the new covenant relationship. Certainly, there are differences or elements of discontinuity. In my study of the prophets, I defined several such elements of *continuity* and *discontinuity*.[9] The elements of *continuity* are:

1. the covenant is between *Yahweh and his people*;
2. the covenant is an administration of *grace and promise*;
3. the people of God receive and cultivate the *kingdom of God* in godly living;

The elements of *discontinuity* in this renewal are:

1. the *internalization* of God's will;
2. the *democratization* of the people of God;
3. the emphasis on God's *sovereignty* (monergism);
4. the extent of blessing in the *messianic kingdom*.

The "new covenant" is a renewal of the relationship between God and his people. But it is not a completely new arrangement; rather, it is a confirmation of existing relationships. In some way, the post-exilic community must already have shared in the

---

[9]VanGemeren, *Interpreting the Prophetic Word*, 313–16.

renewal of relationships. If not, what renewal of covenant could they have been a part of? Certainly, the prophecies go beyond the period of restoration! They also go beyond the present era of the gospel because they anticipate the fullness of redemption in the state of *visio dei*. The prophetic word points beyond the restoration from exile—even beyond the present era of grace—to an eternal state in which the joy of the saints will be full and their sanctification complete. How else can we take Jeremiah's words, "No longer will a man teach his neighbor . . . because they will all know me" (31:34)?

Consequently, Moo's "ashes of the old" in the pre-exilic prophets cannot refer to the whole Mosaic administration. The ashes were the result of Israel's rebelliousness, guilt, and exile. They had broken covenant. In God's grace, he renewed the covenant, restored the people to the land, and extended benefits to the post-exilic community *in fulfillment of the words spoken through the pre-exilic and exilic prophets*. The history of redemption requires that proper attention be paid to the progress and unfolding of God's plan of redemption in the era of 538 B.C. to the coming of Christ.[10]

Jesus' teaching on the law is fully consonant with the prophetic hope. In the Sermon on the Mount, Jesus roots himself in Moses while applying the law in the light of the moment of his presence. The Son has come! If people really had listened to Moses, they would have heard the Son. His message is in continuity with Moses (Matt 5:17–19). To make Jesus a "law-abiding" citizen of the kingdom may avoid the accusation that he was antinomian or a Marcionite. However, Jesus goes further by claiming that the children of the kingdom must follow him in following Moses because the Father, who speaks through the Son, has also spoken through Moses and the Prophets.

I conclude by leaving the reader with the two points of tension in the teachings of Jesus. On the one hand, he taught that the new era is here: "The Law and the Prophets were proclaimed until John. Since that time, the good news of the kingdom of God is being preached, and everyone is forcing his way into it" (Luke 16:16). On the other hand, he affirmed the continuity of the law: "It is easier for heaven and earth to disappear than for the least stroke of a pen to drop out of the Law" (v. 17).

---

[10]W. VanGemeren, *The Progress of Redemption*, 300–24; *Interpreting the Prophetic Word*, 183–87.

Response to Douglas Moo

Greg L. Bahnsen

Readers owe their gratitude to Dr. Moo for the marvelous bibliographical work that is reflected in his essay. Christian scholars who wish to explore in greater depth theological and exegetical issues pertaining to biblical law will find a wealth of guidance for their research here. As a Christian, I would add my own personal appreciation for Dr. Moo's clear devotion to the superiority and unsurpassed excellence of Jesus Christ and the culminating age of redemption that has been inaugurated by his death, resurrection, and ascension. We are fully agreed in our worship of Christ in whom all of God's promises have been affirmed and confirmed (2 Cor. 1:20)—that he has the preeminence, not Moses; by comparison to the new covenant in Christ, that which went before was a ministration of condemnation (2 Cor. 3:3–4:6), so that we now exult in knowledge of the glory of God in the face of Jesus Christ!

As a Christian scholar, my assessment of the clarity and cogency of Dr. Moo's theological constructions and conclusions would, at places, need to be a bit less enthusiastic. Hopefully we can mutually serve, sharpen, and teach each other in this dialogue.

The original proposal for this book which was sent me in 1990 said that Dr. Moo would argue for a modified "Lutheran" approach to Law and Gospel, but very early in his essay Dr. Moo makes clear that he rejects the very manner in which Lutheran theology poses the question of "Law and Gospel." He maintains that these terms denote not general theological categories (i.e., commanding and promising aspects of Scripture, whether in Old or New Testaments), but rather the "periods of time" before and after the coming of Christ. In light of that assertion diligent and analytical readers should go back and examine Dr. Moo's essay to see if he himself is consistent in portraying the New Testament use of the word "law" as denoting the time period before Christ. He is not—not even close. Toward the end of his essay, for example, he writes: "I think, then, that not being under the law means not living under the regime or power of the law."

Moo begins his essay with this general statement: "I will argue that the New Testament writers view the Mosaic law within this salvation-historical framework and relegate it *basically* to the period of time before the coming of Christ" (emphasis added). A few sentences later he says "Law and Gospel *primarily* denote . . . two successive eras in salvation history" (emphasis added). But just how much latitude is allowed by his qualifications? There is no way of telling—and accordingly no way of assessing the truth or accuracy of his claim; it is just too slippery. Would he still say the New Testament writers "basically" use the word "law" for the pre-Christian time period if they do not do so in a large or majority number of cases? If it is not their most common usage, is it "primarily" the way they write?

As a friendly and constructive critic, I would suggest that throughout his essay Moo too often succumbs to dialectical, vague, or equivocal expressions that leave his reader unable to tell exactly what he is claiming or to judge its truth. Take another example. Moo asserts that "before/after" conceptions within the New Testament have to do "not with the experience of the individual," but with a corporate focus on God's people (or the world). Notice clearly what he denies. Then in the very next sentence he dialectically takes it away: "This is not to deny, of course, . . . that the biblical writers often [often!] describe this transition in the life of the individual." First we have a categorical assertion, then an emphatic ("of course") denial of what was just claimed! So just what is it that the writer is really saying? He advances a resolution in his next sentence: Moo wishes to place "more importance" on the corporate conception than on the individual. That is, his statements reduce to a claim about *emphasis*—something that is notoriously subjective, outside publicly verifiable analysis, and thus unhelpful in theological polemics. Diligent readers should ask, again, how much latitude is permitted in this author's claim about emphasis? There is no way of telling. Did he offer any kind of warrant for his own judgment about the New Testament emphasis? If the New Testament writers turn out to use the individual conception about as readily as they use the corporate conception of before/after, would Moo still claim the latter has "more importance"? What *kind* of greater "importance" does he have in mind, anyway? He does not say.

Here is another case of conceptual confusion. Moo emphatically and repeatedly states that drawing a distinction between "moral" and "ceremonial" laws is illegitimate and impossible. "This distinction does not hold up under close scrutiny," he declares. He insists that the law must be treated as "a unity" and not divided up into "parts" or "different kinds of laws." Logically then, whatever is said about certain laws (e.g., they are abrogated by Christ's work) must be said about all of the laws; they are a "unity." As my essay indicates, I believe the text of Scripture is against Moo here regarding a conceptual distinction (theologically necessary) between moral and ceremonial (redemptive) laws. But I wish to point out something further, something on which Moo himself equivocates. In the conclusion of his essay, when trying to soften the antinomian-sounding character of his claims, Moo makes this remarkable statement: "I am not, then, suggesting that the essential 'moral' *content* of the Mosaic law is not applicable to believers." Now the law is *not* for him an unbreakable "unity"! Moo believes that he is able to draw a conceptual distinction between the "moral content" of the Mosaic law and that content of the Mosaic law that has been redemptive-historically terminated—even though he had earlier declared that precisely this distinction "does not hold up under close scrutiny." Moo gives back with one hand (a moral law distinction or category within the broader law) what he took away with the other.

Are the above examples simply infelicities of expression? Maybe. But after reading the essay over and over again, it does not seem to me that they are. The generalizations, crucial claims, and conclusions that the author propounds are too often marked with the same vagueness and equivocation. In short, the line of reasoning or argumentation found in the essay lacks clarity, warrant, and coherence.

Because space is limited, let us look at what is perhaps the most crucial illustration of this defect. Throughout his essay Moo argues that New Testament Christians are not morally bound to the commandments of the Mosaic law. Consider some of the assertions he makes: "Christians are not, according to Paul, bound to the law of Moses." "I have argued that Paul is 'against the law' as a continuing binding authority for Christians." "Christians . . .

are no longer subject to the Mosaic law in the most general possible sense." At its extreme Moo insists that subjection to the law of Moses is "an all-or-nothing proposition"—in which case, as he explicitly writes, New Testament believers are "free from that law, *free from all its commandments*" (emphasis added). But does he really mean this? Does he bite the bullet? One of the Mosaic commandments is a prohibition of bestiality (Ex. 22:19; cf. Lev. 18:23; 20:16). According to Moo's principle, Christians today are "free from" that commandment! Indeed, because it is an all-or-nothing matter, Moo insists that we must not be morally bound by the Mosaic prohibition of bestiality, or else we are obligated to circumcision, tabernacle, Levitical priesthood, sacrifices, and all the rest of the old covenant. Another of the Mosaic command-ments is a prohibition of cursing a deaf person (Lev. 19:14). According to Moo's principle, Christians today are "free from" that commandment! Indeed, because it is an all-or-nothing matter, Moo insists that we must not be morally bound by the Mosaic prohibition of cursing the deaf, or else we are obligated to circumcision, sacrifices, etc.

But of course not even Moo accepts what Moo has written here. He does not, after all, really believe that Christians are "free from all [the Mosaic] commandments." At the end of his essay he contradicts what he has written earlier and modifies his view: "I argue that we are bound only to that which is clearly repeated within New Testament teaching." Indeed, he here concedes that "the detailed stipulations of the Mosaic law *often* reveal principles that are part of God's word to his people *in both covenants*" (emphasis added). This is a massive conceptual shifting of ground. First we are told that absolutely none of the Mosaic commandments is morally binding. Then we are told that many of the Mosaic commandments (cf. "often") are morally binding today. "Many specifically Mosaic commandments are taken up and included within this 'law of Christ'" to which all believers are bound, according to Moo. This is incoherent. Logically Moo cannot have it both ways. Early in his essay, Moo wrote that the challenge before him was to find a theological framework which is capable of organizing the biblical texts about the law "into a coherent picture." It is now evident that he has failed to do so.

Let us continue our analysis. My best guess is that Moo would choose the second position (whatever is repeated is binding) over the first (all-or-nothing, we are free from all the Mosaic commandments). Of course, even this does not save him from the *reductio ad absurdum* that we are free from the prohibitions of bestiality and cursing the deaf—because these are not, it turns out, repeated in the New Testament. Some evangelicals would attempt to argue, in a self-defeating way, that these prohibitions *are* repeated in the New Testament, but in the more generalized form of the prohibition of "fornication" and exhortation to "love." However, such a line of thinking would concede that the New Testament concepts of fornication and love are defined by the details of the Mosaic law, thus presupposing the continuing validity of that law.[1] However, this tactic is unavailable to him. The position that he finally maintains in the essay is that we are bound only to that part of the Mosaic law that is "clearly repeated" within New Testament teaching (rather than generally covered by a broader word or concept).

Even more devastating to Moo's dispensational principle regarding the Mosaic law (binding only if clearly repeated) is the fact that it stands squarely in contradiction to the declaration of Jesus himself: "I tell you the truth, until heaven and earth disappear, not the smallest letter, not the least stroke of a pen, will by any means disappear away from the Law, until everything is accomplished. [Therefore][2] anyone who breaks one of the least of these commandments and teaches others to do the same will be called least in the kingdom of heaven" (Matt. 5:18–19). It could hardly be clearer in this text that Jesus does not presume that all of the law has been laid aside except those portions that come to be repeated. *His is exactly the opposite presumption.* All of the details—down to the least letter of the least commandment—are binding until the end of the universe. For us to believe otherwise about any detail will then require authorization from the Lord himself.

Just here we again run up against the vague, equivocal, and unwarranted character of Moo's theological and exegetical generalizations or conclusions. I have cited Matthew 5:18–19 against his principle that we should presume discontinuity unless a Mosaic commandment is repeated in the New Testament. I think it is as plain as the hand before my face that Jesus in this text does not teach discontinuity with the Mosaic commandments, but upholds

---

[1]In the very same fashion theonomists could argue that *all* of the Mosaic commandments are reintroduced into the New Testament under the general rubrics of "love," "fornication," etc., which defeats the whole purpose of the dispensational restriction that only those laws that are "repeated" are binding today.

[2]The word "therefore" (Gk. *oun*) has unjustifiably been left untranslated in the NIV text.

their every minute detail—their "original form" as written, if you wish. So what does Moo make of that text in his essay? Notice this. He admits that we should "probably" understand that Jesus here taught the "continuing authority of the law." That admission is in itself decisive against the position Moo has championed.

So how does he attempt to rescue his view from biblical refutation? He concludes his discussion of the passage with the claim that Jesus in Matthew 5 does not call us to do the Mosaic law "in its original form," but only "as fulfilled by Jesus." Such a remark rests on the assumption of discontinuity between original/fulfilled forms of the law, which makes sense only if one thinks about elements of the law that were redemptive foreshadows, like sacrificial requirements. The "original form" of meeting God's demand for shed blood (i.e., animal sacrifices) has been replaced by a "fulfilled form" of meeting that demand (i.e., Christ's once-for-all death on the cross). But we should not ignore the fact, overlooked by Moo, that the text and context of Matthew 5:17–19 show the focus of Jesus' instruction to have been, not the redemptive provisions, but the ethical instruction of the Old Testament. His discourse mentions nothing pertaining to atonement, foreshadows, or prophecy, but is rather about lifestyle: "good works" (v. 16), "righteousness" (v. 20), and distortions of the moral code (vv. 21–48). So with respect to the moral content or requirements of the Mosaic law—and even Moo draws such a conceptual distinction, as we saw above—just what does Moo mean that Christians are *not* to do the law's demands "in its original form" *but* by contrast in its "fulfilled form"? The original form of the Mosaic commandment prohibits sex with animals; does the "fulfilled" form remove that prohibition? How then are they set against each other? The original form of the Mosaic commandment prohibits cursing deaf people; how does the "fulfilled" form change my duty in this regard? It does not. That is the whole point of the declaration of Jesus in Matthew 5:17. He has come to "fulfill" the law by "filling up the full measure" of its original demand (before scribal rationalizations, externalizations, and qualifications: cf. vv. 21–48). Contrary to Moo, Matthew is not here using *pleroō* ("fulfill") in an "eschatological" sense, meaning to accomplish what the Old Testament "prophesied." Each instance of this word in Matthew must be understood within its own context—for example, Matthew uses it in a general sense for "filling up" a fishnet in 13:48. It is not a word that always connotes prophecy-fulfillment.

And contrary to claims made by Moo in his discussion of the

antitheses of Matthew 5, the moral content of what Jesus sets over against the instruction of the elders *can* indeed, in each case, be found in the Old Testament itself, when not corrupted in the manner of the Pharisees. Moo cannot deny *some* kind of continuity between the teaching of Jesus in the Matthew 5 antitheses and the moral instruction of the Old Testament. He maintains that in Matthew 5 Jesus was "making demands to which the law pointed forward." But according to Moo, the teaching of Jesus is "more forthright"; his teaching "can hardly be said to grow directly out of the Old Testament." This then leads Moo to draw an incoherent conclusion. He claims that "Jesus 'fulfills' the law not by explaining it . . . but by proclaiming the standards of kingdom righteousness *that were anticipated in the law*" (emphasis added). If Jesus proclaimed not some new standards for the kingdom but what was already germinally present in the law, then what he did is precisely to "explain" the law. The reader is baffled to understand exactly what Moo maintains since he uses such words in odd ways.

But there is more. Moo has asserted that the teaching of Jesus did not "grow directly out of the Old Testament." Notice the crucial word "directly" in the claim. Just what does it mean? That Jesus did not verbatim quote the Old Testament? But that would hardly carry any importance or significance whatsoever, provided that he upheld the original demands of the law and did not cancel or change them. One simply cannot do the kind of solid, detailed study of the New Testament for which I would credit Moo as a Christian scholar without running into New Testament texts which, without straining to evade it, clearly endorse, uphold, or utilize the Old Testament law. The diligent reader will notice that the recurring way in which Moo deals with this evidence is identical to the way in which he handles Jesus' reaffirmation of the Old Testament law, namely, by alleging that the texts in question do not advocate using the Old Testament law in a "direct" way. At the outset of the essay he states his intended conclusion: "I will argue that the Mosaic law . . . is no longer, therefore, *directly* applicable to believers" (emphasis his own). Similar statements appear throughout. For instance: "this fulfillment [of the law in Christ] means that this law is no longer a *direct and immediate* source of, or judge of, the conduct of God's people." Or again: "Christians should not look directly to the Mosaic law as their authoritative code of conduct." Moo cannot escape the fact that James upholds the authority of the law for the Christian, but he then qualifies that fact by stating that James "is not speaking of the law of Moses simply and directly." And in his conclusion, Moo again states: "The Mosaic law is not a *direct and immediate* source of guidance to the new covenant believer" (emphasis his).

The pernicious thing here, and the difficulty for any reader, is that nobody can tell in any objective way what this claim about "directness" by Moo means. The problem is not that his claim is mistaken, but worse, that it has no clear meaning in the first place. Where within the biblical texts in question does he derive his interpretative claim that these texts repudiate (or say anything at all about) an alleged "direct" use of the law? Just what would count as this abhorred "direct" use? As we have seen above, Moo's use of a qualifier like this is dialectical, vague, and equivocal. What is the criterion of "directness" being used by Moo? What are the limits of "directness"? What is the salient or defining mark of a "direct" versus "indirect" use of the Old Testament law? Nobody can tell, and thus Moo's vague and emotive claim cannot be assessed. One suspects that this repudiation of any "direct" use of the Old Testament law is little more than (unintentional) shorthand for identifying those who disagree with Moo's own use of the law; unlike him they make an inappropriately "direct" appeal to the Old Testament. This is the deadly vulnerable, Achilles' heel of Moo's entire discussion.

At the beginning of his essay Moo indicated that his aim was to find a coherent framework for understanding the various New Testament texts about the Mosaic law "*without* imposing forced and unnatural meanings on those texts." However, by inserting into texts that uphold the Mosaic law the textually unjustified qualifier "but not directly," Moo is doing the very thing he deplores. It seems this artificiality is what leads to the equivocal statement of his conclusion at the end of the essay. On the one hand "the Mosaic law in itself is *no longer binding* on the Christian" (emphasis added), asserts Moo, who nevertheless goes right on to affirm (dialectically) that this is not to deny that "individual commandments within that law *may*" (emphasis added) be binding on the Christian! No and yes both. It is hard to make this intelligible, but let us try.

Moo here speaks of the Mosaic law "in itself" not being binding. Elsewhere he writes that the "locus of authority" has shifted from Moses to Christ. So then, might the "direct" application of the Old Testament law that he intends describe a Christian obeying (or exhorting others to obey) a commandment in a spirit which says, "It makes no difference to me what Jesus or his apostles may say about the matter, for I appeal directly to the authority of Moses as sufficient reason to submit"? If so, then Moo's point was simply too trivial for him to have labored to make. What Christian, after all, would advocate going "directly" to Moses and ignoring the Lord Jesus Christ? Christians throughout the history of the church who have advocated the authority of the Old Testament law in Christian moral instruction, such as the Reformers or Puritans, have not (as a generalization) done so because they make Moses the locus of their authority! Rather and more realistically, they have done so only because their true Lord and Authority, Jesus Christ, directs them to honor and obey the moral commandments of Moses. That is, they do not "directly" go to Moses, but go to him only because of Christ and with respect for what he or the apostles taught that might alter the application of what Moses required.

At another point Moo sets a "direct" appeal to the Old Testament law over against interpreting the Mosaic commandments in light of the redemptive-historical phenomenon of Christ. As his whole essay testifies, he wants to argue for a redemptive-historical understanding of the Mosaic law's demands. But again: Just how (or why) is it thought that redemptive history changes the moral content—the practical ethical duties—revealed in the Mosaic law (which reflects, as Moo's essay openly admits, the very righteousness of God)? Moreover, what precisely is meant by a "redemptive-historical" interpretation of the Old Testament law (as opposed to a "direct" use)? Early in his essay Moo explains that he uses the phrase "redemptive history" for a conceptual framework which recognizes that "salvation [is] the culmination of a historical process which features several distinct periods of time," which sees Christ's death and resurrection as "forming the decisive turning point," and "finds a discontinuity between the time before and time after Christ at the core of the Scriptures"— even though "this is not, of course, to deny the continuity of salvation history." But that description does nothing to identify a distinctive approach to Law and Gospel by Moo. Since *every author contributing to this dialog could say the very same thing*, all of the essays could be described as "a salvation-historical approach."

Moo introduces his essay as "a" salvation-historical approach, but early on in the text the expression has evolved into something more: "I will seek to show in what follows that the salvation-historical approach"—now it is "the" salvation-historical approach of his essay—"is able successfully to explain and integrate the various New Testament data about the Mosaic law and the Christian." But that is unjustified and misleading. Moo's renunciation of a "direct" use of the Old Testament law in favor of a "redemptive-historical" interpretation cannot be said to have established anything like a clear, cogent, or coherent theological alternative.

Response to Douglas Moo

Walter C. Kaiser

Douglas Moo's position is similar to that of Wayne Strickland's dispensational approach. Even though the argumentation in these two essays is different at times, the results are so similar that both may be legitimately labeled dispensational.

As a first step, Dr. Moo divides biblical revelation into two "ages" or "eras," one "before" Christ and the other "after" Christ. Then he makes his most critical move when he separates Law from Gospel, demanding that they be two *successive* eras in salvation history and *not* two constant aspects in God's Word (p. 3). This, of course, is the familiar grid that has been cast many a time over Scripture wherein specific types of revelation are assigned to specific types of people for specific times—a veritable watertight compartment that sees revelation as being a sort of mail that pertains only for the people it was addressed to in those times.

Initially, one might be sympathetic to assigning the Mosaic law to the period before Christ, but to strip those Old Testament saints of the "gospel" runs counter not only to the claims of the Old Testament with its call for faith in the coming Man of Promise (e.g., Gen. 15:6; Hab. 2:4), but it flies right in the face of the Pauline affirmation in Galatians 3:8: "The Scripture foresaw that God would justify the Gentiles by faith, and announced the *gospel* in advance to Abraham: 'All nations will be blessed through you'" (emphasis ours). Moreover, Paul preached the "gospel of God," which "*gospel* he promised beforehand through his prophets in the Holy Scriptures [i.e., the Old Testament]" (Rom. 1:1–2, emphasis ours). Likewise, the writer to the Hebrews was no less shy in affirming that the "gospel" was available to those who lived in Old Testament times, for he wrote in Hebrews 4:2: "For we also have had the *gospel* preached to us, just as they ['whose bodies fell in the desert,' cf. 3:17] did; but the message they heard was of no value to them, because those who heard did not combine it with faith" (emphasis ours).

The amount of discontinuity found in such a radical separation of Law and Gospel into respective eras "before" and "after" Christ will not fit the biblical evidence. The whole essay, then, is set on an incorrect and non-biblical foundation when judged simply by the criteria of where the "Gospel" appeared. This says nothing, for the moment, about "Law."

But apart from the "before" and "after" grid into which this solution of the Law/Gospel is cast, there are at least six major areas where we feel the substance of the essay fails to meet biblical evidence. In our view, it is incorrect to argue that: (1) "the law is associated with doing and not with believing"; (2) "the law promises salvation if it is kept"; (3) " 'law of righteousness' almost certainly refers to the Mosaic law"; (4) "The 'writing of the law on the heart' [of the new covenant in Jer. 31:33 and the so-called 'Zion torah' of Isa. 2:3; 42:4; 51:4, 7; Mic. 4:2] may . . . involve transformation of the actual content of the Mosaic law"; (5)"[Jesus'] teaching is neither a repetition nor an expansion of the law; nor is it based on the law"; and (6) Christ being the *end* of the law in Rom 10:4 means that "the law has ceased to have a central and determinative role in God's plan and among his people." Each of these assertions needs to be vigorously examined under the searchlight of the Word of God.

The Law Is Associated with Doing and Not Believing

To ask whether the law can bring salvation is to ask the wrong question as far as Scripture is concerned—in both the Old and New Testaments! Never does either Testament affirm, imply, or even hint that this might ever have been the case. To appeal, however, as Moo appears to do, to Acts 13:39 ("Through him everyone who believes is justified from everything you could not be *justified* from by the law of Moses" [emphasis ours]) as the basis for "open[ing] the door to making the law, if done in the right way or in the right spirit, a means of salvation," is unfair to the text and to Paul's meaning. Surely the same use of "justified" appears in James 2:23–24: "And the scripture (i.e., the Old Testament) was fulfilled that says,'Abraham believed God, and it was credited to him as righteousness,' and he was called God's friend. You see that a person is *justified* by what he does and not by faith alone" (emphasis ours). The only one I know that feared that James might have claimed that some could be saved, and in that sense justified, if they did good works was Luther. That is why he regarded James as "a strawy epistle" and therefore treated it as being outside the canon. His hermeneutic on Law/Gospel yielded results that tended to demonstrate that there was an error in his approach to this problem.

It is a further error to argue that the writer of Hebrews (10:1–4) corrected the law, as if it had taught that "the blood of bulls and goats [could] take away sins." In fact, the Old Testament never once claimed that the blood of these animals was efficacious. The sacrifices were pictures, types, and models of the one perfect sacrifice that was to come, without which none of those sacrifices would have amounted to a hill of beans. Therefore, the sacrifices were subjectively efficacious in that they pronounced the sinner forgiven and his or her sin forgotten and removed as far as the east is from the west (Ps. 103:12), but nowhere is a case made for the objective efficaciousness of any of the Old Testament sacrifices.

The environment set for the giving of the law was grace. Exodus 20:2 heads the Decalogue with this gracious notice: "I am the LORD your God, who brought you out of Egypt, out of the land of slavery." Moreover, the giving of the Sinaitic covenant is thoroughly interlaced with the repeated affirmations that it was given in the context and with the reaffirmation of the promise made to the fathers, Abraham, Isaac, and Jacob (Ex. 2:24; 3:6; 4:5; 6:2–8).

In fact, the whole structure of the Pentateuch can be shown, as we have argued at length in our article in this volume, to emphasize the necessity of believing. At each of the compositional seams of the Torah, Moses placed this theme of belief (Gen. 15:6; Ex. 4:5; 14:11; Num. 20:12; Deut. 1:32; 9:23). It is as unconscionable as it is sub-biblical to associate the law merely with doing and not with believing. If such a separation had been possible, then why all the fuss and fury from the prophets? Their constant charge was that Israel and Judah had failed to believe the Lord and to perform the law with the motivation of belief and heart attitude. Faith, belief, and the internal response of the heart are foundational and prior commitments to doing or observing the law. They cannot be torn apart and claim to be representing the biblical point of view.

The Law Promised Salvation If It Was Kept

One of the most amazing sections in Dr. Moo's chapter is found under the heading of "The Law's Promise of Life." Even he concludes that "the reader may think that I have . . . affirmed contradictory points"—and I did think that!

But even worse is the confusion about what is taught in the passages cited. Is it really true that Jesus taught that it was "at least theoretically valid" that the rich young man could have attained eternal life by obeying the commandments? And is the Pauline declaration in Romans 2:13b of "righteous" fairly used in this context of earning one's personal salvation by doing works? Or is Paul's statement in Romans 7:10 about the commandment bringing "life" fairly cast in that same orbit of work's salvation?

A thousand times, "No!" If Paul had thought that that is what he had been doing in Romans 2:13b and 7:10, he surely would have been surprised, for in Galatians 3:21b he distinctly denies any such offer (hypothetically or really) in his work or in any one else's ministry (Jesus and the Old Testament included). He cautioned, "For if a law had been given that could impart *life*, then righteousness would certainly have come by the law" (emphasis ours). But note it well: There never has been, nor will there ever be a law by means of which people can get saved and earn eternal life. That should end immediately any and all speculation on whether there ever was a hypothetical offer of eternal life if anyone could ever keep the whole law of God perfectly. It doesn't exist; therefore, theologians ought to desist from even mentioning it—period!

One thing more: Surely the law of God did not affirm such contradictory assertions as "God did not give the law to save his people, and that the law promises salvation if it is kept." These two things *are* as incompatible as one can find anywhere. Both those forms of covenantal theology that appeal to such a device and dispensational theology need to be seriously challenged for ever inventing a "hypothetical covenant [or offer of salvation] by works." In no sense were the words of Leviticus 18:5 ever used as a slogan to express the conditional character of the Mosaic law. As I explained in my chapter, when Leviticus 18:5; Nehemiah 9:29; Ezekiel 20:13, 21; Romans 10:5; and Galatians 3:12 use the clause "live by them," they do not intend an instrumental meaning of the Greek *en* (i.e., "live by means of [doing these things]"); rather they intend a locative meaning: "shall live in the sphere of them" (i.e., in the context of an obedient life that expresses the reality of the faith and belief claimed therein). Thus, the resulting teaching is very much like John 10:10—"I have come that you may have life, and have it to the full."

The law has never served any purpose for justification; but it had an enormous contribution to make in the area of sanctification and living life to the fullest as God had intended for his people to live.

"The Law of Righteousness" Refers to the Mosaic Law

Central to the argumentation of our chapter was the fact that Romans 9:30–10:11 was a central chair teaching passage on Paul's view of the law. All the word studies on "law" in the world would not be worth a snap of the finger in comparison to the contextual considerations in this section.

What could be clearer? The "righteousness" of Romans 9:31 cannot, by any stretch of the imagination, refer to the Mosaic law. It is just the opposite of the "righteousness by faith" (9:30); it was pursued "by works" (9:32), "as if [that were] possible" (9:32); it bypassed the Messiah who was the Stone set in Zion as the only legitimate object of faith (9:33); it was based on "zeal," but it was a "zeal not based on knowledge" of what God had ordained in his word (10:2); and it was a "righteousness" that was "their own," not God's righteousness (10:3). Now if that is not completely antithetical to what God taught and what his law encouraged, what possibly could ever qualify to fill that bill? Is it any wonder that his position wanders so far afield from what the biblical truth teaches? If this point is missed when there are so many caution signs to the contrary, what confidence can we have in other texts where there are fewer qualifying clauses?

Paul did not call for works, rather than faith, from the Mosaic law in Romans 10:31, but he argued that we establish and uphold the law by faith (Rom. 3:31). The phrase in question is best interpreted *"made a law out of* righteousness"—an indirect but nevertheless clear condemnation of the Pharisaic abuse of the law! To cite Ephesians 2:15 as substantiation for this point is to confuse the "commandments and regulations" of the ceremonial law, which are indeed ended, with the undergirding moral law of God. Likewise, Galatians 3:12a must be understood in the context of "all who rely on the law" for salvation vis-à-vis the *tôrâ*'s means of salvation found in the "gospel," as cited in Genesis 12:3 by Paul in Galatians 3:8–9.

The New Covenant "Torah" Is a Transformation of Mosaic Torah

Another embarrassment to this position is that God's *tôrâ* appears as part of the new covenant and the so-called "Zion Torah" of the last days (Isa. 2:3; 42:4; 51:4, 7; Jer. 31:33; Ezek. 11:20; 36:27; Mic. 4:2).

The immediate complaint is that it does not say that it is the "same" *tôrâ* as the one that God gave to Moses. However, since God called it "my law," it would seem that unless we know of another *tôrâ* in the context of these passages, it would be an eisegetical fallacy to import a meaning such as "law of Christ" or a "transformed *tôrâ*" into the meaning package of these eschatological texts. Here is where the use of the New Testament to lead out the meaning of the Old Testament yields poor results. No wonder liberals have rightfully accused us of finding a "flat Bible," so that any reference to the same subject allows for the importation of all the possible meanings ever found in the use of that word in the canon. Thus, the burden of proof is on those who say this law found in the new covenant and the Zion passages is different from the one already known in the text. This solution of multiplying separate realities by dividing up the terms is well known for yielding incorrect results: cf. two new covenants, two peoples of God, two programs of God, three or four gospels, etc.

Jesus' Teaching Neither Repeats, Expands, Nor Is Based on Torah

In Moo's survey of Matthew 5:17–47, in spite of the clear statement to the contrary in vv. 17–20, he decides to limit our Lord's involvement with the Mosaic law to one of "fulfilling" prophecy. What Dr. Moo will do with "the least of these commandments" I have no idea. Even if we are unable to determine definitively what the word "fulfill" means (and I don't think it is all that difficult in the context), the subject is not about eschatological events, but about a "righteousness [that] surpasses that of the Pharisees and the teachers of the law" (Matt 5: 20). That does not look like Jesus was proposing a prophecy conference!

One must not only establish the precise meaning of *plērōsai* ("fulfill") and *katalysai* ("abrogate"), but it is just as important to understand the relationship that exists between the two. Their relationship is expressed in the strong adversative *alla* ("but") and the connective *oun* ("therefore"). Moreover, the antitheses of verses 17, 18, and 19 also prevent us from applying a "prediction/verification" or a "transcending" theme to "fulfill."

Moreover, the contrasts in six "you have heard it said"

statements and our Lord's deliberate rebuttals in Matthew 5: 21–48 are not matters of prophecy, but matters of keeping the law. Jesus challenged the oral law of the Pharisees and the teachers of the law with the way he and his Father had originally stated the matters in the *tôrâ*. He strengthens what had been said, but in no way did he retract, deny, or attempt to distance himself from what he had long ago revealed to Moses. Jesus did repeat the law and expand on it; in no way did he deliberately avoid that law.

Christ Is the End of the Law

Moo argues for a combination of meanings for *telos* in Rom. 10:4. He suggests "culmination" as the best rendering, thereby combining the ideas of "end" and "goal." This has some strong possibilities to it, so long as it does not imply that the Old Testament foundation is thereby scrapped.

However, the explanation of what this entailed for Moo is difficult to follow. In Moo's view, "This does not mean, of course, that the law ceases to exist or even that it has no more relevance to believers. What is suggested, rather, is that the law has ceased to have a central and determinative role in God's plan and among his people." Once again Moo seems to be adopting mutually contradictory points of view. At times it appears that the "before" aspect of the Mosaic law marks it as something that is no longer needed now that Christ has come. But then we are told that the law has not ceased, even though he argued that Romans 7:10 and Galatians 3:12a said that the law had indeed ended. Now it is affirmed that *tôrâ* no longer has a central or determinative role. What role is left? If it cannot determine anything, I should think that the greatest role it could play would be a heuristic role—which is saying very little, if anything.

Why not note that *tôrâ* is not understood to the depth that it is intended to serve until it comes together in Christ? But nothing in Romans 10:4, or anywhere else, limits it to a noncentral or undetermined role. Surely such a conclusion is extrabiblical, or even sub-biblical.

Conclusion

Moo rightly concludes that "many [may] label the approach that I have outlined in the last section 'antinomian.' In a sense, of course, this is fair, for I have argued that Paul is 'against the law' as a continuing binding authority for Christians. But, as I have repeatedly emphasized, the law from which Paul claims Christians are set free is the Mosaic law, the *tôrâ*."

The question must now be asked: But what law does Moo propose to obligate Christians to obey? He answers, "God's law." But that is strange, since I thought that he is the one who gave the *tôrâ*. To make the "in-lawed to Christ" of 1 Corinthians 9:21 and the "law of Christ" in Galatians 6:2 the new law for believers is to invent a replacement theology by making distinctions in terms that are largely synonyms for each other—much the way that some in the past have divided between the kingdom of heaven and the kingdom of God. The terms are different, to be sure; but it remains to demonstrate that the substance is also. What this position owes us is a list of new commandments that goes beyond "love one another" and "bear one another's burdens." Having compiled that list, it must then be shown that all, or most, of the features in that list are brand new and in no way are a renewal and repetition of what was urged in *tôrâ* or in the times "before" Christ.

Moo concludes that the Mosaic law "is not a *direct* [or] *immediate* source of guidance to the new covenant believer." However, he suggests that there is an "essential 'moral' *content* of the Mosaic law [that] is . . . applicable to believers." But this confuses me still more, for now the moral aspect of the unified law can be ascertained and is applicable, but not in any direct or immediate way. Moo concludes, "I am no Marcionite." For this I am glad; but please tell me how his disciples are going to be able to resist Marcionitism, given the force, direction, and logic of his position? Ultimately, Moo is bound only by what is clearly repeated within the New Testament teaching. What advice will he give on marriage to close relatives (cf. Lev. 18), involvement with forms of witchcraft and various forms of the occult (cf. Lev. 19), the case for capital punishment (cf. Gen. 9), or the proscription against abortion (cf. Ex. 21)? Did Americans not learn in 1973 that a New Testament exclusivistic ethic landed us squarely in one of the largest legalized murdering ventures in recent times—now exceeding Hitler's six million Jews sent up a chimney by four times over with some twenty-four million babies going in a bucket? What will it take to wake us up to the narrowness of our views? If this is not a Marcionite view, it is at least semi-Marcionite—and the disciples of our teaching will soon prove what direction it was that we were heading in if we refuse to fully follow the implications of our own thought.

Response to Douglas Moo

Wayne G. Strickland

Douglas Moo has embraced a redemptive-historical approach to the Law-Gospel issue, emphasizing a baseline discontinuity between the periods before and after the incarnation of Christ, a discontinuity between Mosaic Law and the Gospel of Christ. Yet he does not deny all forms of continuity, seeing "one God, one plan, one people."[1] Thus he appears to approach the issue with balance, avoiding the extremes of absolute continuity or discontinuity. His approach is heavily exegetical, and he is to be commended for seeking to allow the major passages to speak without the undue influence of a preconceived theological construct. He has presented a compelling case for the cessation of the Mosaic law. He poses the proper question: "Can we find a framework that is capable of organizing into a coherent picture the various texts about the Mosaic law *without* imposing forced and unnatural meanings on those texts?"

---

[1]It is evident that when eternity is ushered in after the millennial kingdom, there will be one people of God. Likewise, it may be argued that there is one spiritual people of God in this era of the new covenant, since the same offer of the gospel is available to all (whether Jew or Gentile), and they have been joined together in one body of Christ. However, one should not overlook the fact that God distinguishes the church and ethnic Israel. This is demanded by the fulfillment of national promises to Israel (as deposited in the Abrahamic covenant) and the promise of salvation in the future (as described by Paul in Rom. 11). Paul distinguishes ethnic Israel in Romans 9–11, arguing that presently the nation has been partially blinded by God as judgment for rejection of the Messiah.

His major thesis is that the "entire Mosaic law comes to fulfillment in Christ, and this fulfillment means that this law is no longer a *direct and immediate* source of, or judge of, the conduct of God's people. Christian behavior, rather, is now guided directly by 'the law of Christ.'" Indeed this thesis is sustained by his documentation: He has presented an accurate portrait of the relationship between the Mosaic Law and the Gospel; he has properly delineated the role and purposes of the Mosaic law; he has argued convincingly for the cessation of the Mosaic law and the implementation of the "law of Christ" for the modern believer.

Douglas Moo has come to a conclusion antithetical to that of G. Bahnsen, W. VanGemeren, and W. Kaiser. Yet may Douglas Moo claim exclusive employment of the salvation-historical model? To be sure, he does not claim to be the only one utilizing that framework, but it may be that each particular approach represented in this volume claims faithfulness in some measure to the redemptive-historical paradigm. For example, certainly the promise-fulfillment motif of Kaiser is drawn from the history of salvation (*Heilsgeschichte*). In addition, the influence of the salvation-historical motif of G. Vos on Reformed theology is well-known. Moo needs to explain how it is that similar redemptive-historical approaches can yield such disparate conclusions regarding Mosaic law. At any rate, it may be argued that the proper application of the salvation-historical principle drives one to discontinuity, as expressed by L. Goppelt, for example.[2] However, it must be remembered that Daniel Fuller, evidently influenced by the *Heilsgeschichte* theologian O. Cullmann, rejects both the antithesis between Israel and the church as traditionally embraced by dispensationalism and the antithesis between the Mosaic Law and the Gospel.[3] On the other hand, the dispensational model presented in this volume comes to the same basic conclusions as Moo's salvation-history model. Perhaps the reason that the

[2]Leonhard Goppelt, *Theology of the New Testament* (Grand Rapids: Eerdmans, 1981), 1:124–27. Other figures who in adopting a salvation-historical purpose make a distinction between Law and Gospel are: J. C. K. von Hofmann, *Interpreting the Bible* (Minneapolis: Augsburg, 1959), 186; Gerhard von Rad, *Old Testament Theology* (New York: Harper and Row, 1962, 1965), 2:389; Geerhardus Vos, *Biblical Theology* (Grand Rapids: Eerdmans, 1948), 143; and H. Ridderbos, *Paul: An Outline of His Theology* (Grand Rapids: Eerdmans, 1975), 13, 134–35, 157.

[3]See Wayne G. Strickland, "A Critical Analysis of Daniel Fuller's Gospel and Law Concept" (unpublished Th.D. diss.; Dallas: Dallas Theological Seminary, 1986), 42–64.

dispensational treatise and Moo's treatise have concluded similarly that the Mosaic law is not directly binding on the believer today is due to similar stresses on epochal shifts.

There is much to agree with in Moo's essay. His argument for the cessation of the Mosaic law based on the biblical discourses on the purposes of the law and the teaching concerning the law in the new age of salvation are convincing. His focus is on the Pauline contributions, recognizing the greater importance of his statements over Jesus' statements, since sometimes it is difficult to discern whether Christ's statements apply to the pre-cross situation or the post-cross situation. In addition, Paul was specifically addressing the problem of Jews who were requiring the Gentile Christians to obey the Mosaic law. In agreement with Moo, Paul clearly explicates the purposes of the law. Negatively, the Mosaic law was never intended to be the means of salvation, having been given to an already graciously redeemed people. It was designed to reveal the character of God to Israel, to supervise Israel in the time period prior to the coming of Christ, and to imprison the nation of Israel under sin (condemnation). Regarding its supervisory role, Moo accurately portrays the meaning of Galatians 3:24. It was not designed to lead a person to Christ (as implied by the NIV and NASB versions), but to serve as a custodian or tutor *until* Christ came. The surrounding context of the passage clearly demands the temporal nuance.

His analysis of *nomos* ("law") is penetratingly precise. The term *nomos*, when designating the Mosaic law, is not identified with faith or saving power. In agreement with Moo, Romans 3:27 ("a law of faith") and 8:2 ("the law of the Spirit of life in Christ Jesus") do not refer to the Mosaic law at all. Further, Paul does not use the term *nomos* itself as a designation for legalism. The concept of legalistic misuse of the law must be drawn from the context surrounding *nomos*.

His rejection of the threefold distinction of the Mosaic Law into moral, ceremonial, and civil aspects is likewise commendable. He recognizes the difficulty of partitioning the law into these sections in an artificial manner and notes that the Old Testament itself does not use these designations.

Since Paul quotes Leviticus 18:5 twice in his comments on the law (Rom. 10:5 and Gal. 3:12), it is crucial to attain a proper understanding of its meaning and Paul's use of it. In agreement with Moo, the text was addressed to a regenerate group and treats the "continuation of life" rather than the initiation into eternal life. Paul uses it in a way that harmonizes with this original sense. Moo gives extensive treatment of the contribution of Romans 10:4, opting for the cessationist view. He correctly understands Paul as arguing that the Mosaic Law has ended because of the epochal shift from the old covenant to the new covenant, the latter being inaugurated through the death of Jesus Christ. Moo's understanding of the new covenant more accurately accords with the testimony of Hebrews 8 than does the view that maintains that this new covenant is a "reissue of the Mosaic law."

There are some minor areas of disagreement. First, with regard to the purposes of the Mosaic law, Moo seeks to present the law as having no direct applicability to the believer because of the Christ event and its inauguration of a new epoch or age of salvation. Yet he does not articulate the possibility of the law having a purpose that transcends epochs. Paul has shown that the law is not binding for the believer's sanctification, but does it have an abiding purpose regarding sin and holiness? Does it have a revelatory purpose that transcends epochs? In his introduction, Moo raises the issue of the seeming contradictions within the various statements of Paul concerning the law. He mentions Romans 7:12, which says that the law is good. Later in his discussion of Romans 7:7–13, he fails to adequately explain how this may be harmonized with his view of the Mosaic law in the life of the church-age believer. Moo believes that Paul is describing his pre-Christian life under Judaism and the life of other Jews under the law of Moses. That is, he seems to restrict it to the experience of the Jews. Yet later, Paul contends that the law "*is* holy . . . righteous and good." Paul here seems to suggest a purpose of the Mosaic law that abides and transcends epochal boundaries. The same would hold true for the purpose of the Mosaic law as revealing the holiness of God. Keep in mind that Paul argues that "the Law is good if one uses it properly," i.e., it has been revealed for the sinners (1 Tim. 1:8–9). These two purposes of the law are trans-epochal or trans-dispensational.

Two final notes of disagreement that relate to the theological models are in order. Moo appeals for a discontinuity understanding, based on the salvation-historical distinction "before Christ" and "after Christ." He writes: "Basic, then, to biblical revelation, is the contrast between 'before' and 'after' Christ, a contrast between two 'ages' or 'eras.'" To be sure, this is a critical distinction and must be recognized in order to properly understand the Mosaic law and its applicability for the Old Testament saint and the New Testament believer. Yet the case for the temporary nature of the Mosaic law is strengthened if one understands other epochal seasons with corresponding discontinuities. Some in the Reformed camp have argued that the Mosaic moral law is eternal, antedating the Sinai legislation. Yet just as Paul argues that it had a termination, so also pointing to its beginning validates that it is not to be viewed as anything other than temporary. It came in alongside the already existent Abrahamic covenant. The fact that there are features of earlier epochs or dispensations that cease with the end of that period helps in principle to validate the possibility of the cessation of the Mosaic law. Just as God was able to sufficiently implement his moral standards without the Mosaic moral legislation prior to the Mosaic economy, so he is able to communicate and enforce his ethic without the Mosaic covenant after the end of the Mosaic economy.

Further, salvation-historical paradigms suffer to a certain extent from theological narrowness. To be sure, a major emphasis of God is his special intervention in history accomplishing the salvation of his people. Yet dispensational models include the outworking of God's work of salvation in history as part of the broader development of his kingdom. This kingdom is entered by faith in Christ and at present is manifest spiritually in the church. Its development includes the social, economic, political, and ethical aspects that are informed by the Holy Spirit's abiding presence in the saint, empowering the believer to follow the law of Christ. The motivation for service in the kingdom is love: a desire to love neighbor, to bring unbelievers to Christ for salvation, and to encourage their personal growth. The kingdom will be manifest in its physical dimension in the eschaton when Christ will rule personally.

Douglas Moo has served to remind the theological community that there are other theological traditions that position themselves on the side of discontinuity in the Law-Gospel debate: the Lutheran tradition, dating back to Luther's discussions during the infancy of the Reformation; the dispensational postulations, dating back to the time of J. N. Darby; and the salvation-historical representation, dating back to J. C. K. von Hofmann.

SUBJECT INDEX

SCRIPTURE INDEX